ACRS MEMOIRS · VOLUME 2

Continuing the Journey:
The Geography of Our Faith

While the first volume of ACRS (the Anabaptist Center for Religion and Society) memoirs traced the effects of a tumultuous century on mainly rural Mennonites who grew up to become leaders, this second volume goes behind somewhat different scenes. Here readers—and former EMU (Eastern Mennonite University) students—can view what they wish they could have known about the crucial events and questions in the hearts and minds of these church and college administrators, professors, authors, and the ones who became internationalists. What, for example, are the African memories that enrich the stories of one? How did a small Mennonite Lancaster farm girl become not only a well-loved teacher but also the founder of a flourishing organization that works for equal housing and offers counseling and other aid to immigrants and those in need? How did a young Mennonite science teacher find his way into international agriculture? All "of one another," as John Lapp writes in his Introduction about the authors, they nevertheless offer readers new and different ways of seeing as each moved into maturity and special areas of service both within the classroom and far beyond it.

Anabaptist Center for Religion and Society Memoirs

Ray C. Gingerich, Series Editor

This series of autobiographical accounts is typically published by Cascadia Publishing House and copublished with the Anabaptist Center for Religion and Society (ACRS) and Herald Press. ACRS/EMU sponsors the series, determines the particular focus of each set of stories, and in consultation with the publishers, volume editors, and authors, is responsible for the content.

VOLUME 1
Making Sense of the Journey: The Geography of Our Faith
Robert Lee and Nancy V. Lee, Editors

VOLUME 2
Continuing the Journey: The Geography of Our Faith
Nancy V. Lee, Editor

ACRS MEMOIRS · VOLUME 2

Continuing the Journey:
The Geography of Our Faith

*Mennonite stories integrating faith and life
and the world of thought*

Edited by
Nancy V. Lee

Foreword by
Myron S. Augsburger

Cascadia

Publishing House
Telford, Pennsylvania

copublished with
**Anabaptist Center for Religion and Society
Eastern Mennonite University
Harrisonburg, Virginia** *and*
**Herald Press
Scottdale, Pennsylvania**

Cascadia Publishing House orders, information, reprint permissions:
contact@CascadiaPublishingHouse.com
1-215-723-9125
126 Klingerman Road, Telford PA 18969
www.CascadiaPublishingHouse.com

The paper used in this publication is recycled and meets the
minimum requirements of American National Standard for Information
Sciences—Permanence of Paper for Printed Library Materials, ANSI Z39.48-1984.

All Bible quotations used by permission, all rights reserved and, unless otherwise
noted, are from *The New Revised Standard Version of the Bible*, copyright 1989, by
the Division of Christian Education of the National Council of the Churches of
Christ in the USA.

Library of Congress Cataloguing-in-Publication Data
Continuing the journey : the geography of our faith : Mennonite stories inte-
grating faith and life and the world of thought / edited by Nancy V. Lee ;
foreword by Myron S. Augsburger.
    p. cm. -- (ACRS memoirs ; v. 2)
  Includes bibliographical references and index.
  Summary: "Here sixteen Mennonite writers whose careers have been linked
to service at Eastern Mennonite University tell of their life, intellectual, and
faith journeys." "[summary]"--Provided by publisher.
  ISBN-13: 978-1-931038-65-2 (trade pbk. : alk. paper)
  ISBN-10: 1-931038-65-1 (trade pbk. : alk. paper)
  1. Eastern Mennonite University--Biography. 2. Mennonites--Virginia--Bi-
ography. I. Lee, Nancy V., 1931- II. Title. III. Series.

BX8141.C66 2009
378'.071977550922--dc22
[B]

2009031787

To Albert N. Keim (1935–2008),
friend, brother, colleague,
educator, writer extraordinaire,
and the first of the founders of ACRS
to complete his journey

CONTENTS

FOREWORD

A one-hour presentation at a monthly breakfast meeting about one's life is not an easy task, requiring both a return to details of the past and a careful winnowing to separate out the most memorable and significant. Yet the authors of the memoirs in this volume, *Continuing the Journey: the Geography of Our Faith*, have been singularly successful in choosing what to offer from their lives. In turn, readers will discover many of the most stimulating insights and commitments that have enriched the educational milieu of our Mennonite campus. Of great importance and influence is the fact that over half of the group brought significant international experience to their classrooms, laboratory, or library; and several have served in influential administrative roles in at least three Mennonite colleges and seminaries. One has made his major contribution to the EMU campus as one of the founders of ACRS, the Anabaptist Center for Religion and Society.

The sixteen authors are all colleagues with whom I have been privileged to work (here or abroad) and who have challenged and blessed my life. Several of them were encouraging mentors in my earlier years of study at EMU, and some I had the privilege of hiring when I was in administration at the college. We know each other well, and I applaud their willingness to share both their various strengths and weaknesses, revealing the good spirit and forgiving grace that make life in community meaningful.

Each writer maintains her or his own voice; but all of the memoirs convey the authors' integrity, respect, mutuality, faith, and commitment to social mission. Indeed, these autobiographical accounts open many windows on the choices (and their reasons) of persons who have helped shape the lives of young people for several generations in preparing them for service in the cause of Christ. Moreover, if the stories of their students and the subsequent decades of service could also be included, we readers would see more clearly the vision that relates our Anabaptist faith to life in the present.

This volume offers a remarkable insight into the uniqueness that makes a small denomination like the Mennonites relevant as a "free church" in society, a church that strives to engage our times and culture according to the priorities of the kingdom of God, of which we are members.

Sola Deo Gloria!

Dr. Myron S. Augsburger
President Emeritus
Eastern Mennonite University

SERIES EDITOR'S PREFACE

Difficult circumstances and fortuitous happenings sometimes converge. Such was the case with the origin of this series. The earliest of these stories (*Memoirs*, Volume 1) were designed as a way for the founding members of ACRS to develop an appreciation for each other's particular backgrounds and experiences, and to help this group of academics, too frequently living inside their own worlds, to hear each other. From the success of those first self-depicting narratives has emerged the series of "ACRS Monday Morning Breakfast Stories," in which elderly leaders share their stories of the past with an empathetic, engaging audience.

As does the first Memoirs volume, Volume 2 focuses on EMU—specifically on former faculty and administrators. However, the stories have direct appeal not merely to the EMU family, but to all engaged in transmitting the heritage of faith and the cultural wisdom of the past into our present setting, a setting that continues to include fragments of the intimacy of the village that once was. Now, as the stories show, this village community is less sheltered, and its life is played out on a global screen.

Each set of these memoirs documents an era and a people. That is, the accounts offer insight into leading personalities that were molded out of a particular "believers church" past. In their narrations, the contributors choose events they perceive as significant, not only for them but also for their continuing church, as well as their civic community. They thus selectively resurrect the history impinging on their lives as Mennonites and also transform it as they respond to present cultural forms.

In reaching from the past to the present, these stories reflect like a shimmering mirror the geography of tomorrow's faith. The narrative form of these memoirs means, of course, that we readers are given no sacred answers. We are simply presented with the stuff out of which to construct our own responses to today's encounters. Narration provides no dogma; instead, it offers insight, even wisdom for the journey. The focus of future ACRS memoirs will shift, but the overarching purposes will remain constant as the authors seek to make sense of the journey by revisiting the geography of their faith.

To all who have participated in making these narratives available to a larger community we are deeply indebted. We express our gratitude to the founders of ACRS for bringing the series to birth, to the editor of the current collection for nurturing this set of stories into a companion volume, and to our ever-encouraging publisher. Not to be forgotten are the many who carried out the myriad of necessary but unnoticed tasks and have gone unnamed. Most of all, our gratitude extends to each of the storytellers! Composing and sharing one's story takes courage and makes one vulnerable. In strange and revealing ways it lets our companion travelers know who we think ourselves to be. May sharing these stories today with a larger readership far outweigh the risks of transparency and the costs of vulnerability. To the posterity of all who have opened their lives through these pages, ACRS dedicates this series.

RCG

EDITOR'S PREFACE

As Myron Augsburger wrote in his Foreword, the stories are continuing. In them we can find answers to questions like these: How does a little Mennonite girl growing up in a small Virginia village become a professor bringing positive changes internationally in countries like Nepal? How does a librarian become the author of a whole range of history books? How does a young man who loved farming become a president who brought new life to a junior college? What kinds of changes did World War II bring in the lives of many of these peace-committed authors? How did their perceptions of their Christian Mennonite faith change throughout the years?

In Part I of this book, "Making Sense of the Journey ... as Administrators," the authors answer some of these questions as they write of their experiences as provosts, deans, presidents, and leaders of organizations like the Mennonite Central Committee. In Part II, "Making Sense of the Journey ... as Language and Science Teachers," the authors answer both similar and different kinds of questions as they trace their years as teachers and also activists. In Part III, "Making Sense of the Journey ... as Authors," the writers—a librarian and teachers—use the tools of their own literature to pin down historical facts and bring to life new perceptions of their world. In Part IV, "Making Sense of the Journey ... as Internationalists," the authors take us along with their questions and new answers to far countries. Finally, in the Appendix, Ray C. Gingerich, Director of ACRS (the Anabaptist Center for Religion and Society), answers the question of what this group of retired professors is continuing to contribute to Eastern Mennonite University and its broader community.

Calvin W. Redekop, Chair of the ACRS Steering Committee, and those closely involved in the publication of this second volume of memoirs wish to thank these storytellers who have here shared their life journeys.

As with the first volume, special thanks goes to Ray C. Gingerich for his leadership in the ACRS Monday Breakfast Series, from which this second volume also comes. Further, he is the skilled photographer of most of the portraits of the authors; and to him, also, thanks are due for the detailed index.

Jan Luyken's (aka Luiken) historical engraving of Jesus preaching his Sermon on the Mount (Matthew 5, 6, and 7) in the cover design was taken from David Martin (1639–1721), *Historie des Ouden en Nieuwen Testaments: bverrykt met meer dan vierhondred printverbeeldingen in koper gesneeden [History of the Old and New Testaments: translated with over 400 engraved copper plates by Jan Luiken]*, published in 1700 by Pieter Mortier, Amsterdam. Clearly to the authors of the following memoirs, this sermon by Jesus was not a set of unattainable principles but actual ways his followers were to relate to those within and without the people of God. Thanks are due to Calvin Redekop for researching the Luyken volume and to the Menno Simons Historical Library at Eastern Mennonite University for the use of the engravings on this and our first volume.

Again to daughter Suelyn Swiggum goes much appreciation and gratitude for her hours of painstaking work on the cover and interior book design as she prepared the final manuscript for the publisher.

It has been a pleasure to work with Michael A. King, President and Publisher of Cascadia Publishing House LLC, who has brought to this task a vision for the publication needs of ACRS-EMU, as well as high standards and Christian commitment. We anticipate this to be the beginning of a longer cooperative partnership. It is at King's initiative that Volume 1 in this series is being reissued simultaneously with the publication of this second volume.

Finally, as the editor of this volume, I wish to thank my husband, Robert Lee, for both his careful work on his own memoir and also his assistance with some of the editorial tasks—as well as for his being so important in my own journey.

NVL

Of One Another

John A. Lapp

As I mused on this collection of remarkable personal stories, I was struck by how these sixteen individuals found themselves within such a group of memoirists. Such a collection is, of course, not accidental. Each person's story is connected to Eastern Mennonite University. Indeed five of the writers graduated together in 1954. In a more profound manner this group of people, in Pauline language, demonstrate what it means to be "of one another."

As I felt while reading *Making Sense of the Journey: the Geography of Our Faith, ACRS Memoirs 1,* I sensed here again a deep relational quality in each memoir. None of these individuals lived alone, developed alone, worked alone, believed alone, worshipped alone, retired alone. In these active members of Mennonite congregations, the sense of belonging flourished in each of their well-lived lives. Such "body life" was not narrowly conceived nor introverted but spilled over to families, congregations, students, and colleagues, as well as denominational, professional and ecumenical contacts, and communities both near and far. In Pauline language these individuals should be understood as "servants of one another" (Gal. 5:13) surely locally but globally as well.

Being "of one another" raises recurring questions emerging from the intersection of personality and peoplehood. Each of these memoir writers is a professional. By training and lifework they lived by the rules, expectations, and obligations of teachers in higher education. Nevertheless, readers will quickly discover that for all of these storytellers, family and church defined their professional life more than did their career or specialization. One finds hardly any reference to the passion for status or recognition so common among academic and professional colleagues. By no means does this mean the absence of research or retreat from publication. Yet there are frequent references to participation in the peoplehood or a response to the call to serve. None of these writers appears to be driven by compelling ambition or an animating cause other than putting the kingdom of God first. The practice of teaching and the communion found on a communally oriented campus seem to have provided ample motivation and reward for these professionals.

One does wish that these modest personalities might have explored more freely and openly the frustrations they surely felt along the way. There is little if any anger expressed here. Whatever disappointments they must have felt have long been forgotten or are no longer deemed significant. The usual tensions of a campus with colleagues and administrators or between gown and town are not found in these stories. Frustrations with a sometimes repressive church authority or possibly influential anti-intellectual patrons are largely overlooked. There are references to significant growth of understanding and insight but few admissions of failure.

The well-known mid-twentieth century writer Walker Percy once opined, "We hand one another along" and "help others a little bit to find their way." The sixteen writers in this volume surely passed on the craft and character of their disciplines. They made their mark as biologists, writers, theologians, counselors, language artists, sociologists, historians, librarians, home economists, administrators, and missionaries. Each of these individuals touched numerous others with their encouraging critiques and their imaginative leadership. They passed on a set of convictions and modeled a way of being. It would be a treat to hear students and colleagues report how these teachers handed "one another along" or helped them to find their way.

This collection of memoirs represents an enormous gift to the families, colleagues, students, friends, posterity in general. In an age that too often refuses to reflect, it is the distinct contribution of these memoirs to help us understand individual journeys and each writer's sense of achievement. In an age when individuals easily get lost in the maze of institutions, promotional briefings and electronic mechanisms, it is a significant gift to help people remember the defining role of personality. In an age when institutional memory grows shorter and shorter, the Anabaptist Center for Religion and Society has provided an enormous service in offering a platform and publication for helping a community near and far recall those who helped to form the ethos that over several generations impacted a college, a church, a student body, a neighboring community. These gifts are possible because of the mutuality and community these writers found in the practices of their church tradition at Eastern Mennonite University.

PART I

Making Sense of the Journey

... as Administrators

LEE SNYDER

Fortuities and Convergences

I learn by going where I have to go.
– Theodore Roethke
Happiness came to me through a door I did not know I left open.
– Chinese saying
Say yes quickly, before you think too hard.
– Sheri Hostetler

It is said that Ernest Hemingway was once challenged to write a story in six words. He wrote, "'For sale: baby shoes, never used.' Rumor has it that Hemingway regarded it as his greatest work."[1] I will not attempt the six-word approach, but I want to introduce this memoir with six scenes—I use the word "scenes" in quotes because some are more anecdotes or vignettes than scenes, strictly speaking.

Scene I: At the Corner of Diamond Hill and Powerline Road

Here the setting is a little white frame church that still stands at the corner of Powerline Road and Diamond Hill Road, out amidst the rye grass fields and within the shadow of the Cascade Mountains, which border the Willamette Valley. This is Oregon. The Amish-Mennonite congregation was the center of our lives—church and work. The ministers who shared the pulpit had been chosen by lot, and we called them simply "the preachers." But there was one who stood out: John Yoder, the gentle bishop who illustrated his sermons with a raft of stories. He may have been the single person on that pulpit bench who so reflected the humble love of God that some of us were able to find grace and

7

salvation without bitterness about the roles clearly prescribed for the silent and submissive half of the church.

Story would be a shaping force in my life. Through interviewing my eighty-five year old grandfather, Frank Kropf, for one of my classes at the university (when I eventually returned to finish my bachelor's degree), I came to understand more about the strength of Anabaptist beliefs in the life of our congregation and in the commitments of my grandparents and my parents. Sitting there in my grandparents' living room with my questions, I discovered Grandpa needed little prompting as he recalled the family's settlement in Oregon and the early years in the Willamette Valley. While my aunt Berniece attended to the old-fashioned wire recorder and occasionally interjected a comment or question herself, we heard the account of the Kropfs coming by train from Missouri to the Northwest in an immigrant car.

Grandpa rocked slowly as he spoke, sitting in his favorite chair. Behind him in a tall bookcase was an over-sized volume of the *Martyrs Mirror*. As a child, I had never gotten beyond the pictures, grim and gruesome in their portrayal of unspeakable torture and death. I much preferred to page through the *Sears Roebuck Catalog* collection my grandmother kept in the compartment under the window seat.

However, that day there was one particular story my grandfather told that has enlarged my sense of God's mysterious ways of working amidst ordinary lives. During World War I, he recalled, the Mennonites were harassed in various ways for their pacifist stand. They were considered German sympathizers by some because their church services were still conducted in the German language. Considerable pressure grew, also, for the Mennonites to buy war bonds, which they refused to do, greatly irritating the locals.

Tensions mounted, my grandfather recalled; and one morning when he looked up at the church, which was within sight of his living room window, he saw a yellow stripe painted around the building. Going up to examine the situation, Grandfather and his father found the front doors padlocked and a sign above the door: "This church is closed for the duration of the war." As my grandfather described it, "Things went from bad to worse," with on occasion a bunch of rowdies driving by, shooting at their place and at his father's house just up the road.

One day, as my grandfather tells the story, a number of husky young fellows showed up at several places; mob-like, these guys clearly were up to no good. Not finding him at home, they warned his wife that they would be back that night. Indeed, later they returned. All stayed in the car except one big fellow, who approached and asked why they did not fight. Grandpa gave a brief answer, and the fellow said, "You'll have to take the consequences." Then the young man climbed back into the car, and they zoomed out of there, leaving my grandfather and his family in fear as they prepared for bed.

It was years later, Grandpa said, that one of the guys involved confessed what had happened the day they had intended to harm these Mennonites. At each of three places they had been prepared to tar and feather their targets. But when the guys got there, the fellow told Grandpa, "There was a heavenly being that stood between them and us, and we couldn't get ahold of anybody."[2]

Scene II: Great Aunt Daisy's Novels

It may well be that putting together in our own minds a lifetime of novel reading is close to knowing what it must be like in the mind of God.

– Alan Cheuse

My cousins and I were the recipients of a whole series of the Elsie Dinsmore books—those Civil War historical novels of dubious literary merit. (The Canadian award-winning writer Rudy Wiebe, I was startled to learn recently, also delved into the Elsie Dinsmore books, as he describes in his autobiography, *Of this Earth: A Mennonite Boyhood in the Boreal Forest*, Knopf Canada, 2006). For me, Aunt Daisy's books are worthy of note because they introduced me to fiction, to novels. Daisy Speiler, who collected the series, was deaf, one of a number in the Hostetler family who were a part of our congregation.

It should be noted that Daisy, my grandmother Viola, and Ida and Grace (other deaf relatives) married deaf young men with names like Speiler, Toll, Stewart, and Baker, bringing a whole group of "outsiders" into our family and into the church. For the most part, it was a happy blend of one distinctive faith community with another equally curious group who were separate from mainstream society. To the extent that the deaf maintained their own language and social networks, they enriched congregational and community life because they challenged our understanding of "the other."

The dozen or more deaf members sat together each Sunday morning in a designated part of the church sanctuary with their own interpreter of the hymns and sermon. Their very presence signaled inclusion. To accommodate the interpreter for the deaf, men and women were allowed to sit together. This was in contrast to the prescribed seating patterns for everyone else—men sat on the right side and women on the left. In a marvelous way the presence of the deaf congregants, including those young men who did not grow up Mennonite, blurred the lines of inclusion and exclusion that characterized the practices of this Mennonite community trying to maintain a clear separation from the world.

Perhaps it should not surprise me, then, that it was my deaf great aunt Daisy who introduced me to other worlds and times through novels. It was Daisy's taste for historical novels and her generosity in sharing her books (there must have been twenty-five to thirty in the Dinsmore series) that hooked me on fiction. Daisy would handpick particular volumes for us cousins, writing each recipient's name in a spidery cursive on a scrap of paper and sticking it in the book she had selected.

We cousins then borrowed each other's books so we could keep up with the unfolding story of several generations in the postwar South. Thus I got my first introduction to at least some version of that history—the horrific cost of the Civil War within families, the terrifying actions of the Ku Klux Klan, and the suffering endured during the Reconstruction and Carpet Bagger era.

But what really attracted me were the traumas and tribulations of the heroine, whom I identified with to a certain extent, a girl who struggled constantly to be obedient. She could never be good enough to please her father, and this failure caused her considerable anguish. An oldest daughter, I too, could never be good enough. I always seemed to be naughty, to sass my mom, to fight with my sister, perhaps to have my head in a book when I was supposed to be working. Indeed, all of us kids were loud and scrappy. I recall the anxiety I would experience as we headed home from Sunday night or Wednesday evening church, my sister and I in the back seat of our black Chevy waiting for Dad's verdict—were we going to get a spanking when we got home because we had misbehaved in church? Curiously, I remember almost nothing about the actual spankings—mostly I remember the dread.

Only in retrospect did I begin to understand what books meant for Aunt Daisy, who was confined by her deafness. As for me, books became more than escape or entertainment. They gave me a way to see beyond the prescribed boundaries of our little community and to some extent helped me understand myself—though certainly this would not have been a conscious awareness. I shall always be grateful that Daisy found entry into imaginative worlds and shared those with her great nieces. I have sometimes wondered how she got by with this, given our conservative community's suspicion of anything "worldly." But for some reason, my parents did not raise questions about our reading. We had full access to the school library and later to the little town library. Fantasy, adventure, romance (including the *Arabian Nights* and the classic fairy tales) drew me and provided a counterpoint to the books and periodicals my dad enjoyed.

Dad, an avid reader, kept up with fundamentalist and other religious publications. He had shelves of books, which included theology, missiology, and works with a dispensationalist-apocalyptic-prophetic slant. His Scofield Bible was a ready reference. Also, he had a keen interest in medicine and health and could not resist experimenting with any number of home remedies. Dad kept up, too, with farm magazines, church periodicals, the *National Geographic,* and materials on investments. A classy set of the *Encyclopedia Britannica* with gold-embossed spines occupied a prominent place in the study, lined up on the beautifully grained wood bookshelf just made for these enormously heavy volumes. This luxury purchase from a traveling salesman must have provided a rather sharp contrast to the otherwise utilitarian and modest furnishings of our living room and study—what we called "the den." Surrounded by implement calendars or scripture mottos on the wall (remember the glass pictures with the foil backing highlighting a Bible verse such as "Jesus Never Fails"?), I cannot say much about our family's aesthetic sensibilities; but in books and reading materials I had access to what were actually vast resources.

I do not wish to disparage my father's reading tastes—they were wide ranging if a little eclectic. I like that about my dad, his insatiable curiosity and thirst for knowledge. Though he did not have the chance to go to high school, he was one of the best-educated persons I have known. I was lucky to be Lloyd's daughter.

Scene III: *Grandmother and the Coburgs*

Jump ahead a decade or two for Scene Three. I am back in college to finish my bachelor's degree. After one year at Eastern Mennonite College, then marriage at age nineteen followed by the birth of two daughters and a mission-service term in Nigeria, I had an opportunity to become a student again. In 1969 I enrolled at the University of Oregon along with Del, who was returning for doctoral studies. I had met Delbert Snyder in high school when we both attended Western Mennonite, a residential school in Salem, Oregon. Ours was more than a high school romance, though it was that. We shared a commitment to the church, a sense of adventure, and goals for service and continued education.

One day in my senior year, on a chance walk through a little gallery at the University of Oregon student union, I came upon an art exhibit. I was irresistibly drawn to a large oil painting by an Oregon artist, called *Grandmother and the Coburgs.* I could not have explained the impact of what I was seeing. Though somewhat abstract, the representation was a scene I recognized immediately. I knew the contours of the Coburg hills at the south end of the valley as one approached Eugene. There was the familiar cluster of cottonwoods and a little building perched up on the mountainside. I was transfixed by the presiding figure in the painting—the strong profile of a partial blue face dissolving into wispy curtains of rain blowing across the ridges—a mountain view familiar from our farm up the valley. The longer I studied the painting, the more I recognized—though I was still not clear what exactly I was feeling and seeing beyond the multi-variant greens, the deep red and orange, the contrasts of pale yellow and turquoise, light and dark. What William Stafford once said about poems is an apt description of the encounter that day: "There is something about it that won't yield to ordinary learning. When a poem [painting] catches you, it overwhelms, it surprises, it shakes you up. And often you can't provide any usual explanation for its powers."[3]

I know now that the power of this painting was in the gathering up into some connected whole a range of only dimly perceived understand-ings—about what it means to be a child of the West, about the pervasive influence of ancestors, about the breathtaking and ever-changing beauty of the Willamette Valley and the mountains, about the painting's female forms that were hidden and revealed—all of this and more. I simply had to find Del and show him this work; it was the first time a piece of art had ever moved me in this way.

Grandmother and the Coburgs (for me it would have been perhaps *grandfather* rather than *grandmother*) captured in an imaginative way in-expressible questions or forces that were submerged for the most part: matters regarding place, identity, heritage and tradition. (As an aside, my mother is also relevant in this story because she could survey the same mountains out her kitchen window as she kept track of the ever-changing Cascades, in turn fierce or ravishingly beautiful, depending on the weather. I call my mother the "keeper of the weather." To this day, when I telephone my mom, she invariably asks about the weather.)

There is a postscript to this story that explains how I got the painting. We were poor students then, both of us studying at the university full time, assisted financially by work-study and grants. I desperately wanted *Grandmother and the Coburgs,* but could not imagine finding the money for the gallery price. I knew nothing about the protocols for purchasing art, but a knowledgeable friend suggested that it would not be inappropriate to offer less than the price posted, once the exhibit had closed.

So I searched out the artist's address and wrote her a letter, telling her how moved I was by the painting. I offered considerably less than the gallery price, being careful to express a hope that my offer would not offend her. I heard nothing. That was disappointing, but I consoled myself with the thought that at least we had saved ourselves some money we could ill afford to spend on a whim.

Quite some time later the artist telephoned and told me how much she had appreciated my letter. Furthermore, she said, she would have sold me the painting except that someone else had already purchased it. I then put it out of my mind and concentrated on my studies, on the readings and papers for twentieth century literature, English drama, folklore and mythology, and literature of the Bible. These winter term courses would bring me to the completion of my undergraduate require-ments at the University of Oregon.

I skipped the midwinter graduation ceremony because I was still taking classes. But the day the term was over, when I walked into our little house in Eugene, there hanging on the wall was *Grandmother and the Coburgs*. I was deliriously happy to see the painting and overcome by Del's generosity. Perhaps the best part of this graduation gift was Del's ingenious effort to manage the surprise. To this day, he will not reveal the purchase price. I have resigned myself to the fact that he deserves to keep that secret.

Scene IV: Fortuities—the Unlikely Mathematics Dinner

This is Del's story really, but mine, too. The setting was Portland, Oregon. The year was 1968, when we had just returned from a three-year Mennonite Mission Associates teaching stint in Nigeria and Del had accepted a job at Portland's Madison High School. A character in Marilynne Robinson's *Gilead* observes, "There are visions … that come to us only in memory, in retrospect." These visions speak "both of the smallness of human life in the face of great mysteries and of the incandescent glimpse of the sacred … once we quit clinging to this world and our places in it."[4] I love that description because it was indeed *only in looking back* that the mystery and wonder of that particular night in Portland became apparent. It represents only one of many convergences and fortuities that were to mark our journey.

One day Del came home from Madison High, where he was teaching, and reported that the math department head had gotten sick and had invited Del to take his place at a dinner for the winners of a high school mathematics competition. Del had agreed to go and then found himself seated next to a guest from out of town. This was Professor Meier, a person Del knew from previous coursework at the University of Oregon. There was another connection, too. While in West Africa we had learned to know some Lutheran missionaries who, it turned out, were related to Dr. Meier.

So Del and his former professor, over whatever the dinner menu was that night—probably salad and chicken—reconnected. When Del returned home, he told me of the coincidence of meeting Eugene Meier and reported, almost as an afterthought, that the professor knew of some National Science Foundation money available at the university.

Professor Meier had encouraged Del to apply if he wanted to continue graduate studies.

In retrospect, that math dinner was to have enormous consequences for our family. Del was granted a National Science Foundation award so that he could continue his studies. Leaving Portland, we returned to Eugene, where we had lived when we were first married and where Del had completed undergraduate and master's programs. We found a house where our two daughters, Lori and Judy, would be within walking distance of their elementary school. Del continued his studies in math. And the timing was right for me to return to school and finally complete my bachelor's degree—which was to prove essential for future opportunities, of which I had no inkling at the time.

That night changed our lives. What an unlikely succession of events: first the department head's getting sick; Del's being a last minute invitee; then his being seated next to a former professor—who just happened to be there; and finally Professor Meier's giving Del encouragement to apply for the grant funds still available for math and science teachers. All very ordinary and rather small things in themselves. But in many ways that unremarkable evening set in motion a succession of changes that significantly affected our future.

Scene V: "Will you have a good man to work for?"

This scene takes me to a conversation with my mother. "Will you have a good man to work for?" was my mother's question when I told my parents that EMC (Eastern Mennonite College, now University) had approached me about considering the academic dean position. Del and I were back at the University of Oregon on a two-year sabbatical/leave of absence (1982 to 1984) from Eastern Mennonite. We had moved to Virginia in 1972 when Del had accepted a math position at EMC. I had continued my studies in English, enrolling in a two-year master's degree program at James Madison University, before joining the staff at EMC (1974).

Del, who by now had been teaching math for ten years, was being asked to broaden his preparation during his sabbatical so that he could also teach business. I had decided that it was time to work on a PhD after eight years in administration and some part-time teaching. Thus from 1982 to 1984 we immersed ourselves in graduate study. Del completed his MBA while I plowed through the doctoral course work, passed the comprehensive exams, submitted the dissertation proposal, and began the writing.

Somewhere along the way—spring, I think—I received a call out in Oregon from Richard C. Detweiler, the president of EMC, asking if I would consider being a candidate for the deanship. Dean Albert N. Keim had announced he was going back to teaching. I really ought to defer to some of my colleagues back then, but this is my version of the story. I first told Richard Detweiler no; I knew full well the demands of the job. I was only persuaded when President Detweiler called back to say that the faculty was asking me to reconsider. (I knew that any successful dean serves at the pleasure of the faculty.)

That brings me to my mother's question. It was a perfectly logical question from her point of view. It was one that encapsulated all those matters of the Apostle Paul's teaching about order and a woman's place. I did not have the same concerns my mother did, but I was fully aware that I had to face my own fears in moving out of a more private, subservient role to a new leadership position. I had experienced professional growth and immeasurable satisfaction in various roles during eight years at EMU as part-time English and humanities instructor, as administrative secretary, and as assistant dean. I confess it was terrifying to think about assuming a more public role.

Saying yes to the EMU invitation did not lesson my fears. In those early months of becoming the academic dean, when asked to speak, I had to contend not only with shaking knees and pit-of-the-stomach anxiety but also with an irrational sense of vertigo if I were sitting too near the edge of the auditorium's high stage. I would literally need to move my chair back to be sure I would not just pitch right off headlong onto the floor below.

While I was trying to figure out what it meant to be the dean, Richard Detweiler was wonderfully supportive, sensing more than I knew, perhaps, my own uncertainties. He told me once that in my role he did not think of me as a woman. He meant that well. I must give President Detweiler credit; he knew the pitfalls and the obstacles. When he was trying to persuade me to consider the position, he said that he had informally tested with church leaders whether it would be acceptable to

At Eastern Mennonite University, pictured with John Paul Lederach. Photo by Jim Bishop

have a woman dean at EMC. He reported that he had gotten an okay. So yes, the answer to my mother's question was, "I would have a good man to work for."

My own coming to terms with a public role has been more of a journey than a once-and-for-all decision. In this question of public versus private spheres, let me add one more vignette. During a particularly fractious time when the college and what was being taught (specifically in the religion department) were suspect in Lancaster Conference (from which many of our students came), the president, seminary dean and I were invited to meet with the Lancaster bishops. Joseph Lapp, who had become president after Richard Detweiler, seminary dean George Brunk III, and I made our way to Lancaster.

I will not speak for what the seminary dean might have been thinking, but I know that I went into that bishops' meeting with trepidation. We were being called to account. I was the only woman sitting in that room of the Lancaster bishops. As I recall, the kindly presiding leader who was in charge of arrangements suggested in advance that I need not speak. (I do not think I am imagining that, though memory plays tricks.) Somewhere midway through the discussion, up from the basement emerged two or three Lancaster women carrying big pitchers of

Kool-aid. It was time for refreshments. I watched these plainly dressed
sisters who clearly knew their place. I had an overwhelming urge to join
them in the kitchen. At that moment, that is where I felt I belonged.

Scene VI: "Why would you want to do this?"

The final scene, which occurred in November 1995, would be another turning point. I had served as academic dean at Eastern Mennonite University
for more than a decade. I called my mother in Oregon from the Detroit
airport to tell her that I was en route to an interview for the presidency
at Bluffton College in Ohio. I do not remember that she asked any particular questions—she would not have wanted to run up the bill.

One of the commitments Del and I had made early in our married
life was to keep communication open with our parents, though our decisions did not always square with their particular conservative beliefs.
Now I did not want my mom to be surprised if she heard by the grape-
vine about my Bluffton candidacy. I wanted to honor her right to know
what was going on.

Arriving in Bluffton on a cold November evening, Del and I were
directed to the location where we were to meet the Board of Trustees
for the first time. They were about to adjourn from a closed session to
an informal reception to "meet the candidate." We were asked to wait
in the student center lounge. Waiting there with us, we discovered, was
the wife of one of the trustees. We introduced ourselves and got acquainted. This beautiful, elegant older woman turned to me and asked,
"*Why* would you want to do this?"

I was startled by the question and to this day cannot recall what
I replied. Again, this was a perfectly good question—in other words,
"Girl, what are you doing here?" I could not have fully answered it then
because I was still learning about calling, about God's surprises along
the way. And about God's sometimes choosing unlikely persons to be
a part of something much larger than themselves.

Meeting earlier with the search committee, I had had two primary
questions, "Could I do it?" and "Did I want to do it?" I continued to
ask those questions, or some variant, right up until the day I walked
out of the president's office in College Hall because in my ten years at
Bluffton, I was keenly aware that there were many days I could not "do it."
Psalm 139 was a guiding focus for me in those early conversations about

accepting a presidency. In the face of deep uncertainty at times (a fellow president calls it "sheer terror"), I rested in the knowledge that God has something in mind for us before we even have a clue, or, as the Psalmist says, "All the days ordained for me were written in your book before one of them came to be" (Psalm 139:16, NIV). Often in the day to day I would return to Deuteronomy 30:11, seeking reassurance in those words as well: "Now what I am commanding you today is not too difficult for you or beyond your reach."

I find encouragement in Flannery O'Connor's advice: "Be properly scared and go on doing what you have to do."[5] There was often, however, an unexpected in-breaking of grace just when I least expected it—or maybe when I most needed it—and the recognition that in lives of service to God, the Holy Spirit has some part to play. It is the writer Mary Rose O'Reiley who observes that "Humility is sometimes merely the knowledge that something is going on that you are too spiritually opaque to get."[6] At times I experienced that as well. What Anne Lamott called her "two best prayers," I claimed for my own. On most days, they about covered it: "Help me, help me, help me," and "Thank you, thank you, thank you."[7]

Just Say Yes

I cannot explain how a farm girl from Oregon got from scene one to scene six. But I am deeply humbled by the opportunities I have had to serve the church and Christian higher education. Sheri Hostetler's little poem, which I ran across in Ann Hostetler's collection of Mennonite poets (*A Cappella: Mennonite Voices in Poetry*), may offer a partial explanation of the path I have traveled.

Say yes quickly, before you think too hard
or the soles of your feet give out.
Say yes before you see the to-do list.
Saying maybe will only get you to the door,
but never past it.
Say yes before the dove departs for, yes,
she will depart and you will be left
alone with your yes,
your affirmation of what you
couldn't possibly know was coming.

Keep saying yes.
You might as well.
You're here in this wide space now,
no walls and certainly not a roof.
The door was always an illusion.[8]

As academic dean and vice president at Eastern Mennonite and as president at Bluffton University, I was filling a role—as folks frequently reminded me—that was a "first" for a woman at these institutions. Among Mennonite colleges I was the first woman president, a fact that seemed more noteworthy to others than it did to me. However, I was keenly aware that the issue of women in leadership was still a matter of contention in many areas of the church. I gradually realized as dean at EMU that, when it came to constituency criticism, I was somewhat "beneath the radar" because of my academic background. Since I was not a theologian nor was I aspiring to be an ordained minister, I did not attract attention in matters of theology or religion, areas which sometimes evoked controversy. Rather, I could and did respond to periodic concerns out of a direct knowledge of the faculty's deep commitment to their calling and to serving faithfully in their respective teaching roles.

Some of the most satisfying (and most difficult, I should add) encounters were those when I was invited by a critical parent or church member for conversation. By listening, by taking a personal, more relational approach, I could show respect even though I might not agree with them. Often I could address their fears just by sharing my own faith perspective and by reiterating the mission and purpose of the educational enterprise—which included dealing honestly with questions as we sought to prepare students for lives of service.

Through a number of mentors who encouraged me in administration, I discovered a calling and vocation that I could never have imagined for myself. As dean, early on I came across Robert Greenleaf's classic on servant leadership. I found his work a particularly inspiring expression of my own intuitive sense regarding uses or abuses of power and authority. Greenleaf became a rich source in my plunge into the role of vice president and then president. As a woman, I was much more confident in carrying out my responsibilities through collaboration, openness, team-building, and persuasion rather than by the more hierarchical model of "command and control." One of my Bluffton colleagues expressed a similar philosophy in the observation that a leader's job is to listen, learn, respect, and support.[9] I find that a profound insight into effective leadership.

But of course there is the messiness of the work itself: the day in, day out press of problem-solving, encouraging students (and recruiting students), hiring faculty, managing the budget when resources are too often scarce, serving as liaison to the community, attending to accreditation requirements, constructing buildings, and creating visionary yet workable strategic plans. And then there is that much overlooked essential for a successful leader: just showing up—at student recitals, athletic competitions, academic seminars, employee recognition dinners, campus celebrations, concerts and dramas, faculty presentations, and broader community events. This part of the job I embraced, most of the time with enthusiasm. As a result, I was usually in a state of almost constant exhilaration or total exhaustion—sometimes both at the same time.

Working with a team of extraordinary colleagues and with a dedicated faculty—at both EMU and Bluffton—offered rewards beyond expectation. At EMU in my twelve years as academic dean (1984 to 1996), we made great strides in hiring outstanding faculty with advanced degrees. A priority for the board and administration was improving faculty compensation. Three endowed academic "chairs" were established during this period in biology, business, and education, which served to highlight the quality of the programs and to honor faculty.

This was a time when the EMU cross-cultural program was coming into its own, offering all students study opportunities abroad. A Russia and China exchange program, along with the establishment of a sister college relationship with Wakkanai Hokksei in Japan, provided further enrichment for EMU students. An intensive English program was started in 1989, yet another outgrowth of the college's emphasis on cross-cultural education and global awareness.

As dean, I especially valued the opportunity to teach a literature course each year to upper level students; a way to "keep me honest," I told the faculty, in being reminded of the rigors of teaching and of the demand for excellence in the classroom. The course, Women Writers, grew out of a competitive Ford Foundation curriculum grant I received in conjunction with the Duke University-University of North Carolina Women's Studies Research Center. This weekly evening seminar-style course provided invaluable connections with students, both women and men, and gave me the chance to keep up in the field of literature.

The 1980s and 1990s at EMU were times of expanding academic programs. Master's programs were added, and the Adult Degree Completion program was launched. This program appealed to persons in the work force who had never had the opportunity to complete their baccalaureate degrees. It also served to strengthen connections with the area business and professional community. In 1990 the Lancaster Extension Campus was established in Pennsylvania.

One of the most significant program initiatives of this period was the beginning of the Center for Justice and Peacebuilding (initially called the Conflict Transformation Program) under the leadership of Director John Paul Lederach and Associate Director Vernon Jantzi. With a keen sense of the potential global impact of the program, the university engaged a small core of nationally and internationally recognized peace practitioners and faculty to launch the Center.[10]

This program, supported by the Board of Trustees as an appropriate and creative expression of the institution's mission, received significant start-up grants from a number of organizations such as the Hewlett and McKnight Foundations and the Pew Charitable Trust. In addition, MCC (Mennonite Central Committee) provided encouragement and support. A significant donor couple, James and Marian Payne, caught a vision for how they might underwrite some of the costs related to this ambitious project. For me, personally, it was a deeply satisfying experience to be part of the realization of a dream for an EMU peace and justice center rooted in the distinctive Anabaptist faith tradition.

Bluffton—an Unexpected Turn

When I said yes to the unexpected invitation to a presidency, the move from Harrisonburg, Virginia, to northwest Ohio required little adjustment. Yes, we were leaving the beauties of the Shenandoah Valley, but we were settling in farm country. Amidst soybean and cornfields, a college had been founded by the General Conference Mennonites in 1899. We were welcomed by the campus community and soon immersed in the familiar routines of college life. At First Mennonite Church, where we became members, we felt at home with these General Conference Mennonites of Swiss background. Except for less familiar names like Luginbuhl, Pannebecker, Sommer, Neufeld, Krehbiel, or Raid, we could have been in an Old Mennonite community. The church building was a little fancier (with breath-taking stained glass windows and a vaulted ceiling) and the organ a prominent feature of worship, but we sang the same hymns.

On my first day in the President's Office, I received a telephone call from a laundry vendor who had learned that Bluffton had a new president. I told the caller that I was not the one who would make the decision as to who should get the laundry contract. That matter, I said, was in the purview of another office. I hung up smiling, wondering if this laundry entrepreneur thought he would have an edge going directly to the novice woman president or whether he called because he knew that my predecessor, who had attended to many of these kinds of details, would have made the decision. In any case, Bluffton had a new president and a different kind of manager.

More than Buildings

The ten years at Bluffton University was a period of growth for this small Mennonite college, which served not only the church constituency but also students from a wide variety of backgrounds. Attracting students from the region as well as from General Conference Mennonite settlements in Ohio, Indiana, Illinois, and Pennsylvania, Bluffton offered a liberal arts program with a focus on Anabaptist faith values. Actually, it had become a welcoming campus for persons from many traditions, with Mennonites being in the minority. As my predecessor, Elmer Neufeld, used to say, Bluffton is "more than Mennonite." Bluffton University's mission was thus somewhat different from those of the four other Mennonite institutions, where Mennonites represented a majority of the student body. I appreciated immensely that Bluffton could be a place where students of varied backgrounds discovered distinctive Anabaptist values and commitments. In a time of missional focus for the newly integrated Mennonite church (MC USA), Bluffton was attracting future leaders, some of whom would go on to Mennonite seminaries and graduate schools in preparation for serving the church and the world.

Highlights during my years at Bluffton would include seeing

long-held dreams for new facilities finally realized: a state-of-the-art academic center, the dedication of a music recital hall, an expansion of the student center, and construction of a student residence hall. The creation of a Technology Learning Center, along with a Federal Title III grant that provided an infusion of technology funds, transformed the campus. These were much needed developments as the campus celebrated 100 years and the opening of Centennial Hall, a four-story academic building.

While buildings and modern facilities are essential, they do not represent the heart and soul of a campus. When I asked students what they valued at Bluffton, they did mention access to technology and an expanded student center, but they talked about relationships with professors who cared about them, about chapel worship, about an appreciation for campus diversity, about friendships, the honor system, and the value of campus traditions. They repeatedly referred to "community," that nearly indefinable quality of a place that nurtures the heart, mind, and soul.

And so it is with my own story, the continued journey of discovery within the community of faith. There is a certain unfathomable joy in being part of a worthy enterprise that is larger than oneself. For me that has been the church and its institutions. I am irrepressibly hopeful about our institutions, but I am not naïve about the pitfalls and failures. I am reminded of Kathleen Norris's observation that "The church is like the incarnation itself, a shaky proposition. It is a human institution, full of ordinary people ... who do and say cruel and stupid things. But it is a divinely inspired institution, full of good purpose, which partakes of a unity far greater than the sum of its parts. That is why it is called the Body of Christ."[11]

I must pay tribute to Del, best friend and life partner, and to our two daughters, Lori and Judy, who have been my chief encouragers. Through a host of surprising opportunities—a myriad of convergences and fortuities—Del and I have gained an appreciation for risk-taking and for the mystery of the unexpected. And both of us have found purpose and fulfillment in being a part of God's work through the church.

Lee Snyder, April 2007
Revised August 2008

Notes

1 From *Utne,* July–August 2005, quoted in *Context,* November 2005, Part A: 8.

2 The recording of the interview with my grandfather was later transcribed by my aunt Berniece, with this story excerpt published in *Mennonite Life* (June 1987): 11–12. See "An Interview with Frank Kropf," edited by Berniece Kropf Schmucker.

3 Quoted by Kathleen Norris in *Virgin of Bennington* (New York: Riverhead Books, 2001), 104.

4 See "This Poor Gray Ember of Creation," by Thomas Gardner, a review of *Gilead* by Marilynn Robinson, *Books &Culture* (March/April 2005): 15.

5 *The Habit of Being: Letters of Flannery O'Connor,* edited by Sally Fitzgerald (New York: Farrar, Straus, Giroux, 1979), 596.

6 Mary Rose O'Reiley, *The Barn at the End of the World: the Apprenticeship of a Quaker, Buddhist Shepherd* (Minneapolis: Milkweed Editions, 2000), 137.

7 Anne Lamott, *Traveling Mercies: Some Thoughts on Faith* (New York: Anchor Books, 2000), 82.

8 Sheri Hostetler, "Say Yes Quickly," in *A Cappella: Mennonite Voices in Poetry,* edited by Ann Hostetler (Iowa City: University of Iowa Press, 2003), 126. Reprinted by permission.

9 Dr. Karen Klassen Harder, who teaches in the business department at Bluffton University, is credited with this wonderful summing up of the leadership task.

10 For a full account of the beginning of EMU's Conflict Transformation Program, see Ruth Hoover Zimmerman's history, "From Dream to Reality: Ten Years of Peacebuilding," available from Eastern Mennonite University.

11 Kathleen Norris, *Amazing Grace: A Vocabulary of Faith* (New York: Riverhead Books, 1998), 273.

The Days of Our Years ... Fourscore

The days of our years are threescore years and ten; and if by reason of
strength they are fourscore years ... it is soon cut off and we fly away.
– Psalm 90:10

Truly it is in sharing our stories that we begin to understand others and ourselves. My story falls easily into four approximate scores of years: birth to 22; 22 to 41; 41 to 63; and 63 to 80.

My First Score: Farming Finally Interrupted (Birth to 22)

In the decade after World War I, Calvin Coolidge became president in 1923 after the death of Warren G. Harding. Coolidge was sworn into office by his father, a justice of the peace, at 2:47 a.m. by the light of an oil lamp in rural Vermont. Charles Lindbergh, putting the finishing touches on the Spirit of St. Louis, was about to fly solo from New York to Paris.

In the same decade on the sunny morning of April 6, 1927, when the grass was green and lambs were frisking about, my mother gave birth to me, her sixth child. Now Shem and Salome had three daughters and three sons. *Jesse* was the name selected for me by my father, but my two brothers, aged eight and ten, vigorously protested that choice because they viewed a man nearby named *Jesse* as a community tramp. That is how it came about that in my first week of life, my mother, honoring an esteemed cousin and family friend, gave me his name, *Laban*. In the next ten years three more sisters and a brother completed our family of ten children. Our age range was twenty-one years, 1916 to 1938.

One of my early disquieting memories goes back to an event when I was three and a half. Given a four-line recitation for the annual Christmas program, I excitedly memorized my verse and looked forward to the program. But alas! Someone, either in the church or family, decreed, "Laban is too little!" I then discovered I was viewed as small for my age. To me, "too little" translated into "not good enough, inadequate." That sense haunted me into my early teens. For farm boys, physical size and strength forms the ability to compete with siblings and school friends, especially in the area of grade school sports. By late childhood I had adapted in school by avoiding sports, volunteering to be a librarian assistant, and concentrating on homework and extensive reading.

The age three episode illustrates how seemingly trivial family or community events may create influences that form attitudes and shape a life. Except as noted above, my childhood was filled with many wonderful experiences whose emotional tentacles reached into my adulthood.

At age nine when I went with my father to visit my mother's uncle, Crist Bender, we saw a bantam hen with chicks enclosed on the front lawn. Because they intrigued my father, he bought them for me. Thus my "bandy" business unfolded over four years, nurturing responsibility, independence, entrepreneurship, and family status. Mother and I "dressed" many for Bender's store; and each time I brought in a dressed chicken, Fred Bender, the storeowner, would say to the clerk, "Give the boy a dollar." A dream of future possibilities began to emerge. I started saving money to buy a farm!

Between the ages of eight and ten came problems of health and struggles with role and identity in the family—basically efforts to find my niche in the scheme of life. Somehow those struggles were resolved as I found suitable and engaging projects to pursue. It helped to live in the shadow of an older brother. Also, I owe much to my teacher in grades five through eight for providing fine instruction and a good learning environment.

Our family farm consisted of 140 acres, seventy tillable ones and pasture, and seventy woodland. The family milked twenty to twenty-five cows, kept 1000 laying hens, and raised pigs. In the 1930s and early 1940s we milked by hand, gathered, cleaned, and packed eggs, and in the winter months butchered and processed two hogs a week. The milk went through a cream separator, and we churned the cream into butter and fed the skim milk to the pigs.

Our mother often dressed some chickens for sale and in the summer also sold garden produce. Processing and preparing produce for Thursday's trip to town consumed a major block of our parents' time from Monday to Wednesday. On Thursday Papa loaded the produce in the car and spent the day making deliveries to stores on a regular route in Meyersdale, Pennsylvania, or Frostburg, Maryland. Often one of us children accompanied Papa.

To supplement our feed supply for the cowherd, Papa and the two older brothers did sharecropping on several neighboring farms. Our farm power was a team of horses and a 1930s model tractor, later with rubber tires. Making a living and living our lives all blended into one. Most of the time, work and recreation did not have a clear dividing line.

From ages twelve to sixteen I worked with my older brother, Paul, almost continually. In some ways he became a surrogate father. Our activities included daily farm chores, summer fieldwork, care for the livestock, and conversation about the perfect farm. Paul's farm idealism, drawn in part from the *Pennsylvania Farmer* and *Hoard's Dairyman*, became the substance of my life. My models were the successful farmers in the community, farm newspaper pictures and articles, Penn State College, and Mr. McDowell, the county agent.

Supporting this idealism were my mother and Uncle Milt. Especially Mother seemed pleased with the farm side of my dream. After Paul went to Eastern Mennonite School (although he came home part of the time), I worked with Papa on farm chores and summer fieldwork. However, I knew that farming was no longer Papa's first love. He had become busy pastoring men in Civilian Public Service (CPS) camps and attending meetings related to the peace issues arising from World War II. He began attending Ministers' Week at EMS (Eastern Mennonite School, later to become a college, EMC, and a university, EMU). Also, he was on MCC-related committees and came home talking about visits with important people like H. S. Bender, Orie O. Miller, P. C. Hiebert, Henry Fast, and many others. He continued to assist a steady stream of draftees with their Selective Service questionnaires, and he traveled some, holding meetings and Bible conferences.

While I was annoyed by Papa's marginal interest in farming, I was also impressed by his many important assignments. I became his student in Bible reading, Mennonite history, and the study of German.

He often read Paul Erb's *Gospel Herald* editorials aloud at the breakfast table. He had me read books such as *Mennonites in Europe* (1942) by John Horsch; and later in CPS I read the six booklet series, *Mennonites and Their Heritage*, edited by H. S. Bender.

At age fourteen I was one of twelve teenagers who prepared for baptism. Our "bench" of ministers walked us through the *Dortrecht Confession of Faith*, and Papa helped me understand the meaning of faith and commitment. The baptism process was a renewal experience for me. I began a new spiritual journey and tried to understand the meaning of faith commitments in attitudes and daily living.

In 1943 when I was sixteen, transitions in the family and changes in the environment affected my life. The United States had entered World War II; gasoline and commodities were rationed; and there was a general mood of anxiety and uncertainty. An older brother and sister had married; in 1941 Paul had left for EMS in Virginia; and two sisters followed him later. We had bought milking machines and discontinued butchering and the weekly sale of farm produce in stores—our milk and eggs were picked up at the farm and sold to local distributors. With my older siblings gone and Papa traveling some, I gradually became "the man on the farm" though I did not look like much of a man. I was sixteen, but my weight on my driver's license was listed as ninety-eight pounds!

April 6, 1945, marked my eighteenth birthday. World War II ended early in August 1945, but the Selective Service draft continued. On October 5 of that year, at 5:30 a.m. I arrived at Civilian Public Service (CPS) Camp #4, in Grottoes, Virginia. I was eager to go despite my attachment to the farm. I wanted to see—experience—the world beyond the Allegheny hills. Since CPS camps and service centers were beginning to close, I stayed fifteen months in four locations: two soil conservation camps, Grottoes, and Powellsville, Maryland. I also spent four months working in a mental hospital in Providence, Rhode Island, as an attendant in the medical building, where many of the patients were terminal. I wrapped up more than twenty bodies during that time and, with the help of another patient, took them to the morgue. I also spent four months in a Food for Relief processing center in Kalona, Iowa, where John A. Hostetler from MCC-Akron was my supervisor.

In CPS I met a great variety of men from the range of Mennonite and

Amish groups, along with a goodly number from the major Protestant denominations, Jehovah's Witness, and independent churches. Since none of us was free to go home or be away from camp, we had time to read. Professor Hubert Pellman, assigned by EMC to visit CPS men interested in preparing for the GED tests, met with several of us, giving directions on what to read. In February of 1946 I passed the GED tests and now had two dreams: Besides saving money to buy a farm, I was also saving money to attend college. Now I could plan for college rather than just dream about it.

My Selective Service release from CPS came in late December 1946, and I arrived home on January 1, 1947, to face new decisions. My parents and their three youngest children were spending time in Arthur, Illinois, where Papa served as the founding pastor for a group of Old Order Amish people who wanted to begin a conservative conference congregation. Thus our chickens and dairy herd had been sold. Now I agreed to help the family for two years to reestablish these aspects of the farm. Those years gave me a chance to reconnect with the home church and friends and also to develop business and management skills with a new productive dairy herd and a successful broiler operation. My farming instincts were renewed. Should I next attend Frostburg State College part time while farming, accept a job offer as service manager with a poultry company at an excellent salary, or go to EMC? For me a number of roads "diverged in a wood, and I—I took the one less traveled by, and that has made all the difference" (Robert Frost, "The Road Not Taken").

During grade school and college, I memorized a number of poems that have inspired me during my lifetime. I have selected four of these that characterize each score of years. This one is probably from grade four.

Great, Wide, Beautiful, Wonderful World

Great, wide, beautiful, wonderful World,
With the wonderful water round you curled,
And the wonderful grass upon your breast—
World, you are beautifully drest.
The wonderful air is over me,
And the wonderful wind is shaking the tree,

It walks on the water, and whirls the mills,
And talks to itself on the tops of the hills.
You friendly Earth! how far do you go,
With the wheat-fields that nod and the rivers that flow,
With cities and gardens, and cliffs, and isles,
And people upon you for thousands of miles?

Ah, you are so great, and I am so small,
I tremble to think of you, World, at all;
And yet, when I said my prayers today,
A whisper inside me seemed to say,
"You are more than the Earth, though you are such a dot:
You can love and think, and the Earth cannot!"

– William Brighty Rands

My Second Score of Years: From Student to Educator and Administrator (Ages 21 to 41)

Sometimes I muse pensively about where the roads not taken might have led. My return from CPS to the farm was intended to be temporary, but in the two years at home the farm dream from early and mid-teens grew new roots. I experienced excitement, opportunity, and challenge as agriculture-related career opportunities emerged. In the providence of God I finally decided at least to take a break from the farm. EMC was where I needed to go.

On January 27, 1949, I stood in the Records Office while Mary Florence Shenk helped me through the registration process for second semester. I thought the varied experiences of CPS had taught me how to make my way. But college! College teachers and students were not ordinary people like those I knew and had known at home, in CPS, and elsewhere. For a semester I lived in awe of this amazing college environment. In time I learned that the college consisted of real people.

The four years were a joyful journey with studies, extra-curricular events, and friends. Helen Mumaw and I got acquainted in Mrs. Brackbill's Introduction to Literature class, and in late 1950 we began dating. We were in the same college class and in some of the same extra-curricular activities. We graduated in May 1952, and in 1952 to 1953 I attended one year of seminary and was the high school boys' hall manager. Helen and I were then married in June 1953 and in 1955 began welcoming our four children—Phyllis in 1955, Lowell in 1957, Byron in 1959, and Joyce in 1963. They all grew up, married, and had families, giving us ten grandchildren and one great-grandchild.

Helen's degree, the Bachelor of Religious Education, did not give her an employable skill. However, she had taken secretarial studies in high school and was proficient in typing and shorthand. For some years, therefore, she worked as a secretary. Now, newly married, we wondered how to sharpen our focus and get direction for the coming years. Teaching school would pay our college loans and give time to clarify our future direction. Since my parents were talking of leaving the farm, combining beef cattle farming with teaching seemed a possibility for us. In my junior year I had bought two Hereford cows with calves, and the farm dream returned as I neared the end of college.

While Helen and I were pondering the future, Ira Miller, then chair of the Student Personnel Committee, offered me the position of dean of college men. The dean of the college, C. K. Lehman, suggested that I prepare to teach psychology and begin by attending graduate school for several summers.

From 1953 to 1963 my academic life was a rhythm of EMC assignments that gave direction to graduate studies and expanded my EMC role. From 1953 to 1957 I spent summers working on a master's degree at the University of Virginia. At EMC my time was divided between teaching psychology courses and working with student personnel: dormitory management, student activities, and counseling. Later I spent several years as registrar.

In 1958 I enrolled in a doctoral program at George Washington University in Washington, DC, and in the summer of 1959 our family—now with three preschool children—moved to Falls Church, Virginia. In school full time for the next fifteen months, I took a variety of courses in psychology, counseling, curriculum, and student personnel. Professor Mitchel Dreese outlined a package of courses that would fit what my assignment at EMC might be. Dr. Dreese, a long time GWU professor, held appointments in both the Graduate School of Psychology and the

School of Education. Also a consultant in the U.S. Office of Education, he wanted me to learn about the many educational resources in the nation's capitol.

In the 1960s EMC was a member of a consortium of small, private, non-accredited, mostly church-related colleges, the Council for Advancement of Small Colleges (CASC). Dr. Dreese believed a study of the student personnel services in those colleges would be a fitting research project. Through EMC involvement in CASC, I knew the executive director, Dr. Alfred Hill. Under the guidance of these two mentors I designed the research and completed my dissertation, *An Investigation of Student Personnel Work in Selected Small Colleges.* Fifty-one colleges were in the research sample, EMC among them. In June 1963 I received a Doctor of Education degree, EdD, in Counseling Psychology.

After graduating from college, I had, as described, been preoccupied with graduate studies. Now I planned to discontinue student personnel activities and focus on teaching. Our fourth child, Joyce, was born on September 1, 1963. Life, I thought, would be less hectic and we could spend more time with our children!

In 1965–66 I was due for a sabbatical. A professor at Goddard College, Arthur Chickering, whom I had learned to know through CASC conferences, had been awarded grants from the National Institutes of Health and the Ford Foundation to do a five-year longitudinal study on the characteristics of college students. The study was to examine how colleges impact the life and values of their students. Fifteen diverse colleges, including Eastern Mennonite, were selected for the study, covering the continuum from conservative/fundamentalist to liberal/no religious orientation. Now for this sabbatical year, I accepted Dr. Chickering's invitation to be a research associate, joining four other staff members in his Project on Student Development, based at his college in Plainfield, Vermont. It was a good year for my family and for me. I learned some basics of research as I helped to collect and process data and went along to various site visits at participating colleges. Weekends and evenings were free. We took family trips, became part of the community, and experienced something of the ethos of a small New England town.

Returning to EMC the following year, I had no college assignments other than teaching. Now my goals were to do a good job of teaching and to build the psychology department.

Then late in May 1967 I was invited to serve as the president of Hesston College in Hesston, Kansas. Since being the president of anything had not been in my thoughts or my ambitions, this invitation was a total surprise! However, in the middle of June I sent a letter accepting the appointment—to begin one year later on July 1, 1968.

The Hesston College Board of Overseers recommended preparation time during the spring semester of 1968, and Dr. Albert J. Meyer of the Mennonite Board of Education arranged an internship with the Association of American Colleges (AAC). Dr. William Jellema, head of the association and a person with experience in orienting college presidents, agreed to arrange a four month part-time internship for me. I taught two classes at EMC that semester on Mondays, and then each week I spent from Tuesday to Friday in Washington, DC. This orientation was excellent preparation in many ways, including, as it did, an introduction to contacts that would be helpful in the years to come. Many educational agencies have their national headquarters in our nation's capitol, and stopping by the AAC office or attending a meeting there was commonplace for college administrators. I met college presidents and deans, attended meetings and conferences, and listened to administrators talk about student activism on their campuses.

I spent a block of time attending meetings, too, on the nearby Mt. Vernon Junior College campus and talked with a few faculty and administrators there. Dr. Jellema also introduced me to leaders in the Association of Community Colleges and Association of Private Junior Colleges. Getting a sense of who those educational entities were and meeting some of the leaders provided resources that would prove invaluable in the years that followed.

During my twenties and thirties, I experienced questions and struggles as I searched for direction. The uncertain flight of Bryant's waterfowl is descriptive of my experience:

To A Waterfowl

Whither, midst falling dew,
While glow the heavens with the last steps of day,
Far, through their rosy depths, dost thou pursue
Thy solitary way?

Vainly the fowler's eye
Might mark thy distant flight to do thee wrong,
As, darkly seen against the crimson sky,
Thy figure floats along.

Seek'st thou the plashy brink
Of weedy lake, or marge of river wide,
Or where the rocking billows rise and sink
On the chafed ocean-side?

There is a Power whose care
Teaches thy way along that pathless coast—
The desert and illimitable air—
Lone wandering, but not lost.

All day thy wings have fanned,
At that far height, the cold, thin atmosphere,
Yet stoop not, weary, to the welcome land,
Though the dark night is near.

And soon that toil shall end;
Soon shalt thou find a summer home and rest,
And scream among thy fellows; reeds shall bend,
Soon, o'er thy sheltered nest.

Thou'rt gone, the abyss of heaven
Hath swallowed up thy form; yet, on my heart
Deeply has sunk the lesson thou hast given,
And shall not soon depart.

He who, from zone to zone,
Guides through the boundless sky thy certain flight,
In the long way that I must tread alone,
Will lead my steps aright.

– William Cullen Bryant

My Third Score of Years: From College President to Conference Minister to MMA's Vice President of Marketing (1968 to 1990)

Hesston College President, July 1, 1968 to June 30, 1980
On Monday morning, July 1, 1968, Hesston College Board Chair, Howard Hershberger, retiring President Tilman Smith, and former President Milo Kauffman (president 1932 to 1950) gathered at the entrance of the administration building for an informal transition ceremony. Chairman Hershberger made suitable remarks, Smith handed the office keys to me, and former President Kauffman offered a long prayer sounding like Moses' prayer for Joshua! The wives were present in support. After everyone left, I went to my empty office, where I sat for a time in perplexity and awe.

Our family had packed the necessary living assets into a U-Haul truck and left Virginia on June 19, 1968. Helen, her sister, Grace, and the children, followed in our car as we headed from Harrisonburg to Hesston. The temperature was 102 degrees the week we arrived in Kansas. However, oblivious to the heat, our children, then aged four to thirteen, enjoyed exploring the community, finding new friends, and moving into a rented house. The Paul Friesen family, who had four children near the ages of our four, had previously sent letters to Virginia, introducing themselves. Thus our children had instant friends. As the family took root in Hesston, Helen in particular found a new role, a world of friends, volunteer activities, and a niche among faculty wives. As in all moves with young children, there were also challenges.

We made annual visits to Pennsylvania and Virginia to keep in touch with grandparents and extended family. However, opportunities to explore places in the Midwest in addition to a new church, school, and community were compensations for what we had left behind.

As the family settled in, I began testing visions and dreams with reality and tried to find my way at Hesston College and in the community. How does one identify and empower the best resources of a faculty and staff and give them affirmation but yet project a new vision, draw everyone into that vision, and begin to move forward? In July and August I interviewed most of the faculty and staff to get their perspectives on where the college was and what they saw as their own role in its future.

I read documents and reports, trying to understand the past. Thus for my orientation many conversations took place. Imagine, however, the "thrill" of listening to a faculty member in his early sixties comment on his vision thus: "I worked hard over the years and had hoped to take it easy in my remaining years."

Hesston, I knew, had been established in 1909 as an academy and a two-year college. Then in the mid-1960s the academy was phased out; in 1964 the college achieved North Central accreditation; and the first associate degree nursing class enrolled in 1966. Also in the 1960s, two new dormitories and a library were built.

During the 1967–68 school year before our arrival, a faculty group had read Jerome Brunner's *Process of Education*. Now I found openness on the part of many faculty to take a new look at the overall college program, revise the curriculum, and examine how students learn and grow. Nationally the community college ferment was being felt. The U.S. Office of Education was offering small grants for faculty development: seminars, workshops, and consultants available for on campus. All these helped create new vision and energy among the faculty.

We were able to activate a curriculum study committee with major faculty participation and support. In November of 1969 we took a document recommended by the faculty and overseers to the Mennonite Board of Education, *Hesston College in the Seventies*, and it was approved by the MBE. The features of the document included these:

- A clearly defined liberal arts context for the two-year education experience
- A block of four general education courses for all students, *The Foundation Studies*
- Course concentrations designed for transfer students, fitting majors in four-year colleges, especially at Goshen and EMC
- Career-oriented programs leading to entry-level jobs or transfer to state universities.

In planning the curriculum, faculty members had had conversations with representatives of the institutions to which our students frequently transferred.

We looked at the students and asked what would strengthen their educational experience. Hesston College freshman were usually eighteen-to-twenty-year-olds, and most lived in the dormitories. The majority were a long distance from home. Thus we worked at developing a student services department with many on-campus recreational and athletic activities, especially on weekends. The campus atmosphere and dormitory experience were seen as the setting where personal development, socialization, and education occurred; and those on the student services staff were viewed as part of the educational enterprise. Second-year students were carefully selected and given training and coaching as dormitory supervisors and campus leaders.

Junior colleges had been part of American higher education since the late 1800s, most of them independent or private. With the emergence of the public community college movement in the 1960s, there was concern among educational leaders about the quality of education in these new colleges. Four-year institutions had a stake in the educational quality of community colleges because students began transferring to them to continue their education into their third and fourth years. Some students were not well prepared.

In the early 1970s the U.S. Office of Education designed and funded programs to strengthen and provide resources for two-year colleges. Four colleges were selected as resource centers with federally funded staff; three were public and one, private. Each resource center was to provide consulting services on a specialized area of college life. Hesston College was selected as the private college resource center, with a focus on student life. Each year 110 to 120 two-year colleges became part of this consortium, receiving services by way of the four resource centers. This federally funded program continued four years, 1974 to 1978. The funding was designed to help colleges review and upgrade their educational programs. National conferences, workshops, and seminars were offered to colleges in the consortium. Thus Hesston faculty had access to a range of educational resources, and they also served as speakers and leaders in some of these conferences. With a "national center" on the Hesston campus, the faculty received many direct and indirect benefits from being part of this program.

In the late 1970s Helen and I were entering our fifties. Three of our children were in college, and the youngest would soon graduate from high school. We had completed over ten exciting years in Hesston. After considerable deliberation we decided that June 30, 1980, would be the end of our Hesston College adventure. At a Saturday board meeting I indicated my wish to terminate, marking the end of twelve years. On a Monday morning in February, 1979, an early faculty meeting was called to announce I would not accept appointment to another term. I would end my Hesston College adventure on June 30, 1980.

Reflecting on the Hesston College Experience:
Looking Back Forty Years

Distance lends perspective and sometimes enchantment to the view. At forty-one I was young and lacked experience. My leadership background was limited to a small segment of college life at EMC, the classroom, and student life. Now suddenly my responsibilities involved a wider range of leadership—relating to faculty, students, boards, church, the public, and more. These many relationships required that I play varied roles among the different constituencies. Suddenly I was a *leader.* This awareness gradually impacted how I thought about myself, my self-identity. New roles, requiring new skills, became part of the substance of my life.

In 1968 the academy on the Hesston campus had recently been closed. Regional accreditation had been achieved. Some young creative faculty were in their first teaching assignment. Nationally the mood in public two-year colleges was to explore new approaches to teaching, learning, and the management of student life. With some federal grants designed to improve teaching and learning, a number of faculty attended workshops and visited two-year colleges. All this created a ferment of energy and excitement on campus. Student enrollment increased, and the positive atmosphere among faculty and students spread into the church constituency.

Over several years, together we were able to create a climate that encouraged new patterns of teaching and learning, creative relationships among faculty and students, and a refocus of institutional goals. We now presented Hesston College to the church and the Kansas public as a two-year Mennonite college with educational resources and goals that were suitable for an important segment of high school graduates. And slowly this college experience, interacting with faculty, students, and church public, transformed me as a person and the ways I worked with people.

The Hesston experience also led me to reflect on my own faith journey. In the months before moving to Kansas I had several important conversations with J. C. Wenger of the Associated Mennonite Biblical Seminary. I asked him these questions:

"How do I nurture my own faith in preparation for a leadership role?"

"How should I and Hesston College articulate appropriately a biblical faith perspective?"

"How do I lead in creating an environment that nurtures faith among college faculty, drawing faculty and students into the stream of church life?"

"How do we find and foster a biblical position on the theological continuum?"

The conversations with Wenger were important to me personally. However, in time persons on the faculty, particularly those teaching Bible and Mennonite history, led the college in building a biblical-Anabaptist emphasis into the curriculum.

As I worked with faculty and board members, I began to learn the meaning of Romans 12:5–6 (NIV): "... so in Christ we who are many form one body .... We have different gifts, according to the grace given us." The fine achievements of Hesston College were the fruit of many people's exercising their gifts, but out of the many we formed a united effort.

It is now forty years since we began our Hesston College odyssey. There were hard times and failures, of course. We are human, finite. However, there would be no joy or benefit in recounting mistakes or personal failures. God was present, guiding our efforts and always extending his grace.

For me, for us, for our family, the Hesston venture was a positive experience. Here our children moved through the teen years to young adulthood and looked toward their future. Helen and I were looking forward to the next phase in life. Could anything in the future be as fulfilling as Hesston College?

The college continues to thrive under new generations of leadership and always new generations of students, as the following three illustrations show.

Recently in a setting unrelated to Hesston College I met a person who has taught at Hesston since the mid-1970s. He remembers our conversation at the time of his employment, spoke of his fine experience over these years, and thanked me for helping provide a wonderful opportunity that has continued now for more than thirty years.

In the past year I also happened to visit five recent Hesston graduates who had just received college degrees from an outstanding university. They glowed with enthusiasm when speaking of their Hesston College experience, which, they said, had given them an excellent personal and academic foundation.

Recently, too, a Hesston graduate from the late 1970s told me how her personal life, family, and career had been shaped by her two years at Hesston College.

My years at Hesston College were mostly great. Helen and I recognized that our lives had been changed for the better by those years as we saw new opportunities opening, enabling us to use the learning and relationships growing from the Hesston experience. In the seven years since Helen has been gone, I continue to be inspired by the Hesston College community.

South Central Conference, 1980 to 1982

The conference consisted of fifty congregations spread across the Midwest—Kansas, Missouri, Arkansas, Oklahoma, Texas—and in Mexico. Plans were in the works to employ a conference minister, but a needs assessment was deemed desirable. The conference leaders asked me to spend two years visiting the congregations, doing a needs assessment and creating a profile of the congregations. They could then determine the job description of a conference minister and what services needed to be offered. Since daughter Joyce was entering her senior year of high school when I left Hesston College and we had wanted to stay in town at least one more year, I accepted this conference assignment.

I did spend nearly two years visiting the congregations, some of them twice and a few more often. We called and installed eleven pastors in the two years and assisted some congregations struggling with concerns and conflicts. Helen, who was employed as the Activities Director at the Schowalter Villa, went with me weekends when the congregations to be visited were nearby.

Typically I visited a congregation from Thursday evening to Sunday afternoon, meeting both the leadership members and groups of members. The questions discussed included "How is your congregation doing?" and "What do you need from conference?" I then addressed the congregation in the Sunday morning service and shared observations/ recommendations after a Sunday fellowship lunch. It was fascinating to write descriptive reports for each congregation without being judgmental. It seemed important to understand the cultural diversity:

- Many were rural and isolated with Mennonite roots.
- Some congregations had varied denominational backgrounds, both urban and rural.
- Some were Spanish-speaking in south Texas and Mexico.
- Many congregations, Anglo and Hispanic, carried the marks of immigration within the last twenty-five to fifty years.

I made an oral and written report to the conference executive committee, and the congregations continued after my two years much as before. For me it was a fine adventure, but I went always hoping that in a small way the effort was helpful to individuals and congregations in their faith journey.

Mennonite Mutual Aid, 1982 to 1990

One of the marks of Anabaptists in the early years was the way they cared for one another. In the American colonial settlements, congregations and communities helped each other as spontaneous expressions of faith. By the 1930s many communities had local organizations to assist families experiencing fire or storm losses. Soon "auto aid" assistance was also organized. Most of these companies made assessments to members based on losses.

In 1944 a General Conference session (of the Mennonite Church) approved forming a company to assist Mennonites with health costs. Care was taken to designate this assistance as *Mennonite Mutual Aid (MMA)*, not *insurance*. By the early 1980s MMA was providing health coverage assistance to a large number of people among various Mennonite groups. Enrollment and marketing were informal through congregations. In the 1960s the Mennonite Foundation emerged as part of MMA, and in the 1980s investments and life insurance became part of the MMA portfolio.

In June 1982 Helen and I moved to the Goshen, Indiana, headquarters of MMA. Helen worked in the Mennonite Foundation office, and I was to develop a church relations effort to promote the vision of mutual aid and help staff interact with MMA's church public.

As health costs increased, MMA needed to improve its product line and control the cost of health insurance premiums; it also looked for better ways of marketing. In 1984 I was asked to fill the new position, Vice President of Marketing, and form a marketing division. We appointed regional managers across the United States Mennonite population and found local insurance agents approved by local committees to represent MMA. By 1990 forty-seven Mutual Aid Counselors were in place with the assignment to sell and service MMA products. It was the task of the marketing division to recruit counselors, to orient them to the MMA vision, and to offer the technical training needed to sell and service MMA products.

When we began at MMA, we were not thinking much about our older years. We had led several retreats for older people, focusing on retirement. By 1990, however, it felt like our turn. The marketing system and new management at MMA had brought about important changes and improvements. The marketing program was working but required insurance background and further development beyond my skills or interest. Also by 1990 Helen and I were past sixty; in Virginia, Helen's father, in his mid-eighties, was in poor health; our four children were adults living between Kansas and Washington, DC; and our farmstead and land in Virginia were deteriorating. It was time to go back to the Shenandoah Valley—to be closer to family, to reconnect with friends, to rebuild the beef cowherd, and to prepare for our older years. We often read William Cullen Bryant's "Thanatopsis." The last stanza helped us look beyond the present:

> So live, that when thy summons comes to join
> The innumerable caravan, which moves
> To that mysterious realm, where each shall take
> His chamber in the silent halls of death,
> Thou go not, like the quarry-slave at night,
> Scourged to his dungeon, but, sustained and soothed
> By an unfaltering trust, approach thy grave,
> Like one who wraps the drapery of his couch
> About him, and lies down to pleasant dreams.

Left, shown at age 13. Right, sitting with Helen

My Fourth Score of Years: Short Assignments and a Grief (Ages 63 to 80)

While driving the truck to Kansas in June 1968, I had entertained our eleven-year-old son, Lowell, by helping him dream, "When we move back to Virginia, you can drive the truck." Now twenty-two years later, on April 1, 1990, Lowell and his four-year-old son, Tyler, flew from Kansas to Goshen; and Lowell drove the truck, accompanied by Tyler. We arrived in Virginia on April 2, Helen's sixty-first birthday. Four days later I turned sixty-three.

In the twenty-two years since we had left Virginia, so much had changed: people, customs, the city of Harrisonburg. Seemingly our friends had aged! It was fascinating to be a stranger in a place that was home. We moved back into our 200-year-old farmhouse, mowed the weeds, and started rebuilding the beef cowherd.

Over the next ten years, 1990 to 2000, I had various short-term assignments. George Brunk III invited me to serve as campus pastor at the seminary. Soon after our move, Lindale Mennonite asked that I serve part time as interim pastor. District overseer, Sam Janzen, felt I needed clergy credentials and conducted an ordination. In addition, I taught in EMU's Adult Degree Program and served as conference moderator and overseer for six congregations, as well as interim pastor not only at Lindale but also at the Zion, Springdale, and Zion Hill congregations. During these years, I completed a two-year master's degree at the seminary, a program I had begun in 1952.

In February of 1997 in a routine mammogram, a cancerous lump was identified in Helen's left breast. After several surgeries, including a mastectomy, and treatments, she had a time of remission. These were months to reflect on life, ask "what if" questions, read from the Psalms, and draw personal comfort from the Scriptures and music. In November of 2000 she developed unusual motor symptoms and talked of discomfort in her head. After a brain scan we learned that the cancer had metastasized to the brain. Death was imminent—weeks—maybe several months. This was a time for her—for us—to prepare for death. Helen died at 7:50 a.m. on December 14, 2000, at Rockingham Memorial Hospital. As we grieved together her last five weeks, we also rejoiced and celebrated our wonderful forty-seven and a half years together—fifty years together counting our pre-marriage romance.

On Monday evening after the funeral everyone went home. Grieving, like believing and dying, has deep personal dimensions. In the weeks and months that followed, I appreciated the care and support of family and friends. Now I knew that life was temporary, but faith, friends, and time enable healing and rebuilding. There is new life after the death of a spouse ... even without remarriage.

In May 2001, the Maple Grove congregation in Belleville, Pennsylvania, invited me to serve as interim pastor. It was good to leave our home for a time and also Lindale, where Helen is buried. Maple Grove was a fine experience of church. For sixteen months I lived in a farmhouse adjoining the farm where my father had been born 112 years before. Following this time, I served as interim pastor at Weavers Mennonite Church in Harrisonburg and Huntington Mennonite Church in Newport News, Virginia.

The last congregation where I was the interim pastor was in Springs, Pennsylvania, an assignment that ended on October 31, 2006. The farm where I had grown up was one mile west of the village of Springs. The two-room school where I went to first grade in 1933—when Franklin D. Roosevelt was dreaming up the New Deal—was up the hill from the Springs Church. What a wonderful gift to return to the community of my childhood and teen years! I had grown up in the Conservative Conference, but we often went to Springs for special meetings. There I heard A. J. Metzler, Paul Erb, J. Mark Stauffer, George Lapp (India), Ernest Miller of Goshen College, and many others. There I began to sense the answer to the question, "What is a Mennonite?" Returning after sixty years became an occasion for much reflection and joy.

Looking Ahead

For ten months now I have been back home in Harrisonburg, Virginia, in an apartment down the hill from Food Lion. Byron and Deanna bought the farmstead, but I still have some acreage and cows. Most days I go to the farm for one to three hours to check on the cows and do a few small maintenance jobs. I have just entered my ninth decade. Is this the last decade? I think of Psalm 90, which, referring to life after the age of eighty, reads, "It is soon cut off and we fly away" (KJV). How does one live richly, meaningfully, in the last years? I have few responsibilities, but this community offers many opportunities for relationships, enrichment, and exciting activities. The Eastern Mennonite University library is a good place to read. The Lindale Mennonite Church is becoming my primary faith community. Here I pastored, received my ordination, and was conference minister. It was also the place that helped to nurture Helen in her spiritual growth, the church where she grew up. Our marriage ceremony was at Lindale, and Helen is buried in the church cemetery. Three of our children and some grandchildren live nearby as do many friends. I can say only that this is a wonderful, blessed time of life ... despite Helen's absence.

Now at age eighty, *past and future* somehow begin to blend. When God called Moses at the burning bush, Moses protested, "How do I know?" in response to God's call. God answered, "In the future, when you worship on this mountain, *then!* you will know!" Is that the meaning of faith? Helen and I came to many crossroads and prayed, "Which way, Lord?" We moved ahead in faith. Now, looking back, we knew—I know—God was there.

I am much indebted and deeply grateful to the church, the institutions where I served, and to many people, family, friends for giving me (us) the opportunity to be part of so many rich experiences. My life was really *our life*. Helen was a part of supporting and shaping everything over a lifetime. Most of all, I give thanks to God for his grace. I did enough dumb stuff to need lots of grace and forgiveness.

I held Helen's hand as she passed from this life. In the weeks and months that have followed, I often read Revelation 21 to 22 and look beyond this life. Meanwhile in this life one of Shakespeare's sonnets gives an interesting perspective.

That Time of Year Thou Mayst in Me Behold

That time of year thou mayst in me behold
When yellow leaves, or none, or few, do hang
Upon those boughs which shake against the cold,
Bare ruin'd choirs, where late the sweet birds sang.
In me thou see'st the twilight of such day
As after sunset fadeth in the west;
Which by and by black night doth take away,
Death's second self, that seals up all in rest.
In me thou see'st the glowing of such fire,
That on the ashes of his youth doth lie,
As the death-bed whereon it must expire,
Consum'd with that which it was nourish'd by.
This thou perceiv'st, which makes thy love more strong,
To love that well which thou must leave ere long.

– From Sonnets, LXXIII (c.1958, 1609) by William Shakespeare

September 10, 2007
Revised 2008

Photo courtesy of MCC

JOHN A. LAPP

Remember Who You Are: Four Trajectories of My Life

I can still hear my mother's repeated admonition, "Remember who you are." From her, then, comes my title. I could have pursued other trajectories, given extended space. One I like to reflect on is my yen to travel from Richard Halliburton's *Royal Road to Romance* and his *Book of Marvels* to my traveling in fifty-five countries. Another has to do with the places we have lived from Derstine Avenue in Lansdale to Girish Chandra Bose Road in Calcutta and Knollwood Drive in Akron. A third would be to follow the jobs I have held from being a paperboy to an operating room technician to a teacher to an administrator. A fourth would be the political context from Franklin Delano Roosevelt—"the only thing we have to fear is fear itself"—to George W. Bush, who staked his fortune on the politics of fear and of terrorism.

I have chosen, however, to muse on these four trajectories: From Depression Baby to Iraq War Grandpa; From Plains Mennonite Church to Post-Denominational China; From Towamencin Township to Global Mennonite History; From Non-Participation in War to the Nurturing of Dissent in a Peace Church.

My parents also admonished us not to talk about ourselves. Obviously that is impossible when one is invited to be autobiographical.

From Depression Baby to Iraq War Grandpa

Historian David Kennedy writes that in March 1933 "history's wealthiest nation, the haughty citadel of capitalist efficiency, only four years earlier a model of everlasting prosperity, land of the pilgrims' pride, of immigrant dreams and beckoning frontiers, America lay tense and still, a wasteland of economic devastation."[1] Thirteen million workers were unemployed, some without work or income for years. State governors closed banks in thirty-two states. Franklin D. Roosevelt became President on March 4; and on the next day, Sunday, March 5, he declared a bank holiday, which was extended to Monday, March 13.

I was born two days later on Wednesday, March 15, at 527 Derstine Avenue in Lansdale. My parents, John E. (Clemmer) Lapp and Edith (Ruth) Nyce Lapp, had waited nearly seven years for this tiny five-pound boy. I was longed for and lovingly cared for.

Fast forward to September 20, 1990, when our son John called from Jerusalem to say that our first grandchild, Sophia Marie, had just been born in a Palestinian maternity hospital. A week later Alice and I were in Galilee, where they lived; and Alice stayed with the new baby and Sandra while I visited Mennonite Central Committee (MCC) projects in Jordan, Syria, Lebanon, and West Bank. Then Alice rushed home, repacked her suitcase, and went to Madison, Wisconsin, where our second grandchild, Sarah Margaret, had been born to our daughter Jennifer, married to Robert A. Lerch. In January 1991 John, Sandra, and Sophia came back to the United States on emergency leave as Iraqi rockets started landing in Haifa twenty miles from their home in Ibillin, an Israeli Arab town between Nazareth and Tel Aviv where Father Elias Chacour teaches peace and reconciliation. In 1991, 1992, and 1997 three more Lapps and Lerches were born. Then in March 2004 daughter Jessica and Phil Hertzler had our sixth grandchild. Thus our grandchildren began arriving as the sword rattling commenced for the first Iraq War and continued coming as the war was fought by other means—embargos until the invasion of Iraq in 2003 and the subsequent occupation of that country.

Of course, much took place between my birth and the arrival of our children and grandchildren. My parents, John and Edith, lived in the center of Lansdale, a town of 10,000 in the 1930s, their home a house built on what was once Great-Grandpa Clemmer's farm. Born there, Dad was a townie who graduated from Lansdale High School. Mom was a farm girl, an only child, from Harleysville six miles north. I like to recall that my parents lived their entire lives within ten miles of where their seventeenth and eighteenth century ancestors had settled. But how their children wandered!

Eight siblings and two stillborn boy babies followed me. We were a quiet yet exuberant family as we children played and argued but usually followed parental guidance.

In 1939 Mom and Dad decided to move out of town since their Derstine Avenue house had become too small. We now lived on an acre (later four acres) along the Allentown Road—an early Pennsylvania road from Philadelphia to Allentown. A stone marker just down the hill noted it was twenty-five miles to Philadelphia.

The family grew up here. From 1930 to 1940 Dad had a grocery store business, which he sold in order to have more time for the church. On our small rural acreage he tried chickens and turkeys in an effort to earn something to pay the bills and provide work for his children. Mom had a large garden in which we children also worked.

Because of Dad's busyness in church life, Mom carried a heavy load in managing the household. A thrifty, capable traditionalist, she yet found time to be informed by the local papers—*North Penn Reporter* and *Souderton Independent,* as well as the *Gospel Herald*—and she had a regular list of friends she talked with by phone.

In 1952 our grandmother Nyce moved in after the death of Grandpa Nyce. Grandmother Nyce was an important fixture for some fifteen years until, like her mother and later her daughter—my mother—dementia set in, and she moved to the Souderton Mennonite Home. Her participation in family life included paying some of the bills as they accumulated.

Dad was more outgoing and self-assured than was Mom. He knew many people in Lansdale, where he had grown up. Later as he circulated in Franconia Conference and beyond, his list of acquaintances became proverbial. Until late in life he could remember most of the people he had met.

Neither parent was scientific in parenting. They read few books on the topic and did not attend any seminars—they did what came naturally. However, when I started to stammer in the first grade, they listened to the family doctor, who urged them not to force me to write with the right hand. The stammering stopped!

Dad encouraged his children to get an education. While it is true that the memories of my sisters regarding his views of education for them are less positive than those of the sons, Dad and Mom clearly respected their children's differences and did not insist on college degrees. They had much admiration for the one son and one daughter who developed highly successful life niches without college attendance.

Since Franconia had no Mennonite school until I was well along in junior high, I did not attend a Christian day school. Dad then encouraged me to go to a church high school in Lancaster (his preference) or Harrisonburg (my choice). My sister Mary and brother Jim also attended EMHS (Eastern Mennonite High School) in Virginia before Christopher Dock (also a Mennonite high school but in our community) was established.

I continued on to college at EMC (Eastern Mennonite College now EMU, Eastern Mennonite University) where, after a little dating, Alice Weber and I found each other in Paul Peachey's Marriage and the Family class. I liked her creativity and assertiveness. She decided, after sitting behind me in that class, that she could tolerate the cowlicks. We took this course in the winter of 1954 and decided to marry in 1955. Meanwhile, I graduated in 1954 and immediately went off to Cleveland in I-W (the approved alternative service category for conscientious objectors to military conscription).

Connecting with Alice brought me into another family circle—the Webers and Hostetters—that proved intensely stimulating. This was Lancaster. I had grown up in Franconia. Both Pennsylvania areas in those days had fairly distinctive Mennonite identities. Actually, Alice's father's choosing not to attend a church for nearly twenty years presented an interesting situation. Mother Sarah, however, kept the faith at Lititz Mennonite Church.

At that time Lititz was only fifty years old in contrast to Plains' 200 years and many Lancaster neighbors' 150 years. It was a progressive congregation facing numerous obstacles from conference leadership then in a regulative phase. Fortunately for us, we were in Cleveland and later Harrisonburg when the clampdown occurred. Alice tells this story in her 100-year history, *Christ Is Our Cornerstone*, published in 2007.[2]

We spent our first year of marriage in Cleveland, where I finished my I-W term and Alice taught in a rough downtown junior high school.

Then we taught in Virginia for two years—I at EMC-EMHS and Alice at Elkton High School—after which we lived in Lansdale for two years while I attended the University of Pennsylvania and Alice taught at the Eisenhower High School in Norristown. We were again at EMC from 1960 until 1969; and our children arrived as scheduled in 1960, 1962 and 1964.

We now had our own family; and our ever-patient children followed us, mostly me, to Akron, Pennsylvania, from 1969 to 1972 and then to Goshen, Indiana, from 1972 to 1984. They grew up in these years and married in 1984, 1986, and 1994. It is interesting how closely our family patterns followed those of our parents; yet there were differences, the biggest of which was that we moved some thirteen times over considerable distances. Our children watched TV, which we as youngsters had not. They read lots of books but spent less time with newspapers and magazines. They complained that their only vacations were attending church conferences, which, however, our son now inflicts on his children. Charles Pinches in his recent book says, "Family is memory's most natural home."[3]

From the Plains Mennonite Church
to Post-Denominational China

Almost as powerful as family memories is our (my) immersion in and preoccupation with the church. Pauline Clemens Fisher still remembers how as a first grader I fought going to school when there was a Bible conference at Plains! Indeed, we went to church often, and my older siblings and I played church in between. I attended my first Mennonite General Conference in Kitchner, Ontario, as a two-year-old in 1935. The family church was Plains Mennonite, built near the edge of where the Mennonite farms ended and the Welsh-English farms began. A hundred years older than Lansdale, which was established on the Philadelphia to Bethlehem Railway, the congregation numbered 270 in the 1930s to 1950s and included strong families deeply interconnected—Clemmer, Rittenhouse, Cassel, Mininger, Hackman, Rosenberger, Kulp, Allebach, Clemens, and others.

Three months after I was born, Dad was chosen in a lot of six to become a minister at Plains. Four years later he was ordained bishop in the Middle District of (the Pennsylvania) Franconia Conference. From the beginning I was a PK (preacher's kid) and son of a bishop!

I am sure Plains had its problems, but I still look back on it as a model congregation. A family spirit was pervasive. Older men and women taught Sunday school, Bible school, and mid-winter Bible study classes. There was a strong sense of mutuality even though different personality/familial styles were hard to assimilate. The accent was surely on nurture and community rather than on witness and evangelism. Here in 1947 I was baptized into the body of Christ. (I had made a confession of faith at Laurelville Mennonite Boys' Camp the previous summer.)

The ministers at Plains—J. C. Clemens, ordained in 1906 and the first real English preacher, and my dad—were gifted speakers and pastors. Both had exposure to the church beyond Franconia, and both served on church-wide committees. Also, since J. C.'s wife, Hannah, was a first cousin to Dad's mother, Kate Clemmer Lapp, the spiritual and familial ties were deep. Both pastors put a premium on education and wider church connections.

Interestingly, Clemens very early became an outspoken advocate of the amillennial interpretation of the Scriptures. (Sometime I would like to find the roots of his deep conviction.) He had a great influence on my dad, and both men promoted, defended, and argued for amillennialism all their lives. They saw themselves as a kind of defensive duo against the onslaughts of premillennialism and used their influence and authority to quell dissenting voices. Moreover, they frequently joined forces with others—Ira Landis in Lancaster, John Risser in Hagerstown, and Chester K. Lehman at Eastern Mennonite College—who also perceived amillennialism to be the historic tradition of the church against the newer more colorful interpretations.

Also, between 1937 and 1960 Dad and Mom were strong advocates for plain dress (which included a "plain" suit coat for men and a cape dress and a covering or prayer veiling for women). Not one of their nine children was convinced by this urging. Uncle Wilbur Lapp observed that Dad moderated because of the influence of his children.

Dad's real passion—beyond the Bible, wholesome church life, and Mennonite history—was nonresistance and biblical teaching on peace. (These were also J. C. Clemens's interests.) In fact, Dad's older bishop colleagues urged him to become knowledgeable about the peace theme as World War II approached. In 1938 he became a member of the Mennonite Church Peace Problems Committee, on which he served until retiring in the early 1970s. After Harold S. Bender's death in 1962, he chaired what was then called the Peace and Social Concerns Committee.

I recall during World War II how dozens of young men from congregations across the conference came to the house for counsel as they filled out Selective Service questionnaires. Then he became a CPS (Civilian Public Service) pastor, traveling many weeks a year to visit conscientious objectors in camps and hospitals from Maine to Iowa. Later he helped to organize and maintain the I-W network for the church. In this way Dad helped manage the church's non-participation in war from the 1940s to the 1970s.

After Plains and my becoming acquainted with Lititz Mennonite Church and Alice, the two of us became early members of Park View Mennonite Church in Harrisonburg, Virginia. In 1972 we moved our membership to College Mennonite Church in Goshen, Indiana, and then in 1986 returned to Lititz.

Dale Brown observed some months ago that he was accused of being obsessed with the Church of the Brethren heritage. My life has been deeply immersed in the Mennonite church. In a less gender conscious age I would have called myself a "churchman."

But through the years my understanding of church deepened as I was exposed to more and more Mennonite congregations. In Cleveland through our I-W unit and particularly the chorus led by Jay B. Landis, I learned to know the Ohio Mennonite and Amish scene. At MCC (the main Mennonite relief agency) I learned to know the spectrum of Mennonite and Brethren in Christ churches across North America. Later I discovered that most MCC work overseas is done in conjunction with local churches, many of them other than Mennonite. I became more and more conscious of the appeal of the gospel message in the global South and its declining appeal in the North. When MCC was discussing in 1993–94 how to celebrate its 75th anniversary, it decided to make a substantial grant to Mennonite World Conference to establish a global church sharing fund as a deliberate way to highlight the transformation of Christian geography. Alice and/or I have attended Mennonite World

Conference Assemblies in Brazil, France, Canada, India, and Zimbabwe. In 1991 Alice and I attended the World Council of Churches meeting in Canberra, Australia, enlarging our vision ecumenically. In 1955 to 1957 I was part of a group that determined to create a new *Global Mennonite History*, a preoccupation of mine ever since.

Finally, on our recent China trip in the fall of 2006, I was taken by the Chinese church's self-definition as being post-denominational. Fifty years ago Herbert Butterfield called denominations a luxury of European dominance. The church in China, as well as the church in other locations, learned through bitter conflict, persecution, and suffering that the fragmentation of the church is a weakening of the God movement as well as a violation of Jesus' prayer "that they may all be one" (John 17:21).

I am still confident that the believers' church tradition is a necessary expression of faithful discipleship. How that fits in a post-denominational situation is not yet clear to me, but I shall never forget the Russian Orthodox priest who reminded me that the truth of Christ is so great that no one of us or any one tradition knows it in its entirety. We can still learn.

From Towamencin Township to Global Mennonite History

Next to family and church, my chosen identity is as a historian. I do not recall that I made a conscious choice before deciding that the best way to connect my interests in the past was as a teacher, particularly at the college level. Nor do I recall all the ways in which the seed of history enjoyment was planted. It surely had to do with the stories J. C. Clemens told from the Scriptures, *Martyrs Mirror,* and the Mennonite past. My father also had an acute sense of history, frequently noting the significance of this place and that. Dad took each of his older children for an extended half-price train ride before they reached the age of twelve. (Times change. I took our children for a plane ride.) My trip was in 1944 on the Black Diamond from Lansdale to Buffalo and then New York Central to Goshen for a special meeting of Mennonite General Conference. (The church was about to divide, but cooler heads prevailed. At my young age, I was oblivious to the seriousness of the occasion.)

Then the two of us headed on to Chicago on the New York Central and the Rock Island to Iowa City, where Dad participated in a Young

People's Institute at the East Union congregation and where I learned about some of the distinctions between eastern Mennonites and mid-western Amish Mennonites. On we went to Denison, Iowa, on the Chicago and Northwestern Railroad. Here Dad visited the Franconia men at a Civilian Public Service camp, James Clemens, J. C.'s youngest son among them.

During a Chicago layover, we visited the Field Museum of Natural History. In those days and perhaps today, there was a very large reconstructed dinosaur that dominated the spacious opening gallery. Dad's word was that this was quite imaginary, that only a few bones existed, and that surely the world was not as old as listed. One of the books on his shelf that I had paged through was a militantly anti-evolution tract called "Monkey Mileage: From Amoeba to Man," my first introduction to this controversial subject.

One of the really special persons who nurtured my historical interests was the principal of the Towamencin Township Elementary and Junior High School, J. Henry Specht. He seemed then to be a gruff, traditional leader to be feared. He was also the local historian writing a master's thesis on the history of our township. He had become the principal of the Kulpsville School by the time I transferred there in March 1939, when we moved out of town.

Mr. Specht, as we called him, must have noted my interests; for by the time I was in the ninth grade, he had organized a history club. We met on Wednesday afternoons, and he told us stories and took us on hikes around Kulpsville, an eighteenth-century village much older than Lansdale. We visited a Revolutionary War graveyard on the Allentown Road and the Detweiler farmhouse (my neighbor friend's grandfather's farm) which Washington had made his headquarters for several days after the Battle of Germantown. Our best walk was to the Towamencin Mennonite Meetinghouse and graveyard, where there were more Revolutionary War graves, including that of General Francis Nash, for whom Nashville is named. This was heady stuff!

Some Wednesdays we were excused from classes early to go by train to Doylestown, Norristown, and Philadelphia. I remember the quaint Merer Museum, the Commercial Museum, and above all the University of Pennsylvania Museum with its rich collection of Egyptian, Mesopotamian, Greek, and Roman antiquities.

To top it off, Mr. Specht established a history award for Towamencin graduates—we had only ten grades. He gave me the first and perhaps the last such award—Stewart Holbrook's new book, *The Story of American Railroads*,[4] which moved me pretty far along on the decision to pursue history.

I had some good teachers. At Eastern Mennonite College Paul Peachey sparkled in church and Mennonite history. Harry Brunk, a fine historian there, was, however, preoccupied with an ill wife during my college days. Carlton Wittlinger, a visiting professor from Messiah College, was an inspiring classroom teacher. At Case Western Reserve University there was Arvil Erickson, a specialist in modern English history, whose course, however, on Russia was insightful. In the middle years of Dwight D. Eisenhower's presidency, Erickson quipped, "There is nothing so simple as a military mind." Donald Grove Barnes respected my interests in British evangelicals and social reform. Harvey Wish helped me understand the dynamics of progressivism and the New Deal. John Hall Stewart was especially complimentary of a paper I did on the Enlightenment roots of humanitarianism. I likely should have done my doctorate under one of these since at the University of Pennsylvania I never really found such kindred spirits. My major professor there, Holden Furber, however, did suggest a church or mission dissertation topic. He was a specialist in the history of India and generously supported my dissertation research and writing.

Why did I choose Case Western Reserve University and the University of Pennsylvania? One reason for doing my I-W alternative service in Cleveland was to go part time to school. My dad did not want me to go to Columbia University because, although John Dewey was not in the history department, he taught there. After I was admitted to doctoral programs at Duke and Penn, Dean-Elect Ira Miller said categorically that Penn would be better than Duke. I managed to secure a Pennsylvania State Senatorial Scholarship to pay the tuition at Penn, and Alice taught at Norristown's Eisenhower High School to pay our bills. She also then and now types my papers.

In high school I was preoccupied with local history. I can still get enthusiastic about Montgomery County or Lancaster County as fertile sources for research and writing. Surely it was Paul Peachey's classes in college that deepened my interest in the history of the church and demonstrated the relevance of sixteenth-century insights for the twentieth-century situation. The intellectual and social dimensions of church history became very appealing.

But no singular theme emerged until I chose to pursue the Mennonite Church in India as my dissertation topic. Melvin Gingerich at the Archives of the Mennonite Church and Nelson Springer at the Mennonite Historical Library in Goshen found more than enough material for the dissertation. I discovered then the richness and problems of the church's encounter with a new culture. I found that mission history had to deal with the sending bodies and their contexts and with the receiving peoples and their contexts. Theological, ecclesial, political, diplomatic, and cultural issues had to be explored. Nevertheless, my dissertation, published in 1972, would be far different if done today. I laid out the mission process in considerable detail, but I did not capture the receiving side very well. I learned in a powerful way that missions are temporary, the church and the kingdom of God are the goal.

When I came back to EMC, Paul Peachey was gone and Grant Stoltzfus was here. Grant was a soul mate with whom I shared many interests and convictions. He was a reformer and a devoted Mennonite. Our almost daily conversations for nine years were extremely stimulating. His widespread knowledge of the Mennonite and Amish past, as well as his awareness of contemporary church politics, inspired new angles for my lectures and writing.

Along with history I had always had a great interest in contemporary affairs. We had no radio or TV when I was growing up, but we had three newspapers, all the Scottdale Mennonite periodicals, plus *The Pathfinder*, a progressive news magazine. The paper route of the *Philadelphia Bulletin* and *North Penn Reporter* gave me the opportunity to keep up with the military operations of World War II, which became a good vehicle for learning geography. I was especially interested in politics. Dad never voted, but he took me to Lansdale in 1944 to get a paper at six o'clock in the morning to see if Franklin D. Roosevelt had beaten Thomas Dewey. He did not like Dewey's mustache. In those days he thought Calvin Coolidge and Robert Taft were the ideal politicians. I, too, was enamored with Taft and went to Madison College (now James

Madison University) to hear him in 1952 when he campaigned here in the Shenandoah Valley.

In 1963 Dan Hertzler, the editor of *Christian Living*, asked me if I would review a new book by Edgar Snow, *Red China Today: The Other Side of the River*,[5] on Mao Zedong's China. I seized the opportunity and, as I was wont to do, was quite positive toward the left-leaning study. Apparently this did not disturb Dan because he soon asked if I would be prepared to write a monthly column on current affairs for *Christian Living*. Thus from 1963 to 1980 I dutifully did this chore, which I actually found to be an energizing task. Grant Stoltzfus showed me how to clip newspapers and magazines to good avail. Usually I thought of the topic, collected furiously, and then wrote.

I succeeded Dean Carl H. Kreider of Goshen College in writing this column. He once told me some friendly critics thought his columns were socialistic and mine even more radical! However, I suspect my reputation in *Christian Living* had more to do with the invitation later to be dean of Goshen than anything else I had done up to that time. Also, two of my books were heavily dependent on my *Christian Living* columns.

Teaching history at Eastern Mennonite College during the 1960s was exciting in every way. The students were eager, the times sparkled with debate, and I was more than ready to challenge existing interpretations of controversial questions. I liked to paint a big picture and develop appropriate generalizations. History of Civilization was a favorite course, and the history seminar was a good venue for exploring the research process and making sense of one's findings. We had excellent majors in those days (and likely still do) who became historians, teachers, lawyers, pastors, researchers, school principals, and deans. Inevitably I developed a lasting interest in how a committed Christian deals with historical realities.

But, alas, when I responded to the call to administration first at Goshen and then at MCC, my connection to history took second and third places. I did only occasional, short-term research; and I found it difficult to maintain interest in the monthly column, especially after *Christian Living* changed its focus from community to family. I did manage to do occasional book reviews for the *Mennonite Weekly Review*, *Mennonite Quarterly Review*, *International Bulletin of Missionary Research*, etc.

In retirement I have continued to write occasional articles of a historical nature. Also, I have found a new project—the *Global Mennonite History*. I am the organizer and fundraiser for this and do coaching and minor editing. Two good volumes have been published.[6] Now I am patiently waiting for the Latin America and Asian materials to come in for their volumes. The North American volume is well under way.

My being a historian gave me credibility as an administrator and surely added to my life both depth and a way of seeing. I cannot imagine a better orientation for MCC leadership. It was good training for the inevitable reports.

From Non-Participation in War to the Nurturing of Dissent in a Peace Church

Another source of my identity is as a peace advocate and sometime activist. This, as I noted earlier, was also a passion I had observed in my father. When Dad was helping the church find ways not to participate in World War II, I was a student in an enthusiastically patriotic elementary school where the students were taught about war and organized to sell war bonds. Classes had competitions to collect scrap metal, tin cans, and milkweed. Understanding that this stuff was all about fighting a "total war," Dad prohibited my participation. This was perhaps the first time I realized how different Mennonites were—their stance clearly went beyond dressing differently. As I also learned, that difference is hard to accept in a nationalistic society, no matter how democratic it is, and I felt the sting of ridicule and name-calling. I saw, too, that not all the Mennonites at Kulpsville School drew the same lines as did my parents.

I have never forgotten the alienation I felt at that time. Apprehensions of a forceful personal witness became embedded deep in my psyche. We were also shown a number of wartime movies like *The Battle of Midway*. I was not supposed to attend any movies. However, by 1945 with my paper route I had gained enough financial independence to pay the dime or quarter to see some films, much to the chagrin of my sister Mary and our parents. Their position was correct, but I did not want to pay the price of dissent. That surely was a major reason for my wanting to go to a Mennonite high school.

I do not recall much from Eastern Mennonite High School or Eastern Mennonite College on peace themes until I was a college senior. Then Paul Peachey and Irvin Horst brought to campus new passion as a result of their years in post-war Europe. Peace permeated their identities and teaching.

While some fellow students chose to serve their conscientious objector service abroad in PAX (a Mennonite wartime relief organization), I decided to be a domestic I-W. I chose this in part because I had a college debt to pay off and in part because I was now dating Alice. Interestingly, one day John Mumaw called me into his office to tell me that there was a Christian high school in the country of Lebanon that needed teachers. He thought I might be interested. I demurred but have often wondered how my life might have been different had I accepted. I have always enjoyed my subsequent visits to Lebanon even at the beginning of the 1982 Israeli invasion.

During my two years of alternative service, I learned how little awareness some I-Ws had of the peace tradition and witness, but the fraternity was warm and memorable. The real education of our I-W group in Cleveland came as we experienced for the first time racial injustice on a large scale. Other than we I-Ws, the people who staffed the university hospitals at the lower levels were largely black, and they taught us new lingoes and communication skills as we worked side by side. Sometimes we attended Gladstone Mission, where Vern Miller and others were carving out a congregation in a black society. We were not always sensitive, however, to Vern's focus on developing an indigenous congregation.

Alice's teaching in Brownell Junior High gave us new insight into inferior education and educational facilities. When she took me to see the movie *Blackboard Jungle,* I could not take the raw reality. She said it was even worse at her school than that portrayed on the screen.

Back at EMC in 1960 we were caught up in the Kennedy-Nixon campaign. By now I had decided it was okay to vote, that being one way to work for peace and racial justice. Apparently some of my political analysis got back to my parents, so the night before the election my mother called. She was quite agitated about the election and worried that I would vote. I teased her awhile and finally admitted that since I was not registered, I could not vote. She said, "Praise the Lord."

Race became a big issue on campus in the early sixties. We had the Virginia author Sarah Patton Boyle come to campus after she published *The Desegregated Heart*.[7] I well remember her response to a question. "I don't criticize the church because it's the best we have." Then came John Howard Griffin of *Black like Me* fame.[8] But most moving was Vincent Harding, who brought together deep spiritual fervor and social action. I do not recall many specifics on campus other than the persistent conversation. There was considerable opposition in Rockingham County to campus activism.

One very rewarding work in the community was the creation of the Rockingham Council on Human Relations. Harold Lehman, Samuel Horst, and I went to visit Charles Zunkel, a leading Church of the Brethren pastor, hoping he might be a good ally. Indeed he was interested and soon became our chair. A black pastor, Richard Bell from the AME congregation, built connections with the black community. Others may recall what achievements there were if any of the Rockingham Council; I suspect we helped a little in creating a climate for the inevitable integration of the city and county schools. Now the massive resistance for which Virginia was so well known seems like a very long time ago.

In August 1963 a carload of us went to Washington to participate in the famous march and hear Martin Luther King's great speech. About the same time I started representing the Rockingham Council at meetings of the Virginia Council of Human Relations. That opportunity gave me a good feel for the extent and depth of the movement for racial justice.

In the mid-1960s the war in Vietnam and the political campaigns of 1964 and 1968 overwhelmed some of our activism for racial justice. I have a distinct memory of discussing with Edgar Metzler then how we could balance and prioritize our concerns about nuclear proliferation and race and whether our focus should be on the larger society or renewing and enriching the life and voice of the church. In 1964 the Committee on Peace and Social Concerns became quite energized against the Barry Goldwater presidential candidacy. I have wondered whether that illustrated a tipping point that was too conspicuously political and partisan.

In the midst of this boisterous decade I managed to finish my dissertation. Meanwhile, there was considerable tension on campus between the students and some faculty activists on one side and the traditional separatists and quietists on the other. In the summer of 1968 Bill Keeney called me from Bluffton College to ask, in his position as the chair of the MCC Peace Section, if I would consider becoming the head of the Peace Section, a responsibility that appealed to me. After some discussion, I secured a two-year leave of absence from EMC, an absence that turned out to be permanent.

At EMC I had been on a number of committees and tasted what administration might be like. At MCC I became an administrator and learned that art primarily from William Snyder. Bill had been at MCC for twenty-five years and had already served as executive secretary for twelve years. He was a formidable force who often disagreed with the peace section activists—William Keeney, Edgar Metzler, John H. Yoder, Frank Epp and others. Something in me said I had to bridge that gap, so I took a different role from being the protagonist I sometimes represented at EMU. Moreover, Bill Snyder and I shared an insatiable interest in what was going on. He knew far more of what was going on in American churches, not only in the Mennonite denomination, than I would ever master. He was also very political in the best sense of that word. Within MCC this meant finding a balance among the members of this inter-Mennonite organization.

But one of the first principles of inter-Mennonite politics I learned from my father. He told me once that as long as a Mennonite Church individual—Orie Miller—was executive secretary of MCC, then the chair of the MCC had to be from another group—Mennonite Brethren P. C. Hiebert or Brethren in Christ C. N. Hostetter. When General Conference Mennonite Bill Snyder became executive secretary, then the Mennonite Church's Ernest Bennett or Newton Gingerich could be chair. It was just like balancing the U.S. Supreme Court geographically and ideologically.

The Peace Section faced major issues in 1969, the biggest of which was the growing draft resistance movement. Frank Epp, a half-time peace section staff in Ottawa, spent considerable time with those who fled to Canada. Walt Hackman, also from Plains, who served half time on the Peace Section and half time with the Mennonite Church Committee on Peace and Social Concerns, ran the draftee counseling service of MCC. Walt was my primary associate at MCC. While a student at EMU, he and Paul Miller from Holmes County, Ohio, had spent the summer of 1966 in Mississippi as part of a large student program there. Now he worked hard to keep resisters out of jail. My contribution was to write a statement—"The Draft Ought To Be Abolished"—for presentation in Washington and discussion in the churches.

Bill Snyder was sometimes agitated about the Peace Section activism regarding the war in Vietnam. MCC workers and Eastern Mennonite Board of Missions and Charities missionaries were becoming very vocal peace workers in Vietnam. The Peace Section board and Frank Epp in particular were urging them on. One day Bill Snyder announced that MCC was going to reduce Vietnam from being a priority and increase the visibility of the Middle East program. This would begin with Frank Epp, who would become a special resource, leading a tour and writing a book eventually known as *Whose Land Is Palestine?* I became the Akron liaison, going with Frank on the tour he led in 1969 and making the Middle East a peace section priority. The Middle East has been with me ever since and included a sabbatical there in 1978–79.

A third issue on the peace section agenda was getting the Washington office established. Delton and Marian Franz—both of whom died recently—moved to Washington and began that ministry in 1968. My task at Akron was to help define the parameters and priorities and to serve as a reference point at Akron. This proved to be a very positive part of peace section work and has developed far beyond what I could have anticipated.

During my second year at Akron, the incoming president of Goshen College, Lawrence Burkholder, asked me to consider becoming academic dean there. Like many administrators, he did this without consulting sufficiently at Goshen, so he had to cool the process until he had faculty support. I decided to ask EMU to extend my leave for one year to see what would happen at Goshen. A number of friends encouraged this move, which we made in 1972. I view the Akron years as good training in administration and diplomacy and as a time for integrating peace activity more deeply into MCC and Mennonite ways of thinking.

The most positive side of peace activity at Goshen was sustained interaction with a strong nuclei of Goshen faculty who were long-time peace proponents. Atlee Beechy, J. R. Burkholder, Guy Hershberger,

Norman Kraus, Cal Redekop, and Lawrence Burkholder were only six of these. Conversations with these people had a great deal to do with the development of my thinking about peace. During this time, there was interest in developing a peace studies program, and a minor was launched at the college.

In 1980 I was invited to replace Bill Snyder as executive secretary of MCC. Henry Weaver, who had been provost at the college, had left Goshen in 1979; and since by 1980 I had served only one year as provost, it did not seem like a good time to leave. Furthermore our youngest daughter, a junior in high school, said we could go but she would not move. Thus we decided to stay put but did accept the second invitation in 1984.

My twelve years as executive secretary of MCC were the culmination of my interest in church and peace. I was now more mellow and less anxious about myself or about changing the world or the church. I decided that peace was indeed a multi-layered concept that ought to be the driving force wherever and whenever. When a British Methodist missionary once asked me in Croatia to define the irreducible essence of the gospel, the Spirit inspired me to say, "God was in Christ, reconciling the world unto himself" (II Corinthians 5:19, KJV). Peace is godly; peacemaking is the work of Christ, and whether it is personal or socio-political, peace has historical and cosmic significance.

I tried to keep this vision at the forefront throughout my MCC experiences. Sometimes it was sharply evident. A big issue at MCC in 1985 was "development" that Pope Paul VI called "a new name for peace." I saw that vision and practice at work at a new water catchment dam in Burkina Faso. On that visit I witnessed a great controversy between the villagers who controlled the dam and the Fulani tribesmen who wanted to water their animals there. The dam was right on the 12th parallel north, which divides the Islamic North from the Christians of Central Africa. The situation demonstrated how development requires peace building.

The MCC experience also taught the fragility and precariousness of peace. In 1993 the Oslo accords were greeted with enormous enthusiasm. Some Mennonite business leaders, especially in Canada, invited me to join them to visit Israel-Palestine in 1994 to explore how business could be part of the reconciliation process. We had a stimulating trip,

With youngest grandchild, Nicholas Hertzler

but nothing happened. All Oslo did was to precipitate Intifada II. The chaos goes on. Peace is a witness as well as a strategy.

A few weeks ago I read a review of a new edition of Aldo Leopold's *Sand County Almanac*. This ardent conservationist observed sixty years ago that "nothing can be done about conservation without creating a new kind of people."[9] Peace, peacemaking, peace building—whatever terms we prefer, deal with vision, ethical practice and embodiment. That has been the Mennonite insight that continues to be so urgent.

Conclusion

Several years ago I wondered what might be an appropriate epitaph on my tombstone. Not wanting to claim very much, I wondered whether it ought to be "He made the system work." I suspect that is my main achievement as an EMU faculty member, as the executive secretary of the MCC Peace Section, as dean and provost of Goshen College, and as executive secretary of MCC. I tried to add a sense of humor and with a little passion promote the vision of "a new heaven and new earth." The Afghan author Khaled Hussein's character Rabin Khan in *The Kite Runner*, put it well, *"There is a way to be good again."*[10]

Wendell Berry, at the beginning of his novel *Hannah Coulter*, has Hannah saying, "This is my story, my giving of thanks."[11] Every day I become more conscious that I belong to many and have benefited from many. All I write should be understood as an expression of appreciation: for my spouse—partner of fifty-one years; for parents and siblings; for at least five congregations and two long standing small groups; for friends, teachers, mentors, and colleagues; for children, in-laws, and grandchildren. These and even more are part of the web of my life, my "community of memory."

The story I have told needs considerable amplification. I have said very little about the content and style of my administration in two major Mennonite institutions. I have not commented on strain, stress, or failure although they have sometimes been very real. Maybe someday I will find it easier to explore them. But now I want to emphasize how blessed I have been in the words again of Hannah Coulter, "Fortunate beyond anything I might have expected or ever dreamed" (43). My greatest satisfaction has been the deep privilege and joy of participating in the narrative of the Bible. Paul Hanson describes *The People Called* as those of every age who define themselves "primarily in relation to its participation in God's purpose for the world."[12] That is the meaning I ascribe to my life.

December 11, 2006
Revised 2008

Notes

1 David Kennedy, *Freedom from Fear: The American People in Depression and Wars, 1929–1945* (New York: Oxford University Press, 1999), 133.

2 Alice Weber Lapp, *Christ Is Our Cornerstone: 100 Years at Lititz Mennonite Church* (Morgantown, PA: Mastoff Press, 2007.)

3 Charles Pinches, *A Gathering of Memories: Family, Nation, and Church in a Forgetful World* (Grand Rapids, MI: Baker Publishing Group, 2006), 10.

4 Stewart Holbrook, *The Story of American Railroads* (New York: Crown Publishers, 1947).

5 Edgar Snow, *Red China Today: The Other Side of the River* (First published in 1963, the next edition, New York, NY: the Penguin Group, 1970; a revised edition, New York, NY: Random House, 1971).

6 John A. Lapp and C. Arnold Snyder, editors, *Testing Faith and Tradition: A Global Mennonite History Series: Europe;* and Alemu Checole, et. al., *Anabaptist Songs in African Hearts* (Intercourse, PA: Good Books, October 2006).

7 Sarah Patton Boyle, *The Desegregated Heart* (Charlottesville, VA: University of Virginia Press, 1962).

8 John Howard Griffin, *Black like Me* (San Antonio, TX: Wings Press, 1977).

9 Aldo Leopold, *A Sand County Almanac, and Sketches Here and There* (New York: Oxford University Press, 1987).

10 Khaled Husssein, *The Kite Runner* (New York: Penguin Group, 2003), 2.

11 Wendell Berry, *Hannah Coulter* (Washington, DC: Shoemaker and Hoard, 2004), 5.

12 Paul Hanson, *The People Called: The Growth of Community in the Bible* (Scranton, PA: Harper Collins), 545.

GEORGE R. BRUNK III

I'd Rather Be Teaching

I am a Denbighite—born in 1939 and reared in the small but vibrant
Mennonite community in southeastern Virginia named Denbigh. We
called ourselves, a farming community a short distance from Newport
News, a Mennonite colony. I have a clear memory of the exact, albeit un-
marked, boundaries that separated our colony from the "outside world."
Looking back, I consider this division both a bane and a blessing. It was
a bane because it created a certain sense of distance from and suspicion of other people and their world. It has taken a lifetime of experiences, some of which will be narrated below, to work at the necessary
de-tribalizing. On the other hand, colony life was a blessing because it
formed a powerful sense of identity-in-community. We were not a people
who floated along with the currents of the culture around us. We had a
particular calling as a Christian community with distinctive values of
nonconformity and nonresistance.

Early Formation

Here in the years of World War II and the early Cold War, the 1940s, I
was preserved from the nationalistic and military fervor even though
we lived with the constant rat-tat-tat of the shooting range at nearby Fort
Eustis and the roar of military airplanes just above our heads as the pilots
practiced landing at the Patrick Henry Airbase. The world was near and
yet so far away. (Actually, it has been my observation that our distinctive
identity as a peace-loving people has turned out to help us, in contrast to
average citizens, more easily break out of our cultural particularity and
appreciate the strange and new. For example, I am grateful that, in spite

73

of growing up in the near Deep South, I was taught to respect African Americans and to appreciate their particular way of being church.)

I was born into the home of minister and church leader George R. Brunk II. Because of my father's long absences in his itinerant preaching, my mother, Margaret Suter Brunk, was the *de facto* head of the home. She did the rearing of the five of us siblings and administered the discipline. However, one strategy of discipline was to keep a record of our misdeeds and remind us that Papa would get the full story when he returned! We older siblings even learned some parenting skills by helping to care for the younger ones.

Church life was everyday fare in our home. Many visitors spent time here, and the conversation typically centered on church life and concerns. My siblings and I were eager eavesdroppers on these conversations, which left the indelible impression that the real values of life concerned the church, her faith and her faithfulness. And since these visitors arrived from near and far, I came to realize that there was a larger church reality beyond my colony.

A silent presence in our home was also formative for me—books. My grandfather, George R. Brunk I, was a self-educated lover of books. My father had lots of *his* books, as well as his own, in large bookcases throughout our home. I loved to pull the books from the shelves and browse through them. They offered heavy theological subject matter in multi-volume treatises by the great Christian writers of the past, and I found delight in trying my theological milk teeth on the profound ideas. Especially impressive were the handwritten notes in the margins of almost every book. Obviously Grandfather enjoyed those ideas and had his own strong opinions about them. I soon learned, for example, that he could smell Calvinism a mile away and that it elicited heated criticism in the margins! This was exciting. The excitement about books and ideas captured me and has never let me go. Moreover, it fed my penchant toward a more intellectual mode of being Christian. Ideas, I understood, were not just mental gymnastics; they had the power to generate action and change reality.

But there was the mundane side of life. We lived on an orchard farm that Grandfather had planted and that Papa had taken over and was running—largely by the proxy of hired help first and then his boys when we were still of a rather tender age. I remember operating the farm equipment from the time I could reach the pedals and depress the clutch. The summer that my older brother, Gerald, turned fifteen and got his driver's license and I was thirteen, we operated the peach orchard while Papa was away preaching under the big tent. We did all the spraying and the picking, as well as the peddling of peaches to the stores in the nearby city. We grew up early in those days as we learned how to manage a business operation and how to deal with manipulative and dishonest businessmen. All of which, minus the bad characters, stood me in good stead in my leadership responsibilities of later years.

It has been noted that our lives are not defined primarily by unusual and extraordinary events, as we are prone to think. The meaningfulness of life is best perceived in the accumulative effects of the ordinary and routine, those things that seem insignificant at the moment but turn out to constitute collectively the weightier aspect of existence. This discernment continues to ring true. Still, particular events often come to symbolize that larger meaningfulness most clearly. I have selected several of these, along with broader descriptions, to attempt to characterize my life story—within appropriate limits.

When I was a pre-schooler (I do not remember my exact age), I was one of several youngsters in my community who contracted infantile paralysis (polio). It was a long battle with my family rallying to my aid even as they endured the quarantine placed on our house. For a time I was in the hospital with little contact with anyone except the occasional visits of my parents. My only views were the huge Newport News shipyard out the window and a dying polio victim in an iron lung across the hall through the room door. The Lord spared me in that ordeal, and I suffered practically no permanent effects. Or should I say, no permanent physical effects. That experience, I perceived in more adult years, had had the effect of instilling in me a sense of purpose about life. Why had I lived when others had not? In 1995, when I survived near death from bacterial meningitis, an exclamation point was added to that sense.

For good or ill, I am also the product of Mennonite education. For nineteen straight years, except for my junior year in public high school, I was a student at a Mennonite church school from elementary school through seminary. For eight consecutive years this education was on the campus of Eastern Mennonite: the senior year of high school, four years of college and three years of seminary. Whatever this institution makes of its students had ample opportunity to be impressed upon me. Understandably these years were deeply formative for my life. In them I moved from being a shy farm boy unaccustomed to much social interaction to someone with a degree of confidence in public speaking and leadership. Somewhere in those years there developed a strong sense of personal vocation for a leadership ministry role in the church. I was not sure of the exact form it would take, but I sensed that it would have something to do with teaching sooner or later.

One of things that I began to come to terms with in those years was the fact that I carried a name with considerable freight attached to it. Not that I spent much time being self-conscious about it. After all, it was just the normal state of things for me. But one day I found myself sitting in the office of the dean of students, Laban Peachey, under discipline for being late in returning my date to her dormitory. At a certain point Laban changed the subject and asked me point blank what it was like to carry the name of a well-known grandfather and father. As I recall, I answered him much as I would answer today. I am not particularly conscious of this fact in decision making, which is not the same as saying that it has not had a determining role. I have tried to live out of integrity to what I am within myself. On the other hand, I gratefully acknowledge the influence of the past generations. I consider my father to have been the most influential person in my life. It is one of those cases where divine purpose (the secularist would say environmental determinism) and human freedom are inseparably and inscrutably intertwined.

I have not reacted negatively to needing to live in this ancestral shadow. Indeed when name recognition brings me opportunity, I have tried to take it as an unmerited gift and make the best of it. Likely my name has closed some doors, but I am not aware of many instances. Thankfully, only on rare occasions has someone used what the previous generations stood for to attempt to leverage my action. I have come to believe that the highest respect I can pay to my forebears is not to duplicate exactly who they were and what they said but to attempt to be, as they were, an innovative and creative person within our common faith tradition. I perceive myself to be in continuity with the previous

Pictured with parents and siblings in front of the house trailer they lived in during summer travel in the tent revival work. In the back, George II and Margaret. In the front row, youngest to the oldest from left to right: Barbara, Conrad, Paul, George III, Gerald.

generations, but not a carbon copy of them. This perspective is after all not unique to my circumstances. At the heart of all Christian existence is the characteristic that philosopher John Milbank has called "non-identical repetition." We replicate in our lives the spirit of a long story of faith, but we do that with integrity only if we do not simply duplicate the past.

Concurrent with my school years was the experience of traveling with my father during the summer in his tent revival and evangelism work. This was an unbelievable opportunity to become acquainted with most of the major Mennonite communities in North American in the various denominational groupings and with many leading personalities in the church. As in the farm work back home, my father pushed us children into roles and responsibilities quite beyond our age. Given my bent for things mechanical, I worked with the tent equipment and kept things running smoothly. It was quite a learning experience in leadership to direct a large group of men in erecting or dismantling the tent. But there were also opportunities for public ministry at the margins of the tent services. Leading in prayer meetings and occasionally even preaching in local churches pushed me out of the nest when wings were still weak.

Sitting under the preaching and teaching ministry of my father for most nights in the summer had its inevitable impact, essentially positive as I view it. He was a gifted communicator and, as one might expect of a revival preacher, he made ready use of rhetorical techniques to persuade and move. But this rhetorical power was the servant of thoughtful, in-depth content reflecting biblical knowledge, theological education, and life observation. I never got tired of hearing him preach, even though I was familiar enough with some sermons to want to remind him when it was time for a certain illustration! And seeing many persons deal-ing with the place of God in their lives created a white hot furnace in which my own spirituality was refined and forged. In light of the pro-found influences of those many summers "under the tent," I have jok-ingly observed that cutting open the heart of my faith would probably reveal a pattern of canvas. Of course much maturation and refinement has transpired since that time, but I perceive all that to have been built on the same foundation.

Italian Interlude

Near the end of my seminary years, we were approaching the important decision point about what comes next. I say "we" because by this time I was married to Erma Hess, whom I had met in college. Much to our surprise the Virginia Mission Board approached us about our possible interest in an assignment in Italy. I had been thinking of graduate school and eventual teaching or some intervening pastoral role before further schooling. Yet something seemed right about a mission assignment at this stage, and we started moving in that direction.

But a moment of turmoil awaited us. President Mumaw at Eastern Mennonite College (now University) asked if I would consider the position of college pastor. I thought some open discernment on the matter would be appropriate; however, the ensuing conversation among the parties involved did not lead to clarity. After some time of personal reflection and prayer we decided to stay with the decision to go to Italy. Thus in 1964 we left for Italy with our five-month-old son, Douglas.

The six years in Italy, most of which were in the city of Palermo on the island of Sicily, offered a great stretching and learning experience, as cross-cultural experiences typically are. Our time there forever cancelled out a great part of our provincialism. After six months of language study in the culture-rich city of Florence, we slowly moved into the pastoral leadership of an already established Mennonite congregation in Palermo. I was also the communication link between the U.S. mission boards and several points of mission-sponsored ministry in Italy. I loved the language and the pastoral work. We learned to love the people and their culture.

I do not consider that I was a particularly good missionary in the usual sense of the word. Others who followed were more gifted in outreach and church growth. To my surprise, judging by the comments people made, even my pastoral work did not make as much impression as the example of our marriage and family life! Still I have not the slightest regret for those years. Serving in Italy set a lasting missional stamp on my faith, to say nothing of a lasting taste for Italian cuisine! Yet I had never thought of the mission field as my ultimate vocational destination. Teaching was rooted deeply in my consciousness—in fact, one of my best contributions in Italy has likely been my multiple teaching sojourns in Italy since returning to the States. Thus it was that at the end of the six years, 1970, the time seemed right to return for graduate study in the States. There were now four of us, since daughter Valerie was born in the last year of our Italian stay.

Graduate Education

At this point another important decision had to be made. What field of study should I pursue in further education? My interests could have taken me in a number of directions. Careful weighing led me to decide on biblical studies. There was a strategic dimension in this choice. Given my sense of call to serve the church more than the academy, biblical studies seemed ideal since my academic work would be more immediately accessible and useful to the church. (However, my interests in learning have never been confined to biblical studies. I love to read and reflect on subjects from philosophy to the practice of ministry and mission. I plead guilty to being something of a "jack of all trades and master of none.")

In the process of application for graduate study, I chose to attend Union Theological Seminary in Virginia, where I would focus on the New Testament. For me and my family the four years in Richmond, Virginia, were good years of growth and learning. Fortunately, Erma found a job in the seminary library, which helped to keep us on the same wavelength. Working in acquisitions, she was in a position to order, with official blessing, any library materials I needed! My particular areas of study were Luke-Acts and resurrection beliefs in Judaism, Hellenism, and early Christianity. These areas supported my dissertation project on the Emmaus account of the resurrection in Luke 24. The dissertation was not all that esoteric; nevertheless, in the graduation exercises, the dean stumbled over the title, naming my dissertation as "The Concept of the Resurrection according to the Erasmus (sic) Account in Luke's Gospel."

If, as noted, I chose a more cautious route by focusing on biblical studies, it is also true that I was bold in facing up to the question of Jesus' resurrection, as it were "going for the jugular" of faith. My study and dissertation strengthened (but also nuanced) my belief and confirmed for me the force of the biblical claim that without the resurrection our Christian faith would be "in vain." The resurrection plays a central role in supporting the entire structure of the Christian world view. It looks back to the life of Jesus, validating the claims of his teaching, example, and saving death. And it looks forward to the future, assuring us that God will restore the entire creation to fullness of life and that our present life and work can begin to experience something of the same renewing power displayed in the resurrection.

I can also summarize the impact of the years of doctoral study as the simultaneous growth of appreciation for both the human and the divine qualities of Scripture. And I give witness that this has been my experience throughout the ensuing years of study and teaching. A close study of Scripture reveals that it has been formed through the complex processes of human reflection and historical development. Yet its unequaled insight into the human experience, its persuasive story of God's saving deeds, and its power to effect spiritual change point to a unique divine quality. For me Scripture carries final authority because it faithfully communicates the absolute authority of God.

Out of the formation of my school and life experience I like to identify myself as a progressive evangelical with an Anabaptist orientation: *evangelical* not as a party label but as sign of uncompromising commitment to the gospel of Jesus Christ accessible to us only in the Bible; *progressive* because the Spirit is calling us to fresh and greater faithfulness in the changes of history; *Anabaptist* because its reading of Scripture is persuasive, and it is a home within which to walk as a faithful disciple of Christ.

Academic Teaching and Administration

In another act of Providence, at the end of my graduate study an invitation came from President Myron Augsburger to join the seminary faculty at Eastern Mennonite College. It was the fall of 1974. Thus began the centerpiece of my life and work. I joined a faculty body composed largely of my former teachers, an older group about to enter retirement. The stimulation of classroom interaction with students around significant subject matter was exciting. I indeed loved teaching. This could be a career.

As it was, my career of full-time teaching lasted for all of three years. In 1977 I was asked to assume the role of seminary dean. I was a greenhorn in academic administration although my previous life experience in leadership was relevant. I was rightly appointed to a two-year acting dean status to test the waters. Subsequent to those two years and until 1999, I stayed on as dean, also teaching half time in the early years but less in the later years when there were higher administrative demands. I often threatened to put a note on my office door that said, "I'd rather be teaching." I never did, for the simple reason that I got enough satisfaction from administration to keep me going. I found fulfillment in the challenge of creating those conditions in which faculty could flourish in their teaching and students in their learning. However, since 1999 I have returned to my beloved role of teaching. Now at retirement age and at the time of this writing, I am teaching part time. Teaching is too much fun, too fulfilling to stop too quickly or all at once.

The challenges of those early years as dean were considerable. The seminary was a fledgling program, looking for its place in the sun within the EMC structure, within Mennonite theological education, and within denominational life. There were questioners, detractors, and skeptics along the way, but there were also key supporters; and we persisted, working at clarifying relationships at all the levels mentioned above. A central question had to do with whether the seminary should follow a strategy of institutional autonomy, gradually separating from the college, or pursue the vision of a unified institution of higher education with shared resources. In part for practical reasons, but also out of a sense of stewardship for the church's resources, I supported the vision of a unified institution. The majority felt the same. Over the years this direction was reflected in the change of institutional name to Eastern Mennonite College and Seminary and then to Eastern Mennonite Seminary as a division of Eastern Mennonite University. The challenge in this case is that a professional school for church ministry has a somewhat distinctive educational character and a very different funding structure. Negotiating the administrative issues this raises has been and always will be a challenge.

At the denominational level the discussion in those years focused on the question of how many places of theological and pastoral education the church needed and could afford. This issue meant a lively and sustained conversation with our sister seminary, Associated Mennonite Biblical Seminary in Indiana and with the then Mennonite Board of Education led by Al Meyer. The result of this conversation and mutual planning was to position the two schools to have some differences in educational programs but to allow the church constituency to "vote by its feet" on the question of how many locations of training it wanted. In retrospect the question we debated was somewhat misplaced. The issue that was actually on the horizon was not whether one or two seminaries were needed but whether even more locations and programs were needed and justified.

When I became dean, most of the faculty were reaching retirement; thus a major task was the recruitment of a new generation of teachers. My philosophy of recruitment was clear. We should look for persons with a proven ability to relate constructively to the church and then, but only then, look for those with the strongest academic credentials possible. The first priority for the seminary was to serve the church in the preparation of ministerial leaders. Academics were in the service of the church, not the other way around. Our faculty was the key to achieving this objective. I cannot here mention all of the names of the new faculty and staff, but only register my esteem for all of them and my thanks for their colleagueship over the years. I will cite the names of John Martin and Sara Wenger Shenk, co-administrators in the seminary, whose leadership gifts have been outstanding and who covered many a shortcoming of my own.

There were other challenges. The seminary needed accreditation in order to serve the best interests of the students, and we were able to achieve full accreditation in 1985. Also, during those years, the Mennonite churches of our constituency were gradually coming to appreciate the importance of seminary training for their pastors. This significant change of perspective led to the near doubling of enrollment at the seminary. A different kind of challenge was that through the period of my deanship, the college went through some times of particular financial difficulties. This situation added to the need to put a firm footing under the growing seminary while also managing the inevitable pressure and stress across the institution. Thankfully, this was also a time of strong collegiality in the administrative team. I have in mind presidents Myron Augsburger, Richard Detweiler, and Joseph Lapp; deans Al Keim and Lee Snyder; and provost Beryl Brubaker. These felicitous working relationships are among my fondest memories.

Denominational Involvements

Along with the responsibilities at the seminary, opportunities arose to be involved in church life, especially at the denominational level. These were something of a natural, given my role in theological education leadership; and I saw them as an important way for the church and seminary to relate. Thus I agreed in 1979 to serve on the Council of Faith, Life and Strategy of the (then) Mennonite Church for six years. As chairperson for CFLS, I had the opportunity to sit on the denomination's General Board. In the years from 1987 to 1993 I was again on the General Board, this time in connection with leadership roles on the Board and for the General Assembly (a national gathering of delegates and members from the regional conferences every two years). I served as moderator of the Mennonite Church from 1989 to 1991. Of valued memory is my working relationship with Wayne North, James Lapp, Ralph Lebold, and David Mann. I note in particular two activities in which I participated with delight: helping to develop the study document, "Affirming Our Faith in Word and Deed"; and serving on the committee to explore integration between the Mennonite Church and the General Conference Mennonite Church. In these later years I have served on the Interchurch Relations Committee of the now integrated Mennonite Church USA and as overseer of ordained teaching professors for Virginia Mennonite Conference.

During my active career in the last quarter of the 20th century, the Mennonite Church went through significant changes and continues to do so. As I see it, these changes were rooted primarily in the fact that the church moved out of its relative cultural and social isolation and into greater interaction and engagement with the larger world of ideas, problems and issues. It was a time of mushrooming institutional expansion. Also, a growing mission and service consciousness, the flowering of higher education, and the gradual urbanization of our people were certainly key factors in the change. Now there is hardly a religious, social, or ideological trend that fails to find an expression in our circles or a social problem or political issue to which we do not feel a responsibility to respond in word and deed. This broad awareness and involvement has brought creativity and vitality into the church. It has also brought a high degree of diversity with attendant conflict and fragmentation. Faithfulness and unfaithfulness flow through our midst with such speed and variety that a process of discernment is rendered highly problematical, especially for a church like ours, which disperses authority to all levels of church life. A particularly good example in this time period is the issue of homosexuality, which illustrates our close contact with the wider church and society reality and reflects our difficulty in maintaining unity through an extended time of discernment. Probably one of the most significant constructive responses of the church during this time was the writing of a new confession of faith, approved in 1995. By involving the whole church in conversation over a number of years, the process resulted in a high level of agreement around a document that continues to exercise a converging influence in church life.

This has been a fortunate time for involvement in church leadership. A relative abundance of resources has made possible a wide range of program initiatives. The budgetary struggles, which consumed so much attention, were not so much a sign of a lack of resources and commitment as they were an indicator that our vision was greater than our reach. While the new sense of engagement with the wider Christian and secular world undermined the Anabaptist identity of some, for many it brought an awareness that the peace theology for which we stand is highly relevant for the contemporary world and that many outside our circles are eager to learn from the long experience of the historic peace churches. Indeed, one of the significant changes in recent years has been our openness and desire to interact with Christians in other traditions.

This time of change has also brought stress and fracture along geographical, social, and generational lines. I have not been immune to the latter. My father took a public stance against certain of the changes taking place, such as the unlimited access of women to leadership roles in the church (he supported women in public leadership roles but not as ordained ministers). On that issue and others, I was on a different track and in my leadership roles had little choice but to speak out on the issues. Fortunately we were able to differentiate between public and family roles and thus retain mutual openness and respect for each other.

Thoughts on Teaching

Here at the end of my recollections I conclude with some reflections on the central focus of my vocational life, teaching. I think that one of the reasons I enjoy teaching is that the classroom becomes a place of epiphany. It is for me a place where "the light dawns." In public lecturing and in discussion with class members, flashes of insight come that have resisted discovery in the lonely study. It fulfills for me the principle of life that the greatest joy is found at the place where in giving one also receives. I believe that teaching is important because it creates a context of conversation across the generations about the things that truly matter. Nothing pleases me more than to see young, unsure, and searching students become clear and confident about where they stand and what they should do with their life.

Method in teaching is important. Over the years I have observed that students have moved from greater dependency on the input of the instructor to an acceptance of greater responsibility for their own learning. Students are less passive and more active. This move from teacher-centered to student-centered learning has required a shift in classroom methods that can be a challenge for an old-timer. But for all that, I am persuaded that the most crucial key to good teaching is the instructor's love of the subject matter and a corresponding love for the students. Such love creates a contagious atmosphere in which a process of exchange takes place and students "catch" the same love for knowing and being. Such love is served by method but is not bound by it.

Conclusion

Here then is a snapshot of a life and a career with some insight into the convictions that animated them. I consider that I have been fortunate beyond measure, certainly beyond merit. Divine Providence and the church have been good to me. I have had a good, supportive family. I have not needed to smash doors in search of opportunity. At the same time I have tasted bitter loss. In 2002, after forty-one years of marital and family happiness, my wife lost her battle with cancer. Nevertheless, the Lord "lifted up his countenance upon me" by bringing into my life Ruthann Miller, widow of my good friend and colleague in Mennonite theological education, Marlin Miller. And so I close with a tribute to my marriage companions, for behind nearly every "I" in this story is a hidden "we" of partnership on the path of life.

October 8, 2007
Revised June 2008

PART II

Making Sense of the Journey

...as Language and Science Teachers

My Travels in the "Eastern School"

Henry David Thoreau observed that he had traveled much in Concord, then a town of a few hundred. Like him I have traveled much in one geographical spot—named as it grew, Eastern Mennonite School to College to University (EMS, EMC, EMU). During its founding period, it was known in Mennonite circles as "the school in the East" to differentiate it from two colleges in the Midwest: Hesston and Goshen, especially the latter, which was deemed tainted with worldliness. While my peers in Mennonite land explored European and Asian universities, did mission work or studied missiology, my lot was to stay home and help establish this school in the Shenandoah Valley. The exceptions to my geographically static condition were my sabbaticals in California and Japan and a one-year leave to teach at Goshen College.

I was born in Richfield, a town of about one hundred inhabitants and seven churches in central Pennsylvania. I was the firstborn, but when I was about three, my brother Richard arrived; and during the next years, we became a family of eight children, the youngest born eighteen years after me. We were all needed to run the farm of eighty tillable acres and dozens of livestock—cows, horses, pigs, and chickens—and especially to keep the sheriff from selling the farm to Dad's creditors. After a hiatus of a few years Dad returned to elementary school teaching, to "save the farm," he said.

All the work was done by human hand or horsepower; and all of us children and parents were immersed in barn work, field work, or whatever other work forced itself on us. On this spread, about half a mile wide—with woods on the crest of each boundary—and about three quarters of a mile long, we not only worked but also gathered berries and cherries and, near the center, played whenever we could. We learned firsthand about animal conception, gestation, birth, and death. Free of earthquakes and for the most part of devastating fires and floods, as well of wars and of other social turmoil, these, in Ralph W. Emerson's phrase "sit fast acres," offered us something of the security of Samuel Johnson's Happy Valley, from which Rasselas made his way into the larger world. So this rural world gave my siblings and me a sound start. Hard work, a solid faith, and reality in human relationships opened the way for our vocational and religious growth.

One incident that grew out of our at times dire financial circumstance illustrates the integrity our parents practiced and instilled into us. In order to pay the interest on a mortgage due, Dad slaughtered a cow and had me peddle the meat in a desolate snowy area. Nobody wanted any beef (it was the wrong time of year; everyone had what he needed).

At one house I knocked on the door and was greeted by the owner, who asked, "Was she an old cow?"

I answered, "Not so old."

I took our meat home. Mother canned it, and later we ate it, not asking whether it was prime.

Our Home Had an Education Slant

The atmosphere set by our parents on this "working farm" valued education. As a teacher Dad ordered a big box of books for his school each year from the State Library at Harrisburg, and we at home had the advantage of reading these. But Dad and Mother created an atmosphere of reaching out in reading and going to formal schooling that counted the most. Regardless of the cost, they saw that we boarded the bus daily to the high school fifteen miles away—and enrolled later at Eastern Mennonite School. Dad's reputation for creating winners of forensic and other academic contests with his school rebounded also among us at home. Mother assisted us in our homework, even in Latin and algebra. She had received a teaching certificate from Elizabethtown College and had taught for two years in McAlisterville Elementary School. Later she sometimes substituted for her husband in his school.

I was the first member of our congregation to go to high school and college. Eventually Dad himself got his B.A. in education, and all of his children attended EMS/C. Actually I had the privilege of having him as a student—in my English composition class.

Perhaps it is a negative that none of us children has become a farmer or wife of a farmer—all have been business or professional people.

I Go to High School

Going to high school, though at a small one with about fifty students and limited facilities, energized me mentally. I count my two years of Latin, one of typing, two of science, and two of social sciences a sound basis for later studies. Even typing was a boon, providing training for the keyboarding on the computer I am now using. Two teachers imprinted their specialties on me. Mr. Stoudt gave me the basics of machines and required two nature collections—one of leaves and another of flowers—along with botanic work on living plants. Dr. Zeiders implanted an alternative interpretation of history and social studies. A brilliant man for the one-horse Central Pennsylvania High School, he was apparently too "pink" for Rochester State Normal School and landed back in his home area, the parents of his students unaware that he indoctrinated them with socialism. He implanted in me the habit of questioning what I read and believed whenever nationalism spoke.

My social life was nonexistent. The only girl who was attractive—possibly not only because of her looks, but also her bright mind and gentle manner—was a distant relative. Besides, my brother Richard says he was sent along with me whenever we had a night debate to be sure I did not make some foolish social move. Dad also nixed my taking the part of a silly salesman who had this small part in a play: "I can dance, too." He was not about to let me into the local social circle.

My Religious Life Grows Slowly

My parents came from seriously religious families: Father, LeRoy Shellenberger Pellman, from Lutheran and Church of the Brethren; and Mother, Elizabeth Hart Lauver, from Mennonite, Church of the Brethren, and in Europe, Reformed congregations. Conrad Pellman, the first immigrant of our branch, a Dutch surgeon and a British mercenary in the Revolutionary War, was likely Lutheran. The Mennonite faith, along with educational aspirations, dominated our home. My earliest memories include regular attendance at the Cross Roads Church for Sunday school and worship. Our pastors, farmers of good character and earnest Bible study, were concerned about giving their congregation the truth, albeit in a rather flat style. I respected them, listening, absorbing Biblical stories, sometimes reverting to maps and weights and measures at the end of my Bible, or in the summer enjoying the peaceful fragrant countryside through the open windows. Occasional Bible conventions on a weekend or revival meetings broke the monotony of the preaching schedule. At home we learned not so much actual Bible content as moral certitude and a style used throughout the Lancaster Conference, of which we were a part, known as "taking the Bible as it is."

When I was fourteen, I "stood" at one of our semi-annual revival meetings—this one conducted by John W. Hess, known for his histrionic style that sometimes sent chills of fear through us sensitive youngsters but also set forth the love of God. The hymn the congregation sang as I stood was "Love Lifted Me." Thus in the summer of 1932 I became a member of the Mennonite Church.

I seem to have had a trait related to religious life that even earlier paralleled my rational approach to church membership and other formal religious structures, such as educational institutions, even when I taught there. Marcus Borg, in his *Meeting Jesus Again for the First Time*,[1] describes this perception as the "'numinous,' the awe-inspiring and wonder-evoking 'holy,' ... not an intellectual paradox but an experience of sacred mystery." This explains why I found myself explaining to classes how Emerson and other transcendentalist writers came close to being Christian; they experienced something beyond the tangible; in fact, to some of them the ideal was more real than the "real."

I Go to College

It was a given that I would go to college. My body size and strength, as well as inclinations to mental activity, caused Dad to see I belonged in teaching, not on the farm. Dad planned for me by consulting a friend who was the dean of Susquehanna, a local Lutheran college, to secure a scholarship. That scholarship had been halfway promised when one sweltering August day in 1936, two faculty members from Eastern

Mennonite School raised the dust in our long lane, on a swing through our area to find money and students for their nineteen-year-old institution at Harrisonburg, Virginia, reeling from the Great Depression and suffering limited interest among its small constituency. Daniel Lehman and John Mumaw were keeping their promise to the faculty to do this solicitation to help the college get on its feet. Dad's financial condition almost required that we accept the scholarship at the Lutheran college; but finally some jockeying that included some work/study financing changed his mind, and he gave consent to send me south. (It turned out that I fulfilled the equivalent of the work/study by digging crab grass from the front lawn, later peeling potatoes, and then working in the library.)

Having had a taste of the school's program at the Young People's Institute earlier that summer, I leaped at the chance to try life at EMS, where the official registration for that school year, 1936–37, would number 134 high school and high school Bible students and thirty-eight college Bible and college students, for a total of 172.

There I found that the high school and college students mingled socially and to some extent scholastically. There, also, I changed readily from a loose farm schedule and wide spaces to an exacting, highly controlled regime mostly on one floor and in a small room. The precise schedule ran by bells from the rising hour of 6:30 a.m. to "lights out" at ten p.m. I discovered, too, that a focus on one's spiritual life in the Mennonite way saturated us residents in the EMS dorm. Inner belief in the Christian God worked out in daily living pervaded the atmosphere, though our humanity was not obliterated. Classes, daily chapels, prayer times and all other activities were aimed at nurturing this inner life. At this time in the Mennonite constituency of EMS and for some years to come, most church leaders strongly believed that rules and regulations expressing this inner life were necessary. In fact, the school was thought of by some supporters as a way of "straightening out" young people who needed disciplining.

Hence EMS wholeheartedly accepted the prevailing educational philosophy of *in loco parentis*. Rules of conduct covered most relationships. Mennonite girls and women had to wear the devotional head covering at all times and bonnets when off campus. Length of dress and color of hosiery were special items of concern by the matron of women and the faculty regulating committees. Men were urged to wear the "regulation garb" (a "plain" coat without lapels but with a sort of high round collar) or at least to avoid neckties. All this emphasis was related to usefulness in church work. Feeling the "call" to some kind of such work, I promised God at the first revival meeting at the school always to wear the plain coat. I also let the promise be attached to greater spirituality, a promise contributing to the depth of my later struggles when I was no longer at EMS. Actually, in spite of the rigid atmosphere there was sufficient social and spiritual warmth to make me feel protected and comfortable.

The college classes were enticing, and I dove in with energy and high aims. I borrowed from the library a book on how to study, absorbed it, and applied its principles. I took the required Bible courses: Old Testament History, taught by Dean C. K. Lehman, and Life of Christ, by Menno J. Brunk. Both had advanced degrees: Lehman from Princeton and Brunk from the Dallas Theological Seminary. These were the only Bible courses I took in my entire educational career.

The faculty taught at satisfactory professional levels as far as I knew, allowing for professional idiosyncrasies: Harry A. Brunk (known as Muzzey because of his high regard for one of his teachers at the University of Virginia) impressed his classes by dramatically lowering his voice to a whisper, closing his eyes with his head almost on the desk, and then virtually shouting a fact or the name of a student he thought was not listening. D. W. Lehman began his classes with a loudly sung verse of a hymn and, as did all the other teachers, with an opening prayer. D. Ralph Hostetter conducted his biology and geology courses in a precise fashion. His lectures supplemented the texts, and he led field forays to see botanical specimens in nearby woods and fields. We took geology trips to Tide Springs in the Valley and to the Pautuxent River near Washington, DC, to find fossilized sharks' teeth. Surprisingly, for he was very Mennonite in all practices, he requested in the fall of 1946 to use a biology text written from the evolutionary viewpoint. He said that "the absence of any reference to the theory of evolution" in the text he had used for ten years was "not a strength but a weakness in our teaching," pointing out that students were getting the evolutionary viewpoint elsewhere and that it was better to discuss the question naturally than to drag it into the classroom.

Women faculty were not given due place and honor for their teaching or mentoring. Dorothy Kemrer should have been recognized for her thorough Greek and Latin instruction and Sadie Hartzler for her high school math and literature courses and, most of all, for her caring for the tiny library until it became the building and institution named for her. Later I worked with her on the Library Committee and found her to be up to speed in her stewardship of the library. Later, also, I was honored to have as a colleague in English, the gracious, talented Ruth M. Brackbill, wife of Maurice.

I formed friendships, especially finding one, Grant M. Stoltzfus, an all-around pal. We studied Dale Carnegie's *How to Win Friends and Influence People* and discussed the church teachings and practices, with Grant supplying Harry Emerson Fosdick's sermons for new, stirring religious ideas. The word never got around that we were involved in reading such heresy, and really we did not know how hot a preacher he was!

I became somewhat more socialized and profited by activity in the Smithsonian Literary Society. My wife remembers my giving from memory a sermon by Clovis Chappell well enough that a student who did not know me said, "Who is this Hubert Pellman? Can any good thing come out of Nazareth?"

Then near the end of the first year Grant urged me to ask for a date with this petite, smart, attractive young woman. Fearful because of my total inexperience, I delayed but finally asked her to accompany me on a school trip to Natural Bridge. She accepted; and with the requisite chaperones, one in front and one in the back seat, Grant escorted Ruth Brunk with Mildred Kauffman and me. It was a wonderful day for my first date with my girl.

At the end of my two years of junior college, I left for a more normal world with sadness because of being separated so soon from my new educational, spiritual and social life, and especially from a girl friend.

I Finish My College Education

I then returned home to finish my college education at Susquehanna University. Getting to know my siblings again, probably the only time all eight of us sat around the kitchen table, was good and pleasant. Of course, the barnyard, stables, and fields required muscle and new attention; and I helped in the summers, except for the one when Dad thought it would be good for me to hitch a ride with some nearby students who attended Bloomsburg State College to be as well prepared as possible for teaching—where, I did not know.

My decision to wear the "plain coat," a legacy from EMS, tied me in emotional knots, hindered joy, and accentuated anxiety about getting a job in the only place I knew, a state high school. Actually, I did not need to feel embarrassed by my plain coat: One fellow student from New York City called it "sharp."

At Susquehanna I finished my college courses for a B.A. in history and a state certificate to teach English, social studies, and biology in high schools. My only extra-curricular activity had been debating, which took me on the collegiate circuit and earned me membership in Tau Kappa Alpha, a national debating society.

However, I continued to feel anxious about my vocational future. I do not remember exactly when, but sometime after my graduation in June 1940, EMS invited me to join its faculty. This request gave me direction, and I accepted and prepared to get my M.A. in English at Bucknell University, Lewisburg, Pennsylvania.

Courses in expository writing, Chaucer, Shakespeare, and a seminar in literature kept me busy. The tensions between my Mennonite way of life and the Bucknell world disappeared to a great degree as I anticipated marriage and a job at a place where I felt I could serve wholeheartedly. On June 9, 1941, I heard Commencement Day speeches by Admiral Stark, Chief of United States Naval Operations, and Rufus Jones, a noted Quaker leader, and received my M.A. in English. Two days later, June 11, Mildred Kauffman and I were married at her home, near Manheim, Pennsylvania.

I Teach at EMS, 1941–43

Mildred and I settled into the newly finished apartment of Betty Mosemann's house on Shenandoah Avenue at fifteen dollars per month rent. Our first quarterly check for $250 arrived on time, the first of the $1,000 for my year of teaching. Incidentally, I had taken my position as a kind of Christian mission without asking what my salary would be.

I taught high school junior and senior English classes. Uncle D. Ralph

Hostetter (Mildred's kin by marriage) trusted me with helping in the biology lab and leading students on hikes around the edges of Park View to spot flowering plants and identify trees. This assignment honored me, especially since I knew his great knowledge of his subject.

When I was asked by the administration to join the EMS faculty, the Religious Welfare Committee of the school had the final decision on faculty and administrative employment. A sentence in the Executive Committee Minutes of the Board for a meeting on February 8, 1941, read: "On recommendation by J. L. Stauffer, Hubert Pellman was appointed as teacher if he passes examination." It was signed by A. G. Heishman, secretary. At this point in EMS's history the Religious Welfare Committee had the final word in hiring and firing. I am sure I was aware of the seriousness of my answers from that point of view, but I also know that those answers provided an accurate picture of my convictions then and for many years of my teaching.

I came to EMS when John L. Stauffer was president. President Stauffer, the former superintendent of the Altoona (PA) mission, had a commercial high school degree, excellent common sense, and natural administrative and people management skills. At forty-seven years, Stauffer was mature, experienced, and capable though, like his two predecessors, without higher education in college administration. He was not troubled by any newfangled electronics because they had not been invented. The old land phone sufficed. He conducted faculty meetings every Friday in an open forum style with no committees reporting because they were few and a more direct democratic style prevailed.

Enrollment spread from 144 students in 1938 to 442 in 1948. In 1945 Virginia granted the school rights as a four-year college to grant baccalaureate degrees. Course offerings burgeoned. Stauffer argued in faculty meetings for additions, recognizing that "We can't go back to being just a Bible school." The English curriculum profited by his attitude.

In Stauffer's time there was an increase in women faculty from about one-fifth to one-third. The constitution was revised in 1947 to read that "The literature and textbooks...shall be as free as possible from objectionable theories such as Higher Criticism, Evolution and Calvinism and from unwholesome sentiments so prevalent in much fiction."

By early 1947 Stauffer felt he had "served his time," he said, noting that it was time for a younger man with more formal education especially since the school was becoming increasingly complex in its administrative demands. He had guided the growing school and taught Bible courses in the high school for seventeen years.

The Board of Trustees then appointed John R. Mumaw acting president for the 1949–1950 session and on January 30, 1950, as president.

After the War I Enter a PhD Program in English

In 1942 the World War II draft declared me I-A, able to go into the army. Because of my conscientious objector (CO) status and my draft board's preference for my doing farm work over that in a CO camp, my wife and I with Donald, who had been born in October 1942, were placed on my father-in-law's farm in Lancaster County.

After the close of World War II in August 1945, I was free to begin classes for a doctorate in English. Mildred, Donald, and I still lived at her home; my brother Richard took my place on the farm, and I enrolled for classes at the University of Pennsylvania in Philadelphia. I commuted by rail several days each week until the beginning of 1947, finishing courses and working to pass my reading tests in German and French. This university had a strong graduate English faculty, largely devoted to a historical approach to language (philological) and literature, very much what I needed to help build EMU's English curriculum. My professors were nationally known for their scholarship and taught well. Mildred earned toward our keep by working in a general store. Then in the fall of 1947 we moved back to Harrisonburg, into a new duplex my father had built on Shenandoah Street.

My College Teaching Begins

When I returned to the faculty, I taught college courses only—no high school classes. My heaviest load became freshman college writing— English composition. Beginning with one section, by my tenth year I was teaching three sections each semester—with about one hundred students in that course—besides Advanced Writing and several literature courses. Ruth M. Brackbill and I comprised the English Department. A longtime teacher of Introduction to Literature and other literature courses, though most gracious and beloved by students, she refused to teach any English composition or other writing courses. The hundreds of papers admittedly drained my energy and creativity. The University of Pennsylvania's traditional PhD program, centered on literature from a historical perspective, did nothing specifically designed to prepare teachers—in fact the head of the Graduate English Department declared that he and his colleagues aimed to prepare their students for research, not to make them teachers. Thus I based my composition program on earlier studies at Bucknell, using their rigorous criteria for grading. For example, a C was the quality of a paper that the average student would do when he tried. I gave few A's, probably getting a reputation as a hard grader. To try to offer good courses I joined professional societies, went to conventions, and visited colleges similar to EMC. I cannot recall ever being formally appointed head of the English Department, though at some point I began to be considered such. No matter, the administration did all the crucial work, especially the appointment of new teachers.

James R. Bomberger, a recent recipient of an EdD from Columbia Teachers College, came on board in 1961; and upon him I offloaded the whole English composition program! Now I was free to teach speech, advanced grammar (after Mrs. Brackbill's death), Biblical literature (after her husband's passing), journalism, world literature, Shakespeare, Milton, the earlier periods of English and American literature, and an occasional special literature course. I rejoiced upon immersing myself in these courses. Yes, I stretched myself thin for some of these assignments, but I got up at five o'clock, studied hard, and at the expense of family tried to do a creditable job. The cliché "I learned more than the students did," like all clichés had a truth at its heart.

Especially did the Biblical literature course enlarge my faith borders through the texts I used (Brackbill had used them, and I kept them). Moulton's huge *Modern Reader's Bible*,[2] a translation with extensive essays by the author, forced me to regard the Bible as a book of human origin as well as divine. C. S. Lewis helped specifically and extensively on Biblical inspiration in relation to literature. An Oxford don, an atheist converted to Christianity who at first taught philosophy and then literature at Oxford and Cambridge, he also wrote prolifically in a number of literary forms. His *English Literature of the Sixteenth Century*[3] served as a great reference source as did his many literary essays. *Reflections on the Psalms*[4] helped me in several chapters by describing inspiration in broader terms than I had earlier learned. He wrote "I take it that the whole Old Testament consists of the same sort of material (some of it pretty accurate), poems, oral and political diatribes and what not, but all taken into the service of God's word. Not I suppose in the same way." He said also, "And no good work is done anywhere without the aid of the Father of Lights." He came to view myth as "real though unfocussed gleams of divine truth falling on imagination." He regarded pagan myths as containing a type of which the Scripture story, especially the salvation story of Christ, was the Original, the Real. All this did not make Scripture untrue. Lewis remarked that "Christianity is the Christian creed, but it is also the glorious experience of God in the heart of a believer."

Other religious questions arose. Some students still questioned the value of fiction, which the college constitution banned but gradually allowed if it was "good." I found an argument that quieted most objections: The reader of fiction becomes more human and thus is better able to serve God. President Mumaw opposed theater but allowed drama as literature. Because I taught Shakespeare, he had me write a paper defending the permitted way and opposing the other. By way of confession, I should point out that my graduate studies emphasized earlier literature, avoiding D. H. Lawrence or similar writings, the beat poets, Sartre, and others that during my period of teaching would have caused a ruckus. We had one course of modern poetry and drama, called Modern Literature, I believe, which Irvin B. Horst taught. You will have to ask Omar Eby, Carroll Yoder, Jay Landis, and other later teachers how they handled the avalanche of what in my time would have at least been called "questionable."

My Years at EMC, 1948 to 1965

The president of EMC for these years, as noted above, was John R. Mumaw, who had come to EMC as a student. Uncommitted to Christ and the church, he was influenced by the Christian atmosphere of the college and in the first fall revival meetings had a dramatic conversion. He grew spiritually, gave himself to his college work, and advanced in positions of responsibility until chosen as president. Mumaw quickly laid out organizational charts for the whole administration and faculty showing the responsibilities and powers of all branches of the college, an action that made for efficiency and enabled him to keep everything running smoothly.

As advisor to the college publications—*Weather Vane,* a student-edited and mostly student-written newspaper, and the *Shenandoah,* the college annual—I had to examine and pass on to President Mumaw all issues. He had a keen eye for what the constituency might make of these publications. I recall standing with editor Dan Hess outside the president's door early one morning to review the student editor's case for a doubtful piece for the *Weather Vane.* We did not get the okay we wanted.

At the beginning of Mumaw's presidency he and the whole college underwent a test pushed by a group who had been agitating for another man as the chief leader because they felt the college was "drifting" or leaving the founding principles. Chairman of the Board John Alger, a believer in the president, had the matter defused by taking it to Virginia Conference, which ordered an examination of the whole faculty, as well as of Mumaw. Conference passed a resolution giving "the School, President and Faculty … a vote of confidence and moral support."

In 1948 Virginia Conference gave the college permission to head toward membership in the Southern Association of Schools and Colleges (SAC). After an intensive self-study the high school achieved membership in November 1957. As a result of Dean Ira E. Miller's special efforts while the president was abroad, the Southern Association granted the college membership in 1959 with the proviso that several goals be met. The administrators reached the minimum of $300,000 endowment, one of SAC's requirements.

The college enrollment increased to 602 by 1965, fifty of whom were not Mennonites, about ten per cent of the students. A small number of international students began to come but no African Americans were yet to enroll.

President Mumaw also recognized the beginning of the great changes that came with the sixties, arising in the nation and affecting colleges, even EMC. He noted the necessity of changing from simply "laying down the law" to using persuasion and education to keep students in line as much as possible. Old curricula expanded, and new ones were started: teacher education; graduate Bible courses; the sciences; English; French and German classes; home economics; music; and nursing education.

In addition, faculty changes came about: Several old-timers retired; and a number died—Ruth M. Brackbill, M. T. Brackbill, Ada Zimmerman Brunk, Gertrude (Mrs. Ernest) Gehman, James Gross, and John L. Stauffer. The chief retiree was Dean Chester K. Lehman, and Ira E. Miller, of Messiah College, took his position. A startling fact relating to the faculty was the president's report in 1956 that the teachers' and employees' contributed services amounted to $57,718.23, a sum "about equal to the total contribution from the church." The Board adopted the categories of rank—professor, associate professor, etc.—and by 1965 the titles of "brother" and "sister" had been replaced by the titles of courtesy and professionalism.

President Mumaw encouraged the male faculty members to accept ordination, which would increase the relationship of the college with the constituency. While Mildred and I were attending Weavers Church, my name was put in the lot for a minister in the Middle District. The lot fell on me, and I was ordained on November 8, 1953. In addition to my full-time teaching, I was sent as pastor to open a church that had been closed along the Mt. Vernon Road near Grottoes. Mildred, as well as Eugene and Alice Souder and various EMC students, assisted in this work. I served as pastor there until 1971.

To Mildred and me, an important event during these years was the birth of our daughter, Carol Ann, on February 3, 1951. Though Donald was eight years older than she, he was happy to have a little sister. One disadvantage of so large a gap in their ages was their not having the same interests in playing. However, the inevitable passing of time made the gap less important. Now, many years later, they find pleasure in each other's lives even though they live miles apart. His practice of law and hers of teaching do not create any gap in their relationship.

A Sabbatical—in California!

For my first genuine sabbatical, in the academic year 1964–65, I taught half time at Westmont College, Santa Barbara. We (Mildred, Donald, Carol, and I) crossed the country pulling a tiny trailer, stopping at U.S. parks and other educational spots. Most valuable was living and teaching in an evangelical yet different cultural climate in a year-round Mediterranean setting. Westmont, founded by Mrs. Ruth Kerr (the glass canning jar manufacturer), was modeled somewhat on Wheaton College, and it offered chances for change in our spiritual outlook. A British colleague, Mildred remembers, said we opened up like a flower blooming. The aura of freedom in appearance and many other ways from EMC may be illustrated by what I saw at the fall faculty gathering for the year's planning, which was held at a swimming pool. I was especially impressed on seeing the president, Dr. Voskuyl, conferring with his dean of women in the pool!

The new cultural environment—El Paseo shops featuring Hispanic architecture and educational objects, a lecture at the University of California Santa Barbara by Paul Tillich and the short-term class for pastors he taught, and courses to audit in eighteenth-century art, American literature, and seventeenth-century literature—gave me an academic shot in the arm. While I taught courses at Westmont similar to the ones I taught at EMC, I had more relaxed but generally interested students. Curiously, academic titles for teachers were carefully observed; hence I was usually addressed and referred to as Dr. Pellman. Westmont strove for professional experience and recognition within and outside its campus even though it observed most of the social customs of the region. In this different atmosphere we had a working vacation. The librarian recruited Mildred to assist in the library, where she earned some money and enjoyed making friendships. Carol found an outlet for her creative gifts in several ways in junior high school. Donald attended EMC that year.

I Do Some Published Writing

Back home at EMC I took up my usual load of teaching, including several sections of freshman English that earlier I had taught for more than ten years, as well as Advanced Composition. The only significant writing I had done in that time was my PhD dissertation at the University of Pennsylvania, *Thomas Hooker, A Study in Puritan Ideals*. While I was at Westmont, EMC gave me the opportunity to undertake a big project—to write a history of EMS/EMC for the fifty-year celebration in 1967. I did enjoy the earlier research and found coverage of the later time periods not to be too daunting.

I had an advisory committee of eighteen, including Harry Brunk, history professor at EMC, who gave helpful counsel about tone, style of writing, and honesty in fulfilling the assignment. My colleague, Dr. James Bomberger, edited the manuscript for style; and Mildred encouraged me by once again putting up with my times of frustration and carefully giving advice, doing the index, and praying with me that I would see the project to conclusion. Published by the college in 1967, it was given good reviews in church publications and has been used frequently for orientation and reference.

The greatest changes in the college (now Eastern Mennonite University) were beginning in the mid-sixties when I finished my manuscript. Happily so, for the closer I got to the present, the more difficult it was to get a clear perspective on the institution's direction. Still, the project boosted my spirit professionally. My understanding of the research data gave me a more balanced, more nearly true view of the claims of founders, leaders, and churchmen and women regarding the place and work of EMS/EMC and of church higher education. I saw the tension in issues such as how to be "Christian," that is, fair and considerate of one another in personal relations, and still maintain an efficient, high quality, business-like administration and respectable and even academically superior college. Church pressures on administration and on faculty had resulted in the subtle freezing out of faculty members who were too far "off base" from the church theology or lifestyle. Human feelings, the clash of ideas, and other differences made me ask the question whether there could be a church college run completely on Christian principles. I did not give up on the idea, but the debate within me stimulated personal growth.

Under a New President

Eight years of my tenure reached into the presidency of Mumaw's successor, Myron S. Augsburger. The new president, installed in 1966, was the youngest (thirty-five) and the first with an earned doctorate (a ThD from Union Theological Seminary in Richmond). At his inauguration, the speaker for the occasion, Dr. Hudson Amerding, the president of Wheaton College, stressed the importance of allowing students "to find authentic meaning that belongs to the thinker, the artist, and the free and responsible member of a genuine community." Augsburger responded: "Within a context of freedom a professor can respect a student's opinions while honestly confessing his own stance."

*In a Japanese
garden*

Augsburger's inaugural address signaled some changes while adhering to the reality of the still-sponsored Mennonite college, though leaning toward an *affirming* rather than a *defender of the faith* type. Augsburger changed the college from a forbidding to a leadership stance in drama, intercollegiate athletics, musical instruments, and faculty dress. He admitted to the faculty such newcomers as Professor J. P. Jacobszoon, pastor of Haarlem Mennonite Church, the Netherlands. He had faculty and students study and discuss a book for a week. He worked toward developing the seminary and cut the high school loose from the college. A great change in curriculum was his leadership in establishing interdisciplinary courses, and I was involved in planning and teaching in several. Each had a biblical or theological component.

Outstanding was his dual experience in evangelism and academic study. He had influence among evangelical leaders in Christian higher education and evangelism. With his wife, Esther, he managed in the midst of other heavy responsibilities at a number of times in his life to hold numerous successful tent revivals and citywide preaching missions. President Augsburger also left a strong impression for nonresistance among evangelicals, especially during the Vietnam War.

A Sabbatical in Japan, 1974–75

In 1973, faced with a what-to-do choice for my second sabbatical, I asked a Japanese student in one of my classes where to go. He instantly replied, "To Japan." I pursued the suggestion, thinking life and teaching in a wholly different culture would be excellent for the purposes of a sabbatical. EMC's administration agreed, as did that of Hokusei Gakuen College, of Sapporo, Japan. Yorifumi Yaguchi, then chairman of the English Department, was to be my liaison; and as it turned out, he and his wife, Mitsuko, became and remained Mildred's and my close friends down to this day! We left the details to Hokusei administrators and found ourselves generously treated.

They hired Mildred to teach two courses in oral English, and I had a full teaching load of courses in reading, advanced language, early American literature, and an unofficial course on Saturday in Shakespeare, really just one play, *King Lear*. We lived in an apartment in Sapporo, then a city of about three million, within biking distance or a bus ride to the college.

A group of Mennonite missionaries had gone to Japan after WWII and found welcome partly for the Western cultural assets they would be (on the Mennonite Church agenda, of course, carrying the Christian Gospel). The Mennonite Board of Missions had asked us to be Mission Associates with education as our task. We went to worship at the Shiroshi Mennonite Church, just around the block from our apartment or to the congregation led by the Yaguchis in another part of Sapporo.

Mildred related well to the Japanese, especially the girls with their standards of perfection, and taught oral English effectively. I did a creditable job, I hope, with classes of sixty students in simple English reading, but I did better with my small advanced classes. I had to come to terms with Japanese educational theory that after their excruciating years of extraordinary study, especially in high school, the students needed a rest in their first years of college. Teachers were to go easy in requirements, including grading.

Religion was pervasive in much of the culture, integrated into ordinary life, especially in the tea ceremony, New Year celebrations, weddings, funerals, and sports—*sumo*, for example; and temples and shrines dotted the country. A Buddhist temple adjoined Hokusei, which had been founded by Presbyterians from the United States but now required only some administrators to be Christian; in religion the student body reflected the general population.

Yorifumi Yaguchi, a devout, practicing Christian, had come from a village in the mountains of Honshu, where he was the grandson of a Buddhist priest and thus in line to take his grandfather's position after his (Yorifumi's) father died; we never heard him downgrade his ancestors' faith. His wife, Mitsuko, also never expressed negative ideas or feelings about her mother's decision to remain in the Buddhist faith of her husband, a university professor. Mitsuko herself firmly held to her Christian faith, as did her husband, sometimes leading the Bible study in the small congregation they had gathered in the city. A crucial element of their faith was Christ's teaching of peace. In a phone conversation in March 2004 Mitsuko said that Yorifumi was planning to protest the sending of a small contingent of Japanese soldiers to help "pacify" Iraq.

Reflections on My Sabbaticals and Travel

For Millie and me these close encounters with other cultures and religious practices made a strong impact on our own faith. In California we had lived for a year in a freeing social and religious climate that allowed us to relax and gave us time and incentives to rethink a way of life without the chance to change. Our months in Japan—within a culture greatly fashioned by Buddhism, Shintoism, and a scientific secular outlook—required thinking about Mennonitism in relation to non-Christian faiths. Our time and travel in England and in Europe (in 1979 as leaders of a group of students from EMC) cast us further into other cultures and expressions of faith. No wonder we had subtly changed!

For me the biggest change was indirectly related to faith: I had gained much more self-confidence, self-reliance. I had more freedom of thought and willingness to express new ideas. Although I now had a different structure for my religious life, I never dropped my basic faith in God and in the Christian revelation. Yet I found myself tolerating ambiguities, even within orthodoxy, that is, in traditional Judeo-Christian thought; and I became less judgmental toward those who differed with my interpretations.

Retirement—1984 to Present

On retiring from teaching I became more involved with my family, especially with Mildred, who had retired a little earlier, and with the two daughters of Carol and Robert Mishler—Anne Elizabeth, "Annie," and Mary Kathryn, "Katie." Since they lived across town, we had the joys of their nearness, making them children/grandchildren, though keeping the lines of parenting and grand-parenting clear—at least most of the time. This situation allowed their mother to finish her college work at James Madison University with honors in English studies, her major. Her senior program included a series of her poems, *The Pear Tree*. She also wrote other poetry, which she was given opportunities to read in the academic community.

Mildred and I now have five grandchildren. Nathaniel Monroe was born to Don and Sally Deal in 1974. In 1981 Don married Manon Larin, a French-Canadian ballerina from Montreal. A warm-hearted, expressive, many-talented woman, she brought Genevieve, her daughter by a previous marriage, into the Pellman family. Stefan Hubert was born to Don and Manon in 1985.

I practiced a long-standing hobby, gardening, and at the same time recovered some lost closeness with Carol in her gardens. I always felt such activity a therapeutic pleasure; now I had plenty of therapy with hers and my own garden. After a number of years arthritis hampered these activities and eventually brought us to sell our house, in which we had lived for forty-three years. We moved into a small rented house in the Virginia Mennonite Retirement Community (VMRC), where tiny flowerbeds tax my bendability to plant and tend. Son-in-law, Robert Mishler, has not only worked hard at parenting and running a hardware business but has also responded to our calls to fix things, has given practical advice to this professor/pastor, and has opened new views of the field of creative thought.

The Pellman Language and Literature Endowed Chair was established at my retirement when the Board of Trustees named me Professor Emeritus of English. In November 1996 the administration also established the Hubert R. Pellman Language and Literature Chair; and on November 21 the Language and Literature Department gave a dinner in Mildred's and my honor. I was aware that the $800,000 toward an endowment goal of $1 million had come from my siblings, many friends, and the addition of seven other department-related endowments and scholarships.

Reading and Thinking in Retirement

For some months after I retired I went lightly on reading. Gradually an appetite for my favorite work and pastime rebounded, and I began reading more than daily and weekly periodicals. Mildred observed that I still read as though I were preparing for teaching. Besides reading recent literary bestsellers, I read a number of theological-type works. Reading a considerable amount of Thomas Merton's writings impressed me with the realities of a faith based on a stream of Christianity that emphasized the intuitive sense of God in the depths of human beings, particularly as guided by contemplation. Merton's writings on social justice spring from his belief that God is in all people, that all deserve the best.

In an old man's fashion I reviewed my life, concentrating on my teaching and the changes in my faith and the relation between them. I realized that being part of a Mennonite institution of higher education in the period in which I served was both advantageous and difficult. Being in one of the liberal arts required creative thinking; being part of a religious denomination that called itself the third way (neither Catholic nor Protestant) required making some new paths, both private and professional. I am no longer pressed to work at the professional aspect. My faith has changed, as the high school and college have changed, along with the church to which it has been related.

To conclude, I would note that my professional and religious life have blended well. Each has strengthened the other. For example, teaching *Paradise Lost* adequately would have been impossible without having considerable biblical knowledge; conversely, Milton's imaginative use of biblical themes, characters, and scenes stimulated my faith. Literature did not become for me a substitute for religion, as it has for many today. Instead it has enabled me to have a deeper understanding of my faith through the writers' fearless, intelligent, and skillful communication of their experience. The religious education that my home and church gave me proved a sound base for the literary thought I experienced in teaching and reading.

I have already shown how I was influenced by C. S. Lewis in my view of the Bible, its inspiration and power. I must add that many writers' use of paradox, imagination, and other literary techniques made the Bible more important than ever to me. These skills enlarged my idea and experience of God and Christ.

Finally, while literature provided enjoyment and increase of faith, it also made me less dogmatic and less judgmental concerning the details of "rules and regulations" and of the faith of others. Grace and mercy have replaced a "know it all" attitude.

A vivid description of the last words of Thomas Hooker, one of the chief leaders in New England Puritanism and the subject of my doctoral dissertation, expressed at least partially the attitude that literature helped me cultivate. According to Hooker's biographer, George Leon Walker, as Hooker lay on his deathbed, one that stood by the bedside said to him, "Sir, you are going to receive the reward of all your labours." He replied, "Brother, I am going to receive mercy."[5]

September 8, 2008
Completed November 2008
with the editorial assistance
of Freda Redekop

Notes

1 Marcus Borg, *Meeting Jesus Again for the First Time* (New York: Harper Collins 1994), 14ff.

2 Richard G. Moulton, *Modern Reader's Bible* (New York: the MacMillan Company, 1943).

3 C. S. Lewis, *English Literature in the Sixteenth Century* (Oxford, England: Oxford University Press, 1973).

4 C. S. Lewis, *Reflections on the Psalms* (New York: Mariner Books, 1964).

5 George Leon Walker, *Thomas Hooker* (New York, NY: Dodd Mead, 1891), 150.

Photo by Elton Horst

A. GRACE WENGER

Walking Barefoot with God

My life journey has not been spectacular: "no dreams, no prophet ecstasy."
Rather it resembles two lines of an Amy Carmichael poem:
Step by step, Lord, lead me onward,
Walking barefoot with my God.
I have never seen far ahead, but at turning points in my life God led me
clearly. Prayer for guidance led to unexpected circumstances that said
to me, "This is the way. Walk in it." Sometimes this prayer began with
an inner conviction. At other times situations drove me to a prayer for
guidance that led to a conviction to act.

Childhood

My life is firmly rooted in the past. As a child I lived on land that had belonged to my mother's family since 1759. About five miles away a cousin
lived on the ancestral Wenger homestead dating back to 1727. There my
father, Elam M. Wenger, had been born and had lived until his marriage.
Within easy walking distance from our house was the Myer family graveyard, where my maternal ancestors were buried. Often our family headed
there on a pleasant Sunday afternoon and read the inscriptions on the
old tombstones. Actually, my education began at Myer's School, named
for the ancestor on whose land the little brick building was erected. And
in the cemetery at our Groffdale Mennonite Church were the graves of
Wengers, the earliest of whom was immigrant Christian.

In our family one of my earliest memories from the year I was two
was the day I heard someone call, "Mabel's home," and we all went to
greet her. Her story is entwined with other family events, beginning

with Father's first wife, Alice Harnish. She had died of peritonitis, leaving two little children—seven-month-old Mabel and two-year-old Esther. Mabel's maternal grandparents took her, the baby, while Esther stayed with Father, in whose home she was cared for by an aunt and later by housekeepers. When Esther was six, Father remarried; and in the next years he and his second wife, Anna Myer, had three more daughters.

After their first child, Edna, was born, they moved to Anna's home farm. Her father was aging, and the son who managed the farm planned to be married and move elsewhere. Part of the responsibility of living on the home farm was not only caring for Anna's father but also for her mentally challenged older sister, Mary. (As a baby she had suffered a long, severe illness that had probably caused brain damage.)

Shortly after this move, Mabel's grandmother died suddenly. Rather than bring the six-year-old into a strange and rather tense environment (for Grandfather Myer was becoming confused and easily disturbed), Father accepted an offer from Mabel's uncle John and his wife to take her. They lived in half of Mabel's grandparents' farmhouse, and their only son, Clyde, was like a big brother to Mabel. For her to live with Uncle John and Aunt Minnie seemed like the best solution.

Alta was born in 1916, shortly before Grandfather Meyer died; and I made my appearance in 1919. When Mabel was twelve, her uncle and aunt decided to move to town. Since our family situation had stabilized by then, she now came home to us, her own family.

We knew that Esther and Mabel had had a different mother: Her picture hung on a wall in the guest room. However, we never thought of them as anything but our full sisters, and Mother was careful to keep the family unified.

Once an old friend whom she was visiting asked bluntly, "Which are your children, and which are Elam's?"

Mother came home and said indignantly, "I was tempted to say, 'I don't remember,' but I said, 'They *all* belong to *both* of us.'"

Our childhood on the farm was a happy one. East of the house was an orchard with big old trees, mostly apple and cherry, some of them excellent for climbing. On the big apple tree just outside the back gate, Father had put a strong rope swing. In the meadow across the road, a little stream offered a delightful place for wading under a large willow tree. In the barn were cats and kittens to love. From both parents we learned kindness to farm animals, as well as to our pets.

Our most unusual pet was Frisky, a red squirrel found as a tiny baby under an apple tree. Eventually he was ready to make his own home in an old oak tree, where he gradually became less and less tame. Finally he refused to come down, but we could hear him chattering high in the tree.

Grade School Days

When I was five, I begged to go to school, not from a love of learning but from feeling lonely without my playmates. When the good-natured country schoolteacher said she would take me, I entered first grade two months after my fifth birthday.

The first page of the primer introduced the little red hen:
The little red hen found some wheat.
She called the cat.
She called the goose.
She called the pig.

I read it glibly. Miss Graybill suspected that I had memorized it and did not know the words. Thus my next assignment was to read the page backward—from the last word to the first. To figure out each word, I had to say mentally the whole page. That teacher should be credited with making me a speed-reader!

During the years on the farm, Father had started a butter, egg, and potato route in Lancaster. Some customers were asking to buy garden vegetables, too; and as the business increased, my parents decided that truck farming would be a good vocation for a farmer who had no sons. For this family of girls, raising and selling vegetables seemed more suitable work than milking cows, making hay, or harvesting wheat. (Teaching children to work was especially important to Father.) Thus, when I was in the fifth grade, we moved to the village of Bareville; and Father soon had the little plot of land back of our house filled with straight rows of peas, beans, and any other vegetable in season. Not one weed was allowed to flourish. In the summer I helped to raise, wash, and sell vegetables; and once a week I took my turn going with Father on the route in Lancaster.

Those were the years of the Great Depression. If a woman came out of her house soberly, motioned Father away from the group of other chatting women, and talked to him privately, I knew her problem. Her husband had lost his job; she had no money for food. Father told her to select what she needed. He then recorded her name and the cost in a little brown book, telling her that she could pay little by little when times got better. Before long, the little book was full of names and amounts. Every customer but one eventually paid her debt in full.

I spent my sixth grade in the two-room schoolhouse that stood next door to our home. The atmosphere here differed from the coziness of the one-room school I knew so well. Our teacher, young and inexperienced, had discipline problems. Fortunately my desk stood near the little bookcases that housed our limited library. After completing my assignments, I could reach over and select a book—and I enjoyed Dickens and Hawthorne, stimulating reading for a ten-year-old.

I had already finished all but the most difficult of our books at home: a Bible storybook, a thick Mother Goose volume, *Grimm's Fairy Tales,* and a few classics by Twain, Barrie, and Dickens that my sisters had won at spelling bees. We also had children's books about animals and religious ones we had "bought" at Sunday school, using tickets won by memorizing Bible verses. Among our favorites was *Mom's Black Book,* a collection of poems she had clipped since girlhood and continued to enlarge. She loved poetry. Often she quoted lines from poems she had learned in school.

Because her mother was an invalid, Mother had had to leave school to help at home when she was only twelve. Now she told us, "When I had to quit school, I said to myself, 'If I ever have children, I'm going to let them go to school just as long as they want to.'" Then her eyes twinkled as she added, "But I didn't know they'd *never* stop."

Spiritual Growth

When I was in the sixth grade, I accepted Christ as my Savior. John W. Hess, who held revival meetings at the Groffdale church that year, was a fiery evangelist. After he made it very clear that I was a sinner and needed a Savior, I stood to announce my decision while the congregation was singing, "Tomorrow's sun may never rise to bless thy long deluded sight." Fear of hell was my primary motive, I am sure, but I knew that I had turned from living for myself to living for God.

The foundation for that decision had been well laid at Sunday school and church—and especially at home. Learning at Sunday school and church was mostly by precept. At home I learned more by example. Material things were not allowed to crowd out spiritual values. Father did not farm tobacco even though most farmers in our area thought the crop essential for success. Mother cheerfully cooked and canned in an old-fashioned kitchen. Indeed, she was amused when anyone suggested that she needed the modern equipment that some friends and neighbors thought necessary. I cannot recall lectures about many things, but it was assumed that we would be obedient, truthful, and kind.

Once when Mother said, "I wonder how that lamp globe got broken," I confessed, "I did it."

Instead of scolding me for carelessness, Mother praised me for telling the truth.

After my early conversion I enjoyed hearing guest speakers at the Groffdale church, especially J. Irvin Lehman and Milton Brackbill, as well as missionaries like George Lapp, T. K. Hershey, and later those from Tanganyika. I remember several influential Sunday school teachers. Words of familiar hymns often came to mind when I needed them, and I started to memorize favorite Bible verses and to pray about daily living. Sometimes I felt guilty about not "witnessing" to classmates, failing to realize that my best witness would have been to be a friend to a girl whom others avoided.

In my early and middle teens, a strong influence that created problems was the teaching at interdenominational meetings. Mabel, who had a car, drove to many such meetings; and we sisters often went with her. There I learned more about the Holy Spirit, victorious living, and complete consecration. My parents also enjoyed listening to this kind of teaching, especially Donald Gray Barnhouse's lectures on the book of Revelation. I too found his teaching very exciting, and I became a convinced pre-millennialist until some years later.

When I told a friend that the prophecies about Christ's second coming would be fulfilled just as literally as those about his first coming, my friend asked with a mischievous look, "Did a *literal* root actually come out of a stem of the man Jesse?"

After that I began to see how much figurative language there is in the prophecies.

The dramatic preaching of these dynamic interdenominational speakers made the low-key sermons at the Groffdale church seem dull. Had it not been for my parents' wise firmness, I would have left Groffdale for some other group. I know that I was guilty of spiritual pride, a feeling that *we* had "the light."

While I was living at home depending on my parents, I could not go against their wishes. As my contacts with the wider Mennonite church increased and I became involved in service, I developed an appreciation for our beliefs. I was never as resentful of "plain clothing" as were some of my friends, probably because my parents were less rigid than most of their contemporaries. Later I was happy to discard "cape" dresses, but changing my hairdo was just too much trouble.

High School and College

While my spiritual life was developing, my academic life was also moving along. I entered the seventh grade at Upper Leacock, a small junior-senior high school with high academic standards. Strange as it seems now, my favorite subjects in high school were science, mathematics, and Latin—and I had four years of each. Since I had always wanted to be a teacher, I expected my next step to be college at EMS (Eastern Mennonite School) in Virginia, where Edna had studied for three years. However, since EMS was not yet an accredited four-year college, she returned to Pennsylvania to take her fourth year at Elizabethtown College—the same year that I was a senior in high school. Edna then suggested that I take a competitive examination for a scholarship that would provide fours years of free tuition at Elizabethtown College. Meanwhile, my high school principal encouraged me to take another competitive examination for a Pennsylvania state scholarship.

I did not hear any results from the state test, but I was awarded an Elizabethtown College scholarship, which, with my parents' approval, I accepted. Then people I respected began to question my decision, suggesting I was materialistic, and their advice made me reconsider. Since I wanted to do God's will, I prayed for definite guidance.

Just as I was about to change plans, I received notice that I had also been awarded the Pennsylvania state scholarship. The announcement had come late because I was in the second place. The winner had chosen to go to Messiah College, which at that time was not accredited and therefore not on the accepted list for state scholarship recipients. I took this unexpected turn of events as the answer to my prayer for guidance.

Though I could not know it then, Elizabethtown College would prepare me to teach at EMS. Since I chose many electives taught by favorite teachers, I earned enough credits in English there to become an English teacher even though my major was elementary education. Had I gone to EMS, I would have taken the two-year elementary education curriculum—and probably would have taught in grade schools all my life.

College was a challenge intellectually and spiritually. The English composition professor had a student assistant responsible for reading the themes, keeping records, and occasionally serving as substitute teacher. Near the end of my freshman year, the professor asked me to serve as her assistant for the next three years. The position, funded by Franklin D. Roosevelt's New Deal, had certain requirements. As I was filling out the application form, I came to a place asking me to sign a statement that I could not stay in college without the assistance of this position. I knew I had to tell the college business manager I could not sign that statement because I had two scholarships and financial support from my parents. However, I was really frightened to go to the office of J. Z. Herr, an enormous man with a long face and perpetual frown.

To my surprise, he said kindly, "I respect your honesty. We'll find a way to pay you out of college funds."

At Elizabethtown I met friends who challenged the basics of Christian faith. I tried to cling to what I thought I believed, but finally I knew I had to face my doubts honestly. I decided to read the four Gospels simply as historical records, not as sacred Scripture, to see what I would discover. Somewhere in Luke I came to the overwhelming conviction that Jesus is who he claimed to be, the Son of God who came to earth as Savior. Since then, I have read that J. B. Phillips said that as he translated the New Testament, he found it had "the ring of truth." I could identify with his testimony.

When someone asked me a few years ago whether I never had any doubts afterward, I admitted that I did. However, the evidence of the resurrection continues to reassure me. Christianity would have been defeated at once if the dead body of Jesus had been found. Certainly the combined powers of the Roman government and the religious leaders could have unearthed any hiding place that the terrified, scattered disciples might have devised. *Finding God at Harvard*, edited by Kelly Monroe, confirms my faith as I read the testimonies of brilliant people who came to faith after carefully examining the Christ stories.[1]

Public School Teaching

After four years of college, including a successful student teaching experience, I was eager for my own classroom. Yet in 1940 positions were extremely difficult to find. Our advisors told us that in addition to sending formal applications, we should visit each school board member personally. I found one in his barn cellar, stripping tobacco.

After asking the questions I expected, he hesitated. "There's one question we ask every applicant," he began. "I'm sure it's not necessary to ask you. But as a matter of form I'll ask: Do you drink or smoke?"

Tables full of trays of prime tobacco leaves sorted by size surrounded us. Instead of saying, "Roll one up, and I'll try," I assured him that I was clean on both counts. I got the job—teaching in a one-room school with fifty pupils in eight grades.

Many of the parents were patrons of the store in New Holland where Esther worked. Soon she told me that customers were saying, "Your sister is going to teach at our school. That's a bad school. Last year's teacher couldn't handle the pupils at all."

I pretended confidence, but I was scared. I confess now that I was far more severe than I needed to be. I actually used physical punishment on three or four of the most defiant students.

Teaching fifty pupils in eight grades was hard work, especially in a building designed for thirty. The playground was crowded; to fuel the Buffalo stove, coal had to be carried in buckets from a dark cellar; and the pay was one hundred dollars a month. Thus one fine April day I decided there had to be an easier way to earn a living. When I heard of a vacancy in the primary grades of a two-room school in Goodville, I applied. Teaching twenty-six well-balanced pupils in four grades there turned out to be a delight.

One Sunday afternoon in the summer after my second year in the new position, as I was relaxing with music and a book, I suddenly had a strange feeling that my life was too easy. Perhaps God wanted me to do more for him. I reminded myself that I was teaching a Sunday school class at the Groffdale church and also summer Bible school in several city missions. Nevertheless, the conviction persisted that God wanted more of my life. I told him to show me clearly what I should do.

Life went on as usual, and I began my third year at Goodville. However, one evening during the first week, I received a long-distance telephone call. A staccato voice announced, "This is Chester K. Lehman from Eastern Mennonite School. We have an increased enrollment in the high school and need another English teacher. Will you come?"

"I can't answer that now, " I explained. "I must discover whether my school board will release me from my contract."

When I visited my director, he was apologetic. "I'd like to help you," he said, "but teachers are hard to get." Since World War II had begun, many college graduates were taking higher paying jobs or joining the Armed Services.

Mr. Burkholder added, "If you can find a substitute, we'll release you."

Next I went to the county superintendent's office, where I learned that an older retired teacher had come in recently to say because of the teacher shortage, she felt it was her duty to offer her services. When I called her, she said she preferred a position nearer her home in Lititz. However, I persuaded her to come with me for one day before she made her decision. At the end of the day she agreed to teach at Goodville.

After telephoning my acceptance to EMS, I went out to buy black hose, and Mother and Alta got busy lengthening my dresses. The following Monday, Father drove me to Harrisonburg. On Tuesday I was teaching English at EMS.

In my thirteen years there I grew spiritually. We were saturated with Bible teaching: in daily chapel, dormitory prayer meetings, revival meetings, Christian life conferences, mission conferences, and weekly faculty ladies' prayer meetings. All were helpful even though the barrage of inspiration often seemed overwhelming. Perhaps most helpful was the experience of leading prayer meetings and counseling students. To be able to share, I had to keep in touch with God.

For a short time I served as the dean of college women, an experience that stretched body, soul, mind, and spirit. Enforcing dress regulations, however, was one duty I could not enjoy. Being "plain" was no problem for me, but forcing others to conform was not pleasant. During my tenure, EMC changed the black hose requirement, so I need to admit some responsibility for what some people saw as the beginning of a landslide toward worldliness.

I spent summer vacations taking graduate courses in English and American literature at the University of Pennsylvania. In 1949, after five or six summers in the humid heat of Philadelphia, I received my Master of Arts degree. To relax and celebrate, in 1952 I went to Europe on a summer work tour sponsored by MCC (the Mennonite Central Committee).

After a quick visit to England, the Netherlands, Belgium, France, Germany, Switzerland, and Italy, I became part of a work camp in Linz, Austria. Three Americans from our tour group joined students from England, Holland, and Germany in excavating cellars for houses to replace the temporary barracks where the refugees lived. We worked with shovels and wheelbarrows, not power equipment. Our dormitory was a schoolhouse, where we slept on cots made beautiful with MCC quilts. Refugee women, using food supplied by MCC, prepared our meals. Once sour beets served on the chipped enamel plates caused an epidemic of food poisoning, more inconvenient than life threatening because there was no indoor plumbing.

We Americans had a brief vacation from work to attend the Mennonite World Conference in Basel, Switzerland. One afternoon, while walking about on the beautiful grounds, I met Lancaster County Bishop Paul Graybill explaining the Lancaster Conference Discipline to a Swiss nurse who was being groomed to serve in Tanzania under Eastern Mennonite Missions. He handed me the pamphlet and told me to answer her questions while he returned to the meeting. I felt like a hypocrite because I had my own questions about the relevance of many of those rules.

In September I returned to EMHS, burned so brown from the work camp that somebody asked, "Is that really Grace?" Teaching became more enjoyable every year. In extracurricular activities we stretched the no-drama rule to its limits, defining as "skits" elaborate dramatizations of classics like "Evangeline" and "The Courtship of Miles Standish."

Then events sent me in a new direction. In the fall of 1955 Mother had several strokes, after which she started to recover—but very slowly in spite of her determination to try routine activities. Also that winter, Father developed pneumonia. Esther and Edna took time off to provide the needed nursing care. Then after Father regained his health, Esther returned to work; but Edna got a substitute to teach at LMS (Lancaster Mennonite School) for the rest of the term.

In Virginia, feeling guilty about not helping, I thought of a solution: If both Edna and I taught part time at LMS, we could care for Mother at home, and neither of us would have to give up the teaching we both loved. (We never considered having outsiders care for Mother since all her life she had been nursing relatives or helping sick neighbors.)

Doris Good, daughter of LMS Dean Noah Good, was then teaching at EMC. One afternoon as we sat side by side in the faculty meeting, I wrote her a note: "Would your father give me a job?"

"Are you joking?" was the note I received in reply.

Afterward I explained our situation. Within a few days a letter from Dean Good assured me that he would be happy to arrange a schedule to meet our needs. Thus in September 1956 both Edna and I were teaching at LMS, she in the morning and I in the afternoon. This arrangement worked very well.

Later in the fall Father died suddenly from a heart attack. Mother accepted his death with courage, and she continued to fight hard to regain her physical dexterity until she became able to do light housework. Then she had two cataract surgeries—before the days of lens implants—and finally a broken hip. With characteristic determination she learned to walk with a walker. Since she was cooperative and cheerful, caring for her was never difficult.

Changes in Family Life

Meanwhile, world events had touched our family. My parents had always been strong supporters of missions. Alta and her husband, Robert Garber, served under Eastern Mennonite Missions in Ethiopia for twenty-four years. In 1938 Mabel had gone to the Belgian Congo under Unevangelized Tribes Mission. In addition to her teaching and evangelism, she cared for a succession of children of African mothers and Belgian fathers. When independence approached in 1960, she had four living with her who knew

no other home. Although her furlough was overdue, she wrote that she
would not leave the Congo unless she could bring her four children. At
once we started gathering the documents she needed to bring her family to the United States.

One justice of the peace shook his head: "You'll never get all those
papers in time," he warned.

Fearing that Mabel might reach this country penniless, I wrote to
an acquaintance at a Mennonite center in New York City, explaining the
situation. I asked him to provide any help she needed. To Mabel I sent
his name and telephone number.

Finally a telegram came: "Arriving New City June– –." The date was
lost. Since it was already the third week of June, we froze a big container
of chicken corn soup and waited.

Late the next Saturday afternoon Mabel called from the Lancaster
Airport. Edna thawed the soup while I drove to the airport to pick up
Mabel, Christine, Louise, Joe, and little Jeannette. They had left the Belgian
Congo on the last plane out before independence, arrived in New York
with only Belgian money, and could find no place open where money
could be exchanged. Fortunately, a Voluntary Service worker had given
them money for tickets to Lancaster.

Mabel's children became an important part of our family, and Mother
had several more years to enjoy her new grandchildren. Then in 1964,
a few days before Christmas, she became sick with what seemed to be
an intestinal disturbance but proved to be a fatal illness. Five days after
Christmas she died.

Early that winter I had become aware that I had a health problem,
and I planned to see our family doctor during the Christmas vacation.
However, because of Mother's illness, death, and funeral, rather impul-
sively I decided to go directly to a specialist. Although tests showed no
abnormality, he decided on exploratory surgery, just to be sure there
was no problem. The result was a diagnosis of cancer, news that I got
on Valentine's Day.

After radium treatment and surgery, I was able to return to teaching before the school term ended. I felt certain of God's direction in the
sequence of these events. Had I been able to follow my original plan to
see a general practitioner, he would most likely have been satisfied with

the negative test results; and the cancer could have reached dangerous proportions before it was discovered.

Cards, flowers, scrapbooks—well wishes of all kinds—came pouring in from friends, students, church members, and neighbors. By June I had decided to go to summer school as a way of announcing that I was well and no longer in need of such loving attention. Since I did not have the energy, however, for graduate study, I registered for two semesters of World Literature as an under-graduate at Millersville State College.

Millersville State College

There I enjoyed the assigned reading, lectures, and even the tests. I found no reason to ask for an interview with the professor. However, the last week of the semester, when we met in the hall on the way to class, she stopped me.

"Miss Wenger, " she began, "I'm curious about you. Are you a teacher?"

I admitted I was.

"Shouldn't you be in the graduate program?"

I explained that I already had my Master of Arts degree.

"Oh, from which university?"

She seemed somewhat surprised when I said, "The University of Pennsylvania."

The second semester I had a different professor. At this time many new Mennonite elementary schools were opening, some with untrained teachers. A few of these beginning teachers took summer courses at Millersville. When the professor looked sharply at me, I suspected he had concluded that I was a farmer's wife who had raised my family and decided to try teaching. He seemed to feel responsible to educate me.

One day he mentioned that in his classes at the University of Pennsylvania, where he was studying for his PhD, there were many priests and nuns. When he asked a priest why they came to Penn instead of to Catholic University, he was told that Catholic University could not afford to employ the best scholars. Penn offered a superior education. Then our professor told us, "It is unfortunate that too many church schools employ uncertified teachers." As he went on at length about the problem, I was chuckling to myself.

Two weeks later, as I finished writing a test, he came to my desk at the back of the room. "I was talking to Dr. LeSage this morning," he began. "She said you have a master's degree in English."

Since his statement sounded like a question, I assured him that I did.

"From the University of Pennsylvania?"

"Yes."

"Well, how would you like to teach at Millersville?"

"I don't think I would," I told him, "because I think church schools need trained teachers."

He laughed. The man had a good sense of humor. "Well, think about it. If you change your mind, let me know."

When I described this exchange to Edna, she said, "Why don't you try it?"

At LMS Dean Noah Good, when told the news, said, "We'd be sorry to lose you, but it would speak well for LMS if Millersville took one of our teachers."

Just a few years earlier I had written a mission study booklet about congregational witness in which I said Mennonites should get out of their comfortable church communities and go where the light of Christ is needed. Now perhaps God was telling me to take my own advice. Again I waited for guidance. I told God if he wanted me at Millersville, he should make the direction clear.

Something unexpected happened on the day of the final examination. Two pages of a long test duplicated on an old-fashioned hectograph machine stuck together, and I missed identifying a page of quotations. When, on my way out of the classroom, another student asked me the source of several lines, I realized what had happened. By then the professor was in his office. I went to explain.

"I'm not asking for a favor," I told him, "but I want you to know what happened."

He looked at my paper. "That's right," he said. "I know you're not cheating. Sit down and finish the test. By the way, if the department chairman happens to come in, may I introduce you as the student I was telling him about?"

The department chairman did "happen" to come in. After we conversed for a few minutes, he asked me if I had changed my mind.

I replied, "I'm considering it." Thus in January 1965 I began teaching English at Millersville State College.

In light of my belief in the separation of church and state, my concern was how to witness in a state institution. When I observed some competition for upper-level courses, I decided to be satisfied teaching freshmen and sophomores. Also, rather than flaunting "high standards" by failing all the students I could, I did my best to help every one succeed. Finally, after learning from student comments how freely some professors in other departments declared their atheism, I felt less hesitant during class discussions to ask a question or make a comment supporting faith. Sometimes students, in evaluating the course, expressed appreciation, never criticism, of such comments.

In the 1960s colleges were emphasizing affirmative action, and I was distressed to see inner-city students, many of them black or Hispanic, be admitted only to drop out in a year or less. When I discovered that such students, if given private tutoring—even just an hour or two a week—could succeed dramatically, I knew that I had found my calling.

I took a year's leave to study English as a second language and as a second dialect. On returning, I asked for special classes of freshman who had scored low on the English entrance exam. Now I had a good opportunity to try out a program I had designed as a project when I was studying at the University of Delaware. Because of the success of this program, the Pennsylvania Department of Education awarded me a Certificate of Excellence in Teaching and also a Commonwealth Distinguished Teaching Chair for the academic year of 1976–1977.

The three years of teaching in this program were exciting but exhausting. After thirty-nine years in the classroom, I felt ready to retire, especially since a young professor who was joining the staff expressed special interest in non-traditional students.

Tabor Community Services

During my years at Millersville, my African nieces and nephew were adjusting to life in America. Ironically, three of them became the first black members at the missionary-minded Calvary Independent Church. When the two older girls married young men from Zaire (the former Belgian Congo), we discovered the ugliness of racial discrimination in housing. For example, one apartment owner assured me, when I called in my Pennsylvania Dutch voice, the apartment was available immediately, the listed price included light and heat, and there were no applicants ahead of me. I had already told him I was calling for my niece and her husband. Now I added, "They happen to be Negroes."

Immediately he became deaf, utterly unable to hear what I was saying.

When I finally got through by shouting, "They're black!" he said, "No, can't rent to them," and hung up.

Eventually both couples got satisfactory housing, but I kept thinking about the many people who face discrimination without *white* relatives or friends to help. As I talked to anyone who would listen, I found a small group who shared my concern. Also, a colleague at Millersville invited me to a Human Relations dinner, where I learned about Opportunity Housing, a fair-housing corporation organized by a group from the Lancaster Friends' Meeting. I discovered that Stanley Kreider, a former colleague at LMS, had been a high school classmate of Robert Neuhouser, the president of Opportunity Housing. Stanley invited Robert to talk to a group of us who were ready for action.

In March 1967 twelve people met at the home of my sisters and me to ask Robert questions and discuss what we could do. Mennonite leader Orie Miller had accepted our invitation to attend. After the discussion each person was asked to write on a slip of paper the amount he was prepared to invest. When $4,650 was committed, Orie Miller advised us to move ahead.

Thus Menno Housing was incorporated on June 22, 1967. M. Elvin Byler, the lawyer who drew up the articles of incorporation, asked to have his legal fees paid in shares of stock. As a member of the corporation, he was elected its first president. Following the example of opportunity housing, we organized as a profit-sharing company with the understanding that any profits would go, not to individual stockholders, but back to the corporation.

As Menno Housing expanded, the officers became aware of some of the limits of a profit-sharing organization. Was it ethical to solicit volunteer labor? Groups from congregations cleaned up properties, scraped wallpaper, painted, and redecorated. Furthermore, a nonprofit organization would be eligible to get government funds to meet the need for low-cost housing. In August 1968 the executive committee (M. Elvin Byler, Grace Wenger, Arthur Voth, Luke Bomberger, John B. Shenk, Orie O. Miller, and Delmar Stahly) decided to form a nonprofit corporation, Tabor Community Services, which within a few months received its charter and began operation. The name *Tabor* was chosen because at this mountain Israel enjoyed a decisive victory over its oppressors (Judges 4), and now in Pennsylvania this group wanted to win a victory over discrimination.

Since many low-income families needed financial counseling in managing their resources to buy and keep up a house, Tabor began a credit-and-home-buying counseling service in 1970. Besides helping the homeless to acquire permanent housing, Tabor soon began rental counseling for families threatened by eviction. The work expanded to include guidance in debt reduction, family savings plans, and ways to achieve financial self-sufficiency. Recent programs provide temporary housing for women released from prison, persons recovering from substance abuse, and those with disabilities.

In the spring of 2007 Tabor's report showed that in 2006 two thousand families or individuals had received help. The little group of twelve who in 1967 invested $4,650 had had no idea of how their vision would grow. God has provided a dedicated staff with vision, business ability, and expertise in dealing with many different kinds of people. As the work enlarged dramatically, my involvement declined; now I am a supportive observer. Full-time teaching left few hours and little energy for Tabor's increasing demands, and I do not have skills needed for the complicated business it has become.

Retirement

Retirement from Millersville did not end my teaching experience. For several years I taught English to two Vietnamese refugee couples sponsored by my congregation. Then in 1981 a new adventure beckoned—a summer in the People's Republic of China. A group of twelve—eight teachers and four assistants—sent by Goshen College flew to the Northeast Institute of Technology (now Northeastern University) in Shenyang for a summer of English classes. Nancy Lee, who was aware of my cross-cultural teaching at Millersville, had recommended me.

Since the People's Republic was just beginning to relax some of the Cultural Revolution excesses, we felt the need to be cautious lest we hinder opportunities for future contacts. When we found we would be welcome at church, we went as a group and had a rich experience. Young people, as well as older ones, filled the church. We heard familiar hymn tunes and observed no shortage of Bibles. One of our group who had served in Taiwan and could understand the sermon gave it a high grade.

Teaching eager students was a delight. As foreign guests we received special deference and many expressions of appreciation. At the end of our weeks of teaching, seeing the Great Wall, the Summer Palace and the Forbidden City were unexpected thrills. Now I find great joy in seeing the growth of the student and faculty exchange programs with Chinese universities.

Going to China interrupted another project I had begun. As early teenagers my sisters and I had learned to quilt. After retirement we made a number of quilts for the annual MCC Relief Sale in Harrisburg. For some time I had played with the idea of making a Pennsylvania Dutch quilt with tulips, hearts, oak leaves, and goldfinches. With an interested friend I went shopping for a background fabric, and we found a yellow calico with a pattern of tiny red and black flowers and leaves. On this I appliquéd solid blue, gold, and red fabric in a design combining several I had studied. The result was a large gaudy quilt, which Esther, Edna, and I quilted.

When we finished it in time for the 1983 sale, I realized that this was the 300th anniversary of the coming of Germans to Pennsylvania. On the pillow throw I found a spot for the dates 1683—1983. To my surprise, the quilt sold for $6,500. Purchased by Merle Good, it is on display at the People's Place Museum in Intercourse, Pennsylvania.

Shortly after this project was completed, Groffdale Mennonite Church asked me to write its history for the celebration of its 275th anniversary—the biggest writing project I had ever undertaken. Through the years I had written articles, Sunday school lesson quarterlies, and mission study booklets; but this assignment was far more demanding.

I became grateful for all the thoughtful persons who had preserved valuable materials. Among the treasures in the safe, I found a 1763 German Bible printed in Philadelphia by Christopher Sauer. Paging

Teaching at Northeast Institute of Technology, China. Photo by Wilbur Birky, 1981

through this massive book, I discovered a piece of paper with writing in German script, a ruling about the colors for sisters' clothing. Also, I found building committee records from 1823, including the cost of every item and the names and donations of all contributors. *Frontiers of Faithfulness: The Story of the Groffdale Mennonite Church* was finished in time for a weekend celebration on November 7–8, 1992. Everyone appreciated the skills of Elton Horst, who did the photography, Dawn J. Ranck, who was the designer, and Ceci Good, who did the cover calligraphy.

Down-Sizing

By this time Esther, Edna, and I were living at the Landis Homes Retirement Community. As we had grown older, keeping up the house and garden in Bareville, where we had lived since 1928, had become a burden. Our names were on the Landis Homes' waiting list, but we decided not to move until after the death of our beloved old house cat, Winnie the Purr. When she became painfully sick one night, we had her euthanized and then informed the Landis Homes Admission Office that we were ready to come as soon as a two-bedroom cottage was available.

In February 1987 we moved into a comfortable cottage there; and Esther got busy with three flower beds, Edna found joy in translating her own version of the New Testament, and I discovered no end to volunteer work, which included writing a history of Landis Homes' first thirty years. To the frequently asked question, "Who cooks?" we sometimes answered, "Whoever has nothing more important to do."

During the 1990s my sisters' health began to decline. Edna developed Parkinson's Disease, and Esther had to be increasingly careful about her heart. Most of my time after 1994 was devoted to their care, which gradually increased until Edna, then Esther, had to move to Health Care (in Landis Homes). As long as they were able, both sisters continued to attend the Sunday morning services at Groffdale with the help of wheelchairs and kind friends.

When they could no longer go to Groffdale, I went with them to the chapel services at Landis Homes. Edna died in 1998, and Esther in 1999.

Caring for my sisters taught me to live one day at a time. I marveled at God's giving physical and emotional strength. Many times as I wondered how to deal with a new situation, he showed the way. Phillips' translation of I Peter 5:7 became my motto: "You can throw the whole weight of your anxiety upon Him, for you are His personal concern."

Shortly before Esther's death, Alta moved into Health Care. A diabetic sore had necessitated the removal of one leg just below the knee. I visited her often and helped when eating became difficult. Robert, who continued to live in the Landis Homes cottage they occupied, appreciated all the help I could give. Mabel, who was at the Calvary Fellowship Home, was diagnosed with lung cancer. Her foster son, Joe, and his wife, Marie, faithfully gave her emotional support and looked after her needs. Both Alta and Mabel died in the spring of 2000. All of my sisters had died in the space of two years and two months. My grief was mingled with rejoicing that they were at home with God and beyond all suffering.

Freed from responsibility for my sisters, I could attend services at Groffdale again. I took my turn teaching the older women's Sunday school class and participated in a small prayer group, which met Wednesday mornings. I was happy to see increasing freedom in worship patterns and less rigidity in discipline. A former high school English pupil proved to be an excellent pastor. After the appointment of a second pastor with special responsibility for work with the youth, young people became more active in worship and outreach.

At Landis Homes, volunteer duties became more demanding. I inherited responsibility for the East Mailroom, where mail is sorted for Assisted Living residents and delivered to those in Health Care. Each morning outgoing mail from these units must be collected. With the help of faithful volunteers, this work moves smoothly. Once a month I serve as the Sunday morning worship leader in East Bethany, the chapel attended by Assisted Living and Health Care residents who are able. On Friday evening several times a year I teach the Sunday school lesson for the following Sunday. Since many residents listen on close-circuit TV, "teaching" becomes a lecture at a podium with a microphone.

An unexpected responsibility came my way when my brother-in-law, Robert, lost his driver's license. I became his chauffeur to doctor appointments, on shopping trips, and eventually to the hospital for a short stay because of heart problems. As his health declined and he spoke of moving from his cottage to a residential room, I was concerned that the change would be traumatic since he had a large accumulation of possessions, even lumber for some projects.

One morning his next-door neighbor called. "This morning at four o'clock," he said, "I saw a light in Robert's dining room. I found him on the floor beside the table. As soon as I touched him, I realized he was gone."

I thanked God for saving Robert from the emotional shock of seeing his precious possessions sold or destroyed. As his nephews and niece began sorting, they invited me to take anything I wanted, suggesting some dishes that Alta had brought from home as a bride. I declared that I needed to get rid of things, not accumulate more.

Right now, that is my major concern—getting rid of possessions. As my balance becomes less stable and my feet more painful, I can no longer keep three flower beds neat. In 2011 my driver's license will expire. To renew it at the age of 92 would be folly. I will need to live where I can walk indoors to the bank, the pharmacy, and a small grocery store. In this December (2008) I will move to a small studio apartment, Harvest View 130.

Finale

I trust that when you read this, I will be settled comfortably. Then I will never need to move again unless I am transported to Health Care. I prefer to go directly to the "building of God, a house not made with hands, eternal in the heavens." Then at last I will see the face of the One with whom I have walked barefoot for many decades.

January 2009
Presented in part on February 9, 2009, by Nancy Lee
with a DVD interview conducted by Alice and John Lapp
and filmed by Elton Horst

Notes

1 Kelly Monroe Kullberg, ed., *Finding God at Harvard* (Downers Grove, IL: InterVarsity Press, 1996).

JAY B. LANDIS

To Enjoy the Work

There is nothing better for a man than to enjoy his work.
– Ecclesiastes 3:22 (NIV)

Family Roots

While I buzzed my toy tractor on the stripping room stairs in the barn cellar, my parents stood near the kerosene heater, sizing and bailing the tobacco that added some welcome income to the dairy and poultry operation on their thirty-acre farm. In the late autumn afternoon I raced my mother to the front yard, hoping that maybe today again my older cousin Bertha might throw me her Popsicle stick from the window of the passing yellow school bus, which in a couple years would stop for me.

My Pennsylvania boyhood home in the Hoover-Roosevelt era of American life was a Lancaster County, East Lampeter Township farm near Mill Creek and a mile or two from Ronks and Smoketown and Bird-in-Hand. It was surrounded by Mennonite and Old Order Amish farms, where the men helped each other at silo-filling and threshing times while the women cooked big meals for these neighbor occasions and kept copious gardens.

The closest neighbors were wonderfully dependable, friendly people who intrigued me with the differences between their Reformed Mennonite Church and our Old Mennonite Church. They had earlier left us to be truer to our forefather, Menno Simons, and now they did not have the Sunday school or revival meetings that we did. Although they refused to come into our churches, we attended their funerals; and once our whole family was invited to the Sunday morning Longenecker's Church wedding of Marie Lahr, who married an Old Mennonite fellow who had turned Reformed Mennonite for her. We knew our Amish neighbors well, too, and they often dropped in to use our telephone.

My father, Martin Sheaffer Landis, and my mother, Esther Mae Good, were married in 1931 on New Year's Day; and I was their firstborn. The Landises gathered annually for a family reunion at the farm home of one of Benjamin and Lydia's ten children, my grandfather the fourth name in the mantra we could all repeat: "Jake an' Ike an' Ben an' Mart an' Phares an' Harry an' Elmer an' Alice an' Cora an' Martha." Katie, my grandfather's twin sister, who had died of diphtheria at the age of nine, made eleven. The Landis reunions were Dylan Thomas "happy-as-the-grass-was-green" occasions on a summer Wednesday. After everyone had enjoyed the dry-ice-packed ice cream that topped off picnic lunch in the corn barn or the tractor shed, we would spread chairs under the shade trees and sing from the hymnals Uncle Elias handed out. Soon the young set would gather around my Grandpa Mart to beg for the traditional peanut scramble, the game with prizes for the one whose luck let him or her find a peanut tied with a black thread. The oldest grandchild of the Landis multitude, I continued to play happily with my dad's first cousins, plenty of whom were younger than I.

Daddy had no siblings, but my mother was also one of ten, the fourth in the Good family *freundschaft*, where there were seventeen of us grandchildren. Mother came from Lititz, where Grandpa Samuel and Grandma Lillian Good lived a block from the Mennonite Church at 246 East Front Street and where my aunts and uncles gathered every Friday night. Here we cousins played kick the can until dark, when we heard the ding-dong-bell of the open ice cream truck on its sweet crawl up Front Street and went off begging our moms or dads for a nickel to get a cone.

A somewhat unusual aspect of my family experience was its composition of three generations in one household: my Landis grandparents and my parents and their three children all lived together. Before my dad was married, his mother—my grandmother—developed a cancerous tumor and needed to have one of her legs amputated above the knee. This circumstance must have directed the decision at the time that my dad and his girlfriend, who had been hoping to be married soon, would move into his home place to ease the difficult misfortune of my grandparents. While this plan of living certainly had its rough times (usually unknown to me) particularly in respect to my mother's place in the household, our three-generation family had lots of camaraderie and happy times together.

A Mennonite Church Childhood

From the 1717 migration of one Jacob Landis, my Landis family traces its history in the Lancaster Mennonite Conference to Mellinger Church; Great-Grandfather Benjamin's funeral in 1916 was the first recorded funeral held in the "new" church dedicated in January 1915. My church life began in this congregation of 500 members with my first teacher, Hettie Landis (this surname is still predominant in the Mellinger mailboxes), in her floor-length, gray, pointy-cape dress with an apron, her prayer covering tied under her chin, clucking over the tiniest boys' Sunday school class. After we dropped our pennies, "every one for Jesus; he will get them all," Hettie handed out those cherished Mennonite Publishing House picture cards. I liked and respected all my teachers—Elizabeth Heller, Lydia Weaver, Tobias Leaman, Bobby Barr, Bernard Kautz—and I waited for Sundays, getting to see my buddies in our Sunday school class, singing out of the *Church and Sunday School Hymnal* or *Life Songs 2*, and hearing a sermon by Preachers David Landis or Harry Lefever, after which Deacon Aaron Groff always testified, "I can bear a hearty 'Yea and Amen' to the message of the morning."

What influence these godly people had upon my young life, along with the teaching and example of my mother and father, I most gratefully acknowledge. I offer two vignettes of Bernard Kautz, the Hungarian Jewish immigrant turned Mennonite who had come as a hired man to the "Bush" Abe and Fanny Landis farm and married Laura Lefever, another Mennonite farmhand; together they reared their family close to Mellinger Church. While Bernard was my teacher, one morning the minister—or maybe the bishop—asked him to stand and acknowledge that he had broken the law by speeding; this confession restored him to communion. Far more significant to me was his weekly practice of transcribing the sermon on small sheets of tablet paper and handing them front several rows to Daniel Rohrer, who was deaf and could only sign. In memory that act can still melt my heart, and indeed it was such examples of service that drew me toward the church. And it was there that as a young boy I experienced a meaningful baptismal service with a large class of young people like myself. I already knew the liturgy—this time meant for me—that Bishop Abe Martin would use: "In the name of the Lord and the name of the church, I offer you my hand—Arise, to a new beginning and a new life in Christ, to which the Lord comfort, strengthen, and sustain you," a walk that I was resolved to take seriously and would constantly need to renew for a lifetime.

Getting on the Bus to School

My life's trajectory begins with watching the yellow school bus that crossed the Mill Creek bridge at the bottom of our hill until finally one morning a couple weeks before my sixth birthday, I climbed on it myself en route to Miss Emily DeLong's first grade room in East Lampeter Elementary School. There in the circle of little chairs in front of the blackboard sat Dick and Jane and Spot, with Miss DeLong's class for reading divided into the Cardinals, the Robins, and the Sparrows. After Miss Reese, who praised me for coloring that robin within the lines, Miss Pontz , our third grade teacher, highlighted music and poetry. We began singing in parts, and she led the whole class in reciting musical poems. In fourth grade Miss Warfel held weekly Current Events, where we were encouraged to bring news items from the *Intelligencer Journal* or *The Lancaster New Era* to share in class. I shocked myself while reading a clipping in 1940 about Japanese cherry trees being chopped down around the Tidal Basin in Washington, DC. The criminals had left a note, "To hell with the Japs." Saying a word so unlike me surprised me so much that I looked toward Miss Warfel and muttered, "That's what it said on the stump." It was this teacher who encouraged the memorization of poetry, and here I seriously began that practice.

In fifth grade Miss Kurkowski opened the works of the greatest of the Renaissance painters, Leonardo da Vinci, Raphael, and Michelangelo. In her class I got picked to be a safety patrolman, an honor; but it later gave me a conscience problem when all the safety patrol children got bused to the high school to watch some movies, an activity I had been taught to reject. This experience might have helped to speed the decision for our family to transfer me to Locust Grove Mennonite School the following year for my sixth grade. I had survived scrap iron drives, buying war bonds, and sitting on newspaper in the halls during air raid drills; but my eleven-year-old conscience forced me to blush shamefully when my Mennonite classmate Alma Buckwalter, the best artist in our class, won the poster contest with her illustrated entry, "Let us tramp the Axis right on their heads." I knew my dad had already taken his John Deere across some back roads to the old Yeates School in answer to the call for local brethren to help transform the grounds for Lancaster Mennonite School to open in 1942. I would be trading public for parochial education for the next eleven years.

Heading Parochial

On my first report card at Locust Grove, Miss Margaret Horst recorded grades as good as they were at East Lampeter, but my conduct line indicated some needed improvement—in language. We had not been too careful around my home—especially perhaps in the cow stable—to avoid expressions like *gee* and *golly* and *heck*. Locust Grove ethos had picked up on these in a hurry. I think now that the Glick and Riehl and Smoker kids were getting away with some things in Pennsylvania Dutch; about all I knew in that department was *scheiss*. Not one to rebel, I flipped the lingo and succumbed to accepted standards of decorum, joining in morning devotions, group prayers before lunch, and sung prayers at afternoon dismissal time.

How we sang at Locust Grove! "Sing the wondrous love of Jesus; sing his mercy and his grace. In the mansions bright and blessed, He'll prepare for us a place. When we all get to heaven, what a day of rejoicing that will be!" In the sixth- seventh-eighth-grade room, Miss Carolyn King (later to be Augsburger) came back from a weekend at EMS (Eastern Mennonite School, now University), joyfully reporting on the alto solos she had sung in *The Holy City*. We heard lots of stories and talks from mission and MCC relief workers, Mennonite historians like Ira D. Landis, and music groups from people who were associated with EMS in Virginia like a men's quartet, one member of whom did chalk drawings while they sang "Throw Out the Life Line" and "The Ninety and Nine." We prepared our own music and religious poetry programs for our parents; one closed with prayerful farewells for a teacher who was leaving us to be sent to an Eastern Mennonite Mission Board field. We built a miniature African church out of sun-dried bricks with a grass roof. I knew all the Tanganyika missionary families and their children's names and was beginning to try to understand the phenomenon talked about in Lancaster Conference churches as the East African revival.

The High School Idyll

Academics at Locust Grove probably were not stellar, but in many ways I think we taught each other along with our committed teachers. We were cliquish, but we nurtured good friendships and bonded in ways that have enriched us all our lives. These relationships we carried from eighth grade across Greenfield Road and down the Lincoln Highway the next year to LMS. The eighth class to graduate from Lancaster Mennonite School, we began the second half of the twentieth century "passing on the faith," as Don Kraybill labels it in his fifty-year history, *The Story of a Mennonite School*.[1] The site was a Mill Creek-watered garden of beauty where competent educators had established a rigorous program of study in the context of a venue to serve and hold the youth of the church, especially in wartime.

A well-loved teacher, Harvey Bauman, who had begun teaching at LMS in our sophomore year, rose to open the first January chapel as we faced the close of our last year. In staccato style with piercing eyes, Brother Bauman declared, "Jesus may come in 1950!" The declaration was repeated before each point of his outline. As one kid in the 250-member student body, I have never forgotten it. Fifty-eight years later I hear it still and think on New Year's days: "Jesus may come in two thousand—dash!" I have not forgotten Harvey Bauman.

Harvey is gone. They are almost all gone—all but J. Lester Brubaker and Don Jacobs—those school-by-the-Mill-Stream pioneers: J. Paul Graybill, Noah Good, Clyde Stoner, Myra Hess, Lois Garber Kauffman, Clayton Keener, John S. Wenger, Martha Mosemann, Amos Weaver, Leah Kauffman Lind, Edna K. Wenger. The poet was Edna Wenger, who sponsored the Stylus Club. She stood one day in chapel and told of a school reunion where a teacher asked all who had come back to stand up if they had remained faithful to the hymn they had sung: "O, Jesus, I have promised to serve thee to the end." Such was the commitment sought.

Sorting the Voices

Lancaster Mennonites at mid-century, if our high school class is any indicator, were still not hurrying to higher education. After that June Monday morning graduation exercise at LMS—where EMC (Eastern Mennonite College, now University) ex-President John L. Stauffer had given the commencement address—I came home, laid down my diploma, and went out to help my dad clean out chicken houses and haul manure. How well I remember the dejection I felt with no assurance that in the fall—or if ever—I would be able to go to college. If I would stick around on the farm, my dad was insinuating, we could think about buying me a car. After all, for things to do beside farm work there was Bob Stetter's chorus to sing with and associated mission possibilities at nursing homes or the almshouse or Green Dragon Market on Friday nights. I could support the Light House Band in Lancaster or explore other interesting possibilities for service at the Vine Street Mission, not to mention being able to be around all those demure young women who had graduated that morning from LMS and who were not going to college.

The Vine Street experience itself embodied a discovery; I should not like to consider the consequences of my life apart from it. When I was twelve, our family had joined several other families in a Sunday school-Bible school and eventual church planting endeavor in southern Lancaster County at a place called Andrew's Bridge, a bi-racial community. The workers helped to provide transportation and other support for families to attend this Mellinger Church outpost. A satisfying experience, our Andrew's Bridge sojourn lasted several years until my father accepted an invitation to consider becoming a mission worker at the Lancaster city church known as the Vine Street Mission. What a reversal from the bends and turns of the rural drive down Route 896 to the Seventh Ward church in the city, lit outside by the neon JESUS SAVES sign and inside with "The Entrance of Thy Words Giveth Light" emblazoned on the wall above the high pulpit! Sometimes I think that the pealing bells of the surrounding churches on Duke and Vine streets as I sat in the Vine Street Mission that first Sunday must have been for me, for a fleeting moment, not unlike the bells and voices that Joan of Arc was sure she heard from her heavenly saints in her country town in France. Unlike at Mellinger and Andrew's Bridge, something was invigorating about this church in Lancaster. What was that Vine Street vision?

Getting to College

During the summer of 1950, Lester C. Shank, probably soliciting students and money for Eastern Mennonite College, appeared one Sunday morning at Vine Street; and I think it was he who left me with an application. So it was that after some extra patches of Silver Queen corn and a couple loathsome months at Neuhauser's Hardware Store in Bird-in-Hand, at summer's end my grandparents and my mother dropped me and my suitcase at Turkey Dorm behind Jacob Shenk's hatchery in Park View, the village home of the college, and drove away. I remember walking up behind the turkey hatchery to be alone, having myself one quick bawl, and never feeling homesick again.

Four of us Turkey Dorm roommates were from Lancaster County, and three of us were LMS classmate hangovers; so much for cross-cultural options, although EMC had begun to welcome international students already in the 1940s and was an early private college in Virginia to welcome African-Americans. I knew that Marjorie Thompson, whom I had known at Andrew's Bridge Church back home, had successfully tested the admission policies to EMC a couple years before. Now I sat by Leroy Buck, a young Harrisonburg black man, in John T. N. Litwiller's Spanish class. Four years later, in 1954 when we graduated, Peggy Webb Howard—whose mother was the well known Roberta Webb—and I collaborated on our class song; at our class night program Peggy led us in "Conquering through Christ." Good news—the chariot was gonna come!

If Daddy had questions about his son's badly wanting to go to college, part of an acceptable solution was my declaring a Bible major. Other LMS classmates' wagons were hitched to different stars: Kenton Brubaker knew science was his field; Virgil Stoltzfus was going to be a doctor as were several other friends back at Franklin and Marshall in Lancaster; and Ada Nancy King was going to be a teacher of deaf children. Bible made my way safer, and I was okay about it. Actually, I was no doubt as pious-appearing as everyone else in daily chapel, evening prayer circles, and dorm prayer circles—all without the new labyrinth, mind you—but I had lots of growing up to do.

I liked to write in Hubert Pellman's English composition class for two semesters, liked it more than most of my Bible courses; and I learned a lot of history and sociology with Harry Brunk, biology and geology under D. Ralph Hostetter, and New Testament Greek from Dorothy Kemrer. M. T. Brackbill's speech and literary interpretation classes ranked high, but Introduction to Literature with Ruth Brackbill gave me the most delight and pointed me in the direction I wanted to go with novels, short stories, essays, and poetry—"Glory be to God for dappled things!"[2] The only research paper I remember writing in my freshman year was for J. Mark Stauffer in an elective music appreciation class; it was about Frederic Chopin, and J. Mark affirmed it in his fine penmanship: "I am delighted with your paper."

Well, we came to EMC for an education that contained more than attending classes or sitting at those ponderous library tables. How many of us tried to do everything? We were Smithsonians (doing our partying at the Pierian Spring!) and Zelatheans (striving, seeking, finding, but not yielding) in contests like the races in *Ben Hur!* We sang in Collegiate Chorus with three weekly morning rehearsals and ladies' or men's choruses the other two mornings before chapel. We went on chorus tours with Earl Maust and J. Mark Stauffer. Students craved positions on the *Weather Vane,* the *Journal,* and *The Shenandoah,* student publications all sponsored by M. T. Brackbill, who wrote a poem, "Lord, I Like It Here." We crammed in as many clubs as we could: missionary, Bible, foreign language, history, the societies—Astral and Avian. Some of us destroyed our erasers to get into Scriblerus. Everyone enjoyed School Day Out with EMC's most delicious cake treat. In the fall and spring we went with College Hikers or Highlanders, and how many YPCA committees could we belong to or join how many Gospel teams? Still there was time for our own planned fun. A group of us could fairly easily persuade A. Grace Wenger to spend an empty Friday evening with us in some dorm lounge taking parts to read *Hamlet.* A. Grace could illuminate for us the more obscure allusions like "to the manner born," "like Niobe, all tears," or "What's Hecuba to him, or he to Hecuba?"

The Surprising Invitation

One warm spring afternoon there came for me a defining moment. Surely not St. Joan again! I had left the library and gone to the fountain under the clock for a drink when an office door in the hall opened and Dean

C. K. Lehman stepped out and accosted me. I was in his ethics class that semester. Now what did he wonder—whether I was going to have my paper, "The Ethics of Studying Literature," finished on time? (As a junior I had added an English major to Bible.) In his forthright style came this question: Would I consider coming back to EMC to teach? The administrators had in mind English in the high school. I would be drafted and need to fulfill my obligation to the U. S. government for two years—but after that ... and would I be willing to find a I-W placement somewhere close to a good university where I could begin graduate studies? I was to learn that about the same time, Dean Lehman had talked with my friend and former roommate John Lapp to offer him an invitation to consider teaching high school history. So much for *The Chronicle of Higher Education* job advertisements in 1954.

John and I got busy in a hurry, sending applications to several schools. Professors Pellman and Brackbill graciously wrote letters of recommendation for me. At that time EMC gave the Graduate Record Examinations, including the area ones, to all seniors at the Dean's Office expense; we had the necessary scores. I remember a trip to Harrisburg for the physical examination. Western Reserve University in Cleveland granted admission to both of us for the fall semester, and The University Hospitals of Cleveland hired two more I-W boys where over a hundred COs were serving their time in the city's hospitals. Western Reserve University—on a joint campus with Case Institute of Technology—was right beside our hospital. John and I rented a room from a Greek family who lived on Cummington Road by the railroad tracks, and Mrs. Nonis collected our rent promptly each Friday.

Cleveland Days

The city had lots to offer I-W boys: recreational arenas, cultural diversity, and endless things to do besides work and study. We lived about three blocks from Severance Hall on Euclid Avenue, home of the Cleveland Orchestra, and could use our season tickets every Friday or Saturday night. One season I auditioned for the orchestra chorus and got to sing Beethoven's *Ninth* under George Szell. I remember, too, the chance to hear Marian Anderson in concert singing "The Erl-King" as well as "He's Got the Whole World in His Hand." The Cleveland Playhouse was also on famous Euclid Avenue; here I saw *Hamlet* for the first time, the lead role played by a fine actor who, after the run closed, was admitted to University Hospitals, where he was to die of throat cancer.

The I-W program itself presented many opportunities for growth. The I-Ws gathered in a storefront on Warner Road on Sundays, and we met there also for rehearsals of the I-W Chorus, Cleveland singers— women and men—who often gave programs in Ohio churches in Holmes and Wayne counties, from which a good many I-W people came. James O. Lehman had been the editor of a Cleveland I-W newsletter called *Cleveland Chimes;* when Jim and Dorothy left to return to Sonnenberg, I inherited Jim's editorial job.

I remember that Hubert Pellman had expressed his confidence to me in Western Reserve's English department, and I found the curriculum exhilarating. In the first course I registered for, Milton and His Times, Raven McDavid took us through all three epics and many of the essays, as well as the shorter poetry. The course helped to remove the trepidation I had about whether I was well enough prepared by my small Mennonite college for the rigors of graduate study. It also did not threaten the faith of this newly-cast-on-the-shores-of-Lake Erie neophyte city dweller. I remember that I did take comfort reading C. S. Lewis' commentary[3] on *Paradise Lost:* no matter how or with what persuasion other literary scholars may read this epic tale "Of Man's first disobedience, and the fruit/ Of that forbidden tree whose mortal taste/ Brought death into the World, and all our woe," about the content of this masterpiece, Lewis had written, "I, in the cold prose, do believe."

My last course in the master's program was a delightful seminar on George Bernard Shaw, who had lived nearly a century and died only in 1950; it was directed by Dr. Arthur Franklin White, a serious devotee of Shaw and a poet who wrote for the seminar students a long poetic souvenir in Shaw's honor. Between Milton and Shaw were quite a few American literature courses, some with Dr. Lyon Richardson, who had written the American survey texts we used and who told me when I was leaving that he would be glad to give me a recommendation to the University of Virginia if I wanted one—that "place over the mountain," he called it. However, I think I knew that teaching high school English the next year would make additional study impossible at that time.

Teaching High School

My teaching load in 1956–57 replicated what A. Grace Wenger had been carrying when she left EMC and returned to Pennsylvania to help care for her ailing father and teach part time at Lancaster Mennonite School. She told me in a letter that she was burning all her old shoes! The loads we were handed in those days! Take my first class of English IV students (who celebrated their fiftieth reunion in October 2007). I had three sections composed of eighty-six seniors, a section of sophomore English, two sections of speech—Oral Expression, it was called—and a Bible class, besides literary sponsorship and faculty committees. Ira Miller, who by then had been appointed the dean, in his kindly way could pile it on unmercifully. I sometimes remembered a Sunday evening back at Vine Street when I was a high school kid moderating a children's meeting and had to take a misbehaving child out of the church. The patriarch-churchman from Chambersburg, J. Irvin Lehman, who happened to be present that evening, comforted or complimented me after the service with the scriptural injunction in Lamentations 3:27: "It is good for a man that he bear the yoke in his youth" (KJV). I was twenty-three. What was this first year of teaching? Every teacher has to have one, but no one would ever ask to repeat it!

In my first seven years, while the high school continued to share space with the college on the main campus, we had many functions together; but gradually President John R. Mumaw helped the high school toward its separate destiny. In the middle of the 1963–64 school year the physical separation occurred although food services, dormitory space, and various other places continued to be used jointly. I shared an office with college teachers Paul Martin and J. Lester Brubaker, along with Clarence Fretz, who kept a cot in the office where he could take a nap every day after lunch. They were helpful colleagues. Meanwhile, Dean Miller, who had enjoyed layering my high school classes with college writing courses, did less of this after the new school brought more separation.

My high school teaching years totaled twelve, and I here express heartfelt appreciation to the directors of the high school who mentored me throughout that time: D. Ralph Hostetter my first year and Harold D. Lehman, Jesse T. Byler, and John H. Krall. In 1958 Harold Lehman led the high school in achieving accreditation by the Southern Association of Colleges and Secondary Schools. How humbly proud we were at that faculty meeting when the committee gave us their report of acceptance, adding that they thought we exemplified that old adage, "plain living and high thinking."

While a good portion of my master's program consisted of American literature study, when I came to the high school curriculum at EMC, the teaching prescription for me was primarily British literature. In two semesters we surveyed the treasures of England from *Beowulf,* Chaucer, and Shakespeare through the centuries to T. S. Eliot, Virginia Woolf, and Bernard Shaw's *Pygmalion.* Like many high schools, we used the Adventures series for literature along with materials for writing and grammar instruction and additional spelling-vocabulary books, actually quite tough ones. I pay homage to Vivian Beachy, my co-teacher in English for those twelve high school years. Vivian had come the year before I arrived, and she modeled excellence in her classes in methods of learning and teaching. When the thousands of EMHS alumni rise to honor the renowned "Miss Beachy" for what they learned with her, I will join that array of appreciative scholars.

A regular component of teaching high school English at EMC meant sharing my classes with the education department's English majors for their student teaching experience. The EMHS students were good sports, and the teachers often added to our classes variety and breadth. Many of them became like colleagues. My gallery of the faithful student teachers reads like Hebrews 11: J. Herbert Martin, Joan Esch Zook, Grace Wideman Herr, Ray Gingerich, J. Allen Brubaker, Paul Schrock, Anna Mary Longacre Brubacher, J. Lorne Peachey, Betty Wenger Good, Helen Longenecker Lapp, Joyce Erb Brunk—"what shall I say more? Time would fail me to tell." By faith we made it together.

Teachers Together

Because I had not yet received a teaching certificate from Richmond, I did not have student teachers in 1957, my first year. There was, however, a particularly attractive senior in English IV and in Oral Expression, who in the next few years would become a teacher in her native Rockingham County, who wrote very good papers, achieved high scores, and held everybody's attention in oral interpretation and speech. Since I was a member of the church-wide Mennonite Youth Fellowship cabinet at the time, I was involved in helping to plan the upcoming summer MYF convention at EMC, and I co-opted some of my recent students to help with the conference. When the planning committee asked that a Virginia MYFer give a welcome speech at the MYF banquet, my eye fell upon the H's in the class roll to my first choice: Peggy Heatwole. Indeed it was the right choice! Soon after the fortuitous banquet, I invited Peggy to go out to dinner as sort of a thank you for what she had done. We drove over to a restaurant along Route 33 in Penn Laird that I thought was called The Golden Lantern. The place turned out to be really The Copper Kettle! We have often laughed about how sometimes our Golden Lanterns have metamorphosed into Copper Kettles.

We were married in the EMC Chapel in 1961, and I know that C. K. Lehman was there although the auditorium had not yet been named for him. Peggy's pastor, Harold Eshleman, performed the ceremony, Ira Miller gave the sermon, and Audrey Shank directed the Vesper Chorus from the balcony in a musical setting of John Milton's poem, "Let All the World in Every Corner Sing." Fourteen years later I gave Peggy this fourteen-line Petrarchan poem:

Sonnet Amoroso

Love, all the world stood up for you and sang—
Green-June Virginia daughter of those bright
Stars over Shenandoah. Candlelight
Hosannas strewed your way and holy rang
Your benediction song. There I too sang
Like Cana's bridegroom when the wine was right
Because the Lord had come. Since that gold night
I do not stop my song or ever hang
My harp on weeping fronds for long. The wise
Days of my life are musical, and fears
Dissolve since your remembered song supplies
My joy. For you I sing. The world who hears
May rise. Today the song is sonnet size:
A morning gift for these first fourteen years.

Peggy joined the Turner Ashby High School faculty in 1961, teaching Latin and English, and we shared the programs of our respective schools. I attended Latin Club meetings with the Latin II patricians and their Latin I slaves, always to be reunited in the manumission ceremony after banqueting in high Roman fashion. There came the autumn semester one year when Mrs. Landis's Latin students came to school one morning, each wearing two pink ribbons. A substitute had filled in for several months until she could return to the Latin classroom, leaving her new babies at home for several hours with the best of care from her sister-in-law, Catherine Heatwole. My EMHS senior English class gave us a playpen. EMC, when a faculty member had an addition to the family, traditionally bestowed $100 to celebrate the new arrival. How welcome was the phone call from Business Manager John Snyder that we would be receiving $200! Also, with a generous loan from the college we were able to exchange our three-room basement apartment for the house on Parkway Drive that became our home for the next twenty-five years.

Things Dramatic

A lingering sense of my personal need to give some time in voluntary service directed us into a sabbatical year in a migrant camp in Caldwell, Idaho, in 1968. Our four-year-old daughters paved the path for us for that MVS experience, relating with neighbors from South Texas border towns who came to Idaho to work on the sugar beet and hops and mint farms of Treasure Valley. At the same time, EMC President Myron Augsburger was asking whether I would consider registering for some academic work in drama—some insulated gloves for picking up that hot potato of the sixties—and join the college faculty. Thus, while in Caldwell I enrolled part time in theater courses at the College of Idaho with enthusiastic Labor Camp children vying for roles in our amateur productions. When we returned to Virginia in 1969, I was assigned a course called Studies in Drama; Ira Miller did not want to take any chances by calling it theater.

The histrionic bent must have always been prevalent at this Virginia college, although its founders and administrators found it troublesome throughout our history. It was John R. Mumaw, after all, who in his early years had hoped to make a life on the stage, we are told. His conversion guided his penchant for acting from stage to pulpit, but the dramatic element was always present. Elwood Weaver of Park View told me that in the thirties students would meet in the old gym for skits, and Indian blankets were the extent of allowable costumes. Some of us remember that the faculty handbook's early description allowed "draping," nothing more. I can remember A. Grace Wenger's high school English classes putting on Longfellow's "Evangeline" with the French soldiers wearing safety patrol belts and badges. In 1959 I had chosen to let the high school seniors put on Rudolf Besier's *The Barretts of Wimpole Street* in the Assembly Room for their spring class dinner entertainment. This is the play about Robert Browning and Elizabeth Barrett's courtship that was printed in their literature book. Irvin Horst, then on the college English faculty, afterward teased me that I had slid drama into EMC under the door.

On the Monday morning after the infamous weekend, I had a summons to Brother Mumaw's office, and his question was not why that play or why had we done it but how come the Assembly Room had been packed out with class members' parents and community folks! Literary societies picked up the practice, and the sixties mounted very good productions: *The Diary of Anne Frank, The Crucible, Antigone, J.B., Murder in the Cathedral,* to name a few. In 1970 the Drama Club had over a hundred members—an evidence of great interest in this art.

My preference came to be teaching drama rather than directing it. Clearly, I did not know enough about it, with fewer theater credits than even a minor in the subject. As literature—the study of drama—I loved it, but I was more than happy to give theater to others like Helen Stoltzfus and Barbra Graber. Albert Keim, the far-seeing, understanding dean, like Euripides, became my *deus ex machina.*

Return for Preparation

In the early seventies, having learned to enjoy participating in the experiment called Gen Ed with its dozen courses required of virtually every student, along with my drama, speech, and writing course load, I knew it was time to go back to graduate school—hence our family's return to Idaho and the excitement of what seemed like a tailored program for me at Idaho State University: literature, an interdisciplinary emphasis, and a pedagogical component. The program also emphasized creative elements and could be broadened to include related fields. I chose speech and rhetoric and drama. The pedagogical segment gave me experience in teaching composition and speech.

At ISU I was able to maximize my interest in teaching along with study in areas in which I anticipated a role back at EMC. Classics in translation occupied lots of time. I took the chance to read Greek and Roman writers, Dante, Cervantes, and the medieval Arthurian legends, as well as writers in classical rhetoric and rhetorical theory and criticism. This literature along with speech and communication course work proved useful in teaching speech both at ISU and back at EMC. I was introduced to new concepts in literary criticism and in the theory of pedagogy. An area of special interest was the teaching of poetry writing. ISU's Doctor of Arts in English program was finally defined by the requirement of three major studies with extensive papers in each, culminating in a scholarly public lecture demonstrating expertise in teaching. After the first semester I had been offered a scholarship, and the program was extremely satisfying, though difficult. One day we received two letters from back East. "Tell Jay not to work too hard," instructed Peggy's mother in Harrisonburg. My mom in Pennsylvania offered Ben Franklin sagacity, "Hard work never hurt anybody." The same day's advice.

The Pocatello years were often Golden-Lanterned. At first Peggy became an assistant to a wonderful elementary principal named Dorothy Frazier, who became her model for years to come. Ann and Jill attended the same school with highly competent fifth and sixth grade teachers. Ann, writing a story one day, went to her teacher for spelling help with a word. It was hard for Mrs. Firkins to understand: the word was "minaswell." In Mrs. Hill's room they danced a lot and sang; but when Mrs. Hill announced the state song, "And here we have Idaho, winning her way to fame," Jill, solidly loyal to her native Virginia, pinched her lips tightly. The kids sang in the Methodist Church children's musicals and had the chance for instrumental instruction in school.

A Pocatello Copper Kettle happened in our final year there. At Franklin Junior High School where Peggy taught, one morning students came to school only to find a gaping hole blasted into the principal's office. Peggy decided then that she would not miss those threatening experiences anymore and accepted a job in career development at EMC for the following year. We never got to see Evel Knievel jump the Snake River at Twin Falls, but we could purchase health foods at his family's store right next to the university; and we got to see Yellowstone and Jackson Hole, the Grand Tetons, Sun Valley, and Craters of the Moon.

The Final Vocational Quest

Back in Harrisonburg, we continued our church life at Park View Mennonite, which has provided sustenance in the years since. Pastoral care has been provided by Harold Eshleman, Don Augsburger, Owen Burkholder, Shirley Yoder Brubaker, Phil Kniss, and Barbara Moyer Lehman. Having moved my membership from Lancaster to the congregation first in 1956, I enjoyed helping with the fiftieth anniversary celebration in 2003. I trace the influences of our congregational life at Park View upon our children as well as what it has meant to Peggy and me, particularly in involvement with the Colloquy Sunday school class. Opportunities to participate in the music and worship programs have been important.

Returning to EMC in 1976, I was able to reunite with colleagues with a renewed sense of purpose in the mission of the school; and, as it turned out, the reunion lasted for thirty more years. I worked about nine years in John R. Mumaw's time, the fifteen years of Myron Augsburger's tenure, seven years with Richard Detweiler, sixteen with Joseph Lapp, and the final three with Loren Swartzendruber (the sequence of the college/university presidents). I know that countless measures of grace were dealt to me through the fifty years of my life at Eastern Mennonite High School/College/University, and I can never express all the gratitude I owe.

Grace was mediated to me by colleagues. My teacher friends: God bless everyone who blessed and challenged my life and work. The English and language departments were close in proximity and in heart—Hubert Pellman, James Bomberger, Omar Eby, Herb Martin, Anna Frey, Carroll Yoder, Lee Snyder, Diana Enedy, Barbra Graber, Ray Horst, Ervie Glick, and Jean Janzen. The more recent comers have become special as well. My many colleagues in the IDS/Humanities deserve my thanks for their mutuality and for the great amount I learned from them: for example, Herb

Swartz and Barbara Fast in Freedom and Order and Ann Hershberger and Ken Nafziger in senior seminars. Fifty years of countless teacher friends—it is indeed an overwhelming memory! Especially was grace accorded near the close of the school years 1979 and 1983, respectively, when Herb Martin and Anna Frey suddenly left our fellowship, and it fell to the rest of us to conclude their work.

And then—the students. In the fall of 2007 the high school class of '57 met to celebrate their fiftieth reunion. Forty-nine years of students had followed them. June Bontrager was in that class of '57. She married that illustrious Oregon student Paul Schrock, and Carmen was their oldest child, a student in my class in the eighties. After graduation from EMC, Carmen married Luke Hurst, Jr. Last year in one of my afternoon speech sections, who walked in, alert, eyes sparkling? Grace Schrock-Hurst! In fifty years, the first and only time—three generations: it had to be time to stop. Two generations happen to many teachers; welcoming the children while remembering the parents, though not unusual or remarkable, does make us conscious of our multiple birthdays. A senior this year, Joe Mason, came to EMU from Philadelphia Mennonite School. When I first met Joe in class and had discovered his origins, I told him that I remembered back at Andrew's Bridge Church in Lancaster County attending his grandparents' wedding! I had also attended his great-grandparents' funerals. Joe could not believe it. If teacher longevity earns one a degree of satisfaction, that diploma should be hung up humbly, with a prayer that justice and mercy have been extended to the Graces and the Joes.

Reflections at Fifty Years

One of my goals through the years has been trying to make names important—to try to identify students by name on the second day of class (enormous IDS/Humanities classes excepted, of course). I wanted to recognize each person and acknowledge his or her presence and importance in that class. In recent years I have experimented in poetry writing with classes by distributing oranges and asking the students to respond to their individual orange with a poem. Later I shared one of mine to illustrate, a sort of memory chain but also meant to be evocative of the really human cast of characters in my classroom theater.

Telling

In OB, they brought Twin Baby A
to my wife from the nursery to be fed.
"But I just fed this baby," Peggy said.
"I don't think so," said the kind attendant,
taking the infant with her anyway.
"Sure enough you did," she laughed upon returning,
holding this time Twin Baby B.

A little period of possession
yields some recognition:
take this orange.

My orange has a flat place
where it wedged beside a sibling
or hung against its branch in a Sarasota grove
or snoozled in a packing crate north to Charlottesville.
Turning in my hand, it grows familiar
until I believe I could distinguish it
out of the thirteen at the table.

For Henrik Ibsen, thirteen at table was portentous.
They say he kept a scorpion on his desk
into whose cage he dropped an orange
wherein the arachnid could discharge its venom.

Imagine, then, Ibsen contemplating
each sad, stung, silent fruit:
unlucky Gregers. Hedda. Mrs. Alving.
Stockman, Borkman, Torvald Helmer.
Each one marked.

Students are the teacher's meat and drink. We walked together and talked together. They gave speeches. I listened to their speeches—thousands of them. They wrote papers. I wrote on their papers. They wrote poetry. They read literature; because I relish oral reading, I often read

Left: Reading with grandchildren Tim and Nate Snider. Right: celebrating retirement with tributes and roses

literature to them—"The grandmother didn't want to go to Florida."[4] They discussed literature and listened to one another. They kept journals. We packed lunches and rode chartered Quick-Livick buses to Washington, DC—EMU's accessible treasure house for the arts—to spend long days seeing plays, studying art, and hearing concerts. One Modern Drama class saw Dustin Hoffman play Willy Loman in Arthur Miller's *Death of a Salesman* at the Kennedy Center—a stop-your-breath performance. A high privilege was the opportunity to accompany students on cross-cultural experiences: the English Room in the Campus Center exchanged for the Barbican Center in London, the Abbey Theater in Dublin, the Royal Shakespeare Theater in Stratford-upon-Avon—or the TV lounge at the Hampstead Heath Youth Hostel in Golders Green, where we held daily classes.

To *experience* the humanities was the thing that counted. If students could feel and hear and find themselves in the writing—the story, the play, the poem—the music, the art, then teaching mattered. "The meaning is in you," Flannery O'Connor said in *Mystery and Manners: Occasional Prose,*[5] and she taught us the way to learn. My students over the years were my greatest gift. The grades they made were the grades I deserved.

They made A's, B's, C's, after a while pluses and minuses. A few settled for F's or NC's. Year to year, fall to winter to spring, their and my successes and failures blended.

But "amid the snows—a rose!"[6] Living next to Ira Miller on Parkway Drive those years, and afterwards at Ira Eby's former place, I was able to observe and learn about roses. I could certainly learn much more. Classes went better with roses. Along with music and writing, rose culture has been a much loved avocation; Eliot and Frost both wrote about merging or uniting the avocation and the vocation. Since Peggy and I both enjoy seeing roses in cobalt blue vases, looking for cobalt became another hobby. An English teacher's life is writing. Stopping to write a poem fulfilled a need, sometimes an assignment from others, sometimes mine. For me, poetry is the genre that nourishes most deeply, though plays will sometimes do. Shakespeare in his plays combines it all.

By whatever threads it was woven, teaching became my vocation. I respect it as a worthy calling. Becky, my ninth-grade granddaughter, is saying she would like to be a teacher. Now she rides the yellow school bus. My mother, born nearly a hundred years ago, would have liked to have been a teacher. She took Latin in her one year of high school; then she needed to quit school, go to work in a garment factory, and give her wages to her pop and mom to help support their large family. In her Latin class Mother may have learned the infinitive *vocare—to call*. Once she told me she had always remembered the Latin word for love: "*amo, amas, amat*," she conjugated. She hoped I would take Latin in ninth grade, which I did, under a *magistra* who loved her work. Because of my mother's influence and the kindness of many, many others, I give thanks for having been permitted to unite the love and the vocation, affirming the wise Preacher of Ecclesiastes, who wrote that "nothing is better ... than to enjoy [one's] work."

November 12, 2007
Revised July 22, 2008

Notes

1 Donald B. Kraybill, *Passing on the Faith: The Story of a Mennonite School* (Intercourse, PA: Good Books, 1991).

2 Gerard Manley Hopkins, "Pied Beauty" in *Poems* (London: Humphrey Milford, 1918).

3 C. S. Lewis, *A Preface to Paradise Lost* (New York: Oxford University Press, 1961).

4 Flannery O'Connor, "A Good Man Is Hard To Find," first appeared in O'Connor's short story collection, *A Good Man is Hard to Find* (New York: Farrar, Strauss and Giroux, 1969).

5 Flannery O'Connor, *Mystery and Manners: Occasional Prose* (New York, NY: Harcourt, 1955).

6 David Hugh Jones and Edwin O. Kennedy, "Amid the Snows, a Rose: A Christmas Anthem S.a.t.b. a Cappella" (Boston, MA: C.C. Birchard & Company, 1944).

Quest and Questions

Some people collect stamps while others collect antique tractors. Perhaps I can claim to collect questions. Here I unpack for you some samples from my collection—some of them my own, many gleaned from others. Fortunately, collecting questions requires less expertise than collecting answers.

Roots

Flash back to 1884. A young couple and three little girls leave their home near Akron, Pennsylvania, to settle on a farm near Newton, Kansas. There my father, Silas J., is born in 1893.

Fast-forward to 1910: My mother, Nellie Showalter, born in 1898 near Singers' Glen, Virginia, is a twelve-year-old when her family likewise leaves the East to settle in Kansas.

In my parents' milieu, children were expected to work for the family between grade school and the age of twenty-one. (Speaking of grade school, my mother earned the highest eighth grade exam scores in McPherson County, Kansas, in the year of her graduation.) Both of my parents, then, entered high school at age twenty-one. My father enrolled at Hesston Academy, to which he pedaled his bicycle four miles each way from his parents' home and from which he graduated in 1918. In 1919 my mother made the grueling three-day train trip to Virginia to enroll at the new Eastern Mennonite School, near her birthplace. After two years there she transferred to Hesston Academy, Kansas, where she graduated in 1923.

Both of my parents took the "normal course," a high school curriculum of teacher preparation. However, World War I disrupted my father's plans for teaching; a few weeks out of high school he was conscripted for military service. Since the army had no arrangement for men who refused to become soldiers, except to bully them, his weeks in military camp were most unpleasant. Eventually the army created a "farm furlough" for the recalcitrant conscientious objectors, and my father went with several others to the Mennonite community near Wellman, Iowa.

Thirty years later, with his voice breaking, he would tell us children how a group of men, angry about the Mennonites' lack of support for the war, threw stones at him and his friends and made death threats until the sheriff arrived to tell the agitators that he would brook no lynching in his county. Question: Since we are grateful for law enforcement, in what way, if any, should we contribute to it? What police actions might Christians support?

After the war Iowa Mennonites hired my father to teach school. Meanwhile, my mother finished her studies; but instead of teaching she got married, fresh out of high school at age twenty-five. The honeymoon was a one-way trip from Kansas to Iowa by Model T Ford on roads turned to mud by October rains. In Iowa the couple took up farming and joined the Liberty Mennonite Church, near South English, where within a year my father was ordained for the ministry.

After five years of marriage there were no prospects of children. From where he lived in Kansas, Grandpa Showalter urged the couple to take a boy from the Mennonite Children's Home in Kansas City "to help with the farm work." They did and named him Emery. Four years later they took a little girl, Hazel, as well. While we always spoke of my older siblings as adopted, after we became adults we learned that they were technically foster children. The Children's Home administrator had advised the couple not to formalize a legal adoption so that if the child ever ran afoul of the law, they as foster parents would not have to assume legal responsibility. Question: Why was "trial marriage" without any binding commitment scandalous while parenthood without a binding commitment was perfectly acceptable? Fortunately, since the 1920s we seem to have learned a few things about every child's need for unconditional love.

Finally, after fourteen years of marriage my mother brought forth their firstborn son. Eighteen months later my brother Allen was born when our parents were forty-one and forty-six. In childhood we failed to recognize that they were old enough to be our grandparents.

Separate from the World

Isolation loomed large in our lives. Grandparents? I saw one grandmother once, when I was three years old. Uncles, aunts, cousins? Most of them lived in other states, and because of farm chores we did not travel. Only one other family from our small church lived nearby, and fifteen miles of dust or mud separated us from the next Mennonite church. We never socialized with our non-Mennonite neighbors; they did nasty things like smoking, drinking, dancing, and going to movies. Fortunately we children had in-house playmates.

Trading farm work did provide some contact with people who were not of our church. Threshing brought neighbor men to our home, probably the only time we ate with non-Mennonites. We assumed that they were watching their language in the presence of the preacher. One neighbor sometimes kidded our father about his cantankerous mules: "A preacher shouldn't have mules—they're too likely to make him swear."

Could our non-Mennonite neighbors be Christians? Our parents admitted reluctantly that some might be "saved." One nearby family was Catholic, and every morning their car passed our house, taking them to Mass. Their faithfulness went unpraised in our home; devotion to a false religion warranted no affirmation.

Since Papa, as we were taught to call him, was usually doing farm work or preparing a sermon, we small children spent a lot of time with our mother. I pestered her with questions: "What makes the bullet fly out of the gun?... Does the stuff inside a *big* clock have to run faster, since the hands have to go farther?... Why does a pull-type corn picker stay out to the side of the tractor instead of following straight behind like wagons do?"

Attending our one-room country school, to which all the pupils walked, brought more contact with other children, but none were Mennonites. Our parents made no issue of the Pledge of Allegiance; each morning we recited, "... one nation, indivisible, with liberty and justice for all." (Since the phrase "under God" was added later, the recent campaign to delete those words is not, for me, the visceral issue it is for some younger people.) During World War II, we did face a weighty question: Should we help in the nation-wide effort to gather milkweed pods for making life preservers for the navy? Our parents concluded that gathering those pods to save sailors' lives was appropriate. Only later did we ask, "Why, then, is the work of a medic, helping wounded soldiers recover, not acceptable?" The rationale that their lives were saved so that they could kill again seemed to apply in one case but not in the other.

Our father had received music training at Hesston under the young C. K. Lehman (who will reappear later in this narrative), and Papa had conducted singing schools in Mennonite churches near Wellman and Kalona. Sometimes on a Sunday afternoon we children would beg, "Papa, give us a music lesson," so he taught us to read notes by the *do-re-mi* system. I laughed with delight the first time we sang a duet, we children on the melody and Papa supplying the alto line.

Our family life suffered an upheaval when I was in the third grade. Pop's pupils of twenty-five years earlier now asked him to be the principal of the new Iowa Mennonite School. He therefore left farming, and we moved to a house where we had electric lights—and a bathroom. The twenty-one unpaved miles to IMS were deemed too many for a daily commute, so during three school years he left home each Monday morning and returned on Friday evening. Also during those years, our country school closed, and a school bus invaded the neighborhood to carry us off to a big town school. There we were more isolated than ever among people who knew nothing of Mennonites. I certainly did not want the other kids to know that we went to church three times a week—and then I felt ashamed for being ashamed of Jesus. Pop's absence during those years contributed to a bleak ambience at home.

When I was eleven, revival meetings at our church brought me a sense of a burden of sin, and I stood to accept Jesus. My younger brother followed suit. As we headed for home after a brief prayer with the evangelist, I was trembling over the enormity of my action. I sensed that my parents were pleased, but typically they said not one word about our decision. We did not talk about personal matters in our home. We had a daily family worship, but that dull ritual prompted another of my childhood questions: "Couldn't we get more work done if we didn't take time for family worship?"

Teen Trajectory

High school brought happier days: I attended Iowa Mennonite School. (My father, lacking any college training, had relinquished the principalship to Paul T. Guengerich and had returned to the farm.) Although many schoolmates at IMS were "worldly" by the standards of my parents, overall I relished a new sense of belonging. For the first time in my life I had meaningful prayer sessions with friends. In chorus we sang selections from Handel's *Messiah*, delightfully new to me. In my senior year we had a new chorus director fresh from Eastern Mennonite College: Dorothy Lehman, now Dorothy Kreider of Harrisonburg. Ada Schrock's English class brought us classic poems such as William Cullen Bryant's "Thanatopsis" and "To a Waterfowl." Miss Schrock's three rules for speaking to a group remain engraved on my memory, perhaps because we so often see them violated: "Stand up to be seen; speak up to be heard; sit down to be appreciated."

Work on the farm provided pleasant interludes in the academic rhythm. My brother could deal with the livestock; I enjoyed plowing, planting, harvesting—anything involving machine operation. I have never fully outgrown that joy; just give me a well-tuned chain saw and a tree to cut up.

At some point in my high school years, a collective shudder ran through many sectors of the Mennonite Church. Rumor said that one of the district conferences was accepting into membership persons who were divorced and remarried even though the first spouse was still living. How could this be, that persons guilty of continuous adultery were given a place in the church? Forty years later that issue and the church's eventual shift concerning it would color my thinking about another major conflict involving biblical authority.

My senior year brought me to a fork in the road. (Yogi Berra said I should take it, but he did not say which fork.) College: Yes or no? If yes, where? What field of study would I pursue? Would I be a misfit? Hesston College would be even more worldly than Iowa Mennonite School; Eastern Mennonite College (now University) not so, but none of my classmates was going there; Goshen College I never considered since all the men there wore neckties; and I certainly would not attend a public institution, where people would deride and challenge my faith.

Pop had once mentioned having considered college study; but knowing of people who had lost their faith while in higher education, he had chosen to avoid that risk. Even at a Mennonite college the danger lurked. Finally I opted for Hesston, not sure that I would continue beyond their two-year program.

College: Bend, Break, or Broaden?

Entrance exams at Hesston indicated that my strongest field was verbal and my weakest, mathematics. Beyond that, career counseling was an undeveloped science at Hesston. I chose the Bachelor of Religious Education program, assuming that even if I returned to the farm, I would be active in the church. Bible classes were my meat and potatoes while music class and choir with Lowell Byler were the dessert, along with arc welding in metalworking class.

In campus life the conservative-liberal divide often threatened. For example, when Hesston initiated intercollegiate sports, I was sure that this was a major step into the "world." It was as obvious as the shorts the basketball players wore.

One musical experience, performing Schubert's *Mass in G,* did pry open a crack in my hermetic worldview. The majestic texts of the Mass— *Gloria* and *Sanctus* and *Miserere Nobis*—were they evil simply because they were in Latin? Since those texts and the exquisite music to which they were attached came from Catholics, how could Catholics be all bad?

On a class trip to Kansas City I used a dial telephone for the first time. Rural Iowa in that era still had hand-crank phones on farmer-owned party lines. Not once during my college years did I attempt to call home, nor did my family ever call me.

After graduating from Hesston, I entered EMC as a junior. Here the campus milieu was more sheltering. For a young man afraid of the big, bad world, this felt good. Clothing styles still supported a separation from that world—although enough students smirked at regulation attire to present another threatening question: If Mennonites eventually succumbed to worldly pressures, where would I fit in? Later I would hear sociologist Grant Stoltzfus talk of the sect cycle, in which a group strongly tied to certain issues separates from the larger society, establishes a unique identity, lives in tension with society, gradually loses

Singing with Clarion Quartet, Eastern Mennonite College, 1959

its fervor about the issues that spawned it, and is finally re-assimilated. We do not talk about that cycle now that Grant is gone. Should we?

On the 1957 junior class trip to Washington, DC, a group of us saw and tasted for the first time that new Italian dish which was nudging its way onto the American menu—pizza.

Church history class led to a question which has nagged me ever since. I. B. Horst told us, "Catholics made the Eucharist the central element of the worship gathering, while Protestants gave the sermon that central place. I am not sure that either of those is appropriate." Question: If we did not count on the sermon to fill the major block of time in our gathering, what would we do? We have become well aware that one-way, lecture-style communication is ineffective for molding values; but we continue to lean on the sermon.

Another question, from Clarence Fretz's Christian Education classes, came with the answer attached: "When is a school not a school? When it's a *Sunday* school." He insisted that we take seriously the church's educational program in terms of setting goals and taking steps to reach them.

Ethics class with the renowned C. K. Lehman brought up a startling issue. Having heard from childhood that verse in Revelation (2:18), "... and all liars, shall have their part in the lake which burneth with fire and brimstone ... "(KJV), we snapped awake when C. K. said, "Some people suggest that in certain circumstances a person might have no moral right to know the truth." You will notice that he phrased this point very obliquely. And he gave it only brief mention, despite its enormous implications. Some issues were apparently too hot to explore in a college that hewed to a line my parents once used in a conversation with their floundering son: "You shouldn't ask that kind of question." Forty some years later an EMU president would confront this attitude, declaring publicly: "If there is an issue that the churches are discussing—*or need to be discussing*—we will talk about it on this campus."

Geology class, with D. Ralph Hostetter, brought to a boil my long-simmering conflict regarding evolution. My home and my church said that all this talk of dinosaurs and millions of years since creation was only the effort of godless scientists to explain away God. Archbishop Ussher, after all, had precisely outlined biblical chronology, indicating that God had created the world about 4000 years before Christ. In geology we learned of the evidence for a much older earth. It seemed that the evidence for science was steadily accumulating. What would we do if all doubt about its truth were eventually swept away? Some said, "In that case, we must reject science and hold to the truth that God has revealed." This brought to mind the child who said, "Faith is believing what you know to be untrue,"[1] as well as the Queen in Lewis Carroll's *Through the Looking-Glass* who claims, "Sometimes I've believed as many as six impossible things before breakfast."

An EMC classmate maintained that God had created the rock strata complete with fossils "to confuse those godless scientists." My faith was wavering, but whatever was left of it viewed God as more eager to promote faith than confusion.

As in the case of C. K. Lehman, we suspected that D. Ralph did not dare to say all that he believed about the topic in question. Ironically, at the time we were tiptoeing around major issues in geology, we were using in Bible classes the *Westminster Dictionary of the Bible*, considered a paragon of conservative scholarship. That dictionary states, "[Ussher's] work…was useful…but it is obsolete." I failed to read my dictionary. Had a Bible professor been so bold as to quote that critique, my struggle to accept a different chronology might have been easier. Even today churches that still see geological age and evolution as red-flag issues might benefit from hearing that Ussher's chronology suffers from serious flaws. Some churches, alas, would probably reject that notion. A few years ago an acquaintance told me that his son was happy at a Christian college in the Midwest "because there, questions about evolution and whether God is a woman don't come up."

To Teach or Not to Teach?

Graduation approached, and I had all but decided to return to the home farm in Iowa when Clarence Fretz invited me to join him at a new Mennonite school at Hagerstown, Maryland. I would teach junior-high singing, English, and wood shop. Teacher training I did not have. I stepped out on faith.

Overnight I was transformed. All my life I had been a Mennonite conservative, but in this context I was a liberal. My car was not black. My "plain coat," I learned, was only a plain collar: a true plain coat had a frock tail and no exterior pockets. Possessing a radio was cause for excommunication. One young woman's candidacy for baptism came under scrutiny because she had gone barefoot while picking berries. A new question stared me in the face: How much conservatism was too much?

The Hagerstown community was and is gracious to me. Friendships have endured in spite of the gulf between their faith practice and mine. Several years ago when I attended a funeral there, my former students made me feel like a celebrity as they stood in line to greet me.

Out of the Box

In my second year at Hagerstown, the military draft board in Iowa beckoned. Remembering an article entitled "Missionaries in Work Clothes," which had sparked the thought that I might find my niche on the foreign mission field, I opted for alternative service in Honduras. Mennonite missionaries there had asked for help in responding to the malnutrition they saw. We Voluntary Service men demonstrated with some success that with herbicides and insecticides people could grow their own vegetables and fruit. Sometimes we built an improved cook stove in a Honduran kitchen, massaging with our bare hands a mix of mud and horse manure and forming it into a firebox to which a stovepipe could be connected.

To the boys who hung out in our thatch-roofed house, we were rich. We each had two pairs of shoes and a wristwatch. We had a radio, a gasoline lantern, and even a kerosene-burning refrigerator. Young men who learned that we received ten dollars a month plus housing, food, and travel expenses said they would be glad for a job like ours.

All around us were questions waiting to be asked, but we lacked training in seeing the forest beyond the trees. Who owned the land outside of the village, and why was none of it available to most villagers? Why was most of that land unproductive—rain forest, or at best, pasture? Why did the locals complain that the North Americans who ran the banana company were getting fat off the villagers' sweat? After all, a job in the fruit company paid four dollars a day while other unskilled work, if any was available, paid one or two dollars. Did we consider that any North American in the company probably earned at least twenty times what the Honduran did?

Learning the Spanish language brought up more questions. Reading II Timothy 3:16 in Spanish hit me between the eyes: "*Toda escritura está inspirada por Dios ... "*—all *writing* is inspired by God? My Bible classes in both high school and college had touted "plenary verbal inspiration" as applying uniquely to the Bible. I recalled a question my brother had raised: "When Confucius writes, 'Since the Divine Being loved us, we should also love each other,' is this writing not inspired, but when John writes nearly the same words, they are inspired?" This question related to the matter of the biblical canon: if the Holy Spirit was capable of inspiring men to write in the pre-Christian era and in the first century after Christ, why did all such inspiration abruptly cease?

Adding to my turmoil over "*toda escritura,*" a missionary of another denomination posed a new question: "How much inspiration did Paul need to write to Timothy to bring along the coat and the books and the parchments that he had left in Troy?" Lectures on plenary verbal inspiration had never explored that idea.

Travel in Central America raised more issues of economics. At bus or train stations boys would besiege us, eager to carry our luggage for a small tip. We were no weaklings—we could jolly well carry our own duffel bags. Then we heard that a Honduran had observed, "You North Americans have so much, and most of the time you won't even let us earn any of it." (Years later, that comment would color my opinions about undocumented immigrants who seek jobs in this country.) When we bought souvenirs in the market, we did not hesitate to haggle for the lowest possible price. On a visit to Guatemala, however, bargaining took on a new aspect when a vendor, despairing over the cutthroat prices we were offering, said to a bystander, *"¿Qué hago? Tengo necesidad."* (What can I do? I need money.)

A malfunctioning machine led to the crowning moment of my two years in Honduras. Two of us Voluntary Service workers were temporarily at the mission station in the town of Gualaco. The mission Jeep, the only vehicle in town, suffered from a chronically discharged battery—a major problem since the village had no electric power to operate a battery charger. Neither was there any mechanic nor any road out to another town. We three amateurs—the missionary and two VS men—set our wits to do battle with the generating system. Many hours later we had reached our wits' end, and two of our little group retired for the night. Reluctant to admit defeat, I lingered. The belt that drove the generator felt slightly loose. Could the problem be as simple as a slipping belt? When I tightened it and restarted the engine, the ammeter needle jumped to full charge. I jumped, too, with elation.

At the end of my term in Honduras I returned to the States, twenty-six years old and still unable to identify any combination of interest and ability that seemed strong enough for a career. I sought again the shelter of EMC, where Dean Ira Miller cobbled together for me a major in foreign languages, combining my New Testament Greek with the maximum of Spanish credits I could earn that year. Music electives filled out my load.

Puzzles and Progress

That fifth year in college brought some resolution to the issues that dogged my steps. James Mullenex, then a young math instructor, turned on a light with his chapel address based on *Flatland*, a small book by Edwin Abbott.[2] Abbott constructs a marvelous analogy of a people who live in a world of two dimensions: Flatland. When a being from a three-dimensional world visits Flatland, the citizens there have no experiential knowledge on which to build a concept of a third dimension. They conclude that up, whatever that might be, is impossible, and they attack the one who tries to help them understand.

The analogy clicked for me: Why should I assume that whatever lies beyond my sensory experience does not and cannot exist? Limited to my three-dimensional world, how can I begin to comprehend a Being of five or ten or infinite dimensions? J. B. Phillips' classic book, *Your God Is Too Small: A Guide for Believers and Skeptics Alike* (1952), took on new meaning. My experience in Central America, where people dressed and thought and lived differently from North Americans, had led to a growing awareness of the enormity of the human family, and *Flatland* prompted an expanded concept of the vastness of the universe and the grandeur of the Creator. All of this reinforced the profound simplicity of a question posed by Laban Peachey: "How much does God care about whether the points on a man's coat collar turn up or down?"

A well-worn adage summarizes my college experience: "The guy who thinks he knows all the answers simply doesn't know all the questions." I came to believe that faith does not require seeing everything in either/or terms; to have faith is to believe in the good in spite of ambiguous areas and incomplete knowledge.

In 1964 I graduated for the second time from EMC, and Belleville Mennonite School in Pennsylvania recruited me to teach Spanish, English, and music. At Belleville I also had a choir to direct; and when my students sang "Joyful, Joyful We Adore Thee," complete with that exquisite syncopation that Beethoven wrote into the "Ode to Joy" of his *Ninth Symphony*, I was on cloud nine.

Clouds, unfortunately, lack the substance required for long term support. Some aspects of teaching I liked, but overall it bogged me down and I sank into depression. My search for a job I could truly enjoy seemed as hopeless as my search for a life companion. I was looking for the perfect girl; but each time I found one, she was looking for the perfect guy. In those dark days I sometimes drew a smidgen of hope from a compliment offered me at EMC by a young English instructor, Jay Landis, who had praised my work as news editor of the *Weather Vane*. Years later I would post this motto at my desk: "Correction accomplishes much. Encouragement accomplishes more."

Housemate David Alleman posed a starkly significant question during our Belleville days: "Does God have feathers?" Even persons immune to poetry can see that Psalm 91:4 (KJV), "He shall cover thee with his feathers," presents poetic, not literal, truth. Dave's question should give pause to Christians who boast, "We take the Bible literally."

My depression deepened. With fear and trembling I sought out a psychotherapist. He asked, "Ray, are you indecisive?" and I said, "Well, yes and no." Fearing I might not survive a third year of teaching, I moved to nearby State College, where I enrolled at Pennsylvania State University to explore my interests in a science career. Would I be able to handle the math?

Two terms at Penn State left me again at sea about a plan for my life—God's plan or any other—so I took a temporary job as a Spanish teacher in a Philadelphia suburb. Then I found a way to explore a science career without more study: I landed a position as a lab analyst in a chemical plant. This job was fun: mixing chemicals, heating test tubes, weighing things down to a ten-thousandth of a gram– –. Meanwhile the good people at the nearby Frazer Mennonite Church reached out to this fearful and lonely bachelor. A friend there introduced me to one Violet Bixler, and—God be praised—our relationship developed into romance and marriage. Question: Given this history, why do my wife and daughters pour cold water on my slightest attempt at matchmaking?

In the new *Mennonite Hymnal* of 1969 I spied a name that took me back to a time when my father had commented on the threat of Modernism in the church. He had mentioned Harry Emerson Fosdick as a leader of Modernism. There in the *Hymnal* was that name—as the author of "God of Grace and God of Glory," widely considered one of the great hymns of the twentieth century. Apparently even Modernists are not all bad.

Two years into our marriage, Vi decided to take a year at Messiah College to complete her degree in nursing. Our relocation brought me the option of exploring my long-standing interest in mechanical work, and I found a job at a Volkswagen shop in Harrisburg. Fixing cars was fun, but I was slow at it; so the following summer I entered a master's program in Spanish at Temple University, hoping to move into college teaching. Literary history left me asking, "Does it really matter that the work of author X shows characteristics of both the Y period and the Z period?" That renowned Spanish novel, *Don Quijote de la Mancha,*

seemed to me a conglomerate of unrelated tales, lacking as badly a sense
of direction as the wandering knight himself. More positively, I learned
that the battle between revealed truth and knowledge gained by the
scientific method had become a hot issue in the Enlightenment and was
not unique to Mennonite churches. The History of the Spanish Empire
course examined imperial greed, violent conquest, church bigotry, a
Euro-centric worldview, and continuing injustice, all relating to things
we had observed in Central America.

Cheney State College, near Philadelphia, called when I had nearly
finished my studies at Temple; Cheney needed an immediate replacement
for a professor who had disappeared. (Later we learned that he was in
treatment for alcohol addiction—a fact that suggests more questions: Why
does the human family fail to label alcohol a dangerous drug, and why
do intelligent people choose to drink, in view of the well-documented
statistic that ten per cent of alcohol drinkers become addicted?)

Teaching at Cheney State brought me a new empathy for minority groups: I was in the white minority. Ninety per cent of the students
were African Americans, heirs of the emotional and cultural baggage
of slavery. Many were earning their own way, working a full-time job
while carrying a full-time academic load. That overload fostered ab-
senteeism and a notable neglect of study outside of class. We teachers
feel successful when our students succeed; at Cheney the success level
lingered at low ebb.

Two events impacted our lives during my five years at Cheney: The
first was the birth of a daughter, and the second was the birth of another
daughter. As a bitter young bachelor, I had said, "Babies are a smelly
mess; when they can walk, they're a nuisance; and when they grow up,
they're a disappointment. Who needs that kind of punishment?" The
memory of that attitude often led me to thankful amazement for the joy
I found in our daughters. Today they are both upright, talented women,
each contributing significantly to her community.

Believing that my history of faith struggles might be helpful to other
young Christians, when we learned that Houghton College needed a
Spanish teacher, I applied. We went to Houghton with some trepidation, knowing we would keenly miss the Frazer Mennonite Church and
aware that Vi would greatly miss the leading-edge nursing environment of the hospital of the University of Pennsylvania. Houghton was in

rural western New York State, thirty miles from the nearest McDonald's and even farther from a Mennonite church. The college was owned by the Wesleyan Church, a conservative branch of Methodists. This was the Cold War era, and one Houghton colleague remarked that the U.S. military filled a God-given role: to hold off the forces of Communism long enough for the Gospel to reach people who would otherwise fall under demonic control.

Most Houghton students were both apt and eager. However, many came from churches that equated God's kingdom with the United States, and most students had little awareness of the world beyond our borders. I found a sense of mission in bringing to their attention real human beings with a real language other than English, people who suffer poverty and hunger and injustice in which our "Christian" nation has often played a part.

Early in our Houghton years, I gave a chapel talk on *Flatland*, developed from the address by Jim Mullenex that had so blessed me at EMC. Chapel planners asked me to repeat that talk several times during our Houghton sojourn.

We attended the only church in town, the Wesleyan Church, but we continued to subscribe to the *Gospel Herald* as a link to Mennonites. A *Herald* article raised a question which thereafter went into my lesson plans every October 12: "Who really discovered America?" The follow-up asks, "As we blithely say 'Columbus discovered America,' what does that imply about the people who were here when he arrived?"

A Houghton student participating in a campus forum opened my eyes to one rationale for Christians to kill their country's enemies. Perhaps he was a Presbyterian predeterminist. "Since God controls everything," he declared, "we cannot kill anyone unless God wills it; and furthermore, the moral onus of killing an enemy rests not on the soldier, but on the ruler who commands the soldier to kill." Question: Whatever happened to individual moral responsibility?

Seeking authorities who buttress our pet ideas can create odd bedfellows. I do not often quote the Pope; but in preparation for a Sunday school class at Houghton, I found a papal encyclical that supported one of my points. Queries the Pope: "If someone has more bread than he or she can eat, and if another person is starving, does the former have a moral right to keep the bread, and does the latter have a moral right to take some if the owner refuses to give or sell any?" Victor Hugo's novel *Les Miserables* comes to mind: Should a person who takes a loaf of bread to feed hungry children be branded a criminal for life?

A Bible professor at Houghton enriched my understanding of hermeneutics. "I believe in progressive or cumulative revelation, not in a flat Bible," he said. "Also, we always need to ask about a given Scripture, 'Does God mean this for all times and all places, or does it apply to a particular circumstance?'" An example might be the repeated New Testament admonition, "Greet one another with a holy kiss." In a chapel service a woman speaking on women's roles in the church told us, "I have a daughter who lived abroad for a time. One day a letter came informing me that she would soon return to the States and would live near me. I did not rush out to the street to see whether the one who brought the good news was a man or a woman."

Each semester Houghton had a "Current Issues Day." One of these explored the theme of the church and homosexuality. Several guests spoke on the power of Christ to change lives, even gender attractions; other speakers declared that our erotic attractions are God-given and unchangeable. This discussion would inform my thinking amid the furor of Mennonite debate on these issues a few years later.

When I reached the age of fifty, I still wondered what I wanted to be when I grew up, so I talked with a psychology colleague, who gave me a personality test. When we reviewed my scores, he minced no words: "Ray, anyone with an introversion score like yours has no business trying to teach." My spouse insists that I am no introvert, but knowing that my test score was significantly higher than that of the average scientist helps me understand why teaching has always been toilsome for me.

Three years later the Houghton College Student Senate awarded me that year's citation for excellence in teaching.

Return to Alma Mater

Since Houghton was Ronald Reagan territory where we often felt out of step, after fourteen years there we were happy to hear of a vacancy in Spanish at EMC. I came for an interview in 1991 during the first Gulf War. Ironically, I knew that this was not my mother's EMC when I spied in the Campus Center a poster urging, "Support our troops!"

Soon after joining the EMC faculty, I found that I needed to upgrade my courses: EMC students could handle in the second-year Spanish course much of the material we reserved for the third-year course at Houghton. The difference, in my opinion, was this: Houghton required two years of foreign language study of every student. Because EMC did not require a foreign language in certain majors, students gifted in areas other than language tended to bypass it. With a higher average level of interest and aptitude in a Spanish class, students could progress more rapidly. In fact, I have mixed feelings about foreign language requirements: We can justifiably argue that no monolingual person is truly educated; however, for some learners, acquiring even minimal skills in a second language is a daunting task.

From Despair to History and Hope

In the fall of 1991 a California researcher made headlines by claiming to identify physical differences between the brains of gay men and those of straight men. For me this was, as Yogi Berra said, *déjà vu* all over again: In the case of evolution it had seemed that scientific evidence was steadily accumulating, and now it seemed that evidence for a biological cause of same-gender attraction was likewise growing. A year or two later someone at EMC organized a panel discussion on the topic. Participants included seminary professor Edward Stoltzfus and campus pastor Bruce Martin, as well as a young man whose name I promptly forgot. His words, however, I cannot forget. I often choke up when I quote him: "My church told me I was an abomination. I did not want to be an abomination, and I prayed fervently that God would deliver me from this. No deliverance came."

How should the church respond to that despairing young man? His plight reminded me of a book by Leslie Weatherhead[3] that examines faith healing in the early church. Weatherhead says that at the outset, the onus of faith for healing rested on the healer. However, within a few centuries that onus shifted to the patient: If no healing came, the patient was blamed for lack of faith. That seemed to be the fate of persons like the young man of the panel. The church was telling them that they had to change, and it preached the power of Christ to change lives; but if no change occurred in spite of repentance, prayer, and every possible resource, the church blamed the one seeking deliverance. "We need to produce on our promise," I thought; "either effect the change the seekers want or accept them as they are."

Not long after that event, the topic became more than academic for Vi and me. Our older daughter told us that she was lesbian. We went through the usual process of mourning and self-searching, in which I poured out my soul in a letter: "Choose carefully, daughter, choose carefully." Later I saw in a new light the matter of "choosing" when a gay acquaintance asked me, "When did you choose to be heterosexual?" I have yet to meet any person, gay or straight, who says that his or her romantic attractions have resulted from choice. Conversely, many gays and lesbians say that if they had a choice, they would by no means opt for a life of harassment and discrimination.

We say we can learn from history. Let us review briefly the church's long history of struggle with change. It started in Jerusalem, where Peter was called on the carpet for eating with Cornelius, an unclean Gentile, "dirty" because he was not circumcised. Later Paul narrowly escaped being lynched for teaching that circumcision was worthless. Early church leaders—as human as we are—laid aside the Scriptural requirements for the bloody sacrifice of animals. The medieval church battled Galileo to hold the line on a geocentric understanding of the universe. Still later many Christians quoted the Bible in arguing that slavery was part of God's plan for humanity. In our day most Mennonites were totally sure that remarriage while one's original spouse was living constituted ongoing adultery.

How did the church manage to shift its position on each of these issues? We need to recognize that Christians have a long history of choosing and using the Scriptures to fit new understandings of God's ways. Call it "new wine in new wineskins" or "cumulative revelation." Sometimes we have set aside a Biblical mandate, as when Peter persuaded the church leaders to lay aside the law that forbade eating with so-called "dirty Gentiles." The Jerusalem Council interpreted the commandment to circumcise boy babies as not applying to Gentile believers, in effect setting aside that Scripture. Surprisingly the church abandoned biblical requirements for animal sacrifices without recorded controversy. At some point Christians stopped stoning to death persons caught in adultery, thus abrogating another scriptural mandate. Reluctantly the medieval church surrendered its firm belief that the Bible described a geocentric universe. Today we disregard Colossians 3:22, which reads, "Slaves, obey your earthly masters in everything …"; and Mennonites in our lifetime have bypassed Jesus' words about remarriage being adulterous.

What lessons can we learn from this history? The answer depends in large part on how we view history. Some people see it in terms of decline and degradation. Others see an ascending pattern of morality. Last summer in France we toured a Roman amphitheater. Hearing of the cruel and bloody events that took place there, I thought, "Fortunately, we've gotten beyond those good old days."

A pertinent question, then, might be this: As the church has changed its standards, have we gained or lost moral ground? When Jewish believers began to eat with Gentiles, did we gain or lose in spiritual quality? When Christians ceased excising foreskins and accepted Paul's doctrine of salvation as a free gift, did we step up or down? When we stopped stoning adulterers, did we lengthen or shorten the reach of God's forgiveness? When the church accepted Galileo's belief in a heliocentric universe, did we augment or diminish our understanding of the Creator? When we recognized that even people who knew no Latin were fully human, did we become more or less like Christ? When the church rejected the Bible's implicit approval of slavery, did we gain or lose moral ground? When we decided that without severing current marriages or splitting entire families, we could offer church fellowship to persons divorced and remarried, did we amplify or reduce our role in God's saving work?

If hindsight indicates that in every one of these cases the church gained moral ground by changing its position, we might well ask why we should absolutely hold the line on matters of same-gender attraction. Rather than stoning children who curse their parents, we now offer them forgiveness and a call to a renewing of their mind. Rather than decrying a departure from biblical standards on divorce and remarriage, we offer blended families support for loving and faithful relationships. Perhaps, rather than bemoaning a moral meltdown, we should ask how we can channel God's grace to *all* people. Perhaps we can help those who seek a change of their romantic attractions to achieve that, while accepting fully those who find such a change impossible. Perhaps we can even join

Peter and Paul in expanding our vision of whom God has made clean, instead of casting out those who have been called dirty.

Conclusion

You have heard my litany of questions, and probably you have deduced that the "quest" of my title alludes to a quest for faith. My childhood faith was tenuous. In my student days my faith was tenuous. My faith is still tenuous, but at least it is more tenable now than it was when I tried to believe things I knew were not true. I am coming to believe with Francis Collins[4] that God has been creating for billions of years and continues to create. This ongoing work suggests that possibly God has not finished with me, either. I wish the same for all of you and for all believers, the church.

January 14, 2008
Revised November 2008

Notes

1 Leslie D. Weatherhead, *Psychology, Religion, and Healing* (New York, NY: Abingdon Press, 1952), 423. Weatherhead attributes this sentence to a schoolboy quoted by William Ralph Inge, Dean of St. Paul's London.

2 Edwin A. Abbott, *Flatland: a Romance of Many Dimensions* (Oxford, England: Oxford University Press, 1963), reissued Oxford University Press, USA, 2008 and www.bnpublishing.net, 2009.

3 Leslie D. Weatherhead, *Psychology, Religion, and Healing* (New York, NY: Abingdon Press, 1952).

4   Francis Collins, *The Language of God: A Scientist Presents Evidence for Belief* (New York, NY: Free Press, 2006).

KENTON K. BRUBAKER

A Few Seasons of My Professional Life

For some reason I thought of the ancient Hebrew philosopher who wrote Ecclesiastes as I contemplated summarizing my life story. He "saw all the deeds that are done under the sun; and see, all is vanity and a chasing after wind" (1:14). Now by nature I am not quite that pessimistic, but I must admit that some projects in my life did not quite work out. There has been considerable "chasing after wind" in my story.

In reminiscing about the seasons of my professional life, I have selected four projects that were very important to me both as an educator and as a faithful consumer of nature: international agriculture, Earthkeepers, experimental vegetable gardens, and the Eden Arboretum.

A former student told me recently that he had observed I was passionate about the subjects I taught and that this passion had been important to him. And I think he was right. I believed deeply in the various projects I undertook and am profoundly grateful for an institution like EMU (Eastern Mennonite University), which allowed me to pursue them. I am also heavily indebted to colleagues like Robert Yoder, Daniel Sutter, Clair Mellinger, Roman Miller, and many others, with whom I worked for over thirty years.

International Agriculture

The oldest of seven children, I grew up with horticulture on a mini-farm north of East Petersburg, Pennsylvania. Both my mother, Helen, and my grandmother, Elizabeth Kaylor, avid flower growers, were competent in the knowledge of the Latin names of many garden flowers. As a child I followed my father, Daniel, through our two acres of gladioli, carrying huge bundles of flowers as he cut them for market. In the winter we grew snapdragons, carnations, and chrysanthemums in our 200-foot long greenhouses. Indeed, I learned to drive negotiating the narrow main street of Manheim and climbing the Mt. Gretna hill on our early Saturday morning trips to the farmers' markets in Lebanon.

One of my organic pest control tasks as a young child was eliminating bumblebees in the greenhouses. Since pollination would cause the flowers to drop prematurely, ruining their commercial value, my next younger brother, James, and I would smash the bees between two sticks as they were gathering nectar and pollen in the snapdragons. We would notch our sticks after each heroic kill, copying the World War II fighter pilots' custom of marking their planes with insignia for each enemy plane they shot down. We were obviously quite impressed with wartime behavior.

Even though radios were not considered appropriate for Mennonite homes in Lancaster County in the mid-forties, we had one; and we listened faithfully every evening as Gabriel Heater described the changing battlefront in Europe. The Battle of the Bulge was especially scary news. Actually, we learned our geography of Europe, North Africa, and the Pacific by studying the daily war diagrams in the *Lancaster Intelligencer Journal*. I was thirteen when the atom bombs were dropped on Hiroshima and then Nagasaki.

It was in high school at LMS (Lancaster Mennonite School) that I came across a book by Ira Moomaw on agricultural missions, and it occurred to me that this could be my career. I could become an agricultural missionary and do my part to alleviate world hunger, probably in Africa! To accomplish this I would of course need to go to college and study scientific agriculture. Three of my best friends at LMS decided to go into medicine. However, I felt that it was more important to work at disease prevention and one way to do this was to improve nutrition, especially among the citizens of the food-deficit countries.

Off to College

Only a few young persons from our East Petersburg congregation had gone to college. Roy Kreider, Paul Swarr, and John Shenk went to EMC

(Eastern Mennonite College, now EMU). My cousins Evelyn and Miriam Sensenig went to that more "liberal" college in Indiana, Goshen, but I chose EMC, enrolling in the fall of 1950. My major was biology, as close as I could get to agriculture—although Wilmer Landis did teach a few courses in agriculture, which I took.

My younger brother, James, who also followed me to EMC, chose pre-med and went on to medical college. It was interesting to observe the effects of our going to college on the social status of our family at church. We had always been one of the poorest families in the congregation. I remember the embarrassment of driving into the churchyard every Sunday morning in our 1929 Model A Ford. Only our elderly deacon had an older model car. Earlier my father had held no positions in the church. However, after his boys went to college, he was appointed Sunday school superintendent; and he blossomed in the role. Although he had completed only three years of high school, he was an avid reader. When we brought library books home from school, he would stay up all night reading them.

Also, my father was a trained Davey Company tree surgeon. I just recently read the letters he wrote while he was in training and in his first year of work for the company in the Hudson River estates around Tarrytown, New York. Unfortunately, the stock market crash of 1929 terminated his career with Davey. He told how some of their wealthy clients committed suicide as a result of the financial disaster and thus the work on their grounds was canceled.

In my junior year at EMC, my friend Stanwyn Shetler suggested that we go to Ithaca, New York, to investigate enrolling at Cornell University. There I knew that I could take more courses in agriculture. We persuaded Perry Brunk, a fellow Mennonite and local businessman, to fly us to Ithaca in his Piper Super Cub. Our flight took place in the winter, and Perry, we discovered, was not used to central New York weather. Just as we approached Ithaca, the plane's carburetor froze and we lost power.

Perry said, "Look for a level spot. We'll have to put her down."

Suddenly I spied the local airport, and we were just able to reach the landing strip. Perry thus learned that he had to keep the carburetor heater on for the trip back, and we followed the Susquehanna River rather than going directly over the mountains as we had done on the way north.

The next fall Stan and I did enroll at Cornell, where I decided to major in agronomy and took a variety of courses in soil science, plant physiology, horticulture, and natural history. Actually, my biggest revelation was the library. I had never been introduced to research and scientific journals at EMC and was fascinated by the articles I found in the Cornell University Library. Entering a contest to write an undergraduate research paper, I read many articles, making extensive notes, and submitted an essay on plant hormones. I think I may have been the first student ever to enter this contest, and the judges found it difficult to believe I did the research; they gave me the second prize. I think it might have been ten dollars.

I came back to EMC the next summer and took the necessary courses to graduate with my class of 1954, along with classmates Elmer Miller and John Lapp, two of the other authors in this volume. I could have continued at Cornell, but my program there required a farm practice internship—a summer on a dairy farm—which I was not willing to do. I felt that having grown up helping with a flower business and milking goats had provided an adequate farm background for me.

I remember one major horticultural mistake at this time in my budding career. I had come home from Cornell at Christmas after a course in plant nutrition and observed that my dad's potted geraniums showed symptoms of nitrogen deficiency. He allowed me to get some sodium nitrate fertilizer and treat them, and I managed to kill all two hundred geraniums! Ever since then I have used fertilizer very cautiously.

Graduate School at Ohio State

I decided to go to graduate school and pursue horticulture instead of agronomy. When I applied to Pennsylvania State and Ohio State, Penn State offered me an assistantship in grape culture and Ohio State, a full Helena Chamberlain fellowship. Of course I picked Ohio State. The fellowship paid $125 a month, which proved adequate for living expenses in those days of $30 a month rent.

I loved graduate school, and I was able to take a great variety of courses outside my department, especially in plant physiology and biochemistry during my five years in Columbus. My advisor, Dr. Alban, wondered why I wanted to take all these courses; but it turned out that they were good preparation for my future teaching career, which spread me over almost the full range of biology and biochemistry.

These were the days of Woody Hayes football at Ohio State University, and Columbus pretty well shut down on football weekends. I actually lived in the stadium that first fall during football season and could watch the games from the Tower Club window. I was also active in the Intervarsity Christian Fellowship, leading singing and serving as president one year. I remember an interview with an Intervarsity staff person who was obviously concerned about my Mennonite theology. She wanted to be assured that I would not promote pacifism in my role as president.

In addition to my course work at OSU, my research focused on chemical weed control for my master's degree (1957) and carbohydrate translocation in tomatoes for my doctorate (1959). I bought a Sears Roebuck portable typewriter and typed my own dissertations with three carbon copies.

After my one year in Columbus, Emma Shetler and I were married. For our honeymoon in 1955 we went to Puerto Rico and visited the Ulrich Foundation agricultural project at Aibonito, thinking it might be a good assignment after my graduation. We were informed, however, that most of the decisions about how to run the project were decided back in Illinois rather than on site. Thus we decided against this opportunity.

Back in Columbus, Emma worked part time as a nurse in several hospitals; and we lived cheaply, riding our bicycles for several years before buying an old 1941 Chevy. Two of our four children were born in Columbus, Karl and Kaye. Karl is now the business manager at Hesston College, and Kaye is an engineering professor at the University of Maryland.

As I was completing my graduate work, I contacted several Mennonite mission boards for possible assignments, but no agriculture assignments seemed to be open at that time. In hindsight, I was a bit ahead of the era when agricultural development became part of Mennonite missions and service. Meanwhile, Dean Ira Miller came to Columbus and asked if I would consider teaching at EMC. I agreed to start there in September 1959.

During our transition to EMC, we lived for a time in East Petersburg, where our second daughter, Jane, was born. She went into horticulture, following her father's footsteps, and is now in charge of plantings on the campus of the University of Oregon in Eugene. Our youngest daughter, Annette, was born in Harrisonburg and is now teaching third grade in Arlington, Massachusetts.

I Begin Teaching at Eastern Mennonite College

My thinking was that if I could not work in agriculture abroad, perhaps I could be involved in training students for such a career. Thus in addition to teaching biology and biochemistry, I was able to introduce courses in soil science, horticulture, pest management, and crop ecology. These courses soon became the basis for a new major in international agriculture, a major that remained in existence for over thirty years, I believe. When my successor left for work with USAID, several members of the department kept some of the courses going. Currently the major has been downgraded to a focus on an ecology major under the rubric of sustainable agriculture, I believe.

Three Years With MCC in the Congo

After my first three years at EMC I asked for a chance to get some practical international experience in MCC/TAP (Mennonite Central Committee's Teacher Abroad Program) in the newly independent Republic of the Congo. I still marvel at Emma's and my decision to take our four young children on this particular project. It was a major undertaking to set up a household in the rain forest of the Ubangi Province in northwestern Congo. We were located in the town of Gemena within the area served by the Swedish Evangelical Free Church and Missionary Covenant missions.

Within days of our arrival, I came down with something we assumed was a stomach virus. Since the presenting symptom was a severe headache, we were surprised at the final diagnosis of appendicitis. Belgian physicians performed the surgery at the local Lovanium University hospital. When the surgeon heard I was in post-op pain, he ordered a sedative, commenting that Americans like lots of pain medication. To add to this rough initiation to life in the Congo, while I was still in the hospital, Emma became ill with a virus-like infection. Our new neighbors, fellow teachers, came to the rescue, however, assuming the care of our children for several days while we were both recovering.

I was assigned to teach horticulture and science at IPOC, *l'Institut Polytechnique Congolais,* one of a series of agricultural colleges being established under a USAID contract administered by the Agricultural Technical Assistance Foundation (ATAF), a Methodist organization out of Los Angeles. I had studied German and Spanish for my graduate work; now I was to teach in French. With a variety of tutors and texts, I did my best. Along with teaching, I was able to do research on vegetable production in a tropical setting, a major challenge. I also received a good introduction to the indigenous agriculture of equatorial Africa.

On the IPOC farm students produced vegetables and eggs. They grew peppers, green beans, eggplants, a type of tropical spinach, and sometimes lettuce. The soil was very acid and leached of nutrients; but with the addition of great quantities of compost, fairly decent yields were achieved. However, green beans and root crops such as carrots suffered from nematodes. One visiting horticulturist recommended burying sugar cane with the seeds, the theory being that the nematodes would eat the sugar cane and burst. We tried the idea but could not decide if it was effective.

As a result of a staff of eight teachers and about 100 students, teaching loads were light. Yet what kept everybody extremely busy was maintaining the facilities, which included eight Ford tractors, seven Chevrolet trucks, and various other pieces of equipment needing constant repair. Much of the time we had to move parts from disabled vehicles to less problematic others in order to keep a few in operation. We constantly ran out of tire-patching material since the tractors would run over sharp points of machete-cut brush and get punctures. Also, the rough gravel roads took their toll on the trucks. Thus we always carried spare parts when we took a trip, knowing we would generally find no repair facilities along the way unless we happened to break down near a Catholic mission.

Unfortunately, after one year the mismanagement of funds by ATAF led to the cancellation of the USAID contract with our supporting organization. Therefore, MCC transferred me to the new Protestant university being set up in Stanleyville (now Kisangani), *l'Universite Libre du Congo.*

Fortunately, our family decided to travel to Stanleyville by riverboat rather than plane. That decision meant we were spared the 111 days of imprisonment and massacre experienced by some of the university staff. We were aware that rebel activity in the eastern Congo could be a threat to Stanleyville, but the university administrators there had assured us that the city was well protected by loyal and well-trained troops. However, just as we were arriving by riverboat, rebel forces captured the city. We learned later that the university dean, Mel Loewen, had been at the dock waiting for us when the city fell and the government troops fled.

We were still several miles away when the riverboat captain got word to turn around. Before he got far, the fleeing national soldiers paddled hastily from the shore in dugout canoes and confiscated the riverboat. The crowded vessel then headed to a port down river. From there our family was evacuated to Leopoldville (now Kinshasa) by a U.S. Air Force crew wearing civilian clothes and flying General Mobutu's private DC-3. Actually, we had met the crew on an earlier trip by General Mobutu to our school at Gemena. One of them, who said he was from York, Pennsylvania, told us his mother wore a prayer cap like Emma's.

As we were about to take off from the airport, some of the local soldiers who had not been paid for a month blocked the runway. They were trying to force the local governor, who was on our plane, to see that they got paid. One of our crew told us not to worry since they were heavily armed and could shoot our way out if necessary. Fortunately, such an action was not necessary.

Assignments as UNESCO Professor in Leopoldville

Upon relocation in Leopoldville, I worked as a UNESCO professor on loan to Lovanium University and the National Teachers Institute. I also was commissioned to write a text for advanced high school students on cell biology (*La Cellule*). (Many years later EMU had a Congolese student who remembered using my text.)

Much of my time was devoted to resettling other missionaries who were fleeing the interior as the rebels moved across the Congo. My most memorable evening was at the Njila airport when the survivors of the Stanleyville massacre arrived aboard the huge C-130s. The first plane to land carried the most seriously wounded. I still have the assignment sheet where I marked an "X" in front of the names of Dr. Paul Carlson and missionary Phyllis Rine—two victims of the massacre. It was nearly midnight when our PAX men assigned to the university, Jon Snyder and Gene Bergman, arrived, having survived.

So was the Congo assignment what I had hoped for, or was there a lot of "chasing after the wind"? Even today, forty years later, it is a struggle to keep institutions like the Protestant university in Kisangani going. Yet, although we had to wait almost a year to go and then after one year had a major change in assignment, the experience was worthwhile in many ways. Some memories are painful; others are enriching. This season included "a time to plant, and a time to pluck up, ... a time to kill, and a time to heal, ... a time to weep, and a time to laugh" (Eccl. 3:2–4).

Further Work in Tropical Agriculture

Because of my interest in tropical agriculture, I have had the opportunity to travel several times to Jamaica and Haiti, as well as go on consulting and study trips to Bangladesh, India, Nepal, Thailand, Philippines, and China. I also helped establish and run the Summer Institute in Tropical Agriculture, which met on our campus and at Goshen and Bethel for a number of years.

Even though recent interest at EMU has focused on peacemaking and conflict resolution, I am still of the opinion that much world conflict and poverty relates to food concerns. People must have food and productive land to produce food and fiber. Thus my concern about world food problems was the stimulus for the course I inaugurated, Food and Population, and also for my students' participation for many years in CROP walks, World Food Day and Bread for the World. I have always had a high regard for Ron Sider's *Rich Christians in an Age of Hunger*,[1] Dr. Lester Brown's annual "State of the World" reports, and the Worldwatch Institute, and faithfully used those materials in my courses, especially in Food and Population.

Earthkeepers

The Earthkeepers paper-recycling program began sometime in the sixties as a cooperative venture between staff and students in the biology and nursing departments. We bought an old VW van, had "Earthkeepers" painted on the side, and loaded it to the roof with the newspapers we picked up in the community. At first we stored the newsprint in an abandoned service station, then a chicken house, and finally a steel warehouse that we constructed in response to the increasing volume of paper. Eventually we acquired a baler and forklift and shipped out truckloads of waste paper to Richmond.

I remember one occasion when my son, Karl, who was then student president of Earthkeepers, and I tried to convince the city fathers to begin a municipal recycling program. Our argument was that newsprint was selling for over $50 a ton and was too valuable to be used as fuel for the city incinerator.

Earthkeepers received several state awards in recognition of our pioneering work in recycling during the time I was advisor to the program. Eventually the business department took over the operation of Earthkeepers, using it as a non-profit business practicum until the city began curbside recycling around 1990. Earthkeepers still continues as a student organization focusing on environmental concerns. Also, David Alliman and now Jonathan Lantz-Trissel have continued the campus recycling effort.

During this time, I wrote a column called "Energy Watch" for the *Festival Quarterly*. I was very pleased to learn at a meeting on the environment several years ago that one of my faithful readers was Amish environmentalist David Kline.

I also served on the original Mennonite Task Force on Environment for a number of years. I am happy to see that this organization has been resurrected with a former student of mine, Luke Gascho, Director of Goshen's Merry Lea Center, in charge.

The Experimental Vegetable Gardens

Just east of the Science Center lay a bit over a half acre of land that my students and I developed into a vegetable gardening project. The original plan was to give practical vegetable growing experience to international agriculture students. It later developed into a research program on organic gardening, a popular topic in the seventies. We eventually had fifteen 10x25 foot garden plots with five different randomized soil treatments: manure, compost, fertilizer, fertilizer+compost, and a no-additive control plot. We planted identical crops in each plot, mulched all plots uniformly, used no pesticides, irrigated with soaker hoses, and carefully weighed the produce, all of which required an amazing amount of work. Work/study student help made it possible. We produced large quantities of tomatoes, potatoes, green beans, peppers, squash, cantaloupes, and sweet corn, which we made available to faculty and staff.

Our results confirmed the value of compost, those plots generally giving the best yields. Especially in dry summers the very high organic content of the compost and manure plots sustained yield probably by conserving moisture. The fertilizer and control plots exhibited a much harder soil texture while the compost and manure plots developed a very fine, dark, friable soil. Just as in much of third-world agriculture, we were able to maintain yield without commercial fertilizer, but the quantity of compost and manure we used was very high.

I spent many hours hand digging or rototilling these gardens for more than ten years, probably doing some of my most satisfying research. When I began my gradual retirement in about 1992, the plots were also retired. Actually they are now buried six feet under the north end of the new soccer field. Final score: Soccer 1, Agriculture 0.

"I saw all the deeds that are done under the sun; and see, all is vanity and a chasing after the wind" (Eccl. 1:14).

The Eden Arboretum

"I made myself gardens and parks, and planted in them all kinds of fruit trees. I made myself pools from which to water the forest of growing trees" (Eccl. 2:5–6).

After retirement I spent about ten years continuing to develop an arboretum to the south of the Science Center. I think it was on Earth Day 1970 that a group of us cleared an area of weedy growth that became the site of the future perennial gardens. At that occasion one of the student volunteers pointed out a unique arrangement of rocks that he thought would make an interesting water feature. Several years later I laid an underground pipeline to carry out his vision. Jacob Schierre, a visiting Dutch engineer, constructed a barrel windmill to pump water to this site, which, however, never worked. Here was a literal "chasing after the wind." I bought a solar pump, which did function nicely until the motor failed, probably due to low voltage in the mornings and evenings. The solar collector is still there, but I have not been able to locate the pump.

We also constructed a pond to irrigate the Aker Hazelnut Grove, and we installed a footbridge over the pond in memory of my first wife, Emma, who died in 1991. The pond has been difficult to maintain but has the potential of being an attractive feature of the campus if there were a constant water source.

I spent the summer of 1994 at the Dyck Arboretum of the Plains, Hesston College, for more experience in arboretum management. One of the special features of the Eden Arboretum was the collection of native prairie plants that I brought from Kansas. I had fallen in love with these prairie plants and wanted to see how they would grow in the Shenandoah Valley, which may have been something of a prairie when the Native Americans managed the local landscape. The prairie garden is no longer in existence, but parts of the perennial garden are still maintained by faculty, staff, and work/study students.

While at the Dyck Arboretum I engaged in a regular correspondence with Shirley E. Yoder, who was serving as associate pastor at Park View Mennonite Church in Harrisonburg. Our friendship progressed to the event of marriage on November 26, 1994. Upon my reaching the age of seventy, Shirley resigned from the church, and we began several years of a variety of special projects together. One of the first was a joint interim pastor position at Jubilee Mennonite Church in Meridian, Mississippi. Later Shirley did additional interims: at Albany Mennonite Church in Oregon; at Carpenter Park Mennonite, Johnstown, Pennsylvania; and at Community Mennonite Church in Harrisonburg, Virginia. We also spent a very cold winter semester at Lithuania Christian College (now LCC International University) in Klaipeda, Lithuania, where Shirley taught writing and I assisted in the library and studied the Lithuanian language, of which I remember one word.

The Park Woods Project

A major project of the arboretum was a comprehensive botanical survey of Park Woods. Thanks to a generous Virginia Department of Forestry grant, I was able to employ a number of students over two summers. We laid out the entire ten acres in ten-meter square plots with a stake at each

On sabbatical: examining a clasping cone flower in Hesston College's Dyck Arboretum.
Photo by Larry Bartel

corner, 400 plots in all. We then measured the breast height diameter of each tree, identified all of the significant trees in each plot, and mapped all the wildflowers. In addition we attempted to introduce wildflowers, shrubs, and ferns that are characteristic of a typical oak-hickory forest, and removed invasive non-native species. We also mapped the soil types. The data we gathered filled six notebooks and represented a significant base study, which Jim Yoder and his current ecology students use.

Very few of the introduced shrubs and wildflowers survived except for the few ferns still present. Most of the failure to grow may be attributed to the unusually dry summers since the project was initiated, I believe. In 2007 Jim Yoder had me introduce the project to his advanced ecology students, and we remeasured most of the "champion" trees. All of them showed significant growth in diameter with the exception of those that had died.

I have been delighted to see Jim pick up this project. Myron Blosser of EMHS (Eastern Mennonite High School) is also using the Park Woods for nature studies. Even though the experimental vegetable gardens were lost to soccer and the valuable Kansas wildflower collection lost to weeds, the Park Woods project may survive. Thus I really do not need to share the despair of Eccl. 2:18–19: "I hated all my toil in which I had toiled under the sun, seeing that I must leave it to those who come after me—and who knows whether they will be wise or foolish. Yet they will be master of all for which I toiled and used my wisdom under the sun. This also is vanity."

The establishment of an arboretum is a very difficult project. It requires major funding and management. Our daughter Jane designed a beautiful plan for an EMU Arboretum for her master's degree in landscape architecture at the University of Oregon. But without a major donor and university commitment, the dream could not be fulfilled. Likewise for the Park Woods' project, pressure for expansion of the campus may doom this fragile ecosystem. It would be great if an easement could be established to protect this resource. However, even its preservation is subject to conflicting ideas of utilization. Several of us want to preserve it as a natural setting, allowing standing and fallen dead timber as a habitat for wildlife. Others want to see it as an urban park with the underbrush removed.

At the 100th anniversary of EMHS/EMU, Park Woods will be remembered as the site of the first classes in the old hotel. Many other historical features can be noted for Park Woods: the first graduation in the tabernacle, the site of the J. L. Stauffer cabin, and Park School. Earlier it was the site of camp meetings, horse racing, and industrial fairs. It is to be hoped that the woods will be preserved for posterity in some manner.

Reflections

As I reflect on these four seasons of my life, I cannot say, "all is vanity and a chasing after the wind." Some things worked out, some did not. As I read and reread Ecclesiastes, I began to sense an underlying sense of humor! As an old man, the philosopher could see that it was good not to take one's self and all one's projects too seriously. I am happy that I could encourage a few students to enter agricultural missions. I am delighted to see our graduates seriously considering and pursuing ecological lifestyles. I even enjoy watching soccer on the new field. I am confident that Eldon Kurtz, Will Hairston, Jim Yoder, and Myron Blosser will do their best to keep our campus "green." That should be enough to satisfy any old horticulturist.

When I contemplate over a half century of relating to Eastern Mennonite University, I am impressed by my personal attachment to and ownership in the institution. When I came as a freshman in 1950, we were barely a college. The library was pitifully small, science facilities were minimal, and intellectual freedom was carefully controlled. Remarkable growth in all these areas occurred over the next decades.

One of the most interesting areas of intellectual development came about in the teaching of biological evolution. When I was a geology student under D. Ralph Hostetter in 1953, the subject was carefully avoided. Years later when colleague Carl Keener and I shared an office in the basement of the old administration building, we had many discussions on our growing understanding of the importance of evolutionary science. Gradually, with the help of scientific scholars in the Christian community, especially through the American Scientific Affiliation, we were able to affirm that indeed God created by evolution. Making a synthesis of the doctrine of God as creator and the science of evolution has been a major intellectual adjustment for many of us at EMU. I often lament the narrow fundamentalist teaching on evolution given to students in many of our Christian schools. Some day many of these persons will realize that the things they were told are simply not true!

Once I was asked to address a Christian Educator's Convention on evolution. I pleaded with the teachers to allow God to create in any way he chose, rather than to give God directions as to how we wanted things done. I think the idea did not go over very well, but one teacher whispered to me on the way out of the auditorium, "What a breath of fresh air!"

Another central theme in my own intellectual development has been a synthesis of the discipleship/simple lifestyle and modern technology/consumerism. As mentioned earlier, I have been strongly discipled by the writing of Ron Sider. This, along with my training and experience in biological and horticultural science, helps me make some decisions about modern controversies. For example, my background in genetics and genetic engineering leads me to realize we have always been doing genetic modification. However, the sophisticated level of genetic modification possible today can be dangerous but is not inherently evil, as the recent list of sins by the Pope seems to infer. It just requires a new level of scrutiny and caution. Moving genes across species boundaries is something nature rarely allowed, and I believe these boundaries serve a useful function. In other words, speciation is important. Furthermore, a gene is not a distinct entity. It may include much genetic material within it and is subject to a host of modifiers in the original species.

My international exposure to the importance of food production for export by developing countries also modifies my response to the current "eat locally" interest. I realize how dependent farmers in Africa and Central and South America are on the export of crops such as coffee and bananas, so I read authors such as Barbara Kingsolver with appreciation but reservation.

EMU has adopted the prophet Micah's recommendation (in 6:8) as an institutional motto: "Love mercy, act justly, and walk humbly with God." This has also been my guiding principle over the past decades.

January 15, 2007
Revised November 2008

Notes

1 Ronald J. Sider, *Rich Christians in an Age of Hunger* (New York, NY: Thomas Nelson, 2005, first published in 1977).

PART III

Making Sense of the Journey

…as Authors

JAMES O. LEHMAN

A Bookworm Finds the Library World

As a farm boy growing up in Wayne County, Ohio, I never would have guessed that as an adult I would become a professional librarian and a researcher and writer of more than ten histories. No, farming meant dairying. However, after seven sons, if my overworked mother needed one of us boys to do the supper dishes, I chose that over milking the cows. I could return to reading sooner. The love of reading came easily to me despite my having no access to a real library or bookmobile. I gave the small number of books at home multiple readings and also became quite familiar with the extremely limited collection of books in the anteroom of my Anderson one-room country school. At a young age I became the proverbial bookworm.

Twists and Turns on the Road to Librarianship and a Mennonite History Author

December 22, 1932, turned out to be a balmy seventy-degree day outside the large old farmhouse several miles from Kidron, Ohio, on the day of my birth. Undoubtedly my mother barely noticed the weather as she recuperated from the pain of a six a.m. delivery of the little person her diary described as a "Big Boy 9 1/2 lbs." Though she had attended a six-week Bible term five years earlier at that faraway Eastern Mennonite School in the Shenandoah Valley, neither she nor Dad could have had any inkling that someday this second son would become a librarian and eventually direct the library of that Virginia school.

This farm boy learned not only to read well but also to relate to his siblings and live through family tragedy. A passel of brothers and later a few sisters helped to knock off some naturally sharp corners as I learned to play fair, share hard work, and work at relationships. But it never seemed really right that as a normal healthy boy, I had an older brother who suffered nearly all his life from severe epilepsy and in midlife the onset of multiple sclerosis. Or that my next younger brother, who had hydrocephalus and never developed beyond the baby stage, died on his seventh birthday. As a youngster then, I learned the importance of family and what it takes for good relationships, important lessons for later life.

From 1949 to 1951, because of their interest in Christian education, my parents happily sent me to the high school division of EMC (Eastern Mennonite College, formerly School, now University) and then two years of college. Dad had barely squeaked through seventh grade because of having to do farm work at home. Despite that, or was it *because* of that fact, he was pleased to help me begin college. With good Mennonite frugality and overloads some semesters, I enjoyed a double major in Bible and teaching, having in mind teaching Bible in a Mennonite high school.

Growing up speaking Bernese Swiss, learning Pennsylvania Dutch from Amish schoolmates, and studying German from E. G. Gehman at EMC helped broaden my preparation for a love of Mennonite history and also eventually stood me in good stead when I almost accidentally drifted into the researching and writing of congregational and community histories. All told, the nine I produced over a thirty-five-year period likely exceeded that of any other researcher and author of this kind of local history. However, since I liked school, my thoughts had early turned toward teaching, not writing history or becoming a librarian. Actually history failed to capture my attention fully for some time. My personal library contains a college textbook in European history on which is plainly penciled on the edge of the closed book, "In case of flood, stand on me, I'm dry!"

But the draft during the Korean War threatened and temporarily altered my direction. In 1953 I dropped out of college and married my childhood sweetheart, Dorothy Amstutz, who like me had grown up in the Sonnenberg Mennonite Church near Kidron, Ohio. After our wedding, my two years of I-W service (alternative service for conscientious objectors to participation in the military) at University Hospitals, Cleveland, Ohio, provided us a taste of city life. Also, someone suggested that the large number of I-W fellows (upwards of 175) working in a half dozen hospitals in the Cleveland metropolitan area ought to have a newsletter. Having already edited a junior high newsletter, *Sonnenberg Sunbeams*, I found it natural to begin *Cleveland Chimes*. Actually, creating newsletters became virtually a compulsion. To this day I am still doing one, the *Shenandoah Mennonite Historian!*

After I-W service I taught school two years at the Sonnenberg Mennonite School near Kidron and then finished college at EMC from 1957 to 1959. Since by that time my interests had changed, I moved to a comprehensive major in the social sciences with a minor in education. Also, in 1957–58 Irvin B. Horst's fine course hooked me permanently on Mennonite history. (Perhaps my fifty page history of the Sonnenberg Church and a good grade were part of this process.)

However, on graduation day in the spring of 1959 came a startling question. That graduation morning in 1959 Irvin and Ava Horst invited Dorothy, our two sons, Lynn and Orval, and me to have breakfast at their home. As we talked about my future plans, out of the blue Irvin asked me, "Have you ever considered becoming a librarian?" That thought had never crossed my mind, but the question lurked thereafter. At that point I had neither interest nor money to pursue graduate education.

Following graduation came another year of teaching at Sonnenberg, during which I was hoping for a position at the newly developing Central Christian High School, slated to open in 1960. In my conversation with the superintendent, Clayton Swartzentruber, about a job there, again came the same surprising question: "Have you thought about or might you be interested in pursuing librarianship?" If the answer was yes, I would immediately have a job waiting for me as a part-time librarian and part-time teacher. With a growing interest in doing a history of the four Mennonite churches of the area, I was excited about this promise of an attractive position at Central Christian in my home community. Dorothy and I had a family of three boys—Lynn, Orval, and Gerald—by that time; and I greatly desired involvement in that new school. Moreover, the Kent State University School of Librarianship at Kent, Ohio, was only fifty miles away. Why not pursue librarianship?

Alas, late in the spring of 1960 came a bit of a lightning bolt. Swartzentruber informed me that Central Christian was unable to open in the fall of 1960 as expected and would not open until 1961. Immediately I dashed down the street to Kidron to speak to my uncle George Amstutz, the principal of the Kidron Elementary School. Might he possibly have a job opening for a year? What a relief when George said that he had an opening for a seventh and eighth grade homeroom teacher for 1960–61! He hired me on the spot!

I did enroll in the Kent State University library school part time as soon as I could. Meanwhile, Swartzentruber suggested that I get a head start on beginning Central's library by ordering the first books while I was teaching at Kidron Elementary. Thus along with a full-time job came the challenge of selecting, ordering, and cataloging the earliest books. I soon convinced Clayton that it was in their interests (and mine!) that we order the new library books through a Barnesville, Ohio, firm that would order the books, catalog them, ship them to Kidron, and have them shelf ready for $1.00 a book. Early on I had taken a cataloging course at Kent State taught by a poor teacher, and I had promptly lost interest in cataloging. Librarians today look at me a bit puzzled when I tell them that, as events unfolded, I never cataloged a single book despite my lifelong profession as a librarian.

Central Christian opened in September 1961, and I settled in for a seven-year hitch that ended in 1968. Teaching American government on the senior level and church history on the junior level, along with being the half-time librarian, went generally well except for one year, 1964–65, when, as a class sponsor, I somehow lost it with that senior class and they teased me, sometimes unmercifully! After their graduation, things were fine at Central.

Two Roads, Two Colleges—EMC or Goshen?

In 1967 came a surprising offer from EMC out of the blue. Linden Wenger, a Virginia Conference bishop and assistant to EMC's president at that time, had come to serve communion at the Virginia Conference congregation that Sonnenberg had become in 1952. President Augsburger, he told me, had authorized him to inquire about my potential interest in becoming a librarian at EMC. To sweeten the offer, they dangled the possibility of my becoming the head librarian eventually. Apparently the administration and faculty were not totally satisfied with the library staff in place at that time, and the invitation contained a hint that a man was needed on the nearly all-female staff.

How does one respond to an offer like that? Furthermore, to complicate things even more, within two months came this offer from Goshen, Indiana. Since Melvin Gingerich, the long-time executive secretary of the Historical Committee of the Mennonite Church, had passed away, that job was open. Was I interested in moving to Goshen and becoming semi-attached to the Goshen College faculty while serving as executive secretary of the Historical Committee? Needless to say, both offers flabbergasted me. Why did these two attractive jobs for this academic greenhorn come my way? I was neither a trained college librarian nor an experienced Mennonite historian quite yet. On top of everything, I enjoyed Central.

By this time Dorothy and I had a family of five children—Lynn, Orval, Gerald, Beverly, and Alan—and were happily involved in our home church. Should we stay where planted or "go east" or "go west"? EMC's offer came with the proviso that they would take me either way: with the master's degree in Library Science I had received in 1965 or, if possible, additional study. Several things pointed eastward. I was an EMC alumnus; in addition, a visit to my alma mater confirmed the fact that it sounded like an interesting promotion to go from secondary librarianship to college librarianship.

At that moment an unexpected possibility for further study turned up. Kent State University began to advertise a graduate federal fellowship for the 1968–69 year open to persons with an MLS and three years of library experience. It carried the attractive plum of a $7,000 grant, virtually equaling the Central Christian salary. I applied for the fellowship and to my amazement was accepted to become the first person at Kent State to land this new fellowship program, which would grant a "Certificate of Advanced Studies in Library Science." That fellowship confirmed our heading eastward. Our children thought it sounded exciting to move for one school year to Kent and then move again to Virginia.

Meanwhile, by 1966–67 the challenge of becoming the researcher and writer of a projected major history of my home community had landed in my lap with the resources of the Kidron Community Council under-writing it. The Sonnenberg-Kidron community was primarily populated by Swiss Mennonites in four Mennonite congregations. Before I would seriously pick up my Kent State studies in the fall of 1968, I finished the final draft of this manuscript and took it to Herald Press at Scottdale. (This thread continues in a later section.)

We moved the family to Kent in August 1968 and nine months later to Virginia. That year at Kent provided me a broadening of perspectives and preparation for academic librarianship along with glimpses of student unrest and protests against the Vietnam War. The fellowship provided generous flexibility for a number of individual studies as well as more graduate courses, including the fine course, Reformation Church History. One could overlook the professor's sparse knowledge regarding the Anabaptist movement since he used a great textbook and knew his subject well otherwise. With great freedom to choose individual study topics, I gained experience in research and writing, producing some half dozen major papers, a few of which eventually ended up published in library journals.

The Early EMC Library World

We arrived at EMC early in June 1969, and I was enthusiastically ready for academic librarianship as my major vocation or profession. However, being slated to teach Colonial American History resulted in my inquiring of my good friend, Grant Stoltzfus, if he might consider swapping with me—let me teach his Mennonite History course while he took the Colonial American course. He cheerfully agreed. Furthermore, a number of Central Christian students had followed me to EMC, some of whom had signed up for Mennonite History. Now, since I had been thoroughly immersed in original research in local history for my Sonnenberg-Kidron book and a number of graduate research studies, I thought my students ought to get a taste of that kind of exhilaration. Hence I required all my students to choose a topic of their interest in Mennonite history and do some original research for a term paper. I continued that kind of assignment challenge for the nearly ten years I taught the course. As a result, the EMC Historical Library became the depository of a number of original term papers. Some were excellent, some good, some mediocre, and now and then one or two poor—like the one whose student author waited until the last weekend to dash down to Blountstown, Florida, do some quick research, churn out a paper, and hurry back to campus. He met the deadline, but the paper showed it, too!

With boundless energy I pursued my new job as assistant librarian, working in the serials department and at other odd jobs. However, I soon discovered myself a bit on the fringes of regular library work because of some discontent by other library staff over my coming; this situation turned out to be a four-year period of patience stretching for me. Meanwhile, interim assignments included some interesting non-library work such as research for Dick Benner and the Development Department—projects like looking for all the Mennonite millionaires in Lancaster County, Pennsylvania, in the summer of 1969. I drove all around the county, only to find people rather tight-lipped about revealing information regarding fellow millionaires!

Also at EMC in one of the early years came the one-year assignment to teach Political Philosophy when the history department spotted the fact that my resume showed a graduate course on that topic. As most professors know, sometimes one is asked to teach a course for which one is insufficiently trained. Fortunately, the students bore patiently with me.

Life provided some interesting experiences in those four years as I waited to see if the head librarian position might materialize—one bit of bait that the president and dean had dangled to help lure me to EMC. Having arrived in 1969 meant that we were here for the unforgettable student library drive in December 1969, when in one weekend the students raised $111,000 to save a federal grant of close to $430,000 for a large new 2.4 million dollar library building. Soon afterwards I sent a memo to the administration suggesting that someone be found to write the history of that momentous event. Predictably they turned around and asked me to do the research and write the story. Never in my life before or since have I researched and written about a historical event that was so dramatic and exciting that it almost wrote itself. The facts flowed onto the pages almost as if by magic. Sometime later Jim Bishop and I did an issue of the *EMC Bulletin* with that report as the feature story. Research and writing had become comfortable.

Another adventure came with the construction of the new library building. I was assigned a job that no librarian should do more than once in a lifetime—moving a library to a new building. At EMC that meant searching for library books all over campus in nearly every building except the gymnasium and a dormitory or two. The next step involved planning how to have them moved into the brand new building so that all the books would be placed in order on the three floors according to the Dewey Decimal cataloging system.

A change in my library role eventually came on July 1, 1973. Sometime after our arrival Dean Ira Miller had begun to pedal backward from the earlier "promises" to me about the head librarian position. And President Augsburger also demurred, not wanting to override the dean. However, when Daniel Yutzy became the dean, things began to move as EMC renamed the "head librarian" position to "library director," some aspects of which I had gingerly and privately suggested. This change meant some rearrangement of library staff relationships, including their loss of direct connections to the dean. My assignment now as the library director was to represent fairly all aspects of the library to the dean.

My new corner office was away from the circulation and reference desks, the scenes of action with students. At that time the circulation and reference desks were also located much farther apart than they currently are. My spacious quiet office was great for a developing avocation—writing congregational histories. However, I moved around the library periodically and scheduled myself at the reference desk in order to have interaction with students.

Director of Libraries at EMC/EMU

I came to enjoy the director's role, which included the twice-monthly jaunt to the dean's office to discuss library matters. For the first time in EMC's history, all of the areas of the library were under the director's purview; these included the Main Library, Historical Library and Archives, Learning Resources, and Curriculum Library. Heretofore, each of those four small "fiefdoms" had all related directly to the dean. In time, the library staff members accepted the changes gracefully. I instituted regular staff meetings, and my style of leadership was to be chairman of the team, giving due respect to the professional expertise of long-term staff.

The corner office became home to both vocation and avocation as I dealt with library affairs from my cluttered desk and worked from that wonderful finely grained wooden table on the other side of the room on my developing avocation—doing research and writing congregational histories. Eventually that table was often piled high, too.

As noted earlier, I enjoy doing a newsletter. One of the needs on campus, I was told, was to promote more frequent and extensive communication with the faculty and administration. That called for another newsletter, *Library Annotations,* two months after I assumed the directorship. I continued it until the spring of 1996.

At that point and at my suggestion, I relinquished my role as director and headed for the archives. It seems that the newsletter began with me and died with me since neither my predecessor nor my successor produced this kind of communication piece. (Of course, for refreshing my memory now for this memoir, the newsletter has become an invaluable tool for reviewing the significant happenings at the library and in the academia on campus.) Over that twenty-three year period, that newsletter and an annual extensive year-end annual report became my primary ways to keep the faculty and administration informed about library news. I included prospective and past budgets and departmental formulas for the allocation of money so that the faculty could assist in building a good book and journal library. All too frequently budgets ebbed and flowed according to the changes in student numbers. When belt-tightening came, I polled the faculty about what journals could be given up and kept them informed about how deeply inflation cut. For example, most chemistry journals finally had to be dropped because their prices went totally out of sight.

Our regular library staff meetings became good times of building camaraderie. Furthermore, I believed that no task around the library was too menial for me, if necessity called for it; and the schedule called for me to be at work as many weekends and evening hours as other staff members. My deliberate attempts to build communication links both inside and outside the library occasionally caused a few waves, but all of us usually soon arrived at smooth sailing. With a good library staff that was generally content there was not much turnover. If we differed on issues, my style tended toward being a compromiser, and I frequently gave up an idea of mine when a better one by a staff member surfaced.

Throughout my tenure as director, I had four supervisors in the dean's office—Daniel Yutzy, Willard Swartley, Albert Keim, and Lee Snyder. Those twice-monthly hour-long talks with the dean were stimulating and enjoyable. I soon learned to respect the busy dean's schedule by preparing carefully and making a list. "Going with the flow" was high priority, even if it brought surprises. Together we wrestled with those periods of riding the undulating waves of budgets or dealing with the staff or building issues that arose occasionally. The deans candidly alerted me to the internal struggles and successes that the administrators at EMC/EMU faced from year to year. Occasionally a dean and I did butt heads verbally. However, I had a tendency perhaps to give in as I learned what battles were worth fighting for and which ones were not winnable. One example of winning several times when an issue came up was the question of whether professional librarians should have faculty status or administrative status. After my departure professional librarians were placed on administrative status.

The library staff clearly enjoyed occupying the new library building in 1971. Almost immediately, in relation to library reference desk procedures, an hourly count of patrons in the library was instituted. This served a double purpose—it got someone going around the building to see that everything was in order, and the count showed us how heavily students were using the new library building. The statistics revealed that the students loved the new building. It then became interesting year after year to see the slow downward slide of library use—if the number of warm bodies in the building hour after hour was any measure of library use. In the first year of doing the count, we had as many as 232 patrons in the library in the evening prime time. During the next few years, it was not unusual for the count to exceed 200 students at evening prime time. Through the seventies library usage kept fairly steady. However, in the eighties the downward slide became more pronounced. By the mid-eighties the high count was 130 students at prime time; and by 1990–91, between seventy and eighty were the high counts. There the numbers stabilized. By the mid-nineties the library staff had gotten tired of this counting business and wanted to drop it. I reluctantly agreed.

Of course, with the advent of more and more computerization and eventually full automation with book records on a campus network, it was predictable that the students would come less often and that library use would decline. However, the librarians thought that other reasons contributed, also. Having taught a Mennonite history course for nearly ten years, I tended to understand the professorial viewpoint to some extent and thus did not always fully agree when the librarians groused that putting books on reserve was all too easy for teachers. We agreed that having books on reserve tended to limit the free rambling and serendipity of library use. The library staff also kept wondering why Eastern Mennonite Seminary professors seemed not to place enough emphasis on wide library use, particularly on the Historical Library, which is the best Anabaptist-Mennonite academic library in the East.

In the late seventies a library staff member polled the EMC and Seminary faculty on library usage. She learned from the fifty-four respondents that over half of them only occasionally or rarely made library assignments. Over seventy-five percent made no regular use of library journals themselves or only used one or two! The puzzle continued. Why was a graduate school like the seminary and later graduate programs not requiring more library use? The ease of interlibrary loans, the advent of computers, and eventually the resources of the Internet have understandably altered library use to a considerable measure. A great deal has apparently changed since I left the directorship in 1996.

After becoming director in 1973, I also quickly became involved in several meetings a year with the library directors of Bridgewater and Mary Baldwin colleges, at which we discussed both positive and negative experiences. Sharing cooperatively with private college libraries soon raised the question of sharing with James Madison University. The attempts I made in the seventies for the easy sharing of resources were stonewalled by the JMU director. However, when they had a change of directors, I quickly made it my business to contact him; and I found the new director most congenial and interested in making arrangements for the easy use of each other's libraries—and it was not just a one-way street. We had found that out long ago as we watched interlibrary loan patterns. The EMC/EMU library had great strengths in religion and history, and other libraries requested our books, too.

A windfall in the fall of 1976 started us down the road of computerization. Along with some 390 other private colleges we were offered an

$8,000 grant to purchase a "dumb" computer that would be hard-wired directly by phone line to Dublin, Ohio, to the wonderful nearly new OCLC (Ohio College Library Center) to catalog our books. Fortunately it was fairly easy to convince the administration to accept this grant, which would begin to revolutionize the library world. It was like moving from horse and buggy days to an early automobile. (Of course it would cost money in future years.) We joined SOLINET (Southeastern Library Network in Georgia), the regional network, to get to OCLC. SOLINET personnel then came on March 18, 1977, to train our catalogers. The staff happily learned quickly, and we were off as we entered the marvelous new world of computer access to a database of two million, eight hundred thousand computerized book records.

Nor was it just a one-way street to get cataloging copy for most of the new incoming books. We immediately began to contribute to the database. The very first original cataloging copy we contributed to the database was for a very rare 1521 book by Hans Füssli, Martin Seeger, and Ulrich Zwingli, *Das hond zwen Schweytzer bauren gemacht,* a book so rare we hid our copy in the Archives' walk-in vault.

What a boon this system became for interlibrary loans! Now we could easily tell what library possessed a given book before we ordered it. Interlibrary loans soon increased by sixty-six percent! Before long the database had four million records and was climbing fast. In time we learned that EMC was one of 1400 libraries in forty-eight states on the system. Within two years (May 1979) we could actually transact inter-library loans with our computer terminal and tell another library what to send us, and vice-versa.

There were also negative things to deal with such as the energy crisis of the late seventies and staff reductions in 1980. Through Robert Lehman's careful monitoring system it became known that the library building was enormously expensive in energy usage. Thus by December of 1977, to counteract the problem, the physical plant people had installed 355 phantom tubes in library light fixtures in place of the forty-watt bulbs. That action lowered total light meter readings, but we did not suffer.

Another negative filtered to campus at that time. We learned that Bridgewater, JMU, and the Union Theological Library in Richmond were planning for or installing electronic "gate keepers" (security systems) at the front doors. Too much library material was walking off. We fought that eventuality as long as seemed judicious. Surely in a Mennonite school we could trust the students and faculty not to walk out of the library with journals or without checking out books! We did an inventory in the summer of 1980. We thought we had 101,618 books on hand by official records, but we turned up a two percent loss. Later we actually counted the books on the shelves and found a two and a half percent loss over the previous decade and a half. We knew that faculty members sometimes carried books to the their offices, simply forgetting to check them out. In fact, on counting day, to my dismay, I discovered a book sitting in my office that had not been checked out. "He has been duly chastised," said the report in the newsletter! After more years of losses, the inevitable had to be faced. In 1985 an electronic system was placed at our front door to curb the hemorrhaging of materials, particularly journals.

Times kept changing, as they always do. In 1981 under pressure from the SGA (Student Government Association), we had to open the library Sunday evenings for student use and later expanded those hours. More details about changing times could be cited, such as the re-allocation of space for the Historical Library, involvement in professional organizations, and staff changes. EMC's undergraduate numbers dropped precipitously in the early eighties. The year 1984 did not see only the burning of the historic old administration building but also the serious lowering of the book budget. Also, it was the year of the largest number of staff changes, among them the retirement of Margaret Shenk, former head librarian, and major changes in Learning Resources with Milo Stahl needing to cease being the director of Learning Resources.

The budgets eventually improved when the student numbers rose, and increasing computerization became the order of the day. As we moved to smarter computers, electronic ordering arrived. By 1987 Audrey Shenk, our "computer guru," set up an acquisitions system that did not just order books, it kept track of accounting figures. Library reporting called 1987 "the year of the computer." However, by 1995 a total automation system made 1987 look pale by comparison.

I went on my second and last sabbatical leave in 1989–90. That and other changes made room for two new professional librarians, Jennifer Ulrich and David Alleman. In my absence for a year, Grace Showalter took over the reigns of the directorship. However, regrettably, on the day she was to retire in 1990, Dorothy and I returned to attend her funeral. As a librarian, she was missed for her expertise in local Virginia Mennonite history.

In 1992 talk became serious about moving toward full automation with an online catalog and other advantages. For several years catalogers had worked furiously at the big hurdle of converting card records to computerized records. By 1993 the subject was the Internet, the "superhighway of computerized information." Someone called it "drinking from a fire hose." Maybe so, but it was time for EMC, about to be called EMU, to drink from that hose. Because of the massive monies needed, EMU managed to land a huge Title III federal grant to help us make the automation leap.

As I nervously eyed this major paradigm shift coming to the library, aware that I was not very skilled in computers, I suggested to Vice-President and Dean Lee Snyder that a new director be found and that I transition into full time archival work. When that change failed to materialize in 1994–95, Snyder requested that I stay on another year to help make the transition into full automation and to establish training patterns. Fortunately, the grant provided monies for the new Information Services Department and for a professional librarian, Dita Leininger, to help us walk through that revolution. I told Dita, "Run with the ball; just keep me informed and involved as necessary." She did. And by 1996 the administration had found Boyd Reese, my successor as library director. That spring I happily retired from the directorship.

But not until we had survived the busiest year of implementing the major sea change in the library world. "Automation has changed almost every aspect of the library's function," said the library systems administrator, Audrey Shenk, as everyone learned new workflow patterns. We climbed a steep learning curve that year. Thankfully, Dita Leininger helped Audrey and Jennifer Ulrich to climb the curve to become fast and most efficient in dealing with automation. Had the library staff succumbed to becoming the "technowizards" who were turning young people into the "point and click generation?" No, we were just climbing the hurdles to keep up with the times.

Regrettably, after I left the directorship, it became evident that the

EMU archivist James O. Lehman (r.) and donor John R. Hildebrand examine the original documents of the Jacob R. Hildebrand journal, source material for A Mennonite Journal: 1862–1865: A Father's Account of the Civil War in the Shenandoah Valley, *published in 1996. Photo by Jim Bishop*

institutional budget would permit archival work to be only half time, rather than full time. I "went with the flow" and eventually retired from EMU in the spring of 2000. Or so I thought. After Dorothy and I returned from a second stint at the International Guest House in Washington, DC, in the summer of 2001, Owen Burkholder, a Virginia Mennonite Conference minister, collared me; and on that fateful morning of 9/11/01, when the U. S. was being attacked, Owen and I were having our conversation interrupted by the news of the moment. Since that time I have been part-time archivist for the Conference, working in the same quarters in the EMU archives.

Mennonite History Involvements

Now to back up time-wise to writing history. The Sonnenberg-Kidron sesquicentennial celebration slated for July 1969 included interest in a full scale history. Backed by Kidron Community Council finances, that book project had a strong base, and I was pleased they had confidence in my doing the research and writing. My contact person, Merl Lehman (no relative), a local journalist very interested in community history and a member of the Council, kept informing the Council as I proceeded. I began to turn up an enormous amount of documentation, bolstered by a whole series of interviews of people with good memories. Occasionally I queried Merl Lehman about whether I should keep going because of so much interesting material turning up. Without hesitation he always replied, "Keep going!" The Council wanted the celebration of the sesquicentennial to be a good one.

Constructing that 384-page history of the community taught me many lessons on researching and writing with care and sensitivity the history of a community that had four Mennonite churches in three different conferences and one that was independent. I was keenly aware that three church splits had fractured that Swiss Mennonite community. Furthermore, I was a member of the pioneer church—Sonnenberg. And to top it all off, the most major split very personally involved my father-in-law, Louis Amstutz, who was the bishop at Sonnenberg in 1936 when that most disastrous church schism occurred. At that point the Kidron Mennonite Church began with the more than 300 members who left Sonnenberg, which was where the leadership stayed. I say "disastrous," because it ripped many families apart. By the late sixties some healing had occurred, but some hurts still festered. Of course you know the worn out cliché that probably applied to me: "Fools rush in where angels fear to tread!" Gingerly I dealt with the stressful times with as much objectivity as I could muster. I also began to realize fully that no historian is without bias.

I had been appointed chairman of the 1969 sesquicentennial and thus got to ride in the first car in the parade through Kidron. A week previous to that July event, it had been my privilege to greet Ohio Governor James Rhodes, who chose to attend the German hymn-sing at Sonnenberg, rather than the sesquicentennial events the following weekend. I escorted him down the aisle through this large meetinghouse full of people to the front bench, and we joined in singing German songs. Governor Rhodes did not do badly with German! I then introduced him to the audience and gave him a copy of a cookbook produced for the occasion and a copy of my newly published history. He, in turn, complimented Mennonites for their fine work with MDS (Mennonite Disaster Service). All these sesquicentennial events occurred in July 1969, several weeks after our family moved to Virginia.

That history is probably one of my best ones. I learned to know the community inside and out and had good help when I had questions. Quietly and surprisingly, this former farm boy, schoolteacher and unknown Mennonite historian had been catapulted into the world of Mennonite history. The Historical Committee of the Mennonite Church, who attended that summer event at Kidron, included historians and professors such as Grant Stoltzfus from EMC and John Oyer from Goshen College. Of course each committee member was given a copy of the history just off the press. I was duly impressed when John Oyer, professor of history at Goshen, opened his copy to the back of the book and scanned the documentation, noting the more than 600 endnotes in the carefully documented history, a large bibliography, and an index.

Then he turned to me and asked, "Where in the *world* did you ever find so much material?"

Taken aback a bit, I mumbled something like, "I just followed my nose, pursued every lead, and kept going," backed, of course, by the Community Council.

I was pleased the following year to be invited to Columbus, Ohio, to have the Ohio Association of Historical Societies present me an "Award of Achievement" for the book, *Sonnenberg, A Haven and a Heritage,* as being "the most substantial, original volume of local history published in Ohio in 1969." Melvin Gingerich, executive secretary of the Historical Committee, reviewed it, and generously called it "a masterpiece of community history."

I completed the manuscript of this book after we moved to Kent. When we took it to Scottdale for Herald Press to print it, they were not a little surprised that I had brought considerably more than a hundred photos to be printed; but after blinking twice, they promptly began to produce a very good-looking hardback history. That book turned out to be a project costing $10,000 in 1969. (Imagine what that cost might be today!) But the Kidron Community Council never flinched at all the sesquicentennial expenses, including the history, thanks to Merl Lehman, the treasurer Bill Moser, and a congenial Council led by George Bixler, the local chief of the quite successful Kidron Body Company.

Further involvements in Mennonite history came as I became a member of EMALA (Eastern Mennonite Associated Libraries and Archives) in the early seventies. Later I became chairman of EMALA for a dozen years. In 1973, the same summer I became the library director, I was also voted onto the Mennonite Church Historical Committee. Being a member of that group became one of the "fun" parts of my avocation since it meant getting to Goshen periodically and to other locations where historical celebrations were held, and the committee meetings were stimulating events. In the seventies the historical interests of the Mennonite Church and General Conference Mennonite Church experienced a warm and exciting courtship. However, after about five years I lost my committee membership, a casualty of Mennonite consciences feeling guilty about the lack of women on church-wide committees. At election time I was slotted for renewal along with my good friend, Carolyn Charles Wenger. Naturally, she was elected. Later, however, in the eighties and into the early nineties I was voted onto the committee again and served during a significant era of staff changes at the Archives of the Mennonite Church at Goshen and emerging new directions for the Mennonite Historical Committee.

Several times Mennonite historians from the U.S. and Canada met for special meetings. A time or two these involved all three major Mennonite groups in North America—MC, GC, and MB (Mennonite Brethren). A special one occurred in 1977. Lawrence Klippenstein from Winnipeg and I put together the programming and shared chairperson duties for a major meeting of the staff from various Mennonite historical libraries and archives. Robert Kreider, the dean of Mennonite historians, and I roomed together at this stimulating event.

After I had completed the Sonnenberg-Kidron history, the news was out, and my name became known as one interested in promoting Mennonite historical interests. Within a few years I began to receive invitations to write histories for Ohio Mennonite congregations. Somehow this "dyed in the wool Ohioan" had not altogether left his home state, and I agreed. In 1974 and 1975, in quick succession I did two short histories: an eighty-eight page history of the Pike Mennonite Church, Elida, Ohio; and a 112 page history of the Crown Hill Mennonite Church, Rittman, Ohio. In 1978 it was the Oak Grove Mennonite Church, Smithville, Ohio. When Peter Wiebe, the pastor at that time, called me one evening in 1977 and asked me to research and write that history, I chuckled with amazement. I knew that congregation had had loads of people for many decades going off to finish college, including famous people like John Howard Yoder and Albert Meyer as native sons. Why not ask one of their graduates?

But Peter insisted. I had only thirteen months to run to Ohio, dig into the research and write a major history (320 pages) of that phenomenally unusual congregation of Amish Mennonite origin. I nearly did myself in, trying to do it in such a short time. I was grateful to Albert Keim, then dean of EMC, for looking the other way when I finally had to take "company time" to get it finished. With a big load of books printed at the Park View Press we made the deadline by twenty minutes to Smithville, Ohio, just in time for me to give the speech assigned to me, "Things I Didn't Dare Put in the Book!"

About this same time I stopped teaching Mennonite history. Dean Keim abruptly announced to me one day that a certain professor needed a full load, and he was giving the course to him. The dean thought I was busy enough anyway. Of course, he was right, but I did regret losing that touch with students.

In 1980 I did another congregational history, that of the Longenecker Mennonite Church, Winesburg, Ohio. Each time I did one I raced back and forth to Ohio several times to research and interview and collect documentation, and when the book came off the press, make another trip to participate in the historical celebration, and sign books. Of course, for research purposes I was situated at the right place at EMC to spend a great deal of time scanning and searching church papers on campus. A number of times I went through many years of the *Gospel Herald* and the *Herald of Truth,* along with turning up other basic sources.

Some of these congregational histories had a recurring theme: tensions and schisms. How should I deal with them? I always tried to listen carefully to voices from both sides and then document my writing thoroughly with endnotes so that readers would know who was saying what. I was passionate about details but always tried to keep the big picture in focus on how a congregation related to the wider church. Along the way numerous people showered me with thanks for doing the histories. But I could also tell a few tales of times I "struck out." Not everyone wanted me to be candid about the tensions and human foibles and negative things that turned up. However, I was thankful to learn that miracles of healing did occur within the congregations.

In 1979–80 I was granted my first sabbatical leave for two terms (EMC was on the three-term system at that time), and Dorothy and I moved to Hatfield, Pennsylvania, for more than four months. Along with working on the Longenecker history, I commuted fifty miles to Rutgers University for two graduate courses; and we spent many hours beginning the research on the Mennonite and Amish experiences during the American Civil War. Then we headed westward. Before returning home we had traveled to more than thirty-five libraries, archives, and depositories, all the way westward as far as Mennonites and Amish had gone in pre-Civil War days, which was to Illinois and Iowa. With a fine-toothed comb we sifted for details. Periodically I laid that project aside to do other histories. In the late 1990s I worked seriously on finding a publisher. Only now, with many twists and turns and the gaining of a co-author, Steve Nolt, history professor at Goshen, has that manuscript, *Mennonites, Amish, and the American Civil War,* finally been published by Johns Hopkins University Press. It came off the press in October 2007.

Back to congregational histories. In 1986 it was the Salem Mennonite Church, Kidron, Ohio, for whom my research took me through General Conference Mennonite publications, including a good German one. In 1990 came another full-length book project, this one for the Bethel Mennonite Church, West Liberty, Ohio. Then I took a rest from congregational histories until in 1998, Lindale Mennonite Church published the history I wrote. This time I had done a Virginia congregation where Dorothy and I have attended ever since our arrival in 1969. To give you an idea of time (although Lindale's fascinating history took longer than most of the others), I logged my time. It took 1100 hours to do that 300-page history! That's 3.6 hours per page. My other histories probably ranged between two and three hours per page. My last congregational history was for the Grace Mennonite Church, Pandora, Ohio, in 2004. Two years earlier I did a full-length book on Mennonite tent revivalism as sponsored by Christian Laymen's Evangelistic Association of Orrville, Ohio, a book that dealt with the meteoric rise and demise of Howard Hammer and the early days of Myron Augsburger's tent revival work.

It has been a very satisfying life to pursue the library profession and the Mennonite history avocation. If I have accomplished anything, it is through the grace of God and his leading, as the Lord and I together activated the supposed 100 billion neurons in my head to thread through the intricacies of life and to put on paper something of how God works through his people.

February 12, 2007
Revised May 2008

OMAR EBY

Memory & Identity

Part I

During Eastern Mennonite University's 1997 commencement, I found myself thinking about that boy who had graduated forty years earlier. Two months later I was in Somalia, a missionary teacher, as Eastern Mission Board (Salunga, Pennsylvania) described me. When I took early retirement in 1999 from the university classroom, I set about studying that boy—a product of Eastern Mennonitism—through the grid of my accumulated years. Often I loved him indiscriminately; often he irritated the heck out of me; often I thought him a fool. Then I sat down and began writing.

I harvested those three years of living in Somalia among a beautiful and exasperating people on the harsh and desolate horn of East Africa. Winnowing the grains of memory, I attempted to resist self-deception, self-congratulation, sentimentality, and narcissism. I suppose sometimes I failed and let chaff get into the polished grain. The attempt to retrieve the honest shape of an earlier life is hard work. Yet I wanted to see the beautiful and the divine intrusion into the mundane, to delight in the glorious trivia of living out those days in that far country.

In these Somali essays I attempt two voices: that of the boy in his early twenties and that of the older man now in his late sixties. The tone is personal and critical, reminiscent and nostalgic, yet lightly mocking even while in a fierce embrace. The stories are like a series of transparencies laid down one on top of the other: the boy's views overlaid by the man's two visits to Somalia in his thirties and then memory laid over everything. Now with more detail and nuance everything should be clearer. Yet I discovered that the historically reconstituted self is still blurred. I worried constantly about the narcissistic seduction of memoir. Still, I wrote. The following essay illustrates something of these themes.

A Distraught Woman[1]

I woke in the pearly morning light of Mogadishu, Somalia, to a woman's wailing, distant but steady. The wail was not raised against her husband's beating; it had no physical urgency. Rather, her keen was of a heart in distress, a spirit broken and without words for grief. When the wail seemed to come nearer, I got up and looked out of my barred bedroom window.

A Somali woman thrashed about on the flat roof of the nearby Lind house, she having climbed the metal staircase against the outside rear wall. She cried and thrust out bare arms towards the pale east. Her hair hung loose, fallen from the tight kerchief all Somali women wore. Staggering to the north edge of the roof, she looked down, her body weaving against the knee-high parapet. I though she might jump. But she turned away and wrapped her long headscarf about her face, blinding herself as she staggered to the west wall. Now I could see her fully as suddenly she again opened her arms, sheathed in the scarf, and threw them up rigid above her head, as though beseeching the fading western star for mercy, for quick death, her life bitter and futile. And then she screeched—a noise prehistoric and inhuman.

A clearly grief-crazed Somali woman on the Lind house roof, she turned again to keening! What could I do? The Lind family was on holiday in Nairobi. I would have to do something. It was another hour before Ali would come to my house. In a fog of irresolution I pulled on shorts and stamped into sandals to go to her. When I came up to the house, I could no longer see her from below. So I climbed part of the way up the steps until my head was level with the roof. She must have heard the metal stairs rasp against the wall, for she whirled and stared at me with eyes wide open, yet flat, dead in a terrible sleep. My heart pounding with fear, I still managed to call greetings to her, quietly, and urged her to come down.

In Mogadishu, Somalia, 1958

If she came however, I had no idea what I would do with her. But she spared me that dilemma, dashing to the farthest corner, all the while wailing. I worried that any moment now someone early on the street below would hear us, look up, and gather a wrong idea. There came to my mind Mrs. Modricker's account of drunken brawls at night in a house of Italian bachelors across the street from the Sudan Interior Mission headquarters. "Lie down! Lie down!" the men yelled as they chased the Somali tarts they had brought home. There was nothing for me to do but to return to my house and await Ali's arrival.

Later he came through the door, shouting with heartless delight. "She crazy! She crazy! Crazy woman on the roof!"

No, he did not know her. But, yes, he had seen her sometimes crazy in the markets until someone came to take her away.

"We must get her down," I said. "This is awful!"

When Ali refused to approach the woman, I suggested he go for the police.

Within minutes he returned, the policeman with him smart in his khaki shorts and blue beret. At first the two men stood below the house and laughed. Something the deranged woman kept repeating—vulgar or incongruous—struck them as hilarious. Eventually the officer, a mere lad, climbed the stairs to the woman, calling and gesturing that she come to him. When she refused, he rushed her. She swirled toward the roof's edge, and again I thought she would jump. But the policeman snatched at her billowing dress and wound her against him. Then shouting and scuffling, the two came down the stairs. The policeman, his voice raised half in amazement, half in anger, called something to Ali. Again their laughter rang out.

Suddenly the distraught woman was docile. But the policeman did not release his hold. In the severe intimacy of his grip, the woman, disheveled and now mute, walked quietly beside him down the sandy driveway to the street. Ali called something to me. The woman shuffled in the sand; she wore only one sandal. I turned away to my house and went inside.

The deranged woman is still shuffling down the mission driveway, shuffling down the mission driveway subdued, shuffling down the mission driveway on one sandaled foot, forever.

I wrote the above account as accurately as I could remember it these forty-five years later. Here in an unedited account is what I wrote home to my parents on an airform dated September 14, 1959:

> Early Sunday morning I saw a woman going all about the Linds' house, looking in the windows and picking up things and throwing other things around. They are still on vacation, so after while I went down to see what it was all about. She had found an old paint bucket and filled it with water and was washing the front porch and steps. I asked her who she was and what she thought she was doing. In Italian she asked me where my mama was. Then she told me that she works here and that I'm to go away. This is not true of course, because the Linds have two men servants. I asked her if she was a thief, and she muttered some incoherent things and kept on washing. There was nothing I could do, and with the house locked I figured it didn't matter.
>
> About an hour and a half later the first Somali student came for worship service, and he saw her and spoke with her. He told me that he thinks she is crazy because she told him that she lives there and he is to go away. He went for the police or someone to inquire about her head. While he was gone, she went up on the roof of the house (it is a flat roof with steps up the back) and began going through terrific movements of her arms, twirling in circles and slinging her arms and skirts; then she would walk around the top very fast.

Finally, a policeman came and another man, and they went up to talk with her. I was afraid she'd jump off when she saw the police coming. But they somehow persuaded her to come down. Then she came walking towards the chapel where I was, and then she ran out the back driveway with the policeman and the other Somali after her. That's the last I saw of her. If she was mentally off, I think it was the first Somali I had ever seen as such. Oh, yes, she told the Somali student that she had just been released from prison and they told her to come here and work at this (Linds') house."

So here is the problem: Which account is true?

I knew that somewhere in my three-year weekly letters to my parents lay an account of this distraught woman on the roof. Deliberately I did not track down that letter, read it, and let it refresh my memory before writing. Rather, I wanted first to see what was in my memory of the incident—the images, the characters, the action, the dialogue, my response and attitude. I was more interested in putting down an accurate memory these forty years after the incident than I was with a historically verifiable record of the occurrence. I was interested in discovering if there was any gap between the two and if so, in teasing out why this might be. Parenthetically I grant that I may have edited the account in the letter home to my parents—as one does when he is a boy. Yet a mad woman on a roof does not seem to be an incident needing to be censored.

So forty-five years after the incident, I find that I am not a reliable eyewitness. Except for the barest facts: once when the Linds were absent on holiday, I had a brief encounter with a crazed woman who had climbed onto the flat roof of their house, and a policeman was needed to get her down. I had forgotten that it was a Sunday morning, that within minutes I alone would conduct the service: lead the hymns, read the scriptures, offer the prayers, give a sermonette. My house servant was not present. I had not suggested the bringing of a policeman. I had forgotten that the woman attempted escape by running from her captors out the upper driveway instead of being escorted by the policeman down to the front gates of the mission property.

In truth I had not initiated any action towards a resolution of the problem: what to do with a deranged woman on our mission house roof in Mogadishu. Rather, I had been my typical self: fearful, passive, inept. That being the case, I am left to wonder why I had unconsciously, during these last four decades, written myself into—if not a lead role—the best supporting male actor of this dramatic episode. Is this the inevitably fated chrysalis a tender psyche spins about itself over the years as a way of surviving, of cushioning itself against the shock of a bald reality? The truth can make one free—yes! But it can also shatter. Thus, to protect against such shattering, does the ego formulate a memory of an incident that is part fabrication and handsomely self-aggrandized?

The gap between the two accounts raises the matter of fact, myth, legend, truth, canon—indeed, to put a theological spin on the memory of the incident, it touches on ontology and hermeneutics. I would have been a most unreliable eye-witness to the life of Jesus, had gospelers Mark or Matthew asked me forty years after Jesus' ascension for accurate accounts of this radical rabbi's miracles and parables. Or it at least raises an ontological question: how closely must the reconstructed narrative match the historically verifiable incident for truth to be not only preserved but also illuminated? Might the memory of an incident recalled forty-five years later have an even greater truth than the bare historical record? Is memory, even an inaccurate memory, one method the psyche employs against the whisper of its own annihilation?

I might console myself with modern theories of memory, as Ellen Ullman reports of them in her *Harper's* (October 2002) article entitled, "Programming the Post-Human."

> According to current research, the contents of human long-term memory are dynamic (not static). Each time we recall something, it seems we reevaluate it and reformulate it in light of everything relevant that has happened since we last thought about that incident. What we then "remember," it turns out, is not the original event itself but some endless variant, ever changing in the light of experience.

Further, perhaps the mere telling of a memory demands its own narrative necessity to get at the truth of an incident—that the truth is of more importance than the accurate catalogue of detailed images: woman, roof top, policeman, the narrative's center of consciousness, a particular September Sunday morning in Mogadishu. There is the kernel of revelation—even the epiphany—coming now forty-five years later: As a Mennonite Christian missionary teacher boy, I was unable to help a grief-frenzied Somali Muslim woman who had climbed onto our mission house roof.

And a second truth: The attempt to retrieve the honest shape of an earlier life is hard work. Even when one resists the seduction of self-deception, self-congratulation, sentimentality, and narcissism, chaff gets into the grains of winnowed memory. One must constantly puff at such chaff to gain the truthful sheen on the historically reconstituted self.

I hope it is a mark of wisdom and maturity to acknowledge that the nature of memory is unreliable, indeed, often deceptive. Finally, somewhere in all this chatter there seems, like the Somali woman on the roof, the jangle of a distraught boy—and an old man.

Part II

Every year, I suppose, hundreds of old English profs retire. Hardly noteworthy. But probably only a few of them keep a journal about their last year in their classroom, teaching writing and literature. I am one of them. I set to the task two or three times a week. The journal is now entitled, "Last Lessons: Watching Myself Retire."

A journal by nature roams among many topics: students, colleagues, administrators, pedagogy, family; the integration of faith and life, of literature and life; a light touch here, a penetrating analysis there; whimsical, conversational, confidential, confessional, poignant, or sharp-tongued; anecdote, commentary, reflection, intellectual inquiry, the voice of a sixty-three year-old man still stumbling towards God. And the new experiences one does not expect after a quarter century of life among students: the social activist, a white Mennonite boy, a biology major, who accused me of racism; the frightened BMOC [big man on campus], a Bible major who sought a loan from me to pay for his HIV-AIDS test; the fundamentalist jock, a chemistry major who insisted on praying for me in my office after the first period on Hemingway.

Here are a few unexpurgated excerpts from "Last Lessons."

TEARING UP FILES
September 3
With little to do on the days between another boring faculty conference and the start of classes, I turn to looking at my files. Particularly those courses I know I'll never again teach: Nineteenth Century British Lit, Public Speaking, Mass Communications, Continental Fiction, and the three Special Authors—Faulkner, Hemingway, and E. M. Forster.

I try to imagine the future: Will I ever again be asked to lead a discussion on Wordsworth's "Intimations of Immortality"? (Students always mocked the title by calling it "Imitations of Immorality"!) Can I tease out that young Romantic's notions about the preexistence of the soul without the aid of my old notes? Will I ever want quickly an illumination of some bit of wrenched syntax in one of Gerard Manley Hopkins' sonnets, say from "The Windhover"?

> I caught this morning morning's minion, king-
>> dom of daylight's dauphin, dapple-dawn-drawn Falcon, in his riding
>> Of the rolling level underneath him steady air, and striding
> High there, how he rung upon the rein of a wimpling wing
> In his ecstasy!...

But who will I be when no longer explicating Browning and Hopkins? This is no time for indulgent lingering. I pitch everything. How hard it is, to shred those good notes on Keats and Browning! But they, too, must go. I tell myself that never again will anyone want to hear me praise that dying youth's loveliness, that elder's tempered wit. I know, too, that I shall forget much about their poetry. Someday in years to come, I will be unable to answer well my own examinations on their poetry, will remember only the trivia about their spectacular lives. But their poems are in books where I can find them when I need the comfort of familiar lines, the nurture of keen metaphor and allegory.

ADULTERY

September 8

Three periods running now we've had extraordinary sessions on Hawthorne's *The Scarlet Letter* in American Fiction. First was an interactive lecture—a too-formal term for my day's rambling about background: Puritanism/Calvinism vs. Transcendentalism/Romanticism. Students readily picked up on questions to pool the class' collective knowledge. For examples: the rise of the Puritans in England with their sincere concerns about the Anglican Church practices that drifted towards the Roman Mass; the hysteria surrounding the Salem witches' trials; the near-Pantheism of the Transcendentalists.

Another period, a five-member team of students directed the class discussion. Granted, three members were particularly capable of prefacing a precise question that elicited more than a mere yes/no answer. As expected, every member of the panel spoke; additionally, more than half the class contributed comments, at times three and four hands in the air at the same time; others just spoke up without waiting to be acknowledged by members of the panel. I, too, joined the discussion at those points where I felt a further question or comment might extend or illuminate a finer aspect of the topic. For instance, some students were particularly hard on the Rev. Dimmesdale—failed to sympathize with him, found him hypocritical, weak, cowardly. Some did not want to wrestle with "Can a person troubled with sin still be a mentor?" Some felt Hester was strong, noble, free-spirited—yet could not answer why she would not reveal the name of Pearl's father, seemed evenly divided over which is the greater suffering: Hester's public shame or Dimmesdale's private torment.

A third period was mine. I set up Nature, Art, Religion, Science on the chalkboard, asking students to assign the name of a main character to each. Easy enough. Then asked them to comment on what the blending of any two produced. For instance, the attempted friendship of Religion and Science (Dimmesdale and Chillingworth), they rightly noted, ends in the arrogant self-appointed right of scientists to probe, define, analyze all reality within their own defined parameters. Similarly, in the wedding of Art and Religion, there is a temptation for esthetics to replace faith, for artistic performance to replace worship. The blending of Nature with Religion tends to revive ancient paganism under new guises, for example, New Ageism.

COUNTRY ROADS

September 15

Teaching three-quarter time this year, I'm trying to claim that other quarter time my own. This semester I have no classes on Tuesdays and Thursdays. On Thursdays I go in to the university at noon, when the Language and Literature Department meets for lunch, "lite" business, and professional gossip. Then stay on for a few hours of deskwork, lesson preps, student conferences. But on Tuesdays I stay home and "do my own things"—affairs totally unrelated to my academic life. Canning grape juice and pears, writing this journal and letters to former student-friends, reading, napping, walking.

I usually drive in to the college to walk the track around the soccer field. But last week I decided to walk the country roads to where my son is farming. Years ago I did all my walking on these roads in the Cooks Creek Church and Burkholder Orchard area. Maybe it's my nerves, but it seems to me the traffic is heavier, faster, with more and more of the large tractor-trailers that haul feed to the poultry villages swooshing by.

I am pleased that the county has not mowed our stretch of the Mt. Clinton Pike. I note the natural bouquets of Queen Anne's lace studded with the blue buttons of chicory weed, the occasional fuzzy mauve flowers of Canadian thistle and burst froth of milkweed pods softening these borderscapes. Yet I am of two minds about walking these country roads. I enjoy the wild flowers and wet weeds until I hear or see traffic coming from two directions. Then, not wanting to join the roadkill, I must step off the paved road into this navel-high nature and risk ankle-twisting terrain. Mostly I stand still, letting the riffled air cool me. Then I return to the roads. I admit the mown stretches of Cooks Creek Road north to Lawrence's farm make for easier walking. But I cry out with Gerard Manley Hopkins:

> What would the world be, once bereft
> Of wet and of wildness? Let them be left,
> O, let them be left, wildness and wet;
> Long live the weeds and the wilderness yet!

HARD SCRUBBINGS

October 13

Mid-day and needing a "centering" experience, I picked up Kathleen Norris' *Amazing Grace* from my office windowsill to read one short chapter. (Actually, I think I'm mocking this "centering" business these days. It is not so much "Who am I? Who am I?" but "Who art Thou? Who art Thou, Lord?" that rings up from my still withered and puzzled soul.)

It contains the following quotation. "They have a kind of polish, a gentle manner that has come from having been hard-scrubbed in the rough and tumble of communal living," she writes of her elderly Benedictine monk friends.[2]

Immediately I began thinking of myself, inevitably, I suppose, if one must resort to spiritual aids at noon to get through another day, even in the "Christian" Academical Village (to sanctify and borrow Jefferson's quaint phrase about his founding-child, the University of Virginia).

So what has happened to me in the "rough and tumble" of the communal living these twenty-seven years at EMC/U? I'm not even sure that life in the Language and Literature Department was all that rough and tumble, when I hear stories out of other collegiate departments—music and Bible, for instance. Yet I must admit to a certain capacity for forgetting the emotional rough stuff that occurred in my life. My wife (Anna Kathryn Shenk, whom I met in 1960 and married in 1962) remembers incidents of brawls with my headmaster at Musoma Alliance Secondary, Tanzania (1966–67), that I have completely forgotten. I like to compliment myself that it is a spiritual grace I have achieved, this not remembering another's sins. When, if the truth were out, it is probably nothing more than the failure of some mental synapses, the failure of some switch of memory to recall from storage, even when probed. Nothing but sheer chemistry. Nothing of *Amazing Grace* practiced on my part at all! So science wins out again—one more spiritual virtue or vice nothing more than a bit of the flow or failure to flow of one's chemical juices? Gad!

"(He) has a kind of polish, a gentle manner … " will hardly be said of me on retirement at the obligatory dinner or, a decade later in the Virginia Mennonite Nursing Home, Oak Lea, stumbled upon by a former fan of Faulkner. Certainly these are not phrases that I think are apt descriptions of myself just now, this year of retirement. Other descriptors—honest and unsentimental words—come to mind, during my moments of "centering" reflections on my own ego. Words like *dour, crotchety, testy, blunt, impatient, irritable, irascible, irreverent*. I am sure my colleagues who attempted over the years to give me a "hard scrubbing" have additional words. (Some not to be written here!)

"What's so amazing about grace?" is that I'm still just simple enough to find a kind of dumb joy in my first Sunday School ditty: "Jesus loves me" (an affirmation whether felt or clung to by one's mere fingernails of faith). "This I know" (a nod to the cognitive). "For the Bible tells me so" (again the gift of grace—granted a favor to believe: that somewhere behind the stories in this ancient text moves the God I know as amazing).

ON TEACHING HEMINGWAY

October 29

I find myself still thinking about the teaching of Faulkner. I'd read nothing of his during my undergraduate days at EMC—even though one of those years he was Writer-in-Residence over at University of Virginia. We read the classics those early 1950s: full courses on Milton, on Shakespeare; the sober-minded fictions of Austen, Thackery, Dickens; the full canon of metaphysical poets, transcendentalists, and the Federalist papers.

I feel that had I a greater intelligence, I might have been a better scholar; I might have followed more closely in the footsteps of my mentor, Hubert Pellman. Studied more attentively the classics and not been distracted by the contemporary writers of the sex and violence so alien to the puritanical years of my Hagerstown youth.

Perhaps I can justify the teaching of Faulkner—his literary stock's climbing rapidly after the publication of Malcolm Cowley's *The Portable Faulkner*—some years after most of Faulkner's greatest novels were already out of print. In the PMLA *(Publication of the Modern Language Association)* Faulkner still holds his place along with Shakespeare and the nineteenth century Russian novelists as the men/works most studied and written about in literary journals. I wet only my toes in this great academic discourse on things Faulkner, finding much of it obtuse. I'd rather do yet another reading of the real thing.

I suppose I can let myself off a bit from this sense of guilt about not teaching the older classics by blaming the pressures on the canon. Feminism and ethnicity rightly needed to join the sacred stable of dead white male authors. Something had to give way for these self-righteous apostolic pioneers of the new politically correct doctrines. So it was good-bye, Chaucer; good riddance, Milton; and watch yourself, Shakespeare! But did I need to be so ready an advocate for the new? Thus, I feel that I, too, am guilty of doing my share of the de-canonization of the Miltons and the Thackerys even while I might claim they were of the British Lit canon. That my greater interests lay with the American writers. Why didn't I run a full course on Emerson, Thoreau, and Whitman? I'd read them carefully, fully; found the experience a pleasure; respected their handling of tough ideas.

But Hemingway! Loathed by the animal-rightists, hated by the feminists, shunned by the high-minded moralists. Even I must admit that I tried not to think about Faulkner (let alone Milton) when I waded into Hemingway country. He seemed thin, mechanical; and while a great stylist, as though he had never found a subject worthy of his skill. The

British novelist Anthony Burgess makes a great claim for Hemingway in the video I use to introduce the author to the class: "Hemingway brought the novel into the twentieth century. While not the greatest novelist, he was the most influential." Even about the latter claim I am not fully convinced— think of Proust, of James Joyce, of Virginia Woolf. As for being the greatest novelist? Even among Americans, Hemingway is not of the rank of Melville and Faulkner.

So why did I teach Hemingway? Partly because of the man, and that not solely because of his macho life: deep sea fishing in the Caribbean; big game hunting on African safaris; European war reporting; wives, women, sons. Rather, my fascination locked in with the reading of a first biography. Here I learned of Hemingway's evangelical home: family Bible reading and oral prayers around the dinner table; church attendance with youth choirs and young people's meetings; no smoking, dancing or drinking allowed; children's tithing their ten cent weekly allowances. What was wrong in that turn-of-the-century mid-western household that would cause the father to shoot himself, as did Ernest? Later a sister and his only brother also killed themselves. (And just possibly the death of his granddaughter was also a suicide.) Why did the eighteen-year-old boy off to his first newspaper job on the *St. Louis Star* draw a line across his life and declare himself finished with Christianity— "that shit they attempt to ram down your throat in your youth"? Might we find clues to any great fears of death and immortality—even of his boyhood God— beneath the fictive veneer of eating and drinking and fornicating in his fiction? In his braggadocio in tales of big game hunting and blue marlin fishing? In the *cojones* of bull fighting and the mutual slaughtering of Europeans in their world wars?

I taught Hemingway because I was filled with a voyeuristic fascination: one of both respect and revulsion. He was, I like to believe, my complete social opposite once he stepped away from his Christian heritage. How had he learned to live and to die without ever reaffirming the Christ of the New Testament and the God of his boyhood?

SHADOW OF DOUBT
December 6
This afternoon, tired of reading student papers, I picked off the window ledge Kathleen Norris' *Amazing Grace.* In a chapter entitled

simply, "God," I read her summary of Moses' call from the Jehovah of the Burning Bush. She then writes:

> Moses understandably wants to know a bit more about this God who is addressing him. He proceeds by indirection. Not daring to ask God who he is, Moses says instead, "Who am I that I should go to Pharaoh, and lead the Israelites out of Egypt?" God's answer is hardly comforting: "I will be with you." And then follows one of the scariest passages in the Bible. God tells Moses that he will know for certain it is God who has called him to this task *only* when it is accomplished. Only when he has brought the people with him to worship on this mountain.[3]

I had an inexplicable stab of terror! I held at bay the shadow of doubt, not even acknowledging its shape. I did not believe that Norris got the proof of Moses' Divine call correct. Pulled from the shelf *The New English Bible*, where it has sat beside *Webster's Ninth Collegiate Dictionary* for twenty-seven years. There in Exodus, 3:12, I read these words:

"God answered [Moses' query], 'This shall be the proof that it is I who have sent you: when you have brought the people out of Egypt, you shall all worship God here on this mountain."

This mission accomplished is proof that God called his servant to that particular task. Scary indeed, for Moses. And scary, too, for a man retiring from a career to which he imagines he was called home from Africa. Is it only to be next summer and the first academic year free of college teaching that I will be given proof that I was not deluded about my call to leave Zambia and return to EMC in 1972?

Whom have I delivered? At whose mountain did we assemble for worship? Still more scary is the possibility that there will never be any affirmation that I have been about my Father's business these past twenty-seven years. That it was all a delusion. Why am I assaulted now with such shadows of doubt, the initial stab of terror only a little abated?

I am a little consoled with reading further about Moses. He was full of worries: Will his own Hebrew people remember this God called Jehovah? Why should they believe such a God would call a bush shepherd to Pharaoh's courts? Doesn't God himself know that Moses is not quick-witted, that he mumbles his words, that he uses wrenched syntax, not having spoken Hebrew for forty years—let alone the Egyptian tongue? "No, Lord," Moses says, "send whom you will"—but not me.

Angry with Moses, God nevertheless concedes to his reluctant servant's wishes; he'd send Aaron to "be the mouthpiece." Reluctantly Moses kisses his father-in-law good-bye; and taking his wife, Zapporah, and his son Gershom and his brothers, he sets his face for Egypt. But this is not a God you should turn your back on! Just when you think you have struck a deal with him and you take your first stubborn steps of obedience, you find that he is still smarting with anger. One reads this scary verse: "During the journey, while they were encamped for the night, the Lord met Moses, *meaning to kill him* ... but ..." (Exodus 4:24).

God is still so seething with anger against Moses that he could kill him! And would have—except for a pagan wife who bloodies her son. Zapporah circumcises Gershom on the spot and touches Moses with the bloody foreskin of their half-caste son and utters some romantic nonsense about "blood-bridegroom by circumcision." From what dark cave of instincts this primitive rite arises in Ms. Moses we cannot know. But it works. A son's bloody penis atones for his dad's recalcitrance. And the Scripture declares, "So the Lord let Moses alone" (4:26).

I say I am a little consoled by Moses' insistence on proof of his calling. Because I, too, have needed proof of a calling and had several even before I asked. I remember how I felt a strange calmness in my spirit the spring of 1972 after reading the mail from the States one afternoon in Kitwe, Zambia.

Casting about for something to do after Zambia, I was only a little interested in returning to college teaching. Yet one week out of the blue come three missiles from EMC: Anna Kathryn's brother airmailed us a *Shenandoah*, the college's yearbook of his graduating class; a college catalogue, which I had not seen for years, arrived by surface mail; and a personal letter from Dean Miller invited me to return to EMC, for the fall of 1972. Six years earlier I had left EMC for Tanzania, for MCC Akron, for Zambia, after a two-year stint at college teaching. Nothing remarkable about that first attempt stayed in my mind over the six years to lure me back to the college classroom; yet I felt a strange nudge, a calm assurance, that I was to return to EMC.

Twice during the next years at EMC I tried returning to Africa. A Fulbright for teaching journalism/mass communications at the University of Nairobi lay but a breath away. I had passed the State Department hurdles and waited for months for some word from Nairobi. Everything was settled: the house rented, the two children enrolled in schools in Africa, Anna Kathryn with a teaching post at an international school, a home for the dog. Finally, down into March, came a telephone call from Fulbright Washington: the University of Nairobi had decided it did not need a Fulbright professor this year. It was a blow more severe to Anna Kathryn than to me. We had wanted to return to East Africa so our children could gain the experience of their mother's childhood ethos. I did not need to read more English-as-a-Foreign-Language essays but was willing to endure that task for a year for the sake of our children's breadth of education.

Since a Fulbright application is valid for two years, I searched their directory the following year. Evelyn Hone College, Lusaka, Zambia, wanted a teacher of journalism/mass communications. I knew that college fairly well from previous visits during my two years in Zambia at the African Literature Centre, Kitwe, on the campus of the Mindolo Ecumenical Centre. But none of us experienced a great thrill thinking about returning to Zambia. Yet we knew Lusaka would be as close to Tanzania as we could get; we'd do Anna Kathryn's African homelands with the children during holidays.

But exactly the same thing happened. I applied for the post, passed the Fulbright Washington hurdles, waited, and waited. Finally, late spring, the Fulbright officials told me they didn't want to send anyone to the Zambian College; they'd heard that it was on shaky grounds, not having paid their teachers for three months or more. So they withdrew the offer, and once again I found myself at home with EMC.

Is that not enough affirmation that I was to continue where I had first been called? Why then, this afternoon—after twenty-seven years—am I so assaulted with the fear that my life has passed in a mission for which I was never called?

Whom have I delivered? To what mountain for worship? Shall I retreat behind metaphor? This, I might say: Dozens and dozens of students have been delivered from the bondage of poor writing (while I taught hundreds and hundreds, not all have yet been delivered from wandering in a syntactical and rhetorical wilderness!). Might also say, hundreds of students have been delivered from the bondage of provincialism by reading novels of another generation, of another ethos, of another gender, of international writers. Might I also say, a few students have been nudged to join me to worship the Lord, to know the discipline of his Silence, and to seek "the hidden god," as Thomas Merton, the contemplative monk describes him? But should one do a metaphorical and personal reading of Moses' calling? Is it an adequate defense to claim that an old writer and an old teacher of literature is inevitably thus afflicted—to read metaphorically and personally, even when he turns to reading Scripture?

The shadows of this morning's doubts lie across my hours for sleep.

Coda

Teaching Fiction and the Old Verities of the Heart
"What would make class memorable for me would be to get a vision for why you think fiction is an important part of understanding and facing our world." Ryan wrote that sentence (plus three more paragraphs) on the mid-term course evaluation my last semester in the university classroom.

Ryan was a bright, thoughtful student with double majors and double minors: biology and international agriculture, missiology, and English. The previous year we had read together British fiction: James Joyce, D. H. Lawrence, Virginia Woolf. Here now the Americans: Hawthorne, Hemingway, Faulkner, and Toni Morrison. Ryan's query brought us together for a three-hour lunch. My arguments? Reading good literature is a pleasure. Enjoying the reading of a story wrought in well-honed language as a pleasure in and of itself. Additionally, if it touches on the human predicament, fine, even if that is not its first mission. Yet I cannot imagine any great literature not grounded in morality. Further, I noted J. S. Bach's motet with its lines by Johann Franck: "Jesus, priceless treasure, source of purest pleasure– –." One doesn't need to attempt a Greek syllogism to meld these three entities into one experience: Logos, Pleasure, and Fiction.

If we do not nurture this God-given capacity for pleasant aesthetics with the good, we will turn too easily for leisure to the vacuous, the frivolous, and the spiritually injurious. The technological wasteland is filled with another kind of pleasure: salacious MTV, passive sports, movies violent and sexual, contemporary Christian music with its mushy melodic lines, and the narcissistic blather of telly evangelists.

Do not ask that the disguise of literature be laid aside so one can talk about urban renewal or about one's self. Set aside all the psychological chatter about self-enhancement, self-fulfillment, self-empowerment. Allow the literature to be a mask, behind from which characters of today and from across the centuries speak to you of their experiencing the human predicament.

This fictive mask is important. I cannot—indeed, will not—preach in my classroom. That would be poor biblical teaching, poor moral teaching, a poor sociology of peace and justice. Even worse, a poor teaching of literature. So my classroom is not a pulpit.

I learned early in the college classroom that I needed to become the best possible teacher I could be—that was my calling, my mission. Only then did I earn the right to give a Christian apology. I was not called to apologetics. If I attempted that, students would yawn; they had heard it all before, from youth pastors and Sunday school teachers. Boring, boring, boring.

Only when I was first the best possible literature teacher I could be—and one with humility, who took pleasure in youth and their muddle of ideas—only then could I give witness to the eternal "verities and truths of the heart, the old universal truths: love and honor and pity and pride and compassion and sacrifice" (lines from Faulkner's acceptance speech for the Nobel Prize for Literature, 1950)—and the transcendent Christ. But this witness was a whisper or a metaphor or in a parenthetical aside, from behind the mask of great literature. Only then did a few students sit up, lean in, to hear of matters more significant and eternal than Faulkner's novel *Absalom! Absalom!.*

I told Ryan of a pre-med senior who in his last semester risked ignoring his advisor and opted for Continental Fiction, team-taught by Carroll Yoder and me, instead of one more course in human anatomy. On the standard form for course evaluations he wrote: "Long after I have forgotten the names of my classmates I shall remember Dimitri, Ivan, and Alexy of Dostoyevsky's novel, *The Brothers Karamazov,* so deeply have they spoken to me this semester."

So from behind the mask of good fiction I tried to demonstrate psychic poise while living with moral ambiguity. Additionally, to witness to the hieratic transubstantiation of a writer's art, to sustain balance in the socio-ecological system, to keep breathing while squeezed by an institution's matrix, to join the community's quest for shalom, to know grace when the transcendent Christ is silent. But first to be an impassioned teacher, transparent before students. Listening to their youthful groanings of visions that could hardly be uttered. Helping them "to speak themselves into existence" (Frederick Buechner). Catching there again a reminder of once when I was young.

Now in retirement I am remembering those good years—when I was privileged to attend that movable academic literary feast. And I am also discovering how rich is the life beyond an EMU classroom. A grandchild with *Goodnight, Moon* stands waiting for an empty lap.

February 13, 2006
Revised 2007

Notes

1 Omar Eby, "A Distraught Woman," *River Teeth* 8.1 (2001). Reprinted with permission of the University of Nebraska Press.

2 Kathleen Norris, "Perfection," *Christian Century* (February 18, 1998), later reprinted in her *Amazing Grace*.

3 Kathleen Norris, *Amazing Grace: A Vocabulary of Faith* (New York: Riverhead Books, 1998), 110.

CARROLL D. YODER

The Road More Traveled By

When ACRS members Edward Stoltzfus and Ray Gingerich asked me to speak to the increasingly popular early Monday morning sharing of memoirs, I hesitated, I refused, I reconsidered, I worried, enough so that even if I finally took courage to say yes, my hesitation itself needs an explanation.

Those pioneers who preceded me have their rewards—photographs, an autographing party, sincere and well-deserved compliments. And, according to Albert Keim's introduction, "the humble self-effacing personalities of the authors are palpable." Not only that—"most of them were movers and shakers in Mennonite institutions."[1] Where do I fit in? Humble and self-effacing, maybe, but a mover and a shaker I am not. I was a farm boy from Iowa who had the sense not to become a farmer, but instead a teacher of French and English at Eastern Mennonite University (EMU) from 1971 until 2004.

Gustave Flaubert once said that he wanted to write a novel about nothing. That was his way of placing form ahead of content. English teachers, who are expected to wax eloquent at every moment, know about that burden. Whatever the content of our writing, it should be presented flawlessly. Maybe you know where this is leading. A life that does not achieve "mover and shaker" status could nevertheless dazzle listeners and readers if it had Flaubert as its narrator. And thanks to my chosen field, literature, I may allow my imagination to usurp the place of various truth claims.

Therefore, I must speak to my friend Ray Gingerich, who set forth the parameters of my talk in a footnote on page eighty-four of *Making*

Sense of the Journey: The Geography of Our Faith: "The stories shared in the ACRS breakfasts are not intended to be a loosely spun fabric weaving together the entirety of life, but rather a more focused pilgrimage of faith and intellectual evolution."[2]

My whole life has too often resembled a "loosely spun fabric," and those who have been in my classrooms know all about my lack of focus. As for my "faith and intellectual evolution," I come down on the side of Sir Philip Sidney in the battle between the poet and the philosopher, perhaps in part because I have always found philosophy to be more difficult than literature. To understand Sartre's existentialism I read *No Exit* or *The Flies* instead of *Being and Nothingness.* As a naïve graduate student, I neglected Roland Barthes and Jacques Derrida because I found their theoretical criticism of little value for doing an *explication de texte* paper (and also because I did not really understand them).

I may appear as liberal to myself, my family and friends, but I am by nature quite conservative. For example, I do not really condone the tearing down of fences between fiction and non-fiction. I am suspicious of postmodernity, whose relativity may hide a lack of responsibility. Writers like to have it both ways: you cannot criticize my creative non-fiction because only idiots make absolute truth claims; nor can you accuse me of slandering because my work is a piece of fiction. And yet I am prepared to defend Sidney and to engage in some hanky-panky of my own in order to enhance this interpretation of my life.

With the merger of the English and Modern Language Departments and the decline of Interdisciplinary Studies, I became more involved in teaching English at EMU during the 1980s. In 1991 I fictionalized some childhood memories, wrote a number of essays, and later began the Writers Read program, which has been in place now for over fifteen years. During my sabbatical year of 1998–99, I revised and added to my fiction while attending a couple of courses offered by the University of Iowa Writers Workshop. After Omar Eby's retirement I picked up his Creative Writing course by default.

As a believer in recycling, I am including excerpts of my fiction that will serve as support for this presentation. I am even offering my service as a psychological literary critic to bridge the gap between my fiction and non-fiction. With Sir Philip Sidney I defend the imagination and assert that lying is allowed because the poet "is tied to the laws of po-esy, and not of history."

So I am warning you that my subject matter itself has the right to be fairly banal if its presentation is acceptable, but I would also admit that a life well lived trumps a life well written. Instead of footnotes or thesis statements I will use italicized excerpts from some of my fiction. I will focus on my childhood because it is the fiction writer's greatest resource.

Born in 1939, I see myself at the center of living history and a living future. The Civil War is pure history because no one I knew person-ally remembers that time. However, the sinking of the Titanic, the First World War, and Lindberg's flight to Paris are events from my living his-tory because they were witnessed by my grandparents and parents. My living future extends through the life span of my grandchildren. Thus I am somewhere near the center of a time line that begins before 1900 and continues to near the end of this century. I am a bridge from my grandparents to my grandchildren, and a part of my life's purpose is to tie those two ends together.

I will introduce you to my parents and paternal grandparents because the focus of this talk is my childhood. In retirement I am much more engaged with my wife, my two sons, Eric and Joel, and their families. I am a slow learner, but I am now more aware than ever of the ways in which Nancy has been the best spouse I could have found. Her sense of organization, culinary skills, love of travel, common sense, patience, and genuine love—these are only the beginning of a long list of per-sonal qualities that have made the last forty years so delightful. I spend a lot of time on the phone with my two sons, and I often marvel at how much we resemble each other for better or worse. Many of my friends and colleagues know how much pleasure my four grandchildren con-tribute to my life.

The Women of My Childhood: Barbara and "Carrie" Yoder

My grandmother, Barbara Miller Yoder, was born in 1880 on the farm that has stayed in our family since 1874. She and her husband, Harvey Yoder, lived in the little house on the other side of our shared garden. Our houses, woodsheds, a smokehouse, a shop, and outhouses were completely enclosed by a well-kept picket fence. Memories of Grandma are associated with ice tea, celery, a low kitchen sink, Bible stories, Pennsylvania Dutch, a butter churn and molds, crocheted rag rugs, fresh baked bread. Grandma worried a lot; in her recurring dreams she was at the wheel of a car, though never having learned to drive, or caught in the throes of an overflowing toilet. The latter reminds me of the name we used for our outhouses—St. Louis. I think this nightmare occurred because when Grandma went to the St. Louis World's Fair in 1904 a few months before she got married, she discovered its flush toilets, one of the technological marvels associated with that event.

Actually my most inexpressible faith longings are associated with Grandma. It is hard to interpret her unconditional love along with her pessimism and sense of guilt. I tried to capture her influence on me and the ambiguity of my feelings in one of my first vignettes—the story of a little boy whose favorite Old Testament story about Elisha and the two bears is coupled with a memory from my childhood: being fed scraped apple from Grandma's table knife. So here comes my first fictional footnote.

He knew the Old Testament story by heart. Disrespectful children, made bold by their number, had deserved their punishment when they followed the prophet Elisha and yelled insults because he was bald like Grandpa. "Go up thou bald head. Go up thou bald head." Sometimes Darrell said the words to himself, tasting their horribleness.

"Wait, Grandma!" He put one hand on the book to study the picture.

Losing his patience, the prophet had turned to face the crowd of children. He pointed a finger at them while his other hand waved his cane, a big tree stick. His angry face was asking God to punish the children. Darrell couldn't see the faces of the children, but he knew that they were wicked and would get what they deserved at the end of the story.

"Why were the children so bad?"

Grandma sighed. "Ach, mein liebe kind. The world's such a wicked place."

"I'm a good boy, Grandma."

"Of course."

"I wouldn't make fun of Elisha."

"No, of course, you wouldn't. So innocent," she said. "Wicked people don't believe in God."

"I'm a good boy, Grandma."

She nodded. "You will always believe in God." Her voice wavered between a question and a command. Darrell turned to the next page where the two she-bears called by Elisha's curses lunged out of nowhere to eat up forty-two of the children. They fell upon the children, the book said.

"Did Elisha go back to get their clothes?"

"Their clothes?"

"Yes, their clothes. The bears wouldn't eat the children's clothes. Elisha could have saved the clothes—given them to the parents."

"I don't know why you always want me to read this story. I'm afraid it'll make you dream."

"But it's a Bible story." There was no argument against his answer. Mama sometimes refused to read fairy stories—"just too awful"—but no stories in the Bible storybook could be skipped over. Again he saw the two bears come crashing through the brush that bordered the road along the woods' edge. Claws ripping, tearing off clothes as the animals ate the forty-two children in a flash. Did any escape? He shuddered, remembering the three-dimensional Tru-View pictures of Goldilocks and the three bears, especially the tenth frame, which he avoided when he was alone in the living room. The one with the bears standing upright, paws stretched out over the poor girl asleep in Baby Bear's bed.

His mouth opened for the last bit of apple. Carefully he licked the last wetness and watched as Grandma placed the table knife beside the paring knife on top of the collapsed peelings now emptied of all their flesh.

My mother, Caroline Maude Slaubaugh, was a resourceful tomboy who could drive a Model T, catch a mouse barehanded, shuck corn, harrow with horses, and get to church on time. She followed her older brother, Jake, everywhere. She disliked her middle name, but since *Caroline* was too formal, everyone called her Carrie. Some wondered if her independent spirit would rule out marriage; but when she and Lester Yoder were driving up one of those rolling hills of Iowa, she did not hesitate to respond affirmatively to his question: would it be okay for a young twenty-two-year-old to marry a woman six years older?

She kept a diary typical of that time period from the age of sixteen until her death in 1983. The litany of work and social activities left no room for feelings. Only by noting the pattern of absences from church could one guess that she was pregnant although she gave birth to five sons between 1939 and 1950.

I recall the contrasting reactions of my mother and grandmother to my arrival home during Christmas breaks while I was a college student. My grandmother's joy at seeing me was tempered by her knowledge of my future departure: "I'm so glad to see you, but I hate to think that you'll be leaving again so soon." My mother adopted quite a different attitude: "I guess Grandma thinks that I don't have any feelings. I'm just as sorry as she is to see you leave, but it doesn't do any good to give in to your feelings." Thus my mother deliberately adopted an optimistic attitude rather than allowing painful feelings to spoil the pleasures of the holiday season.

My most sustained attempt to understand my mother came about in 1994, eleven years after she died of cancer. I was teaching "The Death of Ivan Ilych" by Leo Tolstoy. Did my mother, like Ivan, experience despair, loneliness, and regret? Did she receive grace during her final moments? To what extent does the account of Ivan Ilych's life, "most simple and most ordinary and therefore most terrible," describe a universal experience, one that I cannot confirm or refute definitively and personally until I meet my own death?

Like Ivan my mother was a "capable, cheerful, good-natured, and sociable" person "strict in the fulfillment of what [she] considered to be [her] duty." She took pride in her loyalty to the church, the appearance of her house and garden, the accomplishments of her children. Like Ivan she held the expression of her emotions carefully in check in order to follow through on her goals. Work oriented her existence, whether done for herself, her family, or her church. She loved painting, varnishing, wallpapering, and making minor home repairs. The phrase "everything's a trouble to me" (meaning work) was the closest she came to expressing feelings of depression.

Because my mother had always controlled her environment so effectively, I wondered how she would react to terminal cancer. Would her carefully woven world finally unravel? Would emotions surface that had never before been allowed? She cited Psalm 46 as her favorite scripture. That choice reflected both her determination to conquer negative feelings as well as her faith commitment. While I cannot answer my original question about my mother's state of mind before death, I draw comfort and inspiration from her example.

My story begins with my mother and an old family photo. I pick it up and imagine future pain in Mother's eyes and down-turned mouth. That's because I know her mother will die of cancer within four years, but in 1915 no one smiles for a photographer. One does not desecrate such a solemn occasion. Mother's eyes are focused on the stranger behind the camera, afraid of the lights, uneasy with a man who dares to joke his way across the divide that separates plain Mennonites from the world. She is already cooperative and in control, her outspread fingers clasping knees under the pleats of her skirt, black shoes and black stockings suspended in mid-air between the curved legs of the stool. The photo records a split second of death in time, the price of its preservation for over 90 years.

The Men of My Childhood: Lester and Harvey Yoder

Years ago my father quoted Psalm 16:5–6 as the basis of the personal testimony that he gave at West Union Mennonite Church near Parnell, Iowa, our home church. "The Lord is the portion of mine inheritance and of my cup; thou maintainest my lot. The lines are fallen unto me in pleasant places, yea, I have a goodly heritage"(KJV).

My father knew well the meaning of "lines…fallen…in pleasant places." He pictured those lines as fences and roads cutting across Iowa fields. As a loyal member of a rural Mennonite community, he had a sense of right and wrong that seemed as dependable as the square miles and forty-acre fields. His faith was rooted in the soil of the farm where his mother was born.

Those "lines…fallen…in pleasant places" recalled a white picket fence as well as the barbed wires that kept the hogs, the Holsteins and the Angus in fields and barnyard lots. Straight-line roads, often rutted or dusty, led to his home church and the homes of friends and relatives.

My father's reading of Psalm 16 was biased—shaped by the stability of a lifetime on one farm and formed by the discipline of an extended family and church. The lines and pleasant places and the goodly heritage promised him the fullness of joy in verse eleven, a place at the right hand of God where there are "pleasures for evermore." He appreciated and defended God's boundaries as they were revealed through the Scriptures and Mennonite traditions. He also noted the way that time was moving the fence lines of his existence. Technology replaced the community-based rituals of threshing and corn shucking with efficient combine and corn picker harvesting. It caused him to expand his allotted land to over 400 acres. Horse harnesses, cream separators, iceboxes, and push mowers all disappeared. West Union members lost their distinctive plain clothing, forgot how to speak Pennsylvania Dutch, and watched their young people run to Iowa City for pizza and a movie—enjoyable substitutes for the traditional Young People's Meetings each Sunday evening.

In this next excerpt from fiction, Darrell is telling his Sunday School teacher about his first encounter with field work.

"Think I can disk cornstalks?"

Papa smiled. "Just keep your eye on the line each time you cross the field. Don't overlap too much—just takes extra time and gas. Don't leave any undisked ground either. We don't want skipping or overlapping. All afternoon the phrase rang in his ears: "No skipping, no overlapping."

Setting the throttle at the right speed had been easy; because the field had no big hills, he could leave the tractor in third gear. His turns got a little wide at times, but he was improving. Following the line drawn by the disk was another matter. When he watched back over his shoulder, the tractor slipped off course. Looking straight ahead, he worried about skipping a bit, overlapping too much. Even worse, the wind-whipped dust sometimes swirled in front of him, wiping out his line so completely that he wandered aimlessly, sure that he was leaving large gaps of undisked field or passing over the same ground two or three times. With his back to the sun, the dust settling a bit, he would catch sight again of the swath he had made and would thank God for answering his prayers until the line would suddenly veer to the right or to the left. Should he overlap boldly, setting a straight path across the field or should he follow the curve created by his confusion?

"But that wasn't the worst part."

Clayton grunted sympathetically. "A bad way to start field work."

"I don't understand how it could happen so quick. Just like that I missed a turn—the kind where you turn towards the fence instead of away from it."

"And you hit the fence?'

"Worse."

His words set a scene that flickered in his mind like a bad fluorescent light. "I couldn't hit the clutch." Against the fence, the front wheels were rising, bouncing wildly. "I couldn't hit the clutch."

Helpless, he had held the wheel of his bucking monster, heard a post crack,

watched the fence disappear beneath him, finally found the clutch after the trac-
tor and disk had both invaded Homer Hochstedler's alfalfa field.

"And then...?"

"I drove right back through the fence, kept on disking until Papa came after
he finished the chores. Told him right away."

There had been plenty of time to prepare his story for Papa as the sun fell
behind Honey Joe's hill and he switched on the Ferguson's lights. Although he
could see only yards ahead, he no longer worried about skipping and overlap-
ping. Nor did it bother him that his early turns along the battered fence left wide
patches of cornstalks untouched by the disk.

"I hope your father wasn't too upset. He doesn't seem like the kind."

"No, he hardly said anything."

Neither to Darrell nor to the rest of the family. Between fried potatoes and
rolls, the Saturday supper talk passed safely from one ordinary happening to an-
other, not omitting casual praise for a field well-disked on a March day (colder than
a person would think), assuring Russell that his day, too, would come—maybe
already next year. Later in bed Darrell had strained to hear the soft murmurs
from the open door of his parents' bedroom at the end of the hall.

"I didn't say anything at supper, and Grandpa can fix it on Monday. No
use that the boys find out."

He had blessed Papa's kindness, a kindness that lifted slightly the heavy
shadow of the accident. Papa knew how important it was to save him. Grandpa,
too, would hold his tongue.

Of all my adult relatives, I probably identified most closely with my
grandfather, Deacon Harvey M. Yoder. Heart attacks in 1945 and 1947 put
an end to hard labor, so I remember him as the man who took charge of
the garden tractor, gathered eggs, caught mice with a mechanical trap,
preached occasionally, trapped visiting salesmen into long conversations,
read his Bible faithfully, snored on the sun porch after lunch, ate raw
onions while working in the garden, used a pistol to shoot sparrows that
dared to nest in our martin house, usually coasted his new, black 1949
Ford halfway into a crossroads before stopping, found room in his basement for the resident tramp. Grandpa was conservative, good-natured,
an easy touch. I shared his optimism, love of conversation, generosity
occasionally misplaced, loyalty to the church and family, and indiscrimi-
nate love of food. I hold him responsible, too, for my lack of hair. The

fiction that follows was inspired by a memory fragment about Clayton, a Mennonite boy who went into the army during World War II. Darrell is just outside his pigeon house, listening in to a conversation between Grandpa and Clayton. The latter is feeling ambivalent about returning to the fellowship. When I had my students critique this story, some responded negatively, some positively to Grandpa. Clayton is commenting here on his friendship with an army friend.

"More than a friend—the most unselfish and dedicated man I ever met. A farm boy from near Des Moines. Handsome and gentle, but as strong as Willis Martin." (Grandpa sucked in a breath of appreciation.) "Charlie was a born again Christian."

"So even there in the army you must have had chances to witness."

Clayton's voice betrayed a brittle edge. "I had nothing to tell him. Charlie prayed every night, a lot more than I ever did. He was the good Christian. I wasn't."

"But now you're asking to come back into the church. Des Moines's not far. You could invite him down some time." Grandpa never missed a chance to meet people.

"Charlie's dead." In the silence that followed, Darrell's saw rasped back to life, assuring the men that he was busy with his work outside.

"Dead," Grandpa said. "My, oh. Dead."

"Charlie was fighting for the Lord, for his family, his country. I was just there, going back and forth as loose as a penny in a washing machine."

"Charlie thought he was fighting for the Lord," Grandpa corrected. "But we must obey the Scriptures and harken to the Holy Spirit. Not all who say Lord, Lord—"

"Don't say that, Brother Miller!" Clayton stood up abruptly. He stepped through the doorway dividing the feed room from the pigeon pen, surveyed a row of nests and homemade perches already fastened to the east wall.

"Pigeons! The boy is going to raise pigeons." Darrell wondered why Clayton sounded angry about pigeons. "What for? I learned a lot about those birds when I was in Europe. In the first World War pigeons would deliver messages."

"I've heard about that," Grandpa said.

"Imagine! Pigeons helping our soldiers fight for peace, but really they were just turning tail and flying back home as fast as they could. Like good Mennonites."

"It's their nature. That's why they're called homers."

"I know," Clayton said. "Pigeon races. You know what a stool pigeon is, Brother Miller?"

"A man who betrays ..."

"It's a fake pigeon that draws other birds to their death. That's what I felt like in the army. Too much milk of human kindness and fear ever since I warmed the benches of Hickory Creek Church. I wasn't a good soldier, Brother Miller."

"I'm glad to hear that."

"You don't understand." Clayton was pacing the floor between the feed room and the pigeon pen. "Charlie was no ordinary friend. He was the best friend any man could ever wish for. If God sends him to hell, I'm not standing in line for heaven. It just doesn't make sense."

Grandpa's hands were clasped together, and he was rubbing one thumb against the other to help himself think. "We're living in a fallen world, and we see through a glass darkly; but we have the Scriptures and the fellowship of the believers."

"Charlie was a believer—a better Christian than I could ever hope to be."

"The war's been confusing," Grandpa said. "I'm sorry, but I'm glad that you've come to talk. You said you wanted to come back into the fellowship. Seven years is a long time."

"I want to do what's right, Brother Miller, but it seems like the Scriptures are too small for the mess this world's in. Can I confess to a sin that Charlie thought was a commandment of the Lord? The Bible says there's no greater love than laying down your life for a friend. Charlie claimed that verse. He didn't betray his friends. He wasn't no kissing Judas."

"I'm not asking you to let down Charlie," Grandpa said. "I'm asking you to follow Jesus, who sacrificed his life like a Mennonite. He died for his enemies; he didn't kill them."

"With all due respect, Brother Miller, it seems you've got that backwards," Clayton chuckled. "The Mennonites believed that they were dying like Jesus."

"You have to come of your own free will," Grandpa said. "It does no good to force people."

"Seven years of praying gets a little wearing for a person. I'm tired of hanging on the edge." Darrell waited for Grandpa to say something that would help give Clayton the little shove that he needed to make up his mind, but he said nothing. "You can call on me Sunday, Brother Miller. I don't see any other way

*out of this mess. I'll testify to peace with God and my fellow men and ask to be
received back into the fellowship."*

*Grandpa rose, a hesitant smile on his face, his hands outstretched. "Welcome
home, brother," he said, giving Clayton the holy kiss from the book of James.*

Radios and Revival Meetings

A strong interest in technology runs through our family. My uncle Roy
was an amateur inventor who made money with his ice saw, custom
corn shellers, and balers before he bought a tiling machine and several
Caterpillars. My son Eric designed and built his own house. All that
eluded me completely, not that I didn't have an interest in the subject. I
daydreamed constantly about books, sports, airplanes, radio, and television and was always fascinated by technology even if I did not understand it. As a result I tried all kinds of impractical gimmicks to teach
French, such as dragging a heavy reel-to-reel video recorder and camera
to Quebec in 1972 to record TV programs and interviews. Later I wasted
a lot of time typing out scripts from those programs, photocopying them
onto overhead transparencies, cutting and then Scotch taping them end-
to-end. It was my inefficient system of closed captions in French that
required my presence to make sure that the captions were synchronized
with the dialog. I was always looking for the perfect technique to teach
a language. My love/hate contradictory attitude toward the media (I am
both a consumer and a critic) has become only more exacerbated with
the advent of the digital age.

He often leafed his way through an issue of Popular Mechanics *until he
found an article on how to build a radio. Undeterred by the hopelessness of the
ritual, he would leave the pigeon house with the magazine, propelled by a familiar optimism towards the old shop, which held a table saw, drawers of nails,
nuts, bolts, washers, hog rings, wire, binder twine, electric fence insulators and
spark plugs, oiled shovels and spades hanging from the wall, a workbench with
a vise good for cracking nuts and flattening tin cans, boards of various sizes, a
large iron kettle for making lye soap—everything needed to fix things on the
farm, but nothing to make a radio.*

*Perhaps he thought that sheer determination would work a miracle, causing
the necessary parts to materialize like magic on the workbench in front of him.
But it never did; baling wire and a scrap of plywood could not substitute for the
circles and zigzags of the mysterious diagrams in the magazine.*

He had hinted, asked quietly, and then begged for a radio. Papa said no without sounding upset. Uncle Lloyd had a radio, most of the people at Hickory Creek Mennonite had radios, and two families had television sets. Darrell understood that Papa wasn't interested in radios, nor did he have time to listen to one. "What would Grandpa say?" Papa had asked. He was living on Grandpa's farm and wouldn't do anything to upset him because Grandpa was a good deacon in the church and older and wiser than Papa, who was after all still his boy.

Building a radio was Darrell's only hope. "What's that you've got there?" Grandpa and Papa would ask, hearing music and static coming from the old shop.

Darrell would smile quietly. "Just a radio I put together in my spare time."

"Like his Uncle Lloyd," they would agree, their pride in his accomplishment neutralizing any arguments against a radio.

The 1952 revival campaign of Howard Hammer shook up my home community. Over 900 persons found their way to the altar. Daily conversations were laced with words like *restitution, sin,* and *confession.* I remember the nightly drama in a cow pasture next to the Lower Deer Creek church with a strange mixture of excitement, inspiration, and guilt. Did I really enjoy the sermons, or was my enthusiasm motivated by the comments of friends and family members? Fifteen years later when I was a graduate student at the University of Iowa, I attended a few of George R. Brunk II's revival meetings. My disillusionment then mirrored my early adolescent feelings when I returned to a Nancy Drew book. Was this really the same book that had captured my imagination in third and fourth grade?

Darrell felt rewarded, blessed to see the gathering of the harvest—not a fair-weather fan like Eddy Bontrager, who suddenly supported the Philly Whiz Kids when he realized that the pennant was within their grasp. He had been on Brother Martin's side from the beginning, a spring training prayer partner. He loved the extra innings after the benediction when Brother Jantzi led the faithful in singing "There's Power in the Blood" and "Bringing in the Sheaves," giving the counselors time to guide the seekers to a saving knowledge of God's grace in the room behind the platform. His heart overflowed to see the victorious ones filled with a newfound courage mounting the steps of the platform, then laughing and crying their way through their testimonies.

That was before Brother Martin preached from Psalm 19:12: "Who can un-
derstand his errors? cleanse thou me from secret faults" (KJV). A chasm split
open beneath his feet; the Psalmist spared no one: "Thou hast set our iniqui-
ties before thee, our secret sins in the light of thy countenance." Darrell knew
about his secret sin, took care of it regularly during nightly prayers, but now
Brother Martin was dragging secret sins out into the open, exposing them to
God's light, using them for His glory to bring more souls to repentance. Darrell
shuddered. To voice a secret sin before a counselor—Brother Mast or Brother
Swartzendruber. It was beyond his imagination; only in silent prayers could he
unveil his iniquity. Although the evangelist dropped secret sins the following
night to prey upon familiar vices, Darrell felt his burden grow heavier, dulling
the joy of the late-night victory sessions.

Brother Jantzi had moved the crowd from singing to humming on "Just As
I Am." "He's calling you to come home; this your last night to find your way
back to a Heavenly Father who's waiting patiently with open arms. Come home
to Jesus." Sustained by soft humming, Brother Martin's hushed plea hovered
over the crowd, powerful in its gentleness.

"Oh God!" Darrell felt a desperate prayer rising from within, calling for
courage to defend his enemy, the secret sin, one verse at a time.

Taking the Road Away from Iowa

One of the ways that a writer of fiction cheats is to make the central characters' actions or words carry future significance that would have been
unlikely at the time. The message is implicit rather than explicit. In these
scenes from my childhood I am more interested in linking past memories to my present life than in recalling accurately what I believe took
place. Entertainment, pleasure, insight—call it what you will—trumps
historical accuracy. For example, Philippe Labro, a French journalist and
novelist who attended Washington and Lee from 1954 to 1956, wrote a
coming of age novel thirty years later that included a fine analysis of
racism and the awakening of the civil rights movement—something I
believe he could not have done as a young student in the 1950s. Labro
told me that his anorectic character Elizabeth was partially inspired by
an American au pair girl who lived with Labro's family in Paris. The
main character's description of a trip to Charlottesville to hear William
Faulkner never took place in real life—a fact that Labro asked me not

Working on dissertation, 1973

to reveal, hoping that his readers would assume that he had actually met Faulkner.

Blurring the differences between real life memory and fiction with one eye to the future helps to create a purposeful narrative. As an optimist I have usually prided myself on what I thought was the inevitable direction that my life had taken. When I look back, it seems that I never had to make truly agonizing choices, nor was I tortured by some terrible mistake.

My love of books and a lack of ability or interest in farming meant that I knew from the beginning that I would go to school as long as possible. I lacked the rebellious spirit of an older cousin, so I did not even question the assumption that I would attend EMC (Eastern Mennonite College, later University) in the fall of 1958. For an impractical reader, it made sense to major in English and history. Garrison Keillor would have approved.

I graduated in 1962, the year that the Mennonite Central Committee launched the Teachers Abroad Program in Africa, and I chose the Congo because that provided free French study—a no-brainer decision. I learned that I would be going to Brussels instead of Paris a few days before the boat sailed, and I ended up staying with a family who were running a youth hostel because no one had made definite arrangements before my arrival. Who could have asked for anything better? I practically worshiped a couple of mentors in Brussels and then Kinshasa, David Shank and Elmer Neufeld.

Upon my return I was hungry for graduate training. Again it seemed that there was nothing to decide. I could kill two birds with one stone by studying French literature. Furthermore, in-state tuition, free board and room at home, and a rather sophisticated but traditional European faculty all made the University of Iowa a win-win situation. An exchange program sponsored by the French department sent me back to France for a year as an English assistant in Paris, and then I spent a few additional months in Germany and Portugal.

I began corresponding with Nancy Myers during that time after a mutual friend let me know that she had told Nancy to expect a letter from Paris. So we met at the Philadelphia airport over a year later. It was love at first sight for both of us; I did not mind that we got lost on our way back to her apartment. We found many common values—our Mennonite heritage, commitment to Christian service, love of travel, graduate school, and good food. I knew that we were making rapid progress when Nancy, always fearful of flying, used her tax refund check to pay for a ticket to Cedar Rapids. The ticket and the refund came out the same to the penny.

We got married on June 6, 1970, at Vincent Mennonite Church in Spring City, Pennsylvania. I passed my exams in July; and we moved to Bloomington, Indiana, under a Big Ten program that allowed me to do my doctoral research on the French African novel under Emile Snyder. My dissertation was eventually published years later (in 1991) by Three Continents Press as *White Shadows: A Dialectical View of the French African Novel*. This general survey, inspired by Sartre's "Black Orpheus," included French and African writers from roughly 1880 until 1980, showing how the thesis (white supremacy) yielded to the antithesis (Negritude and anticolonial themes) before moving on to a tentative synthesis (a thematic shift from racism to social and economic issues).

I did not hesitate when Myron Augsburger asked me that winter if Nancy and I would join the EMC faculty for the fall semester of 1971 although I was aware of an opening in French African literature at

Wooster College in Ohio. Later I was invited to apply to Wheaton, but I preferred staying with family and friends in a Mennonite area with a kinder climate.

I am deeply grateful to the EMU community, which allowed me to spend a lot of time in cross-cultural settings. The needs of the school coincided with what I imagined was my "deep gladness," to quote Frederick Buechner. As an unorganized generalist who would prefer to start a new and risky project to finishing the task at hand, I now understand better how EMU sometimes facilitated my weaknesses for its own purposes. I was always ready to try a new course. I did not keep up in my field of French African literature—not too surprising when one realizes that an African literature course (half English half French in translation taught every other year) came out to three percent of my teaching load.

I enjoyed teaching lower level French because of the pedagogical challenges. In the language classroom one may discuss any subject if one has the necessary vocabulary. Unfortunately, most of the time that discussion is limited to what we already know—the sky is blue, the boy in the blue sweater is asleep, etc., etc. Thus the language teacher subverts the intent of language, which is to communicate something significant. The most fearsome enemy is boredom rather than intellectual understanding.

My French load was nicely balanced by a variety of English and interdisciplinary courses. The latter provided a wonderful introduction to teaching as I learned from colleagues—Al Keim, Omar Eby, Herb Martin, Roland Fisch, John Horst, Anna Frey, Arlene May, Steve Dintaman, to name a few. During the mid-1970s, I became obsessed by the winds of behaviorism that tore through campus with all the energy of a George Brunk II revival. That experience did me a big favor: I finally understood why I was in the humanities. It is a long story, but I knew that the winds would turn when Al Keim admitted to me that he did not want EMC measuring his spiritual progress with a behavioral-based module.

From the time that I was a child the year 2004 carried a kind of magic quality for me because I knew that was the theoretical end of my career, so even the decision to retire then was not as significant as I might have imagined. As I watched the widening cultural differences between me and my students, observed how easy it was to become a critical and somewhat indifferent grouch about school matters, I decided that grandchildren, gardening, travel, and volunteer work would provide a good transition.

Difficult choices based upon an aggressive awareness of one's responsibility and a willingness to face failure honestly bring their own rewards. One can make a good case for rebellion, something that is hard to admit when one is raising teenagers, especially those who like experimenting with explosives or motorcycles. I am a little puzzled by my most fictional footnote in this talk, and yet it is something I need to own.

The setting is a funeral in a rural Mennonite church in which the mother responds angrily to the suicide of her son. The main characters are all fictional and serve, I suppose, to surface feelings that I would not normally own. Perhaps my easy and passive acceptance of the direction my life has taken carries some consequences that become most evident in fiction.

Although Darrell's heart had been turned against Bishop Byler, the awful logic of his speech had exposed the weak and wishy-washy arguments of Brother Mast for what they were, a desire to paint over a peeling wall that needed scraping with a wire brush. The bishop's words left no room for escape. The only sound was the rustling of the wind in the cornfield on the west side of the church and the whoosh of a passing car on the gravel road. Grandpa was holding his forehead as if he hoped to shield himself from the tragedy that had been visited upon the congregation. Both of Brother Mast's hands were on the pulpit, clutching it as he often did during his sermons when he was driving home an important point, but this time he seemed to be searching for support, holding on as best he could.

For the first time Darrell succumbed to the full weight of his teacher's useless death. To be sure, the bishop saw it as a warning, one that could compel sinners to stop dead in their tracks and give their hearts to the Lord. His plan might work for regular Mennonite sinners who got an extra boost from Christian teaching at home and in the church, but what was the use of warning the English who weren't able to live up to their strength of their convictions? In the end, Clayton had failed. Brother Mast and Bishop Byler were both making the best of things—holding out a false hope, believing that God would either forgive him or use this terrible sin to straighten out the wayward.

In the middle of the front bench just below the pulpit, Nellie Murphy rose to her feet. The silence that had been focused on Brother Mast fell upon the widow, a small woman in a solid black cape dress. Her white prayer covering blended naturally with her long gray hair twisted into a modest bun. Despite her grief, Nellie Murphy was still in control, an unfolded handkerchief in one hand, the white ribbons from her prayer veiling, two righteous lines against the shoulders of her dark dress. Like the bishop she turned to face the congregation, and her soft voice carried to the back benches of the wing, so quiet was her audience.

"I have nothing to say which is more than the two men who have just spoken." She paused, prolonging a painful silence and imposing on her listeners the memories of a love that had brought a stranger into their midst. It was a silence that carried all the grief and bitterness of more than thirty troubled years between Nellie and Clive, between her family and the church.

Clive Murphy had not been the first to marry into the congregation. The Lamb sisters had both found good husbands at Hickory Creek and had accepted as part of the bargain the covering, the long hair and all the rest of the doctrines and practices of the Mennonite Church. Only occasionally did a flippant but good-natured remark or an unusual dish at a potluck remind the people of the sisters' origins.

With Clive it had not been the same. "A poor soul," Grandma used to say sympathetically. "A poor soul." Nellie was not one to go down without a fight. When Clive began to drink again and wrote bad checks for farm machinery that wasn't needed, she never complained but had a talk with the banker who closed off her husband's checking account. She spent more time in the fields and less in her garden.

"I have nothing to say," Nellie began again. "I mean I've got no advice for Brother Mast or the congregation—not even for Bishop Byler." Her eyes flashed in direct contradiction to her words. "But I've got plenty to say to the Almighty Himself." The preacher and the bishop looked at each other, their animosity swallowed up in mutual fear. What kind of blasphemy was the woman going to visit upon the congregation?

"The Lord has some explaining to do in all this mess. He knows that I never loved two men more than Clive and Clayton. The one's at Anamosa for the rest of his life because he shot a man when he was drunk. That penitentiary took a burden off my back, but it didn't bring any peace to my soul. The other's in a casket, and none of us knows all the reasons for that." Her eyes swept past the bishop. "None of them has anything to do with sin. I never heard a mean

word from Clayton, more than one can say about a some of the saints in this congregation."

"Lord, you know I did my part." For a second Nellie raised her head as if she could see right through the high, plastered ceiling of the church house. *"I led Clive to Hickory Creek, had him baptized, married him, kept in the fold for over ten years, and invested a plenty of prayer time on him. I did just as much for my son. I brought Clayton here every Sunday since he was five weeks old, saw him baptized at fourteen, prayed him back into the fellowship after he came back from the army. I done all I could and then some, but you've not been much help, Lord."*

The way Nellie bore down hard on *"Lord"* made Darrell realize that Hickory Creek was caught up in the middle of a eyes-open prayer, one that had almost no resemblance to what followed Brother Mast's *"Let us pray"* when the congregation rumbled to its knees, foreheads pressed against the backs of varnished benches, ears attuned to a familiar rhythm of thee's and thou's.

Nellie Murphy was talking back to the Lord on His home grounds like some disobedient child or woman rebelling against a father or husband. *"And your people here did their part most of the time,"* she continued, giving the congregation the benefit of the doubt. In her anger against the Lord she was passing over her grievances against family and church members who had been as unsuccessful as she in making Clive over into a full-blooded Mennonite.

"You tell us to ask and it shall be given. I've asked and what did I get—a jail and a cistern, that's what. I'm done with asking. If You didn't see fit to straighten things out while my son was still alive, there's no point in crawling after some Catholic fairy tale like purgatory."

There was no summing up, not even an amen, to alert Nellie's audience to the end of her prayer. One moment she was holding God and the congregation hostage to her recriminations, and the next she was seated again, head bowed, shoulders hunched over her grief and rage.

Brother Mast did the only thing that he could think of to save the situation. He motioned to the octet. *"'My Heavenly Home is Bright and Fair'"* and make it all five verses," he said, retreating to the minister's bench behind the pulpit.

"Two roads diverged in a wood, and I—/I took the one less traveled by,/ And that has made all the difference." Robert Frost (in "The Road Not Taken") makes a good case for creative individuality, but I doubt that his poem tells my story. I took the road more traveled because of the map provided by my faith community. Should I brag or suffer remorse? As a child, like everyone else I felt unique—*apart from* but also *a part of* my people. I assumed that the road more traveled would keep me faithful to God and my community—that it was the right road, the one most likely to bring me happiness and peace of mind. With the passing of time I understand that life is not that simple. There were many roads I could have taken, some more courageous or creative. Occasional regrets do not remove a sense of gratitude inspired by God and sustained by my heritage, family and friends.

April 14, 2008
Revised 2008

Notes

1 Robert Lee and Nancy V. Lee, eds. *Making Sense of the Journey: The Geography of our Faith* (Harrisonburg, VA: Anabaptist Center for Religion and Society, 2007).

2 *Ibid.,* 84.

PART IV

Making Sense of the Journey

... as Internationalists

VERNON E. JANTZI

The Search for Wholeness in the Morass of Mennonite Institutional Life

I stood on a cliff looking out over Saginaw Bay, recalling memories of my childhood and youth while a few paces behind me two men put the final touches on my father's grave in the AuGres-Sims Cemetery. It was May of 1996 and the first time death had come to my immediate family. Then in January 2003 in the middle of a bitterly cold Michigan winter, we reenacted the ritual for my mother to complete the generation of William Troyer Jantzi and Rose Knepp Swartz Jantzi. When I later visited the gravesites in June that year to participate with my three siblings and our children in one of our many family rituals to commemorate important transitions, I suddenly realized in a why-didn't-I-see-this-earlier moment that we Mennonites are clustered in contiguous plots on the edge of this cemetery much as we lived in our "failed Amish community" in the hinterlands of AuGres, Michigan.

My grandparents and their friends had drained the Lake Huron wetlands to build their farms after accepting a homesteading offer by the state of Michigan in the early 1900s. The farms lay nearly side by side in plot-like sections of the Arenac County landscape. They and their children mingled freely with their neighbors on their farms wedged in between or in the middle of Mennonite farms because everyone shared Pennsylvania Dutch as the mother tongue. This little coffin-shaped culture region was mostly Mennonite but included Lutherans and Catholics as well though they were clearly the minority in this tiny Mennonite homeland. In the midst of the cemetery ritual I realized at a much deeper

level than ever before that these were my people and I was their son.
I pondered anew and more profoundly my life's course in Mennonite
community and institutions.

The challenge to tell my story has caused me some trepidation because most of our efforts to recall and share about ourselves are really
exercises in laying presumed facts end to end or side by side like Lego
or Scrabble pieces to make sense of the chaos of life at a given time.
However, such placing of remembered facts does not detract from the
effort to be true to our history; it just means that our history changes
over time and space. What seemed so true back then is today more relative or open to different interpretations, especially when we reflect on
our life events informed by the social sciences. Actually, all of my life
I have gained great satisfaction from inventing or starting something
new, making something really nice, fixing something broken or "taking one for the team"—putting the welfare of the group above my own.
I have enjoyed other people, listening to their stories, sharing laughter
and excitement about the mundane and exceptional in life, and sometimes just sitting quietly together. So I ask anew, "Who am I and why
am I like I am?"

The Foundations of a Social Entrepreneur

The little white clapboard-sided church on Twining Road about a mile
from our farm served as the focal point for a lot of the social activities
of Mennonite and other children and young people in the area, especially before the two-room country school fell to the ax of annexation.
As preadolescents we argued long and hard after church about the best
tractors and cars years before we could drive them.

The Sunday evening children's meeting stands out as one of my
fondest memories as a youngster. We loved to compete in Bible drills to
find the reference read out by the leader. The winner always got a small
reward of some kind. If it was my Uncle Andrew on one of his preaching
forays through Michigan, it was usually a quarter or half dollar. I muse
today about how significant these children's meetings might have been
in fanning my passion to take calculated risks as a social entrepreneur.
After all, if you wanted to beat your friends, you had to be thinking
about where to find a particular book of the Bible so that at the signal

you would head for the right part of the Bible, a split second advantage that often meant the difference between being first or second. Also, after you jumped up, you had to risk that you would find the actual verse on the page by the time the leader called on you to read it.

These were calculated risks, not wild guesses, in children's meeting in church, but what better preparation to live and function successfully in a capitalist world where the ability to take calculated risks is essential? These lessons would serve me well later as I worked to create new programs and practices in the institutions that employed me. With the exception of the value of nonresistance, I now marvel at how readily our nonconformist congregation socialized us youngsters to conform to many of the core values of our society and to be nonconformist in areas that were less vital in terms of challenging the larger economic and cultural system, but very important in drawing the boundaries of the Mennonite community.

Family dynamics probably have an even more significant impact on one's formation than church in small tightly knit rural communities. As a youngster I sat for hours with my mother and Grandmother Swartz, who taught me to be as efficient and creative as possible but still to do a good job. I learned all the tricks of how to peel an apple quickly and not leave much fruit on the peel. I also discovered that when one cuts up peaches or pears to be canned, it is important to make the slices as uniform as possible and then to place them in such a way that the finished product in the glass jars appears like uniform slices, not a bunch of uneven chunks with their pit cavities exposed. The same precision held for quilting. The stitches had to be small and tight. If not, the sewer had to tear them out and do them over again. It was painful to see one's work destroyed but even more painful to destroy it oneself and do it again.

My father loved to invent gadgets, anything that would save labor and increase efficiency. He typically saw life as a puzzle to figure out or a challenge to overcome. My older brother, Marvin, learned how to do mechanical things while I learned to quilt and cut up vegetables and fruits. When my sisters, Sharon and Virginia, eventually pushed me outside, I stepped into my brother's shoes because he had gone away to do his alternative service at Michigan State University in East Lansing, a hundred or so miles away in distance but light years away in world view.

That winter I worked with my father to invent and construct a device to pick up our round hay bales mechanically. He taught me, sometimes less than patiently, to make perfectly rippled seams with the arc welder and to be as proud of them as I was of precisely sliced peaches and pears. However, what I learned most of all was that if a person ran up against a problem or lacked a particular part, an alternative existed; one just had to figure out what it was. Another lesson was that one always approached any problem or challenge with a preferred plan and a reasonable alternative just in case.

Community's Costs and Benefits

I lived and breathed church-based community from my earliest memories. It was far from perfect. We suffered traumas of physical and sexual abuse and infidelity, as well as the rest of the "seven deadly sins." Nevertheless, it was also powerfully redemptive even in its imperfection. Adults and children gathered at the church to worship, work, or play generally in intergenerational teams. (When a total congregation consists of 100 or fewer persons, it means that a large percentage of the congregation participates in these activities.) My father, though not a preacher, often ran the show along with a few other leaders. He always exercised leadership as an opinion shaper and informal leader. If people needed to test an idea or had a problem that needed a solution, they typically showed up at our house. We children learned a lot by listening as we hung around the kitchen table, where most of those discussions took place. Clearly the ability to help one another was among the benefits of community and extended family that we enjoyed.

However, in my early teen years I discovered a facet of community I had not recognized earlier. My parents, along with an uncle and aunt, had become attracted to the ministry of a child preacher and divine healer known as "Little David." I rather enjoyed the music and hubbub of the masses in the Flint City Arena. I had never attended any meetings of this size, so I was excited. This was a new world for me.

However, the church sent small delegations to visit my parents, and I assume my uncle and aunt as well, to ask them not to attend any more of these mass meetings in Flint. My parents disregarded the pleas of the congregation and with my uncle and aunt continued to make the trips to Flint. Soon it reached the point where they were given a choice: Either they quit attending Little David's meetings or they would have to leave the church. After much prayer and weeping my parents submitted, and I learned that even a loving community can be unbending.

I thought that only my type of Mennonites and the Amish set such choices, but eventually I discovered that similar requirements are common to all strong communally oriented groups anywhere in the world. While I had became aware of our great differences with "the world" at a superficial level, I later saw our vast sociological similarities to other tightly knit marginal political, religious, and ethnic communities everywhere. We defined our behavior as faithfulness to God; but to most social scientists, even though we may have been odd, we were nothing more than an interesting sociological example of a particular type of social organization.

Individual costs can be high in community as well. I remember that my Uncle Elmer, who, though in his twenties had not gone beyond the eighth grade, was part of the "lot" with two other men from which our congregation would choose a minister, or preacher, to use our terms. When he opened his hymnal and found the slip, he cried.

Some years later I asked about his feelings when the lot fell on him. He took a deep breath, exhaled forcefully, and said that he was upset and frightened. He was full of questions and doubts. He wondered how he could preach with only an eighth-grade education. How could he preach and also make a living when he did not even know how to farm yet? In his voice I heard the angst of a frightened and disappointed young man whose life dreams had been radically changed by pure "luck of the draw," so to speak. He was definitely not a young man who had pined to be a preacher, but the view was that now by God's grace through the process of the lot, this was his role. In the eyes of someone looking in on us from the outside, the community had traded his birthright to enjoy young adulthood in exchange for a lifetime of servitude in the church.

In fairness to the process of the lot, I should underscore that like most people who make a commitment to community, eventually my uncle was willing to answer the call and step forward. My father provided him with counsel on farming and loaned my brother and me to help with the physical work; and working together on Uncle Elmer's farm, we made the dreadful pleasant. Actually, my uncle became a self-made biblical scholar and the best preacher we had ever heard in our young days, even better than Little David! Moreover, this preacher uncle would be a lifelong mentor and support for me. As a gifted athlete himself, he understood my love for sports and guided me in more positive directions than my enthusiasm and talent would have naturally channeled me.

As I reflect on my uncle's ordination, especially since I have become more aware of how trauma affects our bodies, I wonder if his depression and other symptoms late in life may have been related to the abrupt change in his life chances forced upon him as a young man by the church community. In contrast to his abrupt calling, I marvel at how in one generation the Mennonite Church that I know has gone from our answering the call of the community to serve, often irrespective of our own personal ambition because of the randomness of the lot, to having basically to package and market ourselves today much like any other product in a society of high mass consumption in order to serve the church as ministers. Even missionaries function, far more than we would like, as sales people where they and the Gospel have become more like commodities in the marketplace than essential elements in a relationship in which our salvation is worked out, in part, collectively rather than exclusively individually.

Launching Out

I never thought seriously about going to college after high school even though my teachers all insisted that I should. In fact, like many students, I probably gave it so little thought precisely because of their opinions. I would have much preferred to play baseball and work at whatever job I could find to keep myself alive or to pursue an airline career.

Work in the airline industry lured me because as a youngster I had been impressed by the low-flying Strategic Air Command planes that skimmed low below the horizon and mock attacked our machinery or buildings as they came roaring out over our woods at terrorizing speed. Ironically my brother and I would race to see if we could get run over by the plane's shadow. The planes would sometimes tip their wings in recognition, so we thought, as they sped back to their base about fifty miles away after another completed mission.

Years later as a development worker in Central America and other parts of the world, I would learn that planes like those we loved to "play" with in our Michigan fields would wreak panic and death on helpless civilians and insurgents alike on the battlefields for "democracy and progress" in countries far from the AuGres plains—countries not always eager for the form of democracy and progress our country bestowed upon them. In another of those bang-yourself-on-the-head moments, I realized that the friendly shadow we ran toward in Michigan many years earlier was just one part of a system that extended the "shadow of death," of which the Psalmist writes, to Central America, Sarajevo, Iraq, and countless other places where even God seemed reluctant to protect the innocent as they ran for their lives, terrified of the fate from which far too few freed themselves.

Small Things Make a Big difference

One day a year after my high school graduation, Uncle Elmer wisely said in his own way, "You need to go to college because I think God has something more for your life. You enjoy singing. You did well in high school. You should really go to college some place."

Reluctantly agreeing, I sent my application to Goshen College and received my letter of acceptance and instructions on what to do to get ready for this awesome experience. I was really excited, but in July I discovered to my dismay that Goshen had no men's chorus. I loved men's music and lived for Sunday when we would listen to the King's Heralds men's quartet on the Voice of Prophecy radio program and the Mennonite Hour and its men's quartet, with whom I lustily sang along. I cared little about the sermons, but I enjoyed the music. Faced now with my disappointment about Goshen College, I decided to apply to EMC (Eastern Mennonite College) in Virginia.

Since it was late July by then, I had little hope of getting in; but I knew that EMC had a men's chorus because Bernard and Manny Martin had stayed at our house when Earl Maust and his men came to our church for a program. I would wait an extra year if necessary, but I would go to EMC. In my naiveté I thought that Bernard and Manny were "blameless and without sin," to use a scriptural description. Later life would prove that this was not exactly the way things were even though they were without question good men. Nevertheless, I was accepted and went to EMC. Fate smiled upon me because I had the privilege of singing with

Bernard in the Mennonite Hour choirs and latter bought Manny Martin's house, where my wife and I still live today. My seemingly coincidental switch to EMC set me on a course that I had never anticipated.

At EMC I met Dorothy Leaman, known to most people as Dot. We married in my junior year, and all of a sudden I was mature. Marriage did that for a person in those days! Being at Eastern Mennonite and meeting Dot also brought together two factors that would influence our life significantly. Dot had a strong family connection to the Shenks and other early Eastern Mennonite Mission Board missionaries to Africa. For many people at that time EMC was still known more as a missionary preparation school than a rigorous academic college, so it seemed appropriate that Dot should come to EMC to prepare herself to serve as a missionary some place like her Uncle Clyde and Aunt Alta's.

With Dot's missionary interest and my Spanish language major, we were happy to accept the invitation brokered by Paul Kraybill of the Eastern Mennonite Board of Missions and Mark Peachey of Rosedale Mennonite Missions (RMM) for me to do my alternative service in Costa Rica with the adult literacy program, ALFALIT, founded and run by a Cuban refugee couple forced to flee by the Castro-led revolution. Since Samuel Horst and Samuel Miller, two of my professors at EMC, had greatly stimulated my interest in Latin America, I was glad to start my work in the region under the direction of two very highly educated and dedicated Cubans, Justo and Luisa Gonzalez.

After a few months I left ALFALIT to direct the RMM Voluntary Service Program in Costa Rica when its leader, Elam Peachey, was forced to return to the USA because of illness. Nevertheless, I maintained contact with don Justo and doña Luisa during our time in Costa Rica—still unaware of how much our relationship would reshape my thinking about what we as North Americans could bring to Latin America or any other place, for that matter. Yet I began to question the typical view that development was something that we took to the rest of the world because we had the answers to their problems and all the assumptions behind such an attitude.

Graduate School and Beyond

Dot and I spent three years in Costa Rica with the RMM service program in the 1960s. It was there that we formed life-long relationships with

Costa Ricans and North American voluntary service workers. When we finished in Costa Rica, we moved to Nicaragua in 1967 on loan for three more years from Rosedale Mennonite Missions to resume our work with ALFALIT, the adult literacy program with which we had worked briefly in Costa Rica. Our literacy work in Nicaragua continued to move us in a direction in which our basic understanding of the world would be challenged. This came to a head in early 1970 during a three-week seminar in Cuernavaca, Mexico, with Paulo Freire, Ivan Illich, and Rubem Alves. These three individuals put to the test any vestige that remained of the idea that development and missionary activity was the North's gift to the South.

I returned to Nicaragua disillusioned and spiritually deconstructed, ready for a change. I needed to go to graduate school, where admission turned out to be a challenge since my cumulative GPA of 2.6 was not a strong endorsement of my academic abilities. The follies of youth embedded in my GPA had followed me to Nicaragua and now threatened to sabotage my hopes for pursuing graduate studies.

Quite to my surprise, Cornell University accepted me but needed a sample of my extemporaneous spoken Spanish to see if it would offer me a Spanish teaching assistantship as part of my financial aid package. Since I had just been in Mexico to help with an adult literacy training course, I decided to describe a remote village that I had visited in the *Ixmiquilpan* area there. I detailed how the village had been transformed by the conversion in Arizona of a migrant worker from that village when he had found a Scripture booklet of the Psalms on the road. I described the people, the town, and the changes that had occurred. Later I received the news that Cornell had awarded me a scholarship that would pay all of my expenses and a substantial living allowance for three years with an option for some aid for a fourth year if necessary!

After several months at Cornell, I asked my professor, Dr. Joe Grimes, if he could explain how I had gotten such an awesome scholarship with such an awful GPA. He replied that he had happened to be the person randomly assigned to listen to my tape. To his great astonishment, he knew all the people I described because he had lived in that village for some five years, doing linguistic research for Wycliffe Bible Translators. In light of this highly improbable occurrence, he decided to recommend me for the lucrative University Scholarship because he thought there might be more here than mere coincidence. Thanks to the scholarship and Dot's part-time job, I finished my graduate studies debt free. It was thus possible for me to come to EMC to teach when I completed my PhD rather than accepting the invitation to head for Harvard University with one of my professors who was to direct the Harvard Institute for International Development.

The Eastern Mennonite University Era

One of the reasons I was willing even to consider EMC as a teaching possibility was that in graduate school I had discovered a reframing of faith as the result of reading Thomas Kuhn's *The Structure of Scientific Revolution* (University of Chicago, 1962), which gave me a way to understand faith in the twentieth century. Christian discipleship makes a lot of sense if one views Jesus as a paradigm for life. It makes the person of Jesus rather than the doctrinally defined Jesus central to the church. It dawned on me that this is really what Anabaptism is about. It is about following Jesus in life, which means that a lot of the doctrinal issues will take care of themselves or fade into the background rather than opening or barring the gates of entry to the church.

While at EMU I completed the equivalent of a twenty-some-year PhD study of Anabaptism through team teaching a course with Ray Gingerich entitled Peace and Justice in the Global Context. It was a good experience although sometimes students may have had trouble capturing the passion we each brought to the class in our own way. We were like two football players who psych each other up before the game and then go in and overwhelm everybody on the field. The class preparation was great for us, but the students had to figure out how to deal with the enthusiasm of new discovery that we brought to the class. Because of these newfound insights and the personal and professional energy and encouragement from many colleagues, especially Ray Gingerich and Titus Bender, I decided to stay at EMU when other attractive offers surfaced.

Kenton Brubaker, in his inimitable low-key way, clinched my decision to come to teach at EMC. He was just beginning the International Agriculture major and asked that I come to support the major with my experience and preparation in development. In exchange he promised that he would support me in anything creative that I wanted to do. I am certain that he does not remember the promise, but his support over the years actually fulfilled it.

When I came to EMC to teach, Kenton and others had already begun to reshape the college's image from mainly missionary and service preparation to development. This along with peace and justice would be our distinctive emphasis until the mid 1990s when the Conflict Transformation Program moved us toward peacebuilding, which was complemented by other graduate and undergraduate programs in the professions; but peace became our brand, so to speak.

As I reflect on my years at EMU, I have pondered what causes some programs to be successful and others, not. Timing is indeed everything. Thus patience becomes vital, and good fortune always helps. From a timing perspective, the International Agriculture major fit the times. Increasing world food production, especially in poor countries, was high on the agenda—much as were the United Nations' Millennium Development Goals articulated at the beginning of this century. In the 1970s the Mennonite Central Committee issued its Hillsboro Declaration, which committed the organization to make increased food production the focus of its development work. More broadly the Green Revolution informed and shaped most development work during the sixties, seventies, and eighties. E.F. Schumacher's *Small is Beautiful* emphasized appropriate technology as the key to successful development in poor countries, enabling them to provide food for their entire populations in a sustainable fashion. Earlier I mentioned the need for entrepreneurs like Kenton Brubaker and others to take calculated risks. We did that with the International Development major, and it was successful during its time; but a new time was coming.

Inspired in part by Goshen College's acclaimed Study Service Term begun in the late 1960s, EMU's cross-cultural program and requirement came to fruition in the early 1980s, following a number of years of informal and ad hoc experiences organized at the initiative of interested individual faculty members. The proposed program encountered strong resistance in some sectors of the college because it would interfere with the way we scheduled courses and it seemed to give too much emphasis to the social sciences. The proposal, along with other major changes in the General Education Curriculum, engaged us in discussions and compromises for a number of years. Fortunately, we eventually learned to live with the innovations even though not all the members of the faculty embraced them with enthusiasm and joy. The university had a clear new mission and a program designed to equip us to participate in the world emerging around us or, maybe more accurately, the world that we were becoming increasingly more aware of and more involved in.

The Central American wars of the 1980s and 1990s created the milieu from which the Conflict Transformation Program emerged. It built on the idea of grassroots connections and appropriate technology or culturally sensitive processes that had been central to the International Agriculture major. The new focus attracted me because of my work with land reform in Costa Rica. While there, I had stumbled onto the emerging Contra groups forming in northern Costa Rica. I also met John Paul Lederach at a Thanksgiving celebration in San Jose. After a brief conversation we discovered that we each needed what the other brought for our work to be successful. John Paul's extensive involvement in the Central American peace process helped him articulate more clearly his ideas on peacebuilding. During those years, we kept in contact, and eventually his coming to teach at EMU led to the development of the Conflict Transformation Program, now known as the Center for Justice and Peacebuilding.

While I consider the Cross-Cultural Program and Center for Justice and Peacebuilding two successful efforts, I often wonder about two programs that never got off of the drawing boards. One was an MBA in the mid 1980s that would have addressed the burgeoning interest in upgrading NGO management in the development field. It would have involved a radical restructuring of our program delivery methods, but it was an idea ahead of its time, euphemistically put. I lacked the vision to know how to make it a reality, and no one else picked up the idea.

An experience-based general education program proposal, developed primarily by Wayne Teel in the mid 1990s, suffered a similar fate. We had hoped to give all the students a firsthand experience with environmental sustainability by making it the organizing theme for the general education curriculum. The proposed program included a lot of interaction with Harrisonburg and Rockingham County communities

Return visit to long-term partners in development, Sandra Campos and her mother, in Upala, Costa Rica in 1993.

through hands-on projects ideally suited for students with more action-oriented learning styles.

I take some solace in the fact that later an MBA program did develop even though it did not focus on NGO management needs specifically. However, with no direct connections to the past, the General Education Program ideas reappeared to some extent in the Micah Project's venture learning proposal in 2006. Thus I learned that ideas and change are cyclical and that what we consider success or failure depends a lot on timing, articulation, and the ability to promote an idea in a manner open enough for others to take ownership in it. It sounds so easy, but I still find it hard to hold loosely the ownership reins of an idea that I passionately want to see succeed.

ACRS, the Anabaptist Center for Religion and Society, is an idea whose time eventually came after nearly a decade-long gestation. It emerged from the convergence of two separate streams of thought. I distinctly recall a comment by Shirley Showalter, former president of Goshen College, in her speech at our Fall Faculty Conference that triggered Ray Gingerich to say something like, "I think we need a center at EMU to take advantage of the knowledge and experience of professors who have retired from active teaching but continue to be active scholars." We immediately began to plan how to make it happen. Several years later we were pleasantly surprised to discover that Robert Lee, a long-term missionary in Japan, had come up with a similar idea independent of our discussions at EMU. The impetus of the larger combined group finally helped the idea become a reality. As an ACRS member, I envision a dynamic future for the Center because we have only begun to imagine its possibilities. Once EMU as an institution sees ACRS as an asset rather than a liability, it will do things far beyond what we have ever thought or dreamed.

During my years at EMU, like other colleagues at the university, I received a lot of support from the institution for my involvement in development work and service beyond campus. This enabled me to continue relating to programs and organizations working in development and peace-related activities in various parts of the world where I had contacts. My teaching benefited from the rich insights gained through these connections. These experiences also stimulated me and others to promote innovations on campus to move the university to support peace and justice work more explicitly, beginning with the revised mission statement and support for new programs across campus as departments reframed their offerings and new programs emerged like the graduate Center for Justice and Peacebuilding, the undergraduate Justice, Peace, and Conflict Studies program, new cross-cultural experience options that focused on issues of immigration and migration among other themes, the Inter-Culteral Communicative Competence (IC3) program to engage EMU students via the Internet with students from universities in a variety of areas around the world, and the formation of campus organizations committed to addressing growing environmental issues.

EMU's transition into this new phase has not been without significant stress and tension because of the cultural lag and uncertainty of the larger Mennonite church regarding its identity, niche in the world, and its biblical basis for a twenty-first century ethic. The university now finds itself situated very differently from where it was when the graduates of the 1960s took over the faculty, so to speak, in the 1970s and 1980s. Then an institution committed to preparing students to engage the world passionately through a missiology and service philosophy that grew out of the post-World War II rise of the United States to world dominance politically and economically. Now it has evolved to a university whose philosophy values more explicitly global interdependence and respect for religious, political, economic, and cultural diversity. However, as in the larger Anabaptist world, this evolution is not complete by any stretch of the imagination. Though with perhaps an overgeneralization, one can plausibly claim that the leaders of the transition at EMU drew their inspiration from the critics of the rise of a reformulated civil religion within the Mennonite church following the World Wars. That is, the church and state coalesced ideologically while the separation of church and state was retained at the level of governance. The resistance to this ideological melding came to a head in the 1970s and 1980s and left the Mennonite world divided ideologically and theologically, as evidenced by the voting patterns and political preferences of Mennonites in recent years. EMU finds itself in the middle of this tension as it increasingly tries to orient itself by a missiological and educational philosophy that questions attempts to make the United States a Christian nation called to evangelize the world for democracy and Christianity. I, along with many of my colleagues, have lived that tension at EMU. We see the need to embrace a missiological, development, peacebuilding, and educational philosophy that enables us to work in, but not on behalf of the powers of death and destruction today; but we find it difficult to agree on the true nature of the various powers around us.

Lenses To See a Different Future

My Eastern Mennonite University experience provided both clarity and complexity to my understanding of the world and our role as Christians in it. However, through service in various Mennonite agencies and other non-church related institutions, I learned firsthand about the challenges of being slightly to significantly off center in relation to North American society's dominant values. In the sixties and seventies Dorothy and I worked in Central America primarily with Rosedale Mennonite Missions. Essentially in the eighties and nineties and the early years of the new millennium I served on the Mennonite Central Committee Board and worked with Cornell University and other organizations like the Costa Rican and Peruvian governments in development and peacebuilding.

These experiences introduced me to a world I had never known. In Central America I learned about poverty, illiteracy, and suffering on a scale that I had not seen in North America even though those challenges are here in our midst as well. I became aware of how much the Mennonite Central Committee's response to human need touched and shaped the identity of our European and Russian Mennonite ancestors who fled to North and South America during the World Wars of the twentieth century.

This countercultural and servant identity helped predispose Mennonites to respond naturally and eagerly with disaster and humanitarian assistance in emergency situations because as a people we had experienced and appreciated humanitarian assistance in our times of most urgent need. However, at the same time, our struggles to survive after fleeing war and economic hardship may have also instilled antisocial welfare attitudes in us as a people, at least if the various studies of the Anabaptist/Mennonite denominations in North America are valid. How do we institutionally respond to humanitarian disasters like endemic poverty and malnutrition that have their roots as much in unjust economic and political structures globally and locally as in personal characteristics of those who suffer?

For years I have faced these difficult challenges in my teaching, development, and peacebuilding work at Rosedale Mennonite Missions, Eastern Mennonite University, Mennonite Central Committee, and other settings. Today I still struggle with the dilemma. However, I have found some hope in the idea that we do what we can, when we can, wherever we are. Just as the church in its many forms serves humanity better because we all have different needs and preferences, so in justice work it takes many different approaches at a variety of levels in society, all focused on the same goal, to achieve just and peaceful communities, societies, and world. We simply need to give each other the grace to do what we can do best to achieve a greater degree of personal and social wholeness today.

Looking Back and into the Future

My life has been rich and satisfying even though not without significant pain and difficulties. I have experienced losses because of death, estrangement, and disappointments with opportunities not seized or denied. Thus at this point I look back and lament all those things we have been unable to achieve and put them on the "to-do" list for a future generation.

From Good to Great Institutions?

I lament the fact that, in spite of our family friendly rhetoric, we still do not have a university-sponsored day care service at EMU for faculty, staff, and students. I see a real opportunity when I note how few of our church related institutions, Anabaptist-run businesses, and humanitarian organizations still do not provide day care services for the children of their employees. I recognize the complexities, challenges, and costs inherent in such an endeavor, but hopefully somewhere and sometime in the not too distant future our commitment to strong families will generate in us the creativity and commitment needed to make this part of our institutional ministry and witness.

I lament the fact that we have not been able to convince ourselves that our colleges and universities would be better with less emphasis on intercollegiate athletics or with their total elimination. I fully accept the counter arguments regarding the social benefits accrued from intercollegiate athletics and the importance of physical exercise in wellness, a concept we all embrace. It pains me, as a former athlete, to suggest that athletics as known and practiced in our church-sponsored schools and colleges may actually be an impediment to our goal of promoting intellectual, physical, and emotional wholeness. In fairness to the athletic department at EMU, I applaud the efforts coaches and others put forth to help athletes be students as well. David King, EMU's current athletic director, has brought a breath of fresh air, but we need to reduce dramatically the number of "professional" athletes who attend our colleges. When added to the increasing number of students who go to college because it is "the thing to do," the critical mass of the uncommitted quickly becomes too large relative to the total student body, thus altering the focus and distinctiveness of the college or university.

At EMU, like most other small colleges and universities, we are not large enough to be both a serious university and a sponsor of *semi-professional* sports teams. I use *semi-professional* because far too many of our athletes *pay* us via tuition to let them play with relatively little commitment to academic excellence. More broadly, as colleges and universities we hem ourselves in institutionally by building excellent but costly facilities that will probably keep us from ever seriously engaging the topic of radical alternatives to what we now have regarding athletics. This is a challenge for the entire Mennonite church, not just the high schools, colleges, and universities. It is larger than any particular individual president, dean, or athletic director. If we are serious about this issue, the impetus to address it must come from the grassroots of the Anabaptist population so that administrators know they will not be left hanging if they try to work creatively with their respective institutions and constituencies.

A Light on Those Who Serve in the Shadows

I lament the fact that we have no adequate institutional way to recognize the contributions of a faculty member's spouse, life-long friend, or significant support group to his or her EMU career. This issue is not unique to EMU. It extends to many small businesses, congregations, and organizations that survive and thrive, subsidized by contributed labor of this sort. Our retirement rituals, usually shaped by what larger and more formal bureaucracies would value, typically recognize this invaluable donated service with only a nod or a brief mention. In my case Dorothy, my spouse, has played a significant part in much of whatever success I have had. I would like to see her get some recognition for her efforts. I want the spotlight to shine a bit more on those who often serve in the shadows unremunerated and unrecognized. I also realize that some faculty members do not have a spouse or a significant support group or find themselves positioned differently with respect to their work at EMU. In most small colleges and universities, especially church related ones, we need to recognize publicly the extra burden we expect these persons to carry, simply because they cannot count on the extra support institutions and businesses often exploit. What can we do to transform our religious, economic, and political institutions to live up to the values of equality and worth we so strongly espouse in word, but so freely ignore in deed? This may well be a generational issue that will take care of itself. If so, thanks be to God.

Not Business as Usual

I live with the hope that the issues mentioned above will inspire us to work creatively in the future to address them. However, other creative initiatives at EMU and in the broader church energize me because of the possibilities that we currently sense as within our reach in the Anabaptist community and beyond.

At EMU, as at other colleges and universities, a green emphasis has emerged that affects how we live together in community and in our communities. The idea of developing new environmentally friendly buildings and living patterns calls us to take seriously the Anabaptist emphasis on relationships as the basis for our wholeness, both socially and with the natural environment. The truly Anabaptist component of the green trend is our commitment to relationships as a significant part of our experiencing wholeness. Long after the trend has peaked and a new wave is upon us, we need to retain a sustainable relationship with our natural environment as part of our salvation, or wholeness as Jesus referred to the outcome of his ministry.

I am energized by what I see on the margins of long-established Christian groups. It appears that Anabaptism in its most dynamic form will arise and be nurtured by movements at the periphery of the long established mainline denominations, as well as radical Catholic and conservative evangelical groups, rather than at the core of the Mennonite and Brethren in Christ denominations, which seem to have been increasingly seduced into mainline America by our education and wealth. We in the traditional Anabaptist groups live a form of Anabaptism but often deny its power because of our unwillingness to accept the risks implicit in taking it seriously. A deep Anabaptist commitment will put us at odds with the civil religious merger of certain Anabaptist groupings with the most conservative elements of the political and economic right. We willingly protest abortion at the behest of this merged religious and political right but do not oppose the blatant pro-war positions of those same groups. On the political left, too frequently the opposite holds.

As Anabaptists we have the challenge of cutting across these religio-political currents rather than flowing with them. Ron Sider called for this type of response a number of years ago with his challenge to a "totally pro-life" ethic. Sojourners and other groups have also issued similar calls. As Anabaptists we get the least support for a fully life-giving ethic from uncritically receiving the programs broadcast on religious radio and television stations to which we turn for nurture. As colleges and universities we face a similar challenge, but possibly from the opposite side of the religio-political spectrum. However, I am energized by elements I see in the emergent church movement, even though I have serious reservations about some of the basic assumptions undergirding the movement in relation to the nature of salvation or wholeness in Jesus. Creative art forms such as the musical rap group, Straight Edge, are signs of hope for me because of their crosscutting relationship with the themes and values of dominant North American society.

It is exciting to realize that in the next several decades we will stand on the threshold of a new missiology and way to view the world. We cannot yet see clearly all of its contours, but the rapid global socio-political changes forced upon us have moved us to reexamine what we mean by *witness* and how we live it out in a multiethnic and religiously diverse world. In Anabaptist circles the Mennonite Central Committee has led the way, sometimes in conjunction with our mission agencies, in the exploration of interfaith interaction at a practical level.

To engage seriously in this type of work requires that we rethink the uncritical way in which we have accepted the exclusive claims of Christianity in relation to other religions. To engage seriously other faiths means that exclusivity, be it Christian or other, must be part of the discussion. We need a missiology that provides a space for this type of dialogue. A true dialogue will lead all parties to a much clearer understanding of who each is respectively.

Today organizations and individuals from many religious and political orientations are promoting interfaith encounters. In the Anabaptist tradition, the Mennonite Central Committee has teamed with Conrad Grebel University College and the Toronto Mennonite Theological Centre to provide a space for interfaith interaction dating back to the final years of the 1990s. Various Mennonite mission agencies and even congregations have also promoted exchanges of different types in the past decade or so. EMU has been talking about such an effort since early in the new millennium but has only recently begun to explore seriously the creation of a space for interfaith interaction.

I am energized by the possibility of a center or some other structure at EMU to promote interfaith interaction among the three Abrahamic traditions as a starting point. I believe we need a project like this in order to understand more fully who we really are as Anabaptists in a religiously pluralistic society and world. If we are to engage a religiously diverse world that increasingly frames conflict religiously, we need to learn how to engage in meaningful interfaith interaction. Without denying the significance of Jesus for our transformation, I believe that interfaith interaction will help us find wholeness more fully by engaging with other faiths in a quest to understand and experience the richness derived from sharing each other's salvation story and ethic.

We at EMU along with most of the rest of the North American Anabaptist world have arrived quite late to the conclusion that our salvation is in some way tied to the salvation story of others. At EMU we are now at least five years behind in developing this focus on campus. The discussion has been taking place in some form essentially since the rude awakening of September 11, 2001. Other groups and organizations were engaged in these efforts for years prior to the September 2001 tragedy.

When we at EMU enter at the midpoint or later in an innovation cycle such as this one, we have to think differently about why we should enter. Given the hundreds and maybe thousands of organizations that are promoting interfaith dialogue currently, we can no longer say that it is important for us to engage in interfaith interaction because so few are doing this important task. Today we must be able to identify the distinctiveness we bring to this now widely accepted practice. If distinctiveness for us is our historic peace commitment and our understanding of salvation as deeply rooted in relationships, for example community formed around our commitment to Jesus and his ethic for life, then we will seek together to find ways that lead to peace while we explore the theological traditions that inform our identity and ethics. In the mid-twentieth century H. S. Bender called for the recovery of the Anabaptist vision. Our taking interfaith dialogue seriously in today's world may well lead us to a new discovery of an Anabaptist vision for today. I am happy to have played a role in helping EMU, and MCC to a lesser degree, play a small part in this transforming movement among Anabaptists.

Much of my life and identity has been tied to Eastern Mennonite University, for better or for worse. EMU and my formative years in communities in Michigan and Central America have indelibly shaped me, and hopefully I in turn have helped shape them. My story, though uniquely mine, is in many ways like that of thousands of other fellow travelers who have served in similar institutional and religious settings. I would like to think that, as we continue our efforts to create a more just and peaceful world, Jesus would say of us as he did of the children when he asked people not to get in their way because "of such is the kingdom of heaven" (KJV).

March 10, 2008
Revised January 2009

CATHERINE R. MUMAW

Touched by the World

My story begins with my formative years of growing up in a Mennonite preacher's family in the shadow of Eastern Mennonite School near Harrisonburg, Virginia. My gift of an ability to sing was encouraged then and throughout my life. Spiritual nurturance came from my family, church, and friends in the communities where I lived and worked. For a career, I chose the broad and interdisciplinary field of home economics and was sometimes reminded that one thing was lacking—that I was not a man! In this career, through interactions with people from many cultures and in many lands, I became an internationalist who was challenged and enriched through exposures to different ways of seeing the world and knowing God.

The Heritage of My Formative Years

My father, John R. Mumaw, was the son of minister and farmer Amos Mumaw and his wife, Catharine, who lived in Wayne County, Ohio. Since Amos died when John was only two years old, John's boyhood centered on life on the farm. My mother, Esther Forry Mosemann, the daughter of John Heer and Lillie Forry Mosemann, grew up in Lancaster, Pennsylvania, where her father was a Mennonite bishop and businessman. Although Mother did not work in her father's peanut butter factory, she did work as a clerk at the Mosemann meat and cheese stand on Central Market.

John and Esther met at Eastern Mennonite School (EMS) and were married in 1928. They settled in the village of Park View (later annexed by Harrisonburg), where he was employed by EMS. My father's demeanor was both serious and fun loving. My mother's bent toward seeing the joyful side of life resulted in much laughter, a Mosemann family trait that brightened our family life.

I was born at home in Park View on July 22, 1932, the third of five daughters. Sisters Helen (Mrs. Laban Peachey) and Grace preceded me, and Lois (Mrs. Emanuel Martin, Jr.) and Miriam came after me. At the time, the country was in the Great Depression, and Father—on leave from his job at EMS because there was not enough money then to pay all of the teachers—was attending the University of Virginia. Mother had the help of Leora Tusing, a midwife who wove coverlets in her home on Branch Mountain in West Virginia.

Most of the people who lived on our street were Mennonites; and Park School, the public three-room school we children attended, had mostly Mennonite teachers. Except for when I was in the second grade, all of my elementary school teachers from grades one through seven were Mennonite women.

Park School was known as a "model school" because students from EMS would do their practice teaching at that school. One student, Earl Maust, who later joined the music faculty at EMS, came to my second grade class and taught us how to read music by the *do-re-mi* system. For the next few years I spent more time reading music than reading books!

My sixth and seventh grade teacher, the principal of the school, Elsie Martin, regularly began the school day with a quotation or a Scripture verse like Psalm 16:6. Possessing an advanced degree in education and a love for children, she knew how to achieve effective classroom discipline and also to encourage her students' creative and active involvement in learning.

The environment of EMS, where all of my teachers and most of my classmates were Mennonites, shaped my high school and college years. The required courses included Bible studies and attendance at daily chapel, where at least once a year a talk focused on the school's motto, "Thy Word Is Truth," promoting the message of the inerrant nature of the Scriptures. In my high school senior year at EMS, I took a home economics course taught by Mary Emma Showalter that included food preparation, nutrition, child development and care, house planning, and art in the home. I loved this class and the many projects that we did! However, since I was planning for a career in nursing, I also took Latin with Dorothy Kemrer.

In 1950 I began my college years by enrolling in science classes— chemistry with Henry D. Weaver, Jr., and biology with D. Ralph Hostetter. Near the end of the first semester I took a temporary job at a nursing home, a job that turned out to be a traumatic experience. After two sleepless nights I began to rethink my motivation for becoming a nurse. In truth and in secret, the nursing profession had appealed to me as a way of escape from wearing the prescribed "cape dress" since in wearing a nurses' uniform, I could put away my traditional Mennonite dress. Now one evening before the second semester began, I said to my father that if it did not seem to be too "wishy-washy," I would like to change my major to home economics! He agreed that this would be just fine and urged me to do so. As a result, I wore the "cape dress" for another fifteen years!

As a second-semester freshman, I was in a brand new program. Mary Emma Showalter had been asked to develop a home economics curriculum and was in the process of doing so when I enrolled. After four years of study, in 1954 Doris Good (Bomberger) and I became the first graduates with the General Home Economics major.

Actually, if I had declared a minor, it would have been music. I elected as many music courses as possible—music theory, choral conducting, class voice, and others. Along with singing in choirs, I had opportunities for leading hymns and singing in small groups. Thus I became known as a musician, an identity and a hobby that I carried throughout my life.

The Gift of Music—from Family, School, and Church

Music was always a part of life in the Mumaw family. From the time we were born we heard Mother humming or singing hymns as she worked in the kitchen or did the laundry. We daughters learned to sing along as we worked together at tasks like washing and drying the dishes. Singing was our way of expressing beliefs, of connecting to God, and of sharing spiritual experiences.

Singing was important, also, in our daily evening family worship. Without instrumental accompaniment my father sang bass, and the rest of us filled in the other parts. For Christmas in 1940, when I was eight, each of us daughters was given a copy of the recently published *Life Songs Number Two*[1] with the first name of each person inscribed on the cover in gold letters, e.g., *Catherine* on my book. My youngest sister, Miriam, often selected Number One in the book, the great Fanny Crosby hymn, "God of our strength, enthroned above." That hymn became one of my all-time favorites. It expressed the key ideas of God as the source of life and love, hope and light, unity and safety, joy and praise. The refrain simply stated: "God of our strength, we wait on Thee, Our sure defense forever be."

Outside of family worship, we four oldest girls began to sing together as a quartet. I could read and sing any part, thanks to Earl Maust. Of course, it was no accident that we could sing in close harmony since our parents both sang well. Also, the Mosemanns always included a time of singing when we had our annual Christmas get-together at Grandma's house in Lancaster, Pennsylvania. It was not unusual to find us singing from *The Holy City* choral worship cantata[2] or *David, the Shepherd Boy* cantata,[3] reinforcing our connections to music that two generations of our family had learned at Eastern Mennonite School in the 1920s through the 1950s.

When Miriam was old enough to join our quartet, we became a quintet and looked for music in five parts. We loved our new arrangement of "From every stormy wind that blows." The text, written in 1831, affirmed a Jesus who brings calmness and peace, gladness, a sense of belonging through fellowship with friends, and the assurance of salvation.

Our family's regular attendance at church services on Sunday morning and evening and at Wednesday evening prayer meetings also gave us a chance to get acquainted with a variety of hymns. At Lindale, the 1902 *Church and Sunday School Hymnal*[4] was used for many years after the 1927 *Church Hymnal* was printed. Eventually the "new" *Church Hymnal*[5] and *Life Songs No. 2*, both in shaped note versions, became the "official" hymn books. When *Songs of the Church*[6] was published in 1953, the congregation purchased it, also, and learned Peter Lutkin's benediction, "The Lord bless you and keep you."

Our family sometimes joined in the New Year's Day *Harmonia Sacra*[7] (the oldest Mennonite hymnal published in the USA) singings at Weaver's

Mennonite Church west of Harrisonburg. And whenever the Mennonite Publishing House published new hymnals, we bought them.

Throughout my high school and college years in Mennonite schools, I attended daily chapel services. We sang in every service and used the Mennonite hymnals. I memorized many hymns, even the numbers where they would be found. I sang, also, in some of the choirs and special music groups, including touring choirs, where I learned great choral pieces. The annual Homecoming rendition of *The Holy City* was a unifying experience for the college family and the alumni returning for a weekend of reunions.

After I moved away from my parental home, other hymnals became important. *The Mennonite Hymnal* of 1969[8] was a joint project of several Mennonite denominations while *Hymnal: A Worship Book* (1992)[9] was a joint project of the Church of the Brethren and Mennonite denominations. Some of the hymn texts were edited in response to concerns for more inclusive language. John Wesley would have objected to any changes, but I welcomed them as steps forward in recognition of the new understandings about God and changing attitudes toward women in the Mennonite Church. However, in most Mennonite worship today the "Doxology" is still sung with a patriarchal text. A recent adaptation, however, recognizes the trinity without mentioning a gender for God:[10]

Praise God from whom all blessings flow;
In heav'n above and earth below;
one God three persons we adore.
To God be praise forevermore. Amen

Very recently two other Mennonite/Church of the Brethren songbooks were published: *Sing the Journey*[11] and *Sing the Story*.[12] These books include music from a diversity of peoples, reflecting the more international character of the present-day Mennonite church.

Along the way I found other music opportunities in the community. For example, for many years I directed and sang with music groups for the Mennonite Hour broadcasts, where the focus was on the gospel of Jesus Christ. The music expressed hope and joy, confidence and peace. My Ladies' Chorus at EMC in the early sixties had repertoires that were suitable for church worship.

In the mid-seventies, after many years of choral directing, I was happy to become simply a singer in community choirs and smaller auditioned choirs. Some of these were directed by outstanding Mennonite choral musicians: David Seitz[13] in Virginia and Indiana; Dr. Doyle C. Preheim[14] in Indiana; and Dr. James A. Miller[15] in Oregon. While living in Nepal, I sang with The Kathmandu Chorale, an international group directed by a German choral musician. There we focused mainly on German music literature and some other works of interest to such a choir and community. The experiences of sharing the gift of music with these groups of singers and the audiences who heard them were always special events that were spiritually uplifting for me.

Music as a language can cross boundaries and unite people of all walks of life, of all languages, of all cultures. Through unique cultural expressions, it communicates to the heart and soul of human beings. Music helps to build bridges from one generation to another, to bring comfort, to raise spirits, and to express the deepest feelings of the soul. The ability to participate in it has been a treasured gift in my life.

Finding My Way in a Spiritual Journey

From the time that I was a child, I felt secure with belief in God as creator and protector, in Jesus Christ as savior, and in the Holy Spirit as an indwelling presence. Our family worship at home and our regular attendance at church on Sundays included Bible readings, and the life and teachings of Jesus were to be modeled and applied in daily life. My continuing search to know God and live in the Spirit became a lifelong challenge.

My father, especially, nurtured my beliefs through his preaching in churches and his readings in our family worship. Also, as an ordained minister in the Northern District of Virginia Mennonite Conference, he expected me to join the Mennonite church. On my tenth birthday (1942) I was given my first King James Version of *The Holy Bible*. Soon after that, by my conviction and choice, I was baptized in the chapel of the EMS Administration Building and became a member of the Northern District.

Being Mennonite then involved tangible expressions of "nonconformity to the world," especially in clothing and participation in church life. Therefore, my parents required that I wear the "regulation dress" for women members of the church. This included a "cape" dress and "head covering" for all appearances outside our home. For me these constituted constraints that later affected my sense of integrity and honesty. The cape dress was designed to give expression to modesty and to nonconformity to the women's clothing fashions of the time. To a degree, these goals were achieved.

The teaching about the significance and meaning of wearing a head covering was rooted in Scripture, though its application was never very convincing to me. I noted the explanations of I Corinthians 11:3–16, where women are exhorted to pray and prophesy with the head *covered,* and men are exhorted to pray and prophesy with the head *uncovered.* The interpretation of this passage was extended to require a woman to wear a head covering at all times, not only to be appropriately prepared to pray or prophesy at any time, but also to show her submission to her husband. At the same time I noticed that the men did *not* use the same logic in terms of praying with the head uncovered. They (the men) were allowed to wear hats on their heads at all times, except perhaps when they worshipped in public places. The paradox of this teaching, along with the fact that I was not a married woman, raised questions as to the relevance of this to my personal experience. Nevertheless, I continued to comply with the expectations!

Since my clothing clearly identified me as a Mennonite in 1942 during the early years of World War II, I was among those ridiculed for their identity with the "conscientious objectors" to participation in the military. The nonresistance position of the church was widely taught as young people struggled with the realities of the military draft.

My identity with a specific Mennonite congregation came in my later teen years after my father was asked to join the pastors' team at the Lindale Mennonite Church. Since my name was placed on the membership roll, I could now be a part of a youth group, which included Basingers, Mumaws, Shanks, Shenks, Smuckers, and Wengers. We had Bible studies and social events that included fall corn-husking parties, winter Christmas caroling activities, spring taffy pulls, and summer watermelon feeds. For twenty-five years that church was a place from which I would go and come.

Just before I moved from Virginia in 1974 to Goshen, Indiana, I had a visit from the young pastor, bringing me my certificate of membership. It was his belief that membership should go with the person in a move. I thanked him but requested that he not remove my name from the roll until I gave him notice. It was important to me to maintain my relationship with the Virginia Mennonite Conference because I had property insurance for my house and car with the Virginia Mennonite Aid Plan—available only to conference members. Thus I placed my church membership certificate in the security box of a local bank in Goshen. Two years later I sold my Park View house and no longer needed the house insurance, but I still had auto insurance in Virginia.

Nine years after my move to Goshen I decided to become a member of the College Mennonite Church. As it was the practice to have new members give a brief statement of their spiritual pilgrimage, I spent some time reflecting on my church membership. I discovered that of the forty years that I had been a member of the Mennonite Church, I had spent only twenty years in congregations where I officially had my membership. I was reminded that a year earlier, in 1982, when I had visited Ethiopian refugee camps along the Juba River in Somalia, I had found those pastoral people impressive. Although they had been uprooted from their former homeland, they were a community with solidarity, they were a people of the universe and the earth, they were tuned in to their God, and they were "at home." Each family had come with their *rondaval*[16] transported by camels. For these pastoral people, *home* was wherever they could put up shelter (their *rondaval)* to provide protection; *home* was wherever their people were found; and *home* was wherever they could worship their God and practice their faith in daily life.

Suddenly I saw in the Ethiopian and Somali pastoral people a parallel to my own spiritual sense of being *at home*. I, too, had been a *pastoral* person, beginning in my childhood years when my father was a minister in the Northern District of Virginia Mennonite Conference. Then since the churches did not have assigned pastors, my father's preaching assignments followed a circuit calendar of appointments that included more than twenty churches; and he frequently took our entire family to these churches. I thus learned at an early age that the church was not a single congregation, but many congregations. The church was not a particular place—rather, it was a quality of life that went wherever the people of God would go or gather. A *home church* existed for me wherever people of God were gathered. *Home* was where I could worship God and relate to others who shared my faith. *Home* was anywhere in the universe where I could express my faith in daily life. For me, *being* church was more important than having an official status of membership in a congregation. Nevertheless, the College Church congregation constituted a visible church family; by bringing my certificate of membership, I was again staking my claim to a certain congregation as my *home church*.

This attitude had some advantages for larger church involvement. I served terms on the following boards: the Mennonite Community Association (1970s); the Mennonite Church Council of Faith, Life, and Strategy (1972–75); the Mennonite Mutual Aid Association (1984–87); and Mennonite Economic Development Associates (1992–95).

When in 1987 I moved to Corvallis, Oregon, I did not move my formal church membership. In 1989 I chose to attend the Eugene Mennonite Church even though it was an hour's drive from Corvallis because I needed a church fellowship where I could feel challenged in my spiritual growth. My father's preaching during my formative years had been based on the exegesis of a selected passage of Scripture read in the King James Version. His interesting sermons included many practical applications. Further, I had found my uncle John Mosemann's carefully spoken sermons at the College Mennonite Church in Goshen to be deep and challenging. That was what I needed again.

Ted Grimsrud, author and now professor in the Bible and Religion Department at EMU (Eastern Mennonite University), who was then pastoring the Eugene congregation (also in a university town), preached many deep, thought-provoking sermons with practical applications. Through his ministry I gained an appreciation for *The New Jerusalem Bible* since he frequently read the scriptures in that translation. It was during that time that I was introduced to Marcus Borg's book, *Meeting Jesus Again for the First Time*.[17] This sparked my interest in taking a new look at my spiritual journey. Dr. Borg, a colleague of mine at Oregon State University, occasionally lectured in churches and at special functions on campus. Gradually I was exposed to the work of the Jesus Seminar scholars and *The Five Gospels*.[18]

Soon after that I went to Nepal for a four-year assignment with the support of MCC (Mennonite Central Committee, the denomination's relief organization). Here I saw the total integration of religion with life in the Hindu and Buddhist cultures. I was grateful that many years earlier at Eastern Mennonite College (now EMU), the faculty break-fast discussion group had read books on the five great religions of the world—Christianity, Hinduism, Buddhism, Judaism, and Islam.

I sometimes visited Nepali Christian churches, which met on Saturdays because of the cultural patterns in the Hindu-dominant country. Their enthusiastic singing and sincerity in their worship were always inspiring. I also became aware of some of the hard times the Nepalese Christians suffered as they turned from their Hindu beliefs to become a part of the Christian community. Eventually they called themselves the Nepal Christian Fellowship as a way of overcoming the denominationalism of foreigners. On the Sundays when I was not working, I worshiped with the International Church Fellowship (in the English language) with people from many different denominations and countries. These experiences affirmed for me that the church is universal and God's people are everywhere in the world, proclaiming their faith and doing work in service to God.

When I returned to Oregon, I again attended the Eugene Mennonite Church, now with new leadership. However, while I was away, the Corvallis Mennonite Fellowship had matured from a house meeting fellowship to a full-fledged congregation meeting in Westminster House near the OSU campus and practicing the belief that each member is a minister; therefore, there was no need for a salaried pastor. After a time, I decided to attend this Fellowship regularly. Their pattern of church life was different from anything I had ever experienced. The Sunday morning worship was broadly participatory, depending on voluntary commitments for the worship and other church life activities. The varied worship services involved many age groups, a situation at once refresh-ing and challenging for those who were responsible for the services. A potluck lunch was a regular feature. After each service and before the meal, the congregation stood and formed a circle, joined hands, and sang a meaningful blessing:

May God creator bless you and keep you,
May Christ be ever light for your life,

May the Spirit of love be your guide and strength,
For all of your days. Amen.

Four years ago I committed myself to purposeful spiritual refreshment. Throughout each year I was challenged by books, presentations, and workshops by Marcus Borg on *The Heart of Christianity*,[19] by Bishop John Spong on *Liberating the Gospels: Reading the Bible Through Jewish Eyes*,[20] by Huston Smith on "What's Important to Know About Religion,"[21] and by Karen Armstrong as she spoke about her spiritual journey based on *The Spiral Staircase: My Climb Out of Darkness*.[22] These theologians addressed the pitfalls of the theistic view of God and the implications for the patriarchal church. They also affirmed the importance of cultural context for understanding biblical teaching. They thus challenged me to move out of my theological comfort zone.

Even though some questions remain, I can affirm that I am a part of a global Christian community of believers who know Jesus as a personal friend and Savior. The life of Jesus exemplifies for me the values of peace and justice along with love and respect for others. God is ever present in me. And I am at *home* with the people of God wherever they live and meet.

Dealing with the One Thing Lacking

In 1915 when a Virginia Mennonite Conference committee was discussing the hiring of a person to serve as principal of the new school, Eastern Mennonite School, a candidate emerged who had excellent credentials in every way but one. As a committee member stated, "The one thing lacking is that she is a woman instead of a man– –."[23] A man, J. B. Smith, was hired instead.

I was born a girl/daughter—not a boy/son as my father had hoped. Since there were tasks to be done on our three-quarter acre plot, some of the outside chores that a son might have done were given to me. In addition, I regularly took my turn washing dishes, scrubbing floors, and doing other cleaning jobs in the house. My sisters helped with the cooking and baking for family meals while I sewed some of their dresses.

As time went on, I began to realize that being a woman—*not a man*— could affect opportunities within the Mennonite church as well as in the larger society. I remember that my mother refused to speak publicly in church because she thought it was not an appropriate role for her. She considered her place to be a support at home with the children since my father was often away from home doing church work.

In some respects, my personality was more outgoing than hers. Thus I readily accepted the invitation to lead congregational singing at the Lindale Mennonite Church, and I exerted leadership with singing groups at school and within the family. When in 1954 I took my first teaching job at Lancaster Mennonite School (in Pennsylvania), I was appointed director of two choirs. After my first public performance with a choir, I was informed that being a woman, I should limit my directing pattern to the front of my body; I was not to reach out with a waving motion! From that day forward I tried to restrict my motions to a small pattern in front of my chest, and I certainly did not swing my full body!

About this time a movement was taking hold in the larger society in which women were pushing for equal rights with men. Women, I knew, were often paid less than men for the same or similar job positions. I also observed women teachers at EMS demonstrating how they could be both a professional person and a home manager at the same time. Moreover, since neither Mary Emma Showalter, my home economics professor, nor Mrs. Ruth Brackbill, my children's literature course professor, had children at the time, it was their professionalism that impressed me most.

In college (EMS had become EMC) I chose the home economics program of study. I loved learning about the scientific aspects of foods and nutrition and the psychology of working with young children and encouraging their mental, physical, social, and spiritual development. I loved learning about ways to deal with health problems in a family and about the challenges of money management and making good consumer decisions. I loved learning about the technical and artistic aspects of working with textiles and clothing and home environments.

However, in my senior year of college (1954) I was not sure what I wanted to do for my life career. Nursing and teaching, I knew, were the two fields commonly accepted as appropriate for women. In the end, I turned down the invitation to become the Assistant Manager for Martin's clothing and fabric store in Park View in order to go to Lancaster Mennonite (High) School in Pennsylvania, where I taught home economics for two years and where I soon found out that I preferred working with older students.

After receiving an invitation to return to EMC to teach, I enrolled full time in a master's degree program at Pennsylvania State University. Then in January 1957 I came back to EMC as a novice teacher, excited about being on the faculty in the department where I would now be Mary Emma Showalter's colleague. The students in my classes, I noticed, were mostly women.

In the mid-1960s I paid attention to writings by outspoken feminists such as Betty Friedan's *The Feminine Mystique* (1963). By that time, the women's movement was in its second wave of advocates. Several exemplary women had already shown the way with their unprecedented actions. For example, in 1939 First Lady Eleanor Roosevelt had resigned her membership in the Daughters of the American Revolution after she learned that the great African American contralto, Marian Anderson, was not allowed to sing in a concert in Constitution Hall. Mrs. Roosevelt then arranged for an outdoor Easter Sunday concert at the Lincoln Memorial, where a crowd of 75,000 came to hear the world famous singer. Another courageous woman, Rosa Parks, had taken her stand in 1955 by claiming a seat on a bus in Montgomery, Alabama. These women made remarkable impacts on the civil rights movement for blacks as well as for all women in America.

In 1964 I returned to Penn State for a PhD program in Family Economics and Home Management with, as my major advisor, Dr. Marjorie M. Knoll, respected for the way she helped students to explore ideas and theories in depth. Indeed, all the professors encouraged us students to think for ourselves and to develop our own theoretical frameworks. And since I had been awarded a General Foods Fund Fellowship for each of my two years of study, I could devote full time to my classes and research.

By the time I finished my program in 1967, the women's liberation movement was well under way. The civil rights activities associated with racism also many times encompassed sexism. At EMC, where I was now appointed head of the Home Economics Department, most of the other departments were headed by men. However, since women dominated the profession of home economics, it was deemed natural for this appointment to be given to a woman.

In the next seven years I gradually took on more responsibilities in committees that related directly to the development of the institution.

I remember especially the work of the Faculty Analytic Studies Group: Long Range Planning (1972–74), which involved imagining the future for EMC. In addition, in the early 1970s I was a part of an unofficial self-appointed group of seven faculty men and women who met to discuss issues affecting the morale of the faculty and its effects on the institution. Concerned that good faculty not lose heart, we developed a proposal that we presented to the Committee on Administration. It included calling attention to the discrepancies in the salaries of men and women faculty and a request to organize a Faculty Senate that would have the authority to convene the faculty without administrators so that they could more freely discuss their concerns. As a result, a Faculty Senate was organized, and I served as the chair. In its first year it considered such issues as salaries, sabbaticals, tenure, and promotion. The position of single women also gained attention.

In the early 1970s, when the Mennonite Church was becoming more responsive to the women's movement, I served on the Mennonite Church's Nominating Committee for the 1971 General Assembly at the time of a major denominational reorganization. The ballot needed 125 names, some of whom were to be women and minorities. Since there was no obvious way of knowing where we could find the talent to match the quotas, we worked very hard.

In August 1973 the first *Report from the Peace Section Task Force on Women in Church and Society* was published by MCC.[24] The series, which continued through the 1980s, focused on women's issues; and its title changed to *MCC Committee on Women's Concerns Report*. Also, in the early 1980s women associated with Goshen College or the Associated Mennonite Biblical Seminaries in Elkhart, Indiana, published and circulated several papers addressing women's issues, including Dorothy Yoder Nyce's "Bible, Bishops, and Bombs" (1981),[25] Anna Bowman's "Women and the Mennonite Patriarchy" (1982),[26] and Mary Schertz's "Intersection: Feminist and Mennonite Theologies" (1983).[27] "Which Way Women?" was published in 1983.[28] Mennonite feminists convened in workshops to discuss the issues, and the Mennonite Church now heard women's voices speaking loud and clear, calling for a change in attitude and more equal opportunities in church life.

There is evidence today that some changes have occurred over the past twenty-five years as the work and witness of Mennonite women has come to be recognized through their autobiographies, stories, and appointments to leadership positions in congregations and on church boards. Yet the earlier metaphor of the "glass ceiling" as a constraint to women's advancement was replaced with the image of the "labyrinth," which represented the more complex pathway with many obstacles that women had to overcome before reaching leadership positions.[29] Not only was this true for church women; it was also true in the home economics profession.

The field of home economics did offer many opportunities for women to provide leadership. A few deans were promoted to higher levels of university administration, and in Mennonite colleges the Home Economics Department heads were involved with some leadership activities. As a department head at EMC and at Goshen College, I had the task of articulating how the mission of the college was addressed in department programs. I tried to show how family life was at the core of community life and how the focus on improving the physical, economic, social, and psychological well-being of individuals and households would strengthen family life in congregations and improve the well-being of the larger society. In economics terminology, individuals and families were seen as both consumers and producers. The work of home economists was to help them develop skills for both. As an interdisciplinary field of study, home economics was integrative in nature and appropriately general in scope, especially for small colleges. The more narrowly focused program in nutrition, for example, was also a high priority field of study in relation to family well-being and worthy of a place in the curriculum where resources could support it.

I had no doubts as to the viability of home economics programs in an academic setting and especially so in a Mennonite college. Why, therefore, were such programs eliminated at EMC and GC? Financial arguments can hardly be convincing. Could it be that the economics of the home and dynamics of family life were considered of far less importance and value than the economics of a business and the dynamics of community life? Surely the one is supported by and gives support to the other. Or was it simply that we women were in a disadvantaged position, even a powerless one, when administrative decisions were made to close the programs? Dare I wonder, "If we had been men?"

Becoming an Internationalist

Family and Community Influences

From the time I was three years old I was aware that our family had connections in other countries. Uncle John and Aunt Ruth Mosemann had sailed to Tanganyika, Africa, as missionaries in 1935. Of course, I had no clear perception as to where in the world that was, but I rejoiced with the rest of the family over every letter that came from them. At age seven I "lost" my first grade teacher, Rhoda Wenger, who also went to Tanganyika to teach in the mission school.

In fourth grade I completed a geography project, "Foreign Lands," which included pictures from Asia, Europe, Africa, and North and South America. In fifth grade I memorized the poem, "The Leak in the Dike," about Peter, the Dutch boy who saved his land "with the strength of his single arm!" as he spent the entire night with his hand in the hole in the dike![30]

About this time I became aware of ethnic groups in my own community, Park View. I met "Two Penny George," a black man who often stopped us as we were walking home from school to ask for two pennies. We children knew we could tease him by offering a nickel or a dime. He always refused the dime because, he said, "it is too heavy." And he never took a nickel because he was afraid of the buffalo on it. My mother encouraged us to give him two pennies when he asked and not to tease him as others did.

In fifth grade we read poems about "Indians," and I memorized Longfellow's "Hiawatha's Childhood,"[31] a story that could have happened in the shadow of the Shenandoah Valley's Massanutten Peak. In the poem Hiawatha asks questions, and Nokomis teaches him about the nature around them—trees, water, fireflies, rainbows, wildflowers, and birds—and about the close connection of humankind to other living things—the beavers, squirrels, reindeer, and rabbits, which he called "Hiawatha's Brothers."

International Students, Travel and Study Programs

At EMS we learned to know international students from Transcarpathia, Germany, Korea, Ethiopia, and Japan. Two students from Japan were in my class of 1954—Itoko Maeda and Taizo Tanimoto. In addition, the first African-American graduate of EMC was in our class—Peggy Webb, from Harrisonburg. As these students became my friends, I learned more about cultural differences.

While a graduate student at Penn State, I met two women from other countries who were especially impressive: a Muslim from Turkey and a Hindu from India. They helped to expand my worldview, especially as it related to views about God.

My first trip abroad was in 1960 as a participant in a ten-week summer European voluntary service program co-sponsored by the Council of Mennonite and Affiliated Colleges and Mennonite Central Committee. In the first five weeks we Americans toured several European countries, where I saw some places of my ancestral heritage. In the last five weeks I worked with European volunteers in two different international work camps. The first was in Medemblik, Netherlands, where campers repaired the roof of an eighteenth century "hidden church," so-called due to its disguise in an effort to escape persecution by the magistrates. The second work camp was in Witmarsum, Netherlands, for the purpose of building a Menno Simons Memorial church. I carried bricks and also helped with the kitchen work. It was in this setting that, for the first time in my life, I was asked this question: "Have you written your confession of faith yet?" It came from a twenty-seven year old man who then explained that he had just joined the church and as a prerequisite had written his statement of beliefs. Of course I said, "No," and explained that in the Mennonite Church in the USA we did not need to do that! This question made a deep impression on me and is one that I often have pondered.

In 1972, on my first sabbatical leave from EMC, I visited the Goshen College (Indiana) Study Service Trimester programs in Jamaica, Haiti, Costa Rica, and Honduras. As a result of that research, the Mennonite colleges' Home Economics Department faculties agreed on a 1973 Home Economics Transcultural Seminar in Jamaica, which I directed. This was my first experience of working closely with professionals in another culture. Dr. Thelma Stewart was enormously helpful and hospitable toward my students, who lived with local families during their twelve weeks of study.

Then in 1974 I accepted an invitation to join the Goshen College faculty, where there was a well-established infrastructure for study abroad.

Indeed, in many ways the climate of the Goshen College campus
had an international perspective. Most of the students and many faculty members had lived and/or studied in another culture through the
Study Service Trimester program, and the classrooms were rich with
ideas shared from those experiences.

I again directed a twelve-week Home Economics Transcultural
Seminar in 1975. During this time, I also worked with Jamaican educators in developing a three-week seminar focused on Maternal and
Child Nutrition in Developing Countries. Offered also in the summers
of 1976 and 1977, the seminar included Jamaican teachers, American
college students, and pre-service MCC volunteers assigned to work in
different countries; and it gained a reputation of being enormously successful in its cross-cultural impact on all involved. However, when the
political climate in Jamaica led to logistical uncertainties, the seminar
was combined with a health component—and later also with agriculture and other themes—and offered as an on-campus experience in
transcultural issues.

On my second sabbatical leave in 1982, I traveled in Central and
South America and in Africa with support from MCC to explore the
technology used by rural women for their household tasks (in Northeast
Brazil, Paraguay, Bolivia, Guatemala, Zambia, Zimbabwe, Malawi, and
Botswana). As a result of the contacts arranged by MCC women volunteers, a small booklet was published[32] with suggestions of ways to alleviate the household work of women.

In 1987, with the closing of the Goshen College Home Economics
Department on the horizon, I moved to Oregon State University (OSU),
where that campus environment also encouraged international interests.
I joined a Great Decisions study group in the community using study
materials from the Foreign Policy Association. Retired OSU President
Robert MacVicar brought helpful insights to the issues for study, and
I developed greater awareness of how American politics affects other
countries. By that time I was an "internationalist" who was focused on
how to influence cooperation across national borders. Thinking of this
challenge, I voluntarily developed a Global Issues course on families and
their quality of life in the developing world, a course offered to meet
requirements in the General Education program of all students.

1997 – Signing the Quality Education Project funding proposal in the Mayor's office in Dhulikhel, Nepal, with Kathmandu University Vice-Chancellor Suresh Raj Sharma and Dhulikhel Municipality Mayor Bel Prasad Shrestha as witnesses.

During this time, since federal and other funding was available to support international students, more than ten percent of OSU's graduate students were from other countries. The display of over 100 national flags in the campus Memorial Union gave evidence of the broad variety of cultures represented on that campus over the previous decade.

Working with International Colleagues

OSU faculty reached out to other countries through generous funding from the USAID and other agencies. Two projects that included me and others in the College of Home Economics were (1) the faculty exchange program (USIA funding, 1990 to 1993) with a university in southern India (Avinashilingham Deemed University, Coimbatore, Tamil Nadu), and (2) a university strengthening program (USAID funding, 1992 to 1995) with the University of Malawi in Lilongwe (Bunda College of Agriculture): curriculum development in Family Resource Management and Foods and Nutrition. Through these programs I developed friendships and collegial relationships that resulted in continued professional support.

It was these positive experiences that finally led to my resignation at OSU in 1995 so that I could go to Nepal to work at Kathmandu University

(KU) with support again from MCC. One aspect of my work in Nepal (1995 to 1999) was especially gratifying. The Royal Danish Embassy's development agency, known as DANIDA, was involved in funding girls' education. It was an act of faith when the Vice-Chancellor of KU and the Mayor of the Dhulikhel Municipality (where the main campus was located), along with other community leaders, laid out their ideas for me to shape into a proposal for funding a Quality Education Project for the Dhulikhel schools. Many of the teachers were women who had had little opportunity for self-improvement. A four-year in-service teacher improvement program was funded and resulted in marked improvement in the quality of teaching, attendance of children in the schools, and condition of school buildings.

Another aspect of my work was the curriculum development for graduate programs in education. These were based in the KU School of Education and included a Master of Philosophy, PhD, and Teaching Certificate. With improved leadership in government positions, it would ultimately be the children of Nepal who would benefit from these programs.

In addition, I assisted with the university's request for funding to help build a women's hostel on the campus. This was intended to increase the overall percentage of women students at KU from twenty percent to at least forty percent by providing campus housing. DANIDA again provided funds, and the building was opened the next year (2000).

Those four years in Nepal were rich with cultural contrasts, with shared hospitality, and with the challenges of a work ethic appropriate for the Nepalese culture. My gracious and hard-working KU colleagues were focused on the development of viable programs in the School of Education. It was my belief that the best thing that could be done to help a nation help itself would be to *educate the people*. Today the KU School of Education programs are moving forward with excellent management and leadership.

The university experiences with international colleagues were greatly enhanced by my close associations with members of the International Federation for Home Economics (IFHE), which I joined in 1969 and then in 1972 attended the XIIth IFHE World Congress in Helsinki, Finland. There I met home economists from many different countries.

Meanwhile, the 1970s were times of expansion for the American Home Economics Association (AHEA), which secured funding for an International Family Planning project that empowered and supported women in many countries. The workshops provided materials focused on "Working with Villagers" to help women gain control of their lives for the sake of their families. At the end of that decade, a journalist and women's rights advocate, Perdita Huston, published two books based on her interviews with village women about themselves and their aspirations for themselves and their families.[33] These books gave visibility to women's concerns in developing countries where national development agencies were funding projects. Under the leadership of Arvonne Frasier and others, the "Women in Development" movement became a force for change in the focus for USAID (US Agency for International Development) funding so that women as well as men would benefit from projects to improve living conditions in poor countries. Elise Boulding, a sociologist and peace activist, spoke of women in poor countries as "the fifth world,"[34] meaning that they were the poorest of the poor and usually the most illiterate. She advocated education and economic opportunity for these neglected persons.

More opportunities continued to expand my global perspectives. Besides my sabbatical leave in 1982, I traveled to Porto Alegre in southern Brazil, sponsored by the Partners of the Americas states of Indiana and Rio Grande do Sul. There I observed women whose lives were being transformed by small-scale income-generating projects. They underscored the true value of E. F. Schumacher's philosophy that *Small is Beautiful*,[35] especially when it is applied to family environmental concerns. Later, in the mid-1990s, I served as a consultant for the Women in Development office of the UN Food and Agricultural Organization for Asia, based in Bangkok. My assignment took me to Thailand, Laos, and Vietnam with the mandate to explore the available technology for distance education programs for rural women in that region. The extensive networks in Thailand were models for potential programs in other countries.

For thirty-five years the IFHE gave me many opportunities to interact with professionals from more than sixty countries. The IFHE World Congresses that convened in these years gave attention to education strategies, food security, living conditions and environment, health, technology, and quality of life, families and change, the community dynamics of cooperation and interdependence, partnerships in national development, and relationships with United Nations' programs (e.g., the special years of the 1975 International Year of Women and the 1994 International Year of the Family). Congresses and/or council meetings were held in countries on all the major continents. With each congress came the opportunity to share different perspectives and also to learn about the host country's culture, problems, and programs.

Through these contacts I became more and more aware of the problems that affect families around the globe. Everywhere the home economics profession was influenced by the emancipation of women and the need for women's education at all levels. It recognized and promoted the importance of education for home and family life for both men and women.

Through interactions with people from many cultures and in many lands, I became an internationalist who was challenged and enriched through exposures to different ways of seeing the world and knowing God. As a result, I became convinced that through knowing people in diverse situations and in working with people to carry out a common mission, we contribute to the understandings that promote world peace.

Epilogue

My story as told includes most, but not all, of my life. When I married Clair L. Basinger in 2005, God planted me in a beautiful garden of people. A kind and loving husband, four daughters and sons-in-law, nine grandchildren, and thirteen great-grandchildren extended my family's diversity and loving support for continuing on life's journey. Besides them, I have my sisters and brothers-in-law, nieces and nephews, and a host of friends. Having moved back to the Harrisonburg community, I have come full circle and am now at home again!

December 10, 2007
Revised June 2008

Notes

1 S. F. Coffman, ed., *Life Songs Number Two* (Scottdale, PA: Mennonite Publishing House, 1938).

2 Alfred R. Gaul, *The Holy City. A Choral Worship Cantata* (New York: G. Schirmer). Written before 1913 as Gaul was deceased in 1913.

3 Hezekiah Butterworth, composer, and George F. Root, author, *David the Shepherd Boy. A Cantata in Ten Scenes for Choir and the Choral Society* (Cincinnati: John Church Company, 1882).

4 J. D. Brunk, musical ed., *Church and Sunday School Hymnal* (Freeport, IL: J. S. Shoemaker, and Elkhart, IN: Mennonite Publishing Co., 1902).

5 *The Church Hymnal* (Scottdale, PA: Mennonite Publishing House, 1927).

6 Walter E. Yoder, ed., *Songs of the Church* (Scottdale, PA: Herald Press, 1953).

7 *New Harmonia Sacra, A Compilation of Genuine Church Music,* 20th edition by Noah D. Showalter (Dayton, VA: Ruebush-Kieffer Company, 1942). The first edition was published by Joseph Funk & Sons, Singers Glen, VA, 1832.

8 *The Mennonite Hymnal* (Scottdale, PA: Herald Press, 1969). This hymnal was the successor to two Mennonite hymnbooks, *The Church Hymnal,* 1927, of the (Old) Mennonite Church and *The Mennonite Hymnary,* 1940, of the General Conference Mennonite Church. It was a joint project of several Mennonite denominations.

9 *Hymnal: A Worship Book,* Nancy Rosenberger Faus and Mary Oyer, hymnal project chairs (Elgin, IL: Brethren Press; Newton, KS: Faith and Life Press; Scottdale, PA: Mennonite Publishing House, 1992). It was a joint project of the Church of the Brethren and Mennonite denominations.

10 From the [Goshen] *College Mennonite Church Bulletin,* August 14, 2005.

11 *Sing the Journey: Hymnal: A Worship Book, Supplement 1* (Scottdale, PA: Faith & Life Resources, a division of Mennonite Publishing Network, 2005).

12 *Sing the Story: Hymnal: A Worship Book, Supplement 2* (Scottdale, PA: Faith & Life Resources, a division of Mennonite Publishing Network, 2007).

13 David Seitz directed The Shenvale Singers in Virginia and The Camarata Singers in Indiana.

14 Doyle Preheim directed the Goshen Community Chorale in Goshen, Indiana.

15 James A. Miller directed The Eugene Chamber Singers in Eugene, Oregon. He arranged an exchange with the Irkutsk Chamber Choir in Eugene in 1991 and in Siberia in 1993.

16 The *rondaval* structure, similar to a modern day *yurt*, consisted of rounded sticks tied together at the top to form the main supports for the tarp or scraps of cloth and plastic that were laid on to form a covering, simulating a "traditional circular African dwelling with a conical thatched roof."

17 Marcus J. Borg, *Meeting Jesus Again for the First Time: The Historical Jesus and the Heart of Contemporary Faith* (San Francisco: HarperOne, 1994).

18 Robert Walter Funk, *The Five Gospels: What Did Jesus Really Say? The Search for the Authentic Words of Jesus* (San Francisco: HarperOne, 1997). The Gospel of Thomas is included in this book. Funk is the founder of the Jesus Seminar, based in Sonoma, California, at the Westar Institute.

19 Marcus J. Borg, *The Heart of Christianity: Rediscovering a Life of Faith* (San Francisco: HarperOne, 2004).

20 John Shelby Spong, *Liberating the Gospels: Reading the Bible With Jewish Eyes* (San Francisco: HarperOne, 1997).

21 Huston Smith, *Why Religion Matters: The Fate of the Human Spirit in an Age of Disbelief* (New York: HarperSanFran, 2001).

22 Karen Armstrong, *The Spiral Staircase: My Climb Out of Darkness* (New York: Anchor Books, 2004).

23 Ruth Krady Lehman, "Marion Charlton. 'The one thing lacking is that she is a woman instead of a man.'" In *EMC Bulletin,* "Women Faculty at EMC," Spring 1983, pp. 2–3. Excerpted from Lehman's *"The One Thing Lacking ..." of The Status of Women Faculty at Eastern Mennonite College, 1917 to 1980,"* her thesis for the Bachelor of General Studies (Harrisonburg, VA: James Madison University, 1981). The statement was recorded in a letter written by the school's search committee chairman, dated April 10, 1914. He added, "As for myself, I was so favorably impressed with all her answers that the only regret I feel about it is that she is not a man instead of a woman. After all, she shows herself to be especially well qualified to do so much good as a teacher in her sphere. "

24 In August 1973 the first *"Report from the Peace Section Task Force on Women in Church and Society"* was published by the Mennonite Central Committee in Akron, PA. The series, focused on issues faced by women, continued through the 1980s with an evolution of title to "MCC Committee on Women's Concerns Report."

25 Dorothy Yoder Nyce, "Bible, Bishops, and Bombs." Paper based on an address given at a Goshen College chapel, March 2, 1983.

26 Anna Bowman, "Women and the Mennonite Patriarchy." *Goshen College Bulletin,* March, 1982. Reprint.

27 Mary Schertz, "Intersection: Feminist and Mennonite Theologies" (Elkhart, IN: Associated Mennonite Biblical Seminaries, 1983).

28 Dorothy Yoder Nyce, "Which Way Women?" (Elkhart, IN: Associated Mennonite Biblical Seminaries, 1983).

29 Alice H. Eagly and Linda L. Carli, *Through the Labyrinth: the Truth About How Women Become Leaders* (Boston: Harvard Business School Press, 2007).

30 Phoebe Cary, "The Leak in the Dike." In Miriam Blanton Huber, ed., *Story and Verse for Children* (New York: The Macmillan Company, 1940), 171–173.

31 Henry Wadsworth Longfellow, "The Song of Hiawatha." In Miriam Blanton Huber, ed., *Story and Verse for Children* (New York: The Macmillan Company, 1940), pp. 170–171.

32 Catherine R. Mumaw, *Technology, Women, and Change.* Development Monograph Series 11 (Akron, PA: Mennonite Central Committee, 1988).

33 Perdita Huston, *Message from the Village* (New York: Epoch B Foundation, 1978). Also see Perdita Huston, *Third World Women Speak Out: Interviews in Six Countries on Change, Development, and Basic Needs* (New York: Praeger, 1979).

34 Elise Boulding, *Women: The Fifth World* (New York, NY: Foreign Policy Association, 1980). Headline Series Pamphlet, 0017-8780 248.

35 E. F. Schumacher, *Small is Beautiful. Economics as if People Mattered* (New York: Harper Perennial, 1973). This book is thought to be among the 100 most influential books published since World War II, having been translated into many languages. It critiques the consumption model of Western economies and makes a case for human-scale, decentralized, and appropriate technologies.

Photo by James Gilroy

ELMER S. MILLER

Nodal Points in Personal Maturation

Pre-Teen Imprints

Two experiences from my pre-teen years have impacted my life in particular ways. First, my birth mother died several months prior to my third birthday. I have no memory of her except a lingering distaste for the "parlor" in our house, where her body had lain in a coffin. After her father had died in 1907 during a diphtheria epidemic when she was only four, she had been placed in the Brethren Home in Harrisburg. When she was nine, the Christ Hiestand family took her into their home, where she became a Mennonite and later met my father. Yet I have always felt a close attachment to her birth relatives, whom my family considered "people of the world." To this day I cannot write my name without the middle initial S, which stands for Sarah Schaffner. Physically and mentally the Schaffner dominates the Miller in me. Throughout life I have sensed her presence and communication, particularly in times of stress. However, I also have a strong childhood memory that is far less pleasant.

A clear mental picture I have of the house in which I grew up is the small southeast corner room where I slept. The kitchen stovepipe came through the floor at the far corner from the headrest of my bed. From that corner a swirling white substance would approach ever closer and larger in my sleep until I awoke in a cold sweat crying. When Papa did not hear my cry in the night, I would walk over sleepily to his bed, where he picked me up and carried me back with reassuring words. My new mama, who arrived when I was four and one-half years old, later recalled my appearances at their bed long after she had arrived. The sense of fear and dread generated by that nightmare is still palpable.

After my mother's death, Grandma Schaffner became our family's housemother for twenty months while Papa sought a new wife and mother for us. Grandma loved to tend our baby brother and appreciated my older sister's help around the house. In contrast, nursing me through the terrible twos and threes must have been a chore. In later years she made a quilt for each grandchild but skipped over mine to make sure she had the strength to complete one for my baby brother. Thus my closest personal relationship with a Schaffner was problematic.

Initially I refused to accept our new mama, Ruth Longenecker, but soon learned to love and accept her unreservedly. She immediately accepted the three of us as her very own, never changing her affection toward us throughout her life, even while she was raising the eight children she bore with Papa. My great-great-grandfather, David Miller, had married an Anna Longenecker, and the two family lines intermarried in succeeding generations. Actually, my wife, Lois Longenecker, was a first cousin to Mama Ruth; we had eyes on one another, beginning with the Rudiments of Music Class at Elizabethtown Mennonite Church several years before we were teenagers. After acquiring a car, I dated other young women in Lancaster County and later at Eastern Mennonite College before returning home to marry Lois in the summer prior to my senior year.

The second pre-teen imprint was my conversion experience at seven years of age during a revival campaign sponsored by our congregation, Bossler Mennonite Church. It was truly a sawdust trail in a tent located on the property where my mother had been raised. The preacher was Frank Lehman from York, Pennsylvania. While both he and my family were pleased at my confession of faith, the ministers and bishop expressed concern as to whether I had sufficient knowledge at that early age to understand fully the implications of the stand I had taken. After some deliberation they decided to allow me to participate in the class of instruction for church membership. Depending on my ability to comprehend the church doctrine imparted there, they would baptize me into full membership.

I completed the instruction class with no apparent difficulty and was recommended for baptism. The ceremony took place below Grandpa Miller's mill in a stream where Bishop Noah Risser baptized me with the assistance of the church pastor, Martin Kraybill, who was Papa's first cousin. Water from the stream that rushed over the wheel to grind the feed was poured over my head and shoulders to wash away symbolically my sins and remake me into a new person in Christ Jesus. According to the congregational record, the date was November 5, 1938, which would confirm my recollection of shivering and being rubbed down with big towels.

The mixed message of ministerial exuberance yet concern about the quality of my decision expressed by the ordained men dampened somewhat my enthusiasm for the "new life" and prompted reservations with regard to complete trust in pastoral authority. It may also have instilled the wariness that persisted throughout my youth. A further complication was the fact that my parents sometimes used my conversion experience as a form of social control when I misbehaved, reminding me that I was now a new person whose confession of faith required obedience to the standards of life laid down by my parents and church leaders.

When I was eleven, our family moved north of town and began to attend Strickler Mennonite Church, where Mama's uncle Harry Longenecker and Papa's uncle David Miller were the ministers and Mama's brother Phares Longenecker was the deacon. Thus we had connections to the entire ministerial bench. While rarely expressed openly, there was an inherent division among the congregants into Miller and Longenecker factions. When Uncle Harry preached, there were critical comments from the Miller clan and vice versa. Since our family had kin ties to both camps, I often felt caught in the middle. While I preferred Uncle Dave's preaching and tended to identify with the Millers, my closest buddy, Cousin Marty, was a Longenecker but also with Miller blood since his father, my uncle Phares, was married to Papa's sister—a further example of the Miller-Longenecker intermarriage previously noted.

Teen-age Markings

The decision to attend Lancaster Mennonite School was made *for* me rather than *by* me. Fully conscious of the financial burden it placed on my parents, I would gladly have attended Hershey High. Concerned about the worldly influence of a public high school, my parents had decided to send me to the church school my sister had attended her freshman year. Two positive memories stand out from that year at LMS: (1) my belated discovery of the joy of learning; and (2) the unexpected invitation to sing bass in a male quartet with three seniors.

The law required school attendance until one was fifteen, and my family followed it precisely. At sixteen, it was time to earn one's keep. Despite my strong desire to return somewhere for my sophomore year, my parents decided to hire me out to a potato farmer in our congregation. Sending each of us to church school for four years would have been prohibitively demanding on our meager family budget. There were seven of us, and number eight arrived during the spring term of my freshman year; three more arrived after I had left home. Equally significant was the fact that my parents seriously questioned the need for higher education at the time as did many families in our church and rural community. When my younger half siblings reached high school age, however, a high school diploma had come to be valued more highly. By that time LMS provided financial packages to assist those in need, and most of them completed high school.

During my four years on the farm, where I helped to pick thirty to thirty-five acres of potatoes and milked thirty-six cows twice a day, it became increasingly evident that I had no interest in farming as a career. It was a time of scattered exploration. Shortly before my eighteenth birthday I had saved enough money to buy my beloved 1948 jet-black Aero-sedan Chevy, which enabled me to date widely in Lancaster County and accompany two friends from Bossler Church to Youth for Christ meetings in Lancaster. Discovering fellow Christians who wore worldly clothing and served in the armed forces was a genuine shock, particularly since many of them seemed more committed to their faith than I was to mine! I remember handing out tracts in the city and preaching on at least one street corner.

Abe Gish, married to one of Papa's cousins, taught a Scofield Bible class in our community focused on dispensational theology and premillennialism, which I also attended occasionally with my YFC buddies. Together with Youth For Christ services, the Gish classes served to instill a double dose of fundamentalism into my understanding of the Christian faith. Both offered an intriguing alternative to the persistently boring focus on nonconformity and nonresistance in the weekly sermons at the Bossler and Strickler congregations. When the Marietta Mennonite Church, pastored by John Hiestand, whose family had raised my mother, was expelled from Lancaster Conference for their radio gospel program, I moved my membership there to support them. Also, their doctrinal teaching was more compatible with my growing attraction to fundamentalist theology.

On a sunny Sunday afternoon in June in 1950 Kenneth Good spoke at Elizabethtown Church. His evangelistic message calling for a full commitment to Christian service reinforced what I had been hearing at Youth for Christ, at the Scofield Bible classes, and most recently, in the Marietta congregation. When he asked those who wished to make a renewed commitment to serve Christ wherever it may lead to stand up, I did. The stand unleashed a powerful emotional encounter that radically changed my life forever. I continue to think of it as my second conversion experience. The farmer I worked for also stood, and we returned home in total silence. Throughout the evening chores and dinner I continued to utter not a single word, likely the longest period of silence in my lifetime! Subsequently I walked out the lane and up the small grade beyond to a cluster of trees, where I wrestled with my Creator for hours. On my walk back to my room in the moonlight, one thought sat in large letters in my mind: the need to acquire further schooling. With Papa's cousin Ira Miller's initiative and his sister-in-law Orpha Kraybill's assistance, I took the GRE Test and entered EMC (Eastern Mennonite College, now University) in the fall of 1950, a move that sadly required the sale of my prized Aero-sedan Chevy.

College and Seminary at EMC

My original intention was to take two years of Bible training and proceed to evangelistic work of one sort or another. I approached classes with fear and trepidation, highly conscious of my lack of preparation with only one year of high school four years previously. One positive booster was learning I had passed the College Entrance Exam with no need to take the make-up English Fundamentals course, which some students fresh out of high school were required to do. Getting Bs or higher during my freshman year was also a confidence builder.

It was a thrill to be chosen for Male Chorus with a planned tour to

Canada. Earl Maust asked me to sing bass with the Park View Melodian Quartet during the tour since their bass had left the community to study elsewhere. In time I learned to sing with a Virginia accent as we continued to sing together at college events and on gospel teams until my junior year, when a member of the quartet, Mark Lehman, graduated and I was invited to sing in the Mennonite Hour Quartet.

Traveling widely for the Mennonite Hour throughout the U.S. and southern Canada for my remaining college and seminary years was an enriching experience. It provided a perspective on the differences among Mennonites I had not imagined possible. In Manitoba, for example, being Mennonite meant speaking German and had nothing to do with the clothing one wore or the color of car one drove. At Winkler there were seven different Mennonite churches, five of which cooperated in sponsoring our program. Opening hymns, prayer, and our introduction were all in German. After our quartet had sung "God, the All Merciful," an elderly man raised his hand to ask how many people present remembered singing that tune in Russia under the tsars. Quite a few hands were raised throughout the huge audience; it was an emotional moment! We sang more than one hundred songs from memory, and I recall seeing "Russian National Anthem" under the title of one of them. All the branches of Mennonite churches were supportive of our work with the Mennonite Hour, expanding significantly my appreciation for the term *Mennonite*.

My switch from junior college to a six-year B.A./ThB program had come in my sophomore year sometime after my roommate, Eugene Herr, and I had visited Bob Jones University to determine whether we wished to transfer there. Gene was to become Billy Graham and I, Beverly Shea! On Young People's Christian Association trips to New Market and Mt. Jackson street corners, we practiced our parts on numerous occasions, particularly after I was named president of the association. During those years, we both held firmly to our fundamentalist theology; and I was determined to convert the famous amillennialist, C. K. Lehman, once I had the opportunity to take a class with him!

The opportunity finally arrived in my junior year in his course on ethics. Armed with scriptural quotations, I made a genuine effort to make the case. Each time I cited a text, "Brother Lehman" asked the class to examine the context. Who was the writer, to whom was he writing and with what intention? It was always the contextual meaning of a given citation to which he called our attention. At first it was frustrating, but with time it became intriguing since there was never a debate, merely an introduction to hermeneutics without calling attention to the term. On a weekend visit home I attended one of Abe Gish's classes, and at one point he asked where I stood on millennialism. When I attempted to explain my equivocations on the subject, he quickly pronounced me lost to the cause, and I never returned. Both he and my Youth For Christ buddies had initially expressed their disappointment at my decision to choose EMC over a conservative theology Bible college. However, once I had chosen EMC, my buddies faithfully provided prayer and financial support in times of need.

Needless to say, it was I who was converted. During the following four years, I took every class C. K. offered and learned something fresh in each one. He was also an inspiring song leader who called attention to the text and elicited spirited music. One particular exchange with him left a deep impression that has served me well to this day. Upon being named president of the YPCA, I told him God had told me to open up street meetings in Mt. Jackson. His response was, "Elmer, you must always say, I interpret this to be God's will for my life."

At EMC, also, Greek and Hebrew classes were pure delight, despite their demand on my time. Had I known how to make a living at it, I may well have pursued textual criticism as a career. Paul Peachy opened up a world of thinking that broadened my perspectives on the church and the social order, and I attended all of his classes as well. I would be remiss not to mention the impact Mrs. Brackbill's literature classes had on my approach to a text. By the spring of 1956, when I graduated from the seminary, a world of understanding had opened up that would never close. In my book *Nurturing Doubt* (University of Illinois Press, 1995) I describe a moment alone in the library when it became apparent to me that my view of biblical inspiration had changed in a manner not shared by my professors and fellow students at the time. That moment of exciting insight was overshadowed by an intruding sense of loneliness: there was no one with whom to share my excitement over the joy of discovery.

My initial job offer that spring came from George R. Brunk II, who asked me to become the manager of his tent campaign and back-up song leader. While the offer was far from my thinking at the time, it was encouraging to learn of his confidence in my leadership potential. The second invitation was from a congregation in Oregon; but before Lois and I could travel there to investigate, J. D. Graber (from MBM, the Mennonite Board of Missions) arrived on campus. The invitation to serve with MBM in the Argentine Chaco among the indigenous Toba seemed a perfect fit. The Strickler congregation had supported Uncle Dave's son Sam and Ella Mae Miller in the Chaco; thus the Toba were familiar to me. Uncle Dave often read letters from Sam and Ella Mae to our congregation, and we took regular offerings to support them. I remembered emptying my savings bank for them when they had dinner with us shortly before departing for Argentina. I had also studied Spanish with J. W. Shank, who spoke frequently about the Toba and his experiences in the Chaco.

The icing on the cake, however, was the recommendation to attend the Kennedy School of Missions at Hartford, Connecticut, the following year to pursue training in anthropology and linguistics. I had become aware of the two disciplines only recently and wished to learn more. Furthermore, I had been reading some Tillich and Bultmann on my own and found them intriguing. At Hartford it would be possible, also, to pursue my new theological tastes!

Mission Training

By the time I learned the term *culture shock* in anthropology I had already experienced it at Hartford. The first day of class in linguistics Professor Welmers walked in the door smoking a cigarette. He proceeded to an open window, flicked the butt through it, and returned to the front of the class. Upon fully exhaling the smoke, his first words were, "Let us bow our heads in a word of prayer!" Dumfounded would be an understatement of my mental state at that moment. Ironically, I later learned he was the most evangelical professor on campus!

Both linguistics and anthropology were pure delight. They also proved useful in learning the Toba language and culture. Dr. Paul's course on Latin America provided an excellent foundation in the history and culture of the continent and got me started on a Toba bibliography that years later became a two-volume publication by the Human Relations Area Files at Yale. The search for sources took me to libraries beyond Hartford to Yale and Harvard, to New York and Washington, DC, and finally to the Newberry Library in Chicago. In Argentina I continued the research at libraries in Buenos Aires, La Plata, Cordoba, Resistencia, and Tucuman. The two volumes eventually contained over a thousand items in thirteen different languages, all of which I had translated into English or Spanish and annotated. Along with an historical ethnographic introduction, this work later became my master's thesis at Hartford.

I mention this not to boast about the extensive effort that went into that bibliographic study, but rather to set the stage for discussion of a seminar I had with Professor Leser that perhaps proved to be the most important influence on my intellectual growth, shaping eventually how I came to read texts, including the Bible, and how I continue to read today. The seminar, entitled Critique of Sources, was based upon the assumption that most people read and write uncritically, often stealing ideas and mixing them up with others that simply do not cohere logically or with integrity. Professor Leser had taken his training in anthropology under the famous German scholar Fritz Graebner, and he had received the only PhD in anthropology that Graebner awarded—Graebner felt that no other student had truly earned one.

In the seminar he challenged us to write a paper identifying the copying of a source without proper documentation. I remembered having heard years previously that Anis Charles Haddad's articles in the *Gospel Herald* had relied uncritically on other sources, but I had not thought more about it until this need to find a project for my paper. Since I knew Mama saved back copies of the *Herald* (I always thought partly because the editor, Paul Erb, was a distant relative), I called to ask her to send me a year's supply of them. After extensive reading I latched upon an article Haddad had written on Petra and began to read books on the Middle East like *In the Steps of the Master, In the Steps of St. Paul,* etc. In time I came across a phrase that rang a bell. Haddad was describing his descent into Petra as proceeding "downward ever downward into bleakness and solitude." I returned to the Haddad article, and sure enough there were the identical words. When I showed them to Prof. Leser, he immediately responded, "Search on, my dear friend; the entire article is copied." I did not believe him but continued the search and eventually found all the sources of that article except for sections I attributed to another author whom I could not find. Upon our return to Hartford after our stint in the Chaco, Prof. Leser said a later student had found the source to be *The National Geographic!*

Prof. Leser recommended that I not report this to the editor since he would be upset at his failure to recognize the problem and the author would lose his livelihood. My conscience would not allow me to leave it at that, so I sent Paul Erb a copy of my paper. He was, indeed, chagrined; Mr. Haddad lost his writing assignment but salvaged a job in the publishing shop. The experience was disturbing in many ways, but it taught me a lesson that shaped my reading after that—although I confess to having a sense of losing something of the edge for critical thought over time.

At Hartford we all read Donald McGavran's *Bridges of God* (1981), which stressed an indigenous approach to missions that recognized God's work among the people we were about to evangelize. When I later expressed some ambiguity to Secretary Graber about the missionary role I was expected to perform among the Toba, he responded, "Go and be a brother." With the encouragement and support of the Buckwalter family, that was the principle that guided our interactions with both the Toba and Spanish-speaking Argentines from October 1958 until August 1963.

During our move to Hartford, I asked Lois if she would be willing to discard the prayer veiling. She agreed, with the exception of in chapel, which left me slightly annoyed. When we visited Uruguay en route to the Chaco, I recounted her choice to Dan Miller, who said, "I asked Eunice to abandon it, too, but she refuses. The veiling is supposed to be a symbol of male authority, but in reality it represents insubordination!" Those of you who knew Dan are aware of his wondrously subtle sense of humor.

At Hartford we visited a variety of Christian churches, all of them more ritualistic and theologically liberal than any we had attended previously. In the end we found ourselves most comfortable at a Quaker Meeting, where the highly respected seminary professor, Dean Purdy, tended to break the silence with words of wisdom that set the tone for the services. Public lectures and discussions with seminary students enriched my understanding of the latest trends in liberal theology. Nevertheless, it was anthropologist Paul Leser's classes in anthropology that made the greatest impact on my thinking. While the thought of pursuing his discipline may have crossed my mind, it was not a serious consideration at the time.

From Hartford we proceeded to the Summer Institute of Linguistics at Norman, Oklahoma, for three months and subsequently to San Jose, Costa Rica, for a full year of Spanish language study. In addition to the instruction we received at both locations, our interaction with fellow students was also enlightening. The vast majority of them were fervently evangelical, fitting nicely the profile of a missionary envisioned at Youth For Christ, Scofield Classes, and the Marietta congregation. In fact, the Marietta Church made a commitment to support us in our missionary work throughout our stay in the Chaco. However, by the time we had completed language training, I was aware that our supporting congregation would have been more pleased with the theological stance of our fellow missionary trainees than with our own. My primary discomfort was not in the theology per se, but the lack of interest in and knowledge about the cultures the trainees were about to engage. With few notable exceptions, the indigenous approach to missions appeared to be an unknown, perhaps even an undesired, perspective in Oklahoma and Costa Rica.

Despite this observation, we made genuine friendships and shared spirited worship and play with fellow missionaries in both places. At the University of Oklahoma it was volleyball in the hot sun. I played on Kenneth Pike's team, where my responsibility was to set up the ball for him to spike it! In Costa Rica it was intense language study in the morning and touch football or basketball in the afternoon. We even had a team that played in the city league. Several evenings a week and on weekends we played cards when study assignments were completed. Since many of our closest friends had children, we traveled to their apartments to play after the babies were asleep. With one couple headed for Honduras we played Rook; with another headed for Venezuela we played Pinochle; and with a third headed for Nicaragua it was Canasta. If this appears to be too much recreation for serious missionary training, you must believe me when I affirm it was not. "Hard work and hard play" was the motto, and it was effective both in Norman and San Jose.

Field Experiences

Most significant in solidifying my personal ongoing transformation from a traditional evangelical believer to an eventual one-universe Christian was life among the Toba in the Argentine Chaco. To adapt an old adage, "You can take a man out of the Chaco, but you cannot take the Chaco out of a man." During the years we lived there, I seriously underestimated the degree to which life among the Toba had reconfirmed, even in the process of reformulating, my developing comprehension of "ultimate reality" and sense of responsibility to it. The Overture to *Nurturing Doubt* describes five encounters with the Toba that illustrate examples of interpersonal encounters contributing to this developmental process.

Hunter-gatherers tend to perceive the observed physical universe as Provider, which prompts them to resist with all their heart, soul, and mind the concept of production essential to a market economy. Their relationship with the physical world was established generations ago on the principle of dependence, which makes them vulnerable to exploitation by capitalist entrepreneurs to the point that their worldview is dramatically shaken. Christian missions helped to shake that reality, also, but the Toba have been proactive in their encounter with Christian faith to the extent that they have transformed it to fit their own reality. The form of Christianity that captured their imagination was Pentecostalism in its least institutionalized form. Since I have written about this extensively during my academic career, there is no need to develop it further here except to note it was not until years later, after suffering culture shock upon our return to the United States, that I came to recognize the extent to which interactions with the Toba had contributed to the transformation of my worldview in the late 1950s and early 1960s.

Graduate School and Academia

Upon completion of our term in the Chaco in August of 1963 we proceeded to Hartford in September, where I was awarded a J. B Hartzler Scholarship. During the fall semester, I began to entertain seriously the notion of pursuing a career in anthropology. The two of us resigned then from the Mission Board, and I applied to graduate schools for admission to a PhD program. It was a heady time. The civil rights marches were in progress, and fellow-student Andrew Young spoke in chapel one morning about his experiences marching in Alabama. He explained how the songs we sang in the peaceful setting on campus took on a totally different connotation on southern streets, where he was fully aware that his life was constantly on the line. J. F. Kennedy was killed that semester, and the shock of watching the scenes on our missionary friend's television set contributed to a sense of alienation, both from the Chaco world and the one to which we had returned. Existentialism was an active topic on campus, and I was particularly attracted to Peter Berger's critique of contemporary Christianity. Upon completion of the spring semester I was awarded an M.A. in anthropology.

That summer the Mission Board sent us on a deputation tour to the Board meetings in La Junta, Colorado. I gained the impression, possibly incorrectly, that the churches we visited were far more interested in how many souls were saved in the Chaco than in the actual spiritual life of the people themselves. Upon our return, when we stopped to acquire a projector at the Missionary Equipment store in Chicago, our car was broken into and our worldly possessions stolen, including hundreds of select slides from the Chaco, without which we no longer needed the projector and thus did not buy one. That night we gave a program in North Goshen without our slides or dress clothing. Lois was expecting and had lost her special attire, some of it borrowed. Russell and Martha Hiestand Krabill—she a Hiestand from the family who raised my birth mother—graciously suggested lifting an offering to help us buy clothing.

I entered graduate school in the fall of 1964 at the University of Pittsburgh, fully conscious that my missionary role was low on the totem pole in terms of respect. We had been sufficiently well prepared for life in the Chaco to experience no serious shock upon arrival there. However, nothing had prepared us for that first year's experiences upon return to the U.S., and the shock was far greater, in retrospect, than I comprehended at the time. The temptation to shed all connections to my roots was powerful. I began to question the value of any religious affirmation whatsoever and stupidly announced it freely, alienating not only our missionary colleagues, whom I cared about greatly, but even more significantly, my family.

Papa always called on me to pray at our family outings. When we gathered on Labor Day in 1963, I told him not to ask me to pray before the meal; but he chose to do so anyway. I gave thanks to God for food, friends, health, and the good life, but proceeded to say, "While we thank you for these blessings, we must also fault you for failing to provide these same good things for so many people throughout the world who suffer hunger, sickness, alienation, and loneliness." "Amen" was barely out of my mouth when I began to feel remorse for this insensitive act.

To escape confrontation I followed Mama into the kitchen, where she put her arms around me lovingly and said, "Elmer, when you went to Argentina among those Indians, didn't you say you tried to fit in with the way they thought and lived? Why can't you do the same when you return home?" I returned her embrace, and with tearful eyes simply responded, "Mama, bingo."

In graduate school at the University of Pittsburgh I was prepared for snide remarks about missionaries, but they never came. In fact, several professors commented favorably about the work of missionaries on indigenous languages and cultures. My own extensive field experience was respected and called upon in class. Professor Murdock even published a paper of mine on Toba kin terms, which he asserted to be his first publication of a student's writings. Both of our daughters were born during those two years, contributing to our positive memories of the steel city. We had no health insurance, but the university had a program in which specialists gave their professional service free to graduate students, an unexpected bonus in our time of need.

Shortly after I had enrolled in Pittsburgh, church leaders from the Mission Board and Scottdale asked if we would consider helping to initiate a congregation in the city. Upon making friends with two other Mennonite couples, also in graduate study, we began to meet on Sunday mornings to discuss an agreed upon book. My initial suggestion was *The Stranger* by Albert Camus, which was likely not what the Board had in mind! However, we rapidly proceeded to less provocative materials, and several non-university couples later joined us. Little

Leading a group of Temple University students in Italy (with campus in Rome), here on an outing inPompeii.

did I expect those initial gatherings to evolve eventually into an active congregation! Today it is gratifying to have had a minor role, however incidental, in that development.

During my teaching years later at Temple University, we attended various churches from time to time in search of a home, including Germantown Mennonite, which was exceedingly small and too traditional for our tastes. Each of our daughters had a close friend whose family attended an active congregation, one a Methodist, the other Unitarian. We went to one or the other from time to time. In the classroom I spoke frequently about my experiences as a Mennonite and missionary. In fact, John Hostetler and I were widely recognized as the resident college Mennonite faculty! They had no idea how much better connected Hostetler was than I! When Messiah College established a residency on campus, the administration asked me to serve as a liaison for purposes of integrating the program and assisting students. In retrospect I regret not having been ready for serious dialogue at the time, which could have been mutually beneficial. There were numerous opportunities available but, regretfully, I was not in a mental or spiritual disposition to take advantage of them.

Late in my career at Temple an undergraduate student asked if I had ever considered that God might have me exactly where he wanted! The comment struck a chord that would not fade. When least expected, it nagged at me in ways that I suspect eventually contributed to my return to and membership at Germantown Mennonite. I knew about that church's struggle with Franconia Conference over the sexual identity issue and eventually with the Eastern District as well. Lois and I were friends with Jim and Fern Derstine, who had introduced us to several church member families. But what really sealed the deal was what happened the first time we visited with the intent of supporting the congregation in its stand. Mary Ann Mellinger preached a sermon that knocked my socks off with its integrity and inspiration. When the congregation was invited to the communion table, I proceeded forward to participate, an action that left Lois in a state of shock! We attended regularly from that time forward and joined about a year later when Lois was prepared to accompany me. Richard Lichty, who meanwhile had become sole pastor, made a special effort to incorporate us into the congregation; he even asked me to preach from time to time.

Attending Germantown prompted awareness of what I had missed by failing to commit to a community of faith where my perspectives on living could be challenged and opportunities for spiritual growth explored on a persistently interactive basis. My connection to the larger Mennonite Church community has remained tenuous, owing in part to the alienation some members at Germantown Mennonite continue to experience. However, it is not resentment I feel since we were not with the congregation when the break with Franconia Conference occurred. Rather, my own disconnect from the larger church relates to issues of concern expressed by broader church leadership to which I cannot relate. A year ago I was asked to represent our congregation on the Germantown Mennonite Historic Trust Executive Committee, where I have gained a more positive perspective on fellow Mennonites in the larger church constituency. That experience has been rewarding and broadened my appreciation for more church-wide interaction. Our trip to China in the fall of 2006, sponsored by ACRS (the Anabaptist Center for Religion and Society) and CEE (China Educational Exchange, now MPC, Mennonite Partners in China) has reinforced that impression. In Florida, where Lois and I spend the winter months, we have established a meaningful relationship with the Covenant Mennonite Fellowship, which has also been a boon to our spiritual growth and development.

Some of you may be aware of serious health issues that have plagued my life, beginning in 1975 with the discovery of thyroid cancer. In 1992 it was a head-on car collision that left me unconscious and required extensive stitching over my right eye; in 2000, the discovery of coronary artery disease and my first stent; in 2001, prostate cancer and seed radiation; in 2003, another stent; and in 2004, a double bypass. During the latter period, I also had both cataracts removed and artificial lenses implanted. We will not talk about what all this has done to support the budgets of Temple and University of Pennsylvania Hospitals, but rather what impact it has had on my spiritual growth and development. Certainly it raised my awareness of dependence upon the Spirit of Life for survival on a daily basis, for which I am deeply grateful. I am also more appreciative of good doctors and Temple's super healthcare package, thanks to the Faculty Union, which I did not consistently support! In many ways I think of each new day as a gift not to be taken for granted, although to be completely candid, the awareness tends to be aroused more readily at moments of vulnerability. Certainly tennis has taken on huge importance in my life since it is the best exercise I can count on to provide the stimulation necessary to keep the blood flowing through the arteries at the rate required to keep me healthy.

Finally, the most important and steady influence in my life has been my wife, Lois. From ten years of age (as noted previously), when we both attended a class in the rudiments of music at Elizabethtown Mennonite Church, we have had eyes on one another. Since then, I have always known Lois would be there for me. A more steady rock in my life I cannot imagine. College friends suggested it would be unwise to return to a childhood sweetheart after college years had separated us, but I am eternally grateful I did. We married the summer prior to my senior year. Throughout graduate school, our Chaco experiences, and professional life in academia, Lois has been a pillar of support and encouragement. Our daughters and sons-in-law depend on her as I do, and the grandchildren are at the age where they recognize her steady presence as well. She nursed me through my health episodes with tender and loving care. In many ways our best times together are now in retirement. We have already been at it ten years, and she has not yet indicated boredom; so prospects for the future appear bright! Thank you, my dear Lois.

November 13, 2006
Revised 2008

ROBERT LEE

Seeking the Center, Living on the Margins

Part I, Growing Up (1928 to 1951): Living in Three Worlds

In editing the memoirs in the first volume of *Making Sense of the Journey,* I became aware of how differently my social background influenced my growing up. In particular, I did not need to come to terms with the *tradition*—that strong rural (even for those who were no longer rural) religio-ethnic identity called "Mennonite"—that informed the memoirs of my colleagues.

Although I was born and raised the son of Chinese parents living in a working-class neighborhood in northwest Portland, Oregon, and became a Mennonite city mission convert before I was thirteen years old, I had no strong sense of being raised in one tradition, either the Chinese or the Mennonite. Rather, in growing up I discovered myself living in three worlds or, more accurately, in one world segmented into three societies with three distinct cultures—two mini-societies (Chinese and Mennonite) encapsulated within the larger public society.

In the Chinese familial society I was reared in an immigrant, minimally literate family, the only Chinese family in the neighborhood. As the oldest of four children, I spoke only colloquial Chinese to my parents and only English to my siblings—Jean, Florence, and William. We related to other Chinese families by fictitious kinship, often visiting Chinatown (the center of the Chinese community) for meeting friends, shopping, eating at restaurants, and attending Chinese school.

In the American public or secular society I played with the neighborhood's mostly Catholic children, who attended a parochial school; but I went to a small (for Portland) public grade school with 600 students.

My tiny Mennonite society revolved around the Portland Mennonite Mission, located one block away on the same (Savier) street as our home. This Pacific Coast Mennonite Conference city mission consisted of the mission superintendent and his family, several single women mission workers, a few local working families and individuals, and others who commuted regularly on Sundays from nearby rural Mennonite churches. The mission program revolved around the children's Sunday school, summer Bible school, and neighborhood home visits.

Because there was little overlap among the people in my three worlds, my early childhood was segmented without much conflict into the three societies, each with its distinct culture. Further, because of language problems, my parents did not meet with the mission workers in their home visits, interacted only minimally with people in the neighborhood, and rarely entered into decisions regarding our pubic school education. Thus instead of a family tradition, what became central in my growing up was *going to school* (three schools). Education, both in my childhood and adult life, provided my basic understanding of the social realities of the world.

Along with attending public grade school and Chinese school (evenings and Saturday mornings), I regularly attended the mission Sunday school. One Sunday the teacher asked who wanted to become a Christian...wanted to follow Jesus. To what seemed like a rhetorical question, I (as well as the entire class) quickly responded positively. Thus our beloved teacher, Albert Snyder, who commuted each Sunday, taught the instruction class instead of the resident mission superintendent. He led us through the 1940s' church instruction manual for beginning Christians, which included the usual teachings about God, Christ, the Holy Spirit, and the church under the seven ordinances (baptism, communion, foot washing, marriage, prayer covering, holy kiss, and anointing the sick with oil). The teachings on the seven ordinances were especially helpful since they provided me a conceptual framework for understanding the way of life of this community—their separation from, nonconformity to, and not being unequally yoked to the world. These teachings now made sense of my Mennonite world of separation—the plain dress, non-use of jewelry, refusal to join unions, the rejection of life insurance, etc.

From this instruction class only I received baptism, and it changed my life. I now faithfully stayed for church service after Sunday school and attended Sunday evening young people's meeting, the evening church service, and the Wednesday evening prayer meetings. While in high school I began teaching Sunday school, speaking on the Sunday evening young people's programs, and attending the Conference quarterly mission meetings.

Segmentation/Encapsulation

This social order continued not only through my high school days with changing sets of people but even through my college years. While majoring in electrical engineering at Oregon State University in Corvallis, I found a surrogate home with a local Lee family, commuted twenty miles to the Albany Mennonite church on weekends, and as often as possible returned to Portland to family, to gainful employment at Chandler's shoe store, and to the Portland mission-church. Graduation brought me back home to Portland to work as a system engineer at the Bonneville Power Administration (a U.S. Department of the Interior agency for the design, construction, operation, and marketing of the electrical power of the high-voltage transmission network in the Northwest).

Now, even though my professional career was progressing well, my relationships within my two encapsulated worlds were becoming increasingly tenuous. I seemed to be marking time in my church life. Restless, I applied to the Mennonite Central Committee (MCC) and asked to go to Hong Kong. However, by 1951 all the Mennonite work in China had already been closed (1949), and the MCC work in Hong Kong was also closing down. Instead, MCC proposed my going to Europe.

Part II, Leaving Home (1951 to 1964): Collapsing Three Worlds into One

In the fall of 1951 I found myself at MCC headquarters in Akron, Pennsylvania, for a week of orientation for new workers. Immediately my three worlds collapsed into one. MCC was like one big family with a common faith and a common commitment for service. For the first time for me, community, culture (faith), and work had found a center.

Europe

In Europe I was assigned to Mennonite Voluntary Service (MVS) under Cal Redekop. Here I became part of the MVS caravan, a traveling work-camp team that extended the international summer work-camp program into a continuous series of short-term work camps throughout the year. The MCC-MVS team members served as the core/continuing caravan members, who then included short-term European volunteers and a few MCC-PAX personnel in an annual program, which culminated in the MCC international summer multi-camp program.

At the end of WWII the international work-camp movement brought diverse groups of idealistic young people, as well as refugees, together in physical labor to meet the material needs of recent enemies as a way of peace and reconciliation for both the victims and offenders of war. Christian work camps included Bible study and worship to add a spiritual dimension to the corporate healing process.

In this MVS program I discovered a pattern evolving during each work camp (as I would learn about later in studying small-group-development theory): the creation (birth) of community out of a diverse, often alienated group of individuals, who through daily labor, discussion, study, and worship would form a new community, encounter conflict and (often dramatically) find reconciliation, and finally depart with a fond farewell (death) scene. Thus the work-camp experience became a microcosm[1] of a new way of life for many when they returned to their everyday life.

At the end of summer, just when the MVS caravan members had reassembled to begin their second year of work, Cal Redekop completed his term of service in Europe. MCC then abruptly reassigned the American MVS members, and I was seconded to the World Council of Churches (WCC) as a traveling resettlement officer stationed in Hanover. My new work assignment was to follow up the WWII refugees left behind after the mass overseas resettlement programs of WCC and other agencies. Thus I was constantly on the road to interview refugees in scattered refugee camps throughout the southern half of the British occupation zone.

Toward the end of my two-year term in Europe, for the first time I met personally with Orie Miller, the MCC executive secretary, to seek advice for the future. While many of my MCC colleagues in Europe saw their service as a temporary hiatus in their life, my earlier resignation from my civil service appointment at Bonneville Power Administration was an open-ended one, an opportunity for me to seek the center of my life in service to Christ. To Miller I expressed how meaningful my first year of work-camp experience had been in serving the Mennonite church, but my second-year assignment was disappointing since it separated me from Mennonite fellowship. Miller quickly responded, describing the new MCC plans to meet the tremendous needs of a war-torn South Korea.

Korea

In July 1953 I found myself at MCC headquarters in Akron, and within three weeks I was on a freighter bound for Japan. By August I was in South Korea, where an armistice in the civil war allowed relief work to begin in the South.

In contrast to the orderliness of an occupied and divided Germany (1951 to 1953), South Korea was chaotic. The American military KMAC (Korea Military Assistance Command) and the South Korean army were everywhere, running everything. Although MCC came under the jurisdiction of KMAC—who were responsible for maintaining civil order among the civilian population, especially the flood of refugees (including many Christians) from the North—KMAC showed little interest in MCC activities.

In Korea MCC's long-term project, assigned from UNNRA, was to develop a vocational training school for older orphan boys on an abandoned farm at nearby Kyongsan, a *rehabilitation* project that because of the chaotic situation would require the MCC director in Korea, Dale Weaver, and subsequent MCC staff several years to establish. Meanwhile, Orie Miller was rapidly recruiting new personnel for Korea, compounding Weaver's logistical nightmares of finding sufficient housing, transportation, interpreters, cooks, electricity, etc. Further, the "ugly" foreigners became the constant objects of daily petty and sometimes bold thievery. Under such tensions the newly arriving college-educated MCC workers had difficulty adjusting and finding meaningful work assignments—except the nurses, who responded quickly to the needs of the malnourished "peanut-sized" babies in the many orphanages. In my case, because the MCC warehouses were overfilled with U.S.

government surplus and MCC relief supplies and because no one else seemed interested, by default (at Weaver's request) I volunteered to establish a material-aid *relief* program.

In addition to solving the logistical needs of the MCC Daegu unit and finding appropriate (relief/rehabilitation/development)[2] work assignments for the incoming new workers, Weaver suddenly faced another problem: An MCC-PAX unit—briefly trained under UNNRA to do community *development* work with local farmers, introducing cottage industries, new agricultural methods, etc.—abruptly dissolved when its two college-educated leaders resigned and returned to the States. As a result five disillusioned young PAX men, who did not want to return home but hoped to complete their alternative service, were absorbed into the Daegu unit. At this point J. N. Byler, Assistant MCC Director, arrived from Akron headquarters to resolve the crisis.

After witnessing a month of indecisions and feeling sorry for these young men, I proposed to Byler that these and the other PAX men at the farm (whose program was also not underway) could regroup as a team to expand my material-aid *relief* program. I had in mind my work-camp experience, where work became service and along with Bible study and discussion created a loving community that included both Europeans and Americans. Now here in Korea the PAX men joined a group of Korean college and medical school students, who participated in MCC discussion groups and also volunteered service in our material-aid distribution program. Although the PAX men showed little interest in student discussions, I was impressed by their work ethic. For them, doing a superb job in the expanded relief program (an eight-to-five job) was not sufficient; they expected to do more.

It was these PAX men who agreed to begin a voluntary work camp on Saturdays to help the most needy in this needy world. When the city government periodically cleared out the *hockle-ban* (squatters' shacks) throughout the city, the PAX men went to the outskirts of the city to help a widow build her house. For building materials they collected cardboard and tin cans (corrugated for roofing) from their relief distributions, hauled large flat stones (for a heated *ondo* floor) from the riverbed, and bought the cheapest (tiny 1" x 1") lumber and straw with their own meager funds to build a mud shack. By summer this weekend work-camp idea had expanded into the first annual summer international

work camp in Korea with the addition of Korean student volunteers from
Seoul and Daegu and a talented group of overseas volunteers from the
U.S. Hollywood Presbyterian Church.

In Korea I did not meet personally with Orie Miller but instead received his approval of my activities through Weaver, the Korea MCC
director. Thus the following year, nearing the completion of my three-
year term in Korea, I was surprised to learn from the director that I was
being seconded again, this time to Korea Church World Service (KCWS)
for the remainder of my term.

In Seoul KCWS was a thoroughly Korean-run church agency that
included staff representing CWS/USA and/or WCC in a polar opposite
structure to my European WCC experience. My role was to reorganize
their material-aid program and to serve as a liaison to all the missionary
stations related to KCWS. Although I was again out of the Mennonite
familial world, I was well received by the missionaries and the Koreans—
precisely because I was Mennonite.

In a society divided by civil war and mobilized by the military—
including a closely allied and triumphant (but also divided) Christian
church—some Korean Christians and foreign missionaries found the
Mennonite peace witness an attractive alternative. Thus, as I escorted
J. D. Graber, Mennonite Board of Missions (MBM) overseas director, on
his field tour in Korea, I asked about my serving under Mennonite auspices in Korea. However, at the end of his tour Graber concluded that
because Korea was already well churched, I should instead go to seminary to prepare for missionary work in Japan.

I was disappointed that a Mennonite witness in Korea could not
develop, allowing me to continue to serve in Korea; but at that time
Graber's reasoning in the context of the rapid church growth in South
Korea made sense to me. Ironically, today, years after the MCC work was
totally phased out, the dynamic peace witness of an Anabaptist center
and an Anabaptist church has arisen in Seoul largely through the efforts of Korean Christians.

Goshen Biblical Seminary

That fall (1956) since my training was in electrical engineering, I entered seminary with trepidation, aware that I did not have the proper
prerequisites (a liberal arts and/or social studies major) from my

undergraduate work. However, I again experienced the joy of the collapse of my multi-worlds—a total reorientation into one centered world, especially through the biblical studies in John Miller's survey of the Old Testament, which he titled The Covenant People, and Howard Charles' inductive study of New Testament books.

I recalled that immediately after baptism the summer I was thirteen, I had decided to read the Bible from cover to cover, literally in forty days and forty nights, moving rapidly over the genealogies and dynastic successions. Now suddenly the Bible not only made sense to me but also proved conceptually integrative; that is, it provided a biblical theology to undergird all my academic work under Paul Miller, J. C. Wenger, Dean H. S. Bender, and others.

In addition, on the social side, my roommate invited me to join the John Miller/Virgil Vogt (Concern) house church, which later became the Reba Place Church in Evanston. Here our long evening biblical/theological discussions on such topics like "loosing and binding" (Matt. 16:19b)[3] created an intense fellowship leading to commitment and discipleship not unlike that of my European MCC work-camp experience.

Most important, I met Nancy Burkholder, who was teaching in the college (discussed elsewhere by Nancy,[4] but here I offer my side of the beginning of our friendship). When my best friend at Goshen, Herb Klassen, suggested in chapel that we move forward together to sit nearer a junior faculty member in whom he was interested, I moved beside Nancy. Nancy was indeed lovely, but I was shy.

Although I do not remember our first date, I think it is true that while in the infirmary for the flu, I telephoned her for our first date. I recall hating to be sent to the health clinic because I disliked missing classes. Isolated with a stack of textbooks, I must have found the courage to make the call. Later, in 1958 before Christmas during my senior year, we were married in the Annex area at Goshen College. (The seminary chapel was not yet finished; and the gym, where the Goshen College Church then held its services, seemed too large and unsuitable for a small wedding.)

Just before graduation I talked to classmate John Litwiller, who was seeing Dean Bender about going to Union Theological Seminary (New York) for graduate studies. (He, Orley Swartzendruber and J. R. Burkholder,

I was told, had wanted to build a Mennonite seminary program in South America—an idea that the Mission Board rejected.) I thought going to graduate school would be a great idea, too.

When I met with Dean Bender, he responded sharply, "Who asked you to teach?"

I was taken aback. That pursuing higher education was to acquire credentials to teach had never occurred to me. Rather, because I so enjoyed my seminary education, I wanted an opportunity to continue my studies to better prepare for missionary work. After consulting with MBM's overseas director, J. D. Graber (who had married Nancy and me), we decided instead to go directly to Japan.

On the way we stopped in Portland, Oregon, for my ordination in my home congregation in the Pacific Coast Conference by Marcus Lind, then principal of Western Mennonite High School who had earlier baptized me when he was the superintendent of the Portland Mission. It had been under his tutelage in summer Bible school that I learned my first fifty Bible verses—from Genesis to Revelation—from which I constructed my first biblical theology.

Japan

In the fall of 1959 we enrolled in the intensive Japanese language program at ICU, the new bi-lingual International Christian University in Tokyo. Two years later, in July 1961, we moved to Obihiro in central Hokkaido to replace Carl and Esther Beck, who had left for a North American furlough. Now our "we" had become four with the birth first of Steven Paul in November 1959 and then of Suelyn Virginia in May 1961. Our Robert John (Bobby) would arrive in November 1963.

By 1961 the mission work in Hokkaido radiated from the two earliest centers, Kushiro in the east and Obihiro in central Hokkaido, with new work beginning in Sapporo in western Hokkaido. Instead of a trained pastor-centered church (not practical in rural Hokkaido), the mission moved toward developing lay leadership supported by an itinerant Bible-training program modeled after Howard Charles' earlier (1960) yearlong ministry in Japan. Thus my purpose in coming to Obihiro was not to duplicate the pioneering church-planting role of Carl Beck and other senior missionaries, but to develop the incipient lay-leadership program.

However, during the three-month interlude when the Becks left for North America (April) and when we arrived in Obihiro (July), the congregation's lay leader had become a Communist (so we were told) and disappeared, devastating the congregation. Further, when I visited Taiki, a mission station south of Obihiro, the resident missionaries, Eugene and Louella Blosser, were waiting to see me because they wanted to move to Sapporo for the sake of their children's education. Suddenly I had inherited the responsibilities for two small congregations along with the hope of creating a teaching program.

What should I do? My academic seminary training and lack of pastoral experience had left me unprepared for this moment. Intuitively (and biblically) I liked the idea of lay leadership, supported by my experiences in work camp and the Concern house church, where collegiality (brotherhood) and mutual interdependence (discerning of gifts) became the basis for community (church).

The next three years were indeed busy ones. The young active church members (with a high school level education) became the leaders of the congregations, doing the preaching and visitation work. I supported their work and leadership, including their doing baptisms, communions and marriage ceremonies. I also did my share of the preaching but concentrated my efforts on developing an itinerant teaching program for lay leaders in the Obihiro and later in the Kushiro areas. Together we learned and served.

Reflections on the Japanese Enigma

My world-changing biblical studies at Goshen Biblical Seminary had provided me with a supreme confidence that thought and praxis needed to come together (as in my work camp and Concern experiences) and that missionary work was to teach the Japanese to walk empathetically with me through the pages of the Bible.

This confidence supported my understanding of leadership training in Japan. After surveying a number of Bible schools in Japan at the mission executive committee's suggestion, I was disappointed at the quality of Japanese Bible training, which emphasized more *kunren* (character formation) than biblical study. I was sure that we could teach the Bible better in the itinerant Bible teaching program I proposed in

Hokkaido. However, in teaching the Tokachi (Obihiro) area lay leaders, I soon learned that the best hours were not my lectures but the all-night sessions, often long after I was in bed, when the small group of lay leaders shared their faith and covenanted among themselves concerning their lives and future service in the church. This was *kunren*—Japanese "loosing and binding."

This disjunction between thought and practice was reinforced while I was counseling some applicants for baptism. I was dismayed by how little Bible (and theology) they understood; but I was struck by their personal testimony, their commitment, and the sacrifices they had made in deciding to follow Jesus. In a Peter-like insight, I thought how could I not baptize them! I came to realize that between that first-century biblical experience and the twentieth-century Japanese experience stretched a journey–"from ancient Jerusalem to modern Tokyo"[5]—that I had not yet taken.

Graduate School

As furlough time approached at the end of our first term in Japan, I realized even more that I needed further training. This time I consulted widely with missionary colleagues about where should I go. They suggested that I write directly to several graduate schools.

Responding, retiring Searles Bates at Union Theological Seminary (New York) wrote that he had an outstanding replacement but was not at liberty to name him. Charles Forman at Yale indicated that I could not combine biblical theology and mission but should select a single discipline, either Bible or history, and then write a dissertation related to mission. Richard Shaull (who later became a leading liberation missiologist) at Princeton Theological Seminary discouraged my coming there since he was leaving for South America. Writing from Ghana, R. Pierce Beaver at Chicago answered enthusiastically. Thus I applied to the University of Chicago.

By this time John Howard Yoder, reading my correspondence at the overseas desk of MBM, advised that because my interests were more theological than biblical, I should write to Gordon Kaufman, a Mennonite theologian at Harvard, and Lawrence Burkholder, who had left Goshen College to head the new Department of Church there. Lawrence, whom

I had known during my Goshen Biblical Seminary days, responded positively about Gordon and added that the famous Dutch missiologist J. C. Hoekendijk was joining his Department. Hoekendijk was the magic word. I applied to Harvard—but Hoekendijk went to Union!

Part III: Expanding Horizons (1964 to 1986): Re-imaging the World

My going to Harvard University in 1964 was to prepare for future mission work in Japan. Following Yoder's advice, I shifted from biblical to systematic theology. Further, rather than studying mission and church history in the Department of Church at the Divinity School, I turned to the strong university programs in Asian studies to study Japanese history, culture, religion, and society. Thus instead of a Divinity School ThD program, I entered the Program for Higher Degrees in the Study of Religion, a PhD program in the Faculty of Arts and Science.

Harvard's strengths are its outstanding faculty with whom one can devise an unusual program. In my case the professors who shaped my education were these: Robert Bellah (a Japan specialist), Talcott Parsons, and later S. N. Eisenstadt in sociology; Masatoshi Nagatomi in Buddhist studies (India, China, and Japan) and others in Japanese history; Gordon Kaufman and Richard Niebuhr in systematic theology; and Krister Stendahl (NT) in biblical theology.

In 1964 among theology students the prominence of the "death of God" theologians, including the young Harvey Cox (*The Secular City*) at Harvard, signaled the end of neo-orthodoxy and traditional systematic theology. In the fluidity of the post-modern religious situation, contemporary theology found itself committed to no single paradigm of religious reality; in fact, it understood that religious reality was symbolic and that religious symbols, although constitutive to human existence, were also subject to continual transformation by human beings.

According to Bellah,

> [T]he fundamental symbolization of modern man [sic] and his situation is the dynamic multi-dimensional self capable, within limits, of continual self-transformation and capable, again within limits, of remaking the world, including the very symbolic forms with which he deals with it, even the forms that state the unalterable conditions of his own existence.[6]

This idea struck me as immediately apropos to my own personal history and the problem of postmodern mission in Japan, e.g., the meaning of conversion (changing self-identities) and the need for contextualization of the gospel in Asia.

In addition, under the attack of the analytical/linguistic philosophers, much contemporary theology was reduced to *ad hoc* critical studies. In contrast, Bellah's 1964 article, "Religious Evolution,"[7] along with Clifford Geertz's provocative article, "Religion as a Cultural System,"[8] provided me a *systemic* study of religion.

In short, the multi-dimensional social theory of human action by Parsons, articulated in a historical and comparative framework (Bellah's religious evolution) provided a comprehensive, holistic view of humanity—so much so that I could argue that sociology of religion could converge with a contemporary constructive theology that accepted the historicity of humanity (e.g., Kaufman).[9]

In practice, in my graduate work the study of theory and of theology cross-fertilized. Critical theological studies informed the fine-grained analysis of religious symbol systems; and sociological studies provided a modern understanding of human reality, that is, a new vocabulary for a constructive theology that by-passed the dualisms (neo-Platonic, Cartesian, etc.) that so plagued systematic theology.

Important for my dissertation studies on the individuation of the self in Japanese history was Bellah's discussion of "historic religion" (aka Karl Jasper's "axial age"[10] or Max Weber's "world-rejecting religion"[11]). In other terms, historic ("world-rejecting") religion described the rise of an autonomous centered-self for the *first* time in human history almost simultaneously during the first millennium BCE ("axial age") and independently in three or four widely separated regions of the world (India, China, Ancient Near East, and Greece).

Although the rise of Japanese religion was much later than the axial age, by cultural diffusion religion in Japan today includes axial-age elements from Chinese Confucian and Buddhist religions first introduced in the sixth century and from Protestant Christianity in the nineteenth century. Thus my research project was to fill in with historical studies of the individualization of the self in Japanese history, dealing in particular with the severe problem in Japanese history of the tendency to collapse the personal self into the national corporate identity.[12]

For my dissertation I studied the following examples of historic and
early modern religion in Japan: Prince Shotoku Taishi (574–622) who introduced a state-sponsored Confucian/Buddhist religion from China into
early Japan; Honen, Shinran, and Nichiren, Japanese Buddhist monks
who promulgated Kamakura (Japanese) Buddhism differentiated from
the State (the twelfth to thirteenth centuries); and Uchimura Kanzo
(1861–1930), who founded the Non-Church (Japanese) Christianity.[13]

Teaching and Research

After six years of intensive graduate studies, I felt I needed a change.
Since I was holding a Kent Fellowship (a Danforth Foundation program
to promote undergraduate teaching), I turned to teaching in part to fulfill the obligations of the fellowship and also to complete my dissertation. Although my motivation for going to graduate school had been to
prepare to return to Japan, specifically to do theology in the context of
Japanese civilization, after such a long period away from Japan, I found
that my relations to the Mennonite Board of Missions and the missionaries in Japan had become so attenuated that no interest was shown when
I inquired about returning. Thus my teaching at Amherst College was
soon followed by a research year at the Institute of Advanced Studies
at Princeton and further teaching at the University of Tennessee in
Knoxville (UT), at Boston University (BU) as University Professor, and
at Southwestern University in Texas as the Wilson-Craven Professor of
Religion. What was intended to be an educational interlude became a
period of sixteen years of teaching, research, and networking.

Although trained in Christian theology, I found little opportunity
to teach theology since most departments of religion already had theologically trained faculty. Instead, I was recruited for the new fields in
the study of religion: theories of religion, comparative religion (India,
China, Japan) using a macro-societal, historical, comparative approach;
and advanced studies in Japanese religion and society. What I enjoyed
most were the opportunities for team-teaching, which became my continuing education in which I could broaden my understanding of Asian
civilization through interdisciplinary studies.

In my teaching experience, not only did I learn a great deal about
Asia, but I also became a grant writer. I wrote four successive grants for

Japan Foundation funding of two new faculty positions, library and media support, and two personal NEH (National Endowment for the Humanities) grants to strengthen my Japan specialization. I spent a summer at the University of Chicago in an NEH seminar on political theory in modern Japan and did a three-year, interdisciplinary research project on Japanese Buddhism, discussed below.

In 1973 Robert Bellah invited Whalen Lai, a Harvard classmate, and me to come to the Institute of Advanced Studies in Princeton as visiting members to join a team of Japanese specialists in a collaborative research project. However, political issues within the Institute led Bellah to resign and take the research project with him to Berkeley. Since I had been concentrating on completing my dissertation before coming to the Institute to begin new research, Bellah's sudden departure left me without a clue for a new project. The Institute agreed that I could continue research on my dissertation project.

In spite of Bellah's absence I enjoyed my year at the Institute, especially the daily luncheons with Clifford Geertz and the small band of social science visiting members. Here I learned the importance of scholarly exchange and collaboration in the type of historical, macro-societal and comparative studies that I was attempting. However, because there were no other Japan specialists in our group, I spent much of the time in the libraries, reading volumes of Japanese Buddhist texts.

The idea of group research did not leave me. Later, moving from Knoxville (UT) to Boston (BU) in 1978, I met with Whalen Lai and other former classmates and with Professor Nagatomi, our former teacher in Buddhist studies, to write a team-research proposal to obtain an NEH research grant ($110,000) for a three-year, interdisciplinary study of Japanese Buddhism to strengthen our weakest area, the literary and visual arts.[14] To set this up, I asked Bellah for advice about doing team research. He advised selecting a team of friends: *Friends* (according to Aristotle) enjoy each other's company, are mutually beneficial and share a common (transcendent) cause. I never forgot this advice since it reminded me of my work-camp experience and later guided me in developing collegial working groups in Japan.

While teaching at Boston University, I was invited to interview for the Wilson-Craven chair at Southwestern University, the oldest liberal arts college in Texas. Because of the atmosphere of tension at Boston University among faculty members, departments, deans, and President John Silber, who was in the process of "cleaning house" to transform that university, I decided to go for the interview.

A Turn toward China and Return to Japan

At Southwestern University I hoped to internationalize the curriculum, in particular to establish a modest Asian studies program. To promote interest, I planned a faculty (development) tour to visit the newly opening China, but the dean demurred. Instead, I left Southwestern in the summer of 1983 to attend the Harvard summer MBA program for PhDs and then went to Houston to begin networking to find a position in China. Meanwhile, Nancy found great employment as the coordinator of the large (with over a thousand students) program for non-native speakers of English in the English Department at the University of Houston.

At the same time we attended the Houston Mennonite Church, where one Sunday we met Dale Schum, the MBM personnel director, who was visiting his daughter. After noting our continuing interest in serving under MBM, within a few weeks he had us in Elkhart, interviewing for assignments in Asia. I was assigned to Japan to do research, a task that I was to define there, but Nancy was assigned to teach English in China.

Part IV. Refocusing: One World (1986 to 2003): Contextualizing in Japanese Civilization

In the fall of 1986 Nancy and I returned to Japan under the Mennonite Board of Missions (now Mennonite Mission Network, MMN) to begin a teaching and research assignment that extended over seventeen years. Although stationed in Japan, Nancy (under the auspices of China Educational Exchange—now Mennonite Partners in China) taught English twelve times—for a semester or summer session—at Northeastern University in Shenyang, China, and also returned to Japan to teach at Meiji Gakuin University and Temple University Japan.

During our twenty-two-year absence from Japan, most of the missionary research institutes had disappeared, and the few remaining missionary-scholar friends were now attached to Japanese universities, seminaries, or churches. I found my former Japanese (non-Mennonite) colleagues (although they claimed that they found me!), including Pastor Satoru Kanemoto, my former student at Boston University, who accompanied me to visit Japanese seminaries.

Among the Japanese Mennonites in Tokyo I began my orientation by attending the meetings of the leaders of TAFMC (Tokyo Area Fellowship of Mennonites) and the Anabaptist Center and noted immediately the differentiated structure. Although the members of the two groups were nearly identical, the former group functioned institutionally as a Mennonite conference like those in Hokkaido, Kyushu, and Osaka. The latter group was an informal (volunteer) discussion group that met regularly to study and promote an Anabaptist vision in Japan. Since I was not a leader of a particular congregation, I could not formally relate to TAFMC but could participate freely in the latter group, which we re-named the Tokyo Anabaptist Center (TAC).

After a year, at the request of MBM overseas secretary Ron Yoder, I sent a scenario for developing a collegial style of research and teaching for leadership training at the Tokyo Anabaptist Center. In particular, I specified how the late Takio Tanase, then the pastor of the next door Honancho Mennonite Church, and I could differentiate our work: He would write the catechetical biblical materials for use in the churches, and I would support this with advanced research in the contextualization of the gospel (doing theology) in Japanese civilization. The teaching and implementation of our work would be integrated with the other activities of the members of TAC, who were the leaders or pastors of the TAFMC churches, as well as shared with leaders from the other Mennonite conferences. However, we were surprised when this proposal was rejected at MBM headquarters. Because this was announced as a North American decision, although disappointed, I did not, could not question it.

Since I needed to take time out to rethink my mission assignment in Asia, I decided to accompany Nancy for a semester on my first teaching trip to China. After returning, as I was browsing through my pile of mail, I noticed two ads for teaching positions at different Japanese universities—ICU, where we had done our language study in 1959, and Meiji Gakuin University, the first Christian university in Japan. Even though the application deadlines for both listings were long past, out of curiosity I applied to both schools.

The position at ICU was filled, but I was invited for an interview at Meiji Gakuin, where I learned that the Meiji position had been reopened. I was hired there as a professor in the new Department of International Studies and given a light teaching load with free time to do my own research. Nancy then joined the department's EFL (English as Foreign Language) faculty. All this satisfied Elkhart, but it seemed too easy. I was returning to teaching and research at a major university, although one in Japan.

When I announced my appointment to my Japanese friends, Pastor Kanemoto and others, I was puzzled by their negative responses, "*Mottai nai! Mottai nai!*" which I thought meant "what a shame" or "what a waste." But these people were furious, as if I had committed a sacrilege against heaven (a possible dictionary meaning). Feeling embarrassed and perplexed, I realized that when they had "discovered" me, they had also assumed responsibility for my placement; but I had betrayed their trust when I made a decision without consulting with them.

During the intense discussion, someone from the back quietly suggested, "Why don't you come to Tokyo Biblical Seminary" (TBS)—the Japan Holiness Church's seminary, one of the larger evangelical seminaries in Japan—"just once a week on Wednesdays to teach in the Asia Graduate School of Theology (AGST)?" (How did they know that Wednesday was my only free day during the week?) To this "win-win" solution I meekly agreed.

For more than a year I commuted once a week by train three hours each way from Kamakura (southeast of Tokyo) to Higashi Murayama (northwest Tokyo) to teach at TBS in the recently established graduate program, part of a consortium of graduate theological schools in Asia under the auspices of the Asia Theological Association, the accrediting agency for evangelical seminaries in Asia. The first class consisted of the five full-time TBS faculty members, who did not have doctorates (including the dean, the vice-president, and the future president of the seminary) although all had advanced degrees, and three had ThM degrees from North American schools.

At the end of the term on the very last day, the dean surprised me by asking if I would also teach the next term. Actually, for over a year I was asked on the very last day of class of each term if I would teach again the following term. Then the vice-president inquired if I would leave Meiji Gakuin to teach full-time at TBS to head the AGST program and to establish a research institute. He also indicated that the seminary could not offer a real salary. Fortunately, both MBM administrators Wilbert Shenk and Ron Yoder were then visiting Japan and could provide immediate counsel. They indicated that because we had not come to Japan as self-supporting missionaries, we could receive Mission Board financial support, but they suggested that we ask for housing at the seminary.

Our move to the TBS campus in 1990 led to a productive period for me as well as for Nancy, who continued to teach in China for one semester annually and then summers at Temple University Japan. During this period, I was able to define my research assignment in Japan: (1) to teach in and direct the AGST program at TBS, as well as to teach in the seminary program; (2) to establish TMRI (the Tokyo Mission Research Institute) to advance research and publication; and (3) to participate personally in a church outreach program and, as much as possible, to relate to the Mennonite churches in Japan, primarily through the Anabaptist Center.

In the AGST program I taught the core courses focusing on missiology, methodology, and contextualization in Japanese history, culture, and society. I was aided immensely by the TMRI translation of David Bosch's *Transforming Mission: Paradigm Shifts in the Theology of Mission* (Orbis Books, 1991), which became prerequisite reading, and by team teaching with TBS President Kazuo Kobayashi, a biblical scholar, and with Waseda University sociology professor, Takanobu Tojo, an Anabaptist Center member and Brethren in Christ church leader.

Later two Japanese Mennonites completed their AGST programs—Professor Tojo added two advanced divinity degrees to his doctorate in sociology, and TAFMC pastor Yoshihira Inamine received a DMin degree with a study on *The Significance of Michael Sattler and the Schleitheim Confession for Mennonites in Japan* (in Japanese).

At the seminary, where I taught sociology of religion to seniors, I devised a macro-societal, comparative, historical course: From Ancient Israel to Modern Japan. I also taught an informal course for reading theology in English (using works by John Howard Yoder and others) to prepare those planning to study abroad. From these classes about a dozen went abroad, many to EMU and AMBS; and a few continued to graduate schools for doctorates and have returned to participate in TMRI (discussed below). The latter group is the future seminary faculty, who remain Holiness but now with Anabaptist characteristics.

As noted, a part of my invitation to teach at TBS included the formation of a research institute. Over the years TMRI sponsored a series of forums, conferences, seminars, and other activities to expand horizons and add excellence to the TBS/AGST teaching programs. In particular, to complement my own teaching from an Anabaptist perspective, I established an annual Summer Pastors' Study Conference with visiting guest lecturers from different fields, beginning in 1992 with Willard Swartley and continuing with Alan Kreider, Marlin Miller, Myron Augsburger, Ron Kraybill, Wilbert Shenk, Norman Kraus, Ben Ollenburger, Stanley Hauerwas, David Augsburger, Alan Kreider (again), Glen Stassen, Willard Swartley (again), Howard Zehr, Wilbert Shenk (again), and myself and others in a special conference on the work of David Bosch. For 2009 TMRI invited Mark and Mary Thiessen Nation to teach and commemorate the twentieth anniversary of the founding of TMRI.

In addition TMRI developed a publication program to introduce new ideas into Japan in missiology, biblical studies, history, theology, ethics, counseling, and conflict transformation. These included the following: TMRI's first book, a set of provocative essays by the TBS faculty on *The Japanese Emperor System: The Inescapable Missiological Issue* (1990, E.T. 1995);[12] the translation of works by John Howard Yoder and David Bosch, which were central to my teaching in AGST and later for the formation of the Japan Missiological Society (JMS); and the translation of works of the TMRI guest lecturers to support their summer teaching (A. Kreider, D. Augsburger, G. Stassen, H. Zehr, W. Shenk), including the translation of Willard Swartley's mammoth *Covenant of Peace: The Missing Peace in New Testament Theology and Ethics* (Eerdmans, 2006) by a team of two Mennonites and three recent New Testament PhD scholars, two of whom were Willard's former students at AMBS.

On a personal level a group of lay leaders at the TBS church asked me one Sunday, "What do you do on Sundays?"

I said we usually attended one of the Mennonite churches.

They asked me again, "What do you *really* do on Sundays?"

With friends TBS President and Mrs. (Dr.) Kobayashi (also our medical doctor), 1999

I finally replied that we just attended church, feeling that my Japanese research and teaching activities during the week were sufficient although I knew that all of the TBS faculty and TMRI senior staff were pastors of churches. (In the Japan Holiness Church, seminary faculty in principle are active, experienced pastors all financially supported by their local congregations. Thus their work at the seminary, AGST, and TMRI is truly voluntary service.)

By now I had learned that when a group of Japanese friends surrounded me, this was not just a "happy hour" event: Something serious had been hatched. Their next question was this: Would I lead/preach twice a month for a new English worship service at the TBS church for expatriates and others interested in an English language worship service?

In other words, this was to become one of the more than forty different small groups that make up the present TBS church. These informal groups meet for all kinds of reasons, from prayer and Bible study to flower arrangement, western cooking, hobbies, etc. Although these small groups may have a secular theme, their informal structure provides its members a personal identity in a freely loving community as an alternative to the more oppressive requirements of formal groups, such as the family or the work place. In this way, President Kobayashi explained, he had created an outreach program for the TBS church, which now has over 300 members and a regular Sunday morning attendance of over 200, both large numbers in Japan.

Then in the summer of 2003—because of the importance of David Bosch's epoch book, which had been translated into Chinese (in Taiwan), Korean, and Japanese (by TMRI)—TMRI sponsored and AMBS hosted in Elkhart an "East Asia Theological Consultation: Asian and Alternative Responses to David Bosch's *Transforming Mission.*" Among the forty-nine participants were AMBS faculty (including former TMRI lecturers), faculty and students from two TBS-sister seminaries in Korea, Chinese scholars from Hong Kong and Chengdu, TMRI-related faculty and students from Japan, former American missionaries to Japan, and East Asian graduate and seminary students studying in the USA and Great Britain.[15]

Finally, at the invitation of Pastor Kanemoto, I made a special trip to Japan in January of 2005 to attend his Doctor of Ministry graduation celebration, to be the respondent at the dedication service of the Japanese translation (arranged by him) of a revised version of my book, *The Clash of Civilization: An Intrusive Gospel in Japanese Civilization,* and to participate in a special ecumenical gathering of Japanese leaders, also arranged by Kanemoto and Nishioka, the directors of TMRI. All this took place on a single day with a rolling audience—some participated in all three meetings: the graduation ceremony in the morning, the book dedication in the early afternoon, and the ecumenical gathering in the late afternoon.

To my surprise the ecumenical gathering of Japanese leaders included charismatics, evangelicals, Mennonites, other Protestants, and Roman Catholics, all interested in mission. As the discussion revealed, what had brought this diverse group together was TMRI's outstanding team-translation and editing by Yoshiyuki (Billy) Nishioka of David Bosch's *Transforming Mission.*

In establishing TMRI, one of the goals I had tried three times to achieve now suddenly had an auspicious beginning. On June 17, immediately before the 2005 TMRI summer session, this group created the Japan Missiological Society (JMS) and held its first meeting. The TMRI staff (Tojo, Kanemoto, and Nishioka) not only founded JMS but then also gave leadership to JMS for its first three years, publishing the first two volumes of the new annual *Journal of the Japan Missiological Society* (in Japanese).

Retiring, a Final Personal Reflection

After serving in Japan from 1959 to 1964, 1986 to 1996, and then with yearly extensions, we were retired from MMN in July 2003 after the David Bosch consultation at AMBS. However, in Japan one never actually retires. In my case I was "promoted" to an honorary position as "international advisor" on the TMRI executive committee. My assistant, Pastor Kanemoto, became the new director of TMRI, Dean of Students Billy Nishioka became the new assistant director, and my teaching colleague, Professor Tojo, became the vice-president on the executive committee, replacing me as the Mennonite representative. Thereafter, Nancy and I limited our overseas activity to the annual TMRI summer program in Japan and the annual executive committee meeting until 2006.

In practical terms (apart from the theological and missiological concerns) what did I contribute as a missionary in Japan for twenty-two years, or more problematic, what is a missionary in the postmodern era? Certainly I was not indispensable since I was out of the country frequently enough to know that things did get done when I was away—although often in very different ways, e.g., the collegial versus line authority issue. What I finally realized was that TMRI/TBS functioned like *friends, voluntary fellowships* (since the financial support of TBS faculty and the TMRI staff came from their home congregations and mine from MMN until I was 65). What delayed my actual retirement was that these friends/ colleagues were overworked volunteers and now had even more work. Volunteering and collegiality had made it possible for us together to add a bit of excellence and/or the personal touch that had made a difference in the life of the church. Happily, TMRI became a "success" story and fully integrated into the seminary and church after my retirement. This became possible because the president and other leaders at TBS went to great lengths to accept and support this Mennonite (non-Holiness) outsider.

February 11, 2008
Revised January 2009

Notes

1 Cf. Philip E. Slater, *Microcosm: Structural, Psychological and Religious Evolution in Groups* (New York: Wiley and Sons, 1966).

2 The failure to differentiate the various types of work assignments contributed to the confusion of the newly arriving workers.

3 Cf. "Binding and Loosing" in *The Royal Priesthood* by John H. Yoder, edited by Michael Cartwright (Grand Rapids, MI: Eerdmans, 1994), 323–358.

4 Cf. Nancy V. (Burkholder) Lee, "An Unexpected Life," in *Making Sense of the Journey: The Geography of Our Faith*, edited by Robert and Nancy Lee (Harrisonburg, VA: Anabaptist Center for Religion and Society, 2007), 296.

5 Cf. my Chap. 1: "From Ancient Jerusalem to Modern Tokyo: Contextualization in Japanese Culture and Society" in *The Clash of Civilizations: An Intrusive Gospel in Japanese Civilization* (Harrisburg, PA: Trinity Press International, 1999), 1–15.

6 Robert N. Bellah, "Religious Evolution," *American Sociological Review* 29/3: 372 (1964).

7 *American Sociological Review* 29/3: 358-374 (1964).

8 Clifford Geertz, *The Interpretation of Cultures*, Chap. 4 (New York: Basic Books, Inc., 1966, but circulating earlier).

9 Gordon D. Kaufman, "The *Imago Dei* as Man's Historicity," *Journal of Religion*, 36:157–168; also *Systematic Theology: A Historicist Perspective* (New York: Scribner's, 1968).

10 *The Origin and Goal of History* (New Haven: Yale University Press, 1953), 1f.

11 Chap. XI: "Asceticism, Mysticism, and Salvation Religion" in *The Sociology of Religion* (Boston: Beacon Press, 1922, ET 1956), 166-183.

12 For an incisive study from the Christian side, see *The Japanese Emperor System: The Inescapable Missiological Issue*, edited by Robert Lee (Tokyo: Tokyo Mission Research Institute, 1995).

13 *Religious Evolution and the Individuation of the Self in Japanese History*, PhD Thesis, Harvard University (1974), published in a limited edition by Tokyo Mission Research Institute.

14 Beside our own research and writing projects, the NEH grant supported a series of conferences and seminars that led to the specialized volume: *Flowing Traces: Buddhism in Literary and Visual Arts of Japan*, edited by James H. Sanford, William R. LaFleur, and Masatoshi Nagatomi (Princeton, NJ: Princeton University Press, 1992).

15 Papers were published in a special issue of *Mission Focus: Annual Review*, 2003, Volume 11, Supplement.

The Continuing Story of the Anabaptist Center for Religion and Society

Ray C. Gingerich, Director of ACRS

Today's Anabaptist Center for Religion and Society represents a growing vision for creative intellectual activity after retirement from the classroom—for the integrative re-imaging of faith and life in contemporary academia and church.[1]

However, what really does ACRS represent? And who exactly belongs to it? These are questions that continue to emerge among both the initiated and the uninitiated. Those of us involved cannot look to other campuses and ask how they are handling these matters of identity and belonging. As we continue to watch what is happening to the crowd on the exit side of academic institutions across the nation and the world, we surmise that ACRS is unique. Based on its activities and productivity, it demonstrates the agility of minds, the creativity of thought, and the power of organization embodied in this post-teaching group. Yet neither the larger educational community nor the narrower academic institution provides a historical pattern. Although our orientation is academic, we are not a mini think-tank. We have components of fellowship and personal support; but to think of ACRS as a sophisticated version of a weekly campus Kafe Klatsch would be like referring to a dean's council as powwow therapy.

In an essay in 2006 on the Anabaptist Center for Religion and Society, Calvin Redekop, Chair of the ACRS Steering Committee, attempted to come to terms with this institution in its adolescence: "ACRS continues to evolve. It is still searching for a firm identity. Finding a specific location/ space for an office and meeting place continues to be a concern. A membership structure is still not established, and the relationship of 'ACRS participants' to the larger campus and community is still not clear."[2]

What is, however, becoming increasingly clear is that ACRS is an organization that assures space "for the discourse of the elders."[3] And as such ACRS functions as a catalyst for thinking at the edge of the system with the hope of contributing to the well-being of those institutionally more controlled by protocol, by repetition of practice, and at times by the path of least resistance: cultural accommodation.

ACRS was birthed in a small Mennonite university surrounded by a mainstream culture that is religiously and politically conservative— one that also makes inroads into the Mennonite community. A major challenge for ACRS is the promotion of an Anabaptist understanding of church, community, and higher education within our current context. We believe Anabaptism offers a critical alternative to mainstream American religion and is vital to the integrity of our mission. Moreover, we see the recovery of Anabaptism as essential to the survival of our church institutions. Distinctive strengths of Anabaptism that ACRS seeks to promote on campus and in the Shenandoah Valley include a practiced faith of creation-care and nonviolence with just-peace embodied in a community that offers dignity and respect to all peoples. These we believe are distinctives sought by a wide spectrum of religious and non-religious people today. ACRS believes these Anabaptist distinctives—dimensions of our inherited tradition—not only point toward the direction that we as an American society must travel, but are the road map for EMU to follow in order to lead.

Key Activities

Memoirs

The monthly Monday Morning Breakfast series, in which former leaders of the community share their intellectual and spiritual pilgrimages, has become the event that currently offers ACRS its highest public profile. The collection of stories in the volume you are holding comes as a direct result of these occasions. Begun in 2003 in an effort to help a group of intellectuals—mostly-retired professors in theology, history, and the behavioral sciences—listen to each other not with the intent to gain more knowledge, but in an effort to know better each other's thinking,[4] this series of life stories soon evolved into high-interest gatherings to which spouses and friends were invited. To many of those participating, telling their story offered an opportunity to sketch the evolution of their intellectual pilgrimage, something that up until that point they had found neither the time nor sufficient motivation to do.

Forums, Seminars, Colloquies and Conferences
Early in the history of ACRS we sensed the need to exercise a gift that in the humdrum of activities is frequently overlooked: the gift of convening—calling meetings to order at critical apropos times. Timing has often been of the essence. Larger public events in which a lecture plays a central role are announced as "forums"; public events involving input from several participants and often followed by discussion are publicized as "seminars"; smaller scale events on issues where the key objective is exploratory are labeled "colloquies."

Here is a sampling of these gatherings over the past several years.

- Mennonite World Conference President Nancy Heisey (Chair of EMU's Department of Bible and Religion)[5] reported in an ACRS sponsored forum after returning from an executive meeting in Zimbabwe during one of its many crises. This is the kind of event that, although not sponsored by EMU, holds the potential for being highly educational—religiously, politically, and culturally. In addition, it demonstrates a kind of leadership that we would hope EMU students would see as a model.
- A one-day conference focused on John Howard Yoder's posthumously published work, *The Jewish-Christian Schism Revisited*.[6] This occurred after the work had been published for nearly three years with virtually no one's paying attention to the crucial issues it addresses. Overtly the book stands as an example of interreligious relationships; more indirectly, it provides a remarkable theological platform from which to reassess the entire corpus of Yoder's writings, including the seminal *Politics of Jesus*.
- When an interdenominational, interfaith delegation (including several members from the Harrisonburg community, one from EMU) returned from Iran (and on another occasion from Iraq),[7]

ACRS took the initiative to call a gathering to hear firsthand how the group was received by President Ahmadinejad and the kind of response members of the group held to be appropriate in that context.

- A forum was scheduled on "Understanding Scripture and Interfaith Relationships" with a presentation by Roy Hange, long-term resident of both Syria and Iran, student of Eastern Orthodoxy and of the Muslim faith, and currently pastor of the Charlottesville Mennonite Church and overseer in the Virginia Mennonite Conference.[8]
- Catholic Mennonite dialogue was promoted through a one-day conference initiated by ACRS founding member, Paul Peachey, Professor Emeritus of Catholic University of America, and Peachey's colleague, Father George McLean, also Professor Emeritus of Catholic University of America.[9]
- Professor James Juhnke, scholar of Mennonite history, just returned from an exploratory Russian Mennonite tour in the eastern parts of the former Soviet Union, visited EMU and ACRS.[10] By providing a much fuller and broader historical context, Juhnke is rewriting a chiliastic-visionary segment of Mennonite history.
- A local elder and ACRS member, Harold Lehman, provided the history of Mennonite Conscientious Objectors in WWII.[11] As both a storyteller and a primary researcher, he conveyed an earlier generation's understanding and practice of pacifism.

In each of these events, ACRS exercised not merely its gift to convene but the time and energy to carry through with the necessary logistics. The initiatives came from the chair or the director, as well as from a steering committee member or someone from the community. But ACRS was present to test and to promote the suggestions and to move forward with the necessary arrangements.

An Educational Tour

Through the counsel and leadership of two ACRS members, Robert and Nancy Lee,[12] the first major group activity was a three-week educational tour to China in October of 2006. Because of the Lees' in-depth knowledge of China it was natural that we, during the early formation of ACRS, began to dream of taking this educational venture together under the auspices of ACRS. Through the excellent preparation for the tour organized by the Lees, combined with the outstanding travel arrangements through Myrrl Byler, the Director of Mennonite Partners in China,[13] this was a model educational experience that would be extremely difficult to surpass. Included in the arrangements were four educational exchanges with faculties in Chinese seminaries and universities.

Scholars in Residence

In the spring of 2008 ACRS-EMU hosted its first Scholars in Residence—Dr. Huaming (Lindy) Yang and her husband, Dr. Lin Li.[14] The sponsoring of several visiting scholars on the EMU campus was a direct result of a process begun by members of ACRS' China Educational Tour, who arranged for an exchange with a delegation of faculty and students at Beijing's Institute of World Religions in October 2006.[15] The culminating event of the visiting scholars was a larger ACRS forum entitled, "Religious Identity in an Emerging China" on May 2008. Drs. Yang and Li both gave excellent presentations that appeared to be well received by a diverse community and university audience. At this same forum Ms. Xiuling (Shirlee) Wang, Director of Protestant Affairs for the State Administration for Religious Affairs, also gave a report on her work in China and her experiences in the Harrisonburg/EMU community. So powerful were several of these presentations that the full impact has yet to be absorbed by the EMU community.

In ACRS' evaluation of our Scholars in Residence experience we received very positive and appreciative feedback from our guests. Furthermore, we felt that those of us within ACRS who had mentoring roles had rewarding experiences. Especially satisfying was Robert Lee's work with Dr. Yang in directing her toward a longer-term focus for her work upon return to Beijing—the study of Anabaptist theology and ethics, with particular attention to the writings of J. H. Yoder. But we were less satisfied with the impact our guests from China had on the EMU campus and believe that ACRS must find ways to enhance the presence of future Scholars in Residence. Particularly important in hosting future scholars is that we find ways to create greater interaction between the visiting scholars and the EMU academic community—both among students and faculty.

Setbacks, Losses, and Challenges

In December of 2007 ACRS celebrated the publication of its first series of Monday Morning Breakfast Stories. All sixteen contributors to the volume were present for the celebration. Six months later, June 2008, we were together again: this time for the memorial services of Albert Keim, a founding member of ACRS. Whether as academic dean, as faculty member, or as community organizer, Keim was for many years an intellectual beacon at EMU. On days when his health allowed him to be present at ACRS steering committee meetings, there was an intellectual "zing"—a phenomenon too often lacking in his absence.

A second setback, although of an entirely different nature than the first, has been our inability until now to carry through the sponsoring of a major conference. The vision of re-imaging our world included in its larger scheme a vision to re-image our church. In this was embedded the need for a series of conferences with Mennonite leaders and institutions, with the hope that as the church would re-image the world, its own self-image in the context of its mission in the twenty-first century would be transformed. In retrospect I hear the echo: "These ACRS folks really took themselves seriously!" Need I report that the re-imaging project was stillborn?

A more reasonable project in its scope—and hence perhaps an even more serious disappointment—has been our inability to pursue the wider story of Harold S. Bender, the leader in a segment of Mennonite history that seems to be rapidly escaping our reach. This failure is due to what continues to feel like the untimely death of Albert Keim. The purpose of the project was to throw a wider historical net than Keim had used in his definitive monograph of Bender (Herald Press, 1998) and to draw on the stories of Bender's still-living contemporaries, while also engaging the vision of a younger set of scholars. Keim was pleased with this approach, and planning was well underway. But since he is gone, no one has had the courage to touch it.

Envisioning the Future

As ACRS envisions its focus for the future, it is attempting to expand the Anabaptist umbrella within and beyond the Mennonite tradition. Phases of this work in which we are currently engaged include the following:

- ACRS seeks to strengthen EMU's academic program by focusing on the need for research, writing, and publishing. Where the gathering and the production of knowledge fail to be fostered, not only does teaching become anemic but also education and Anabaptist understandings remain largely insular. In response to this situation ACRS is seeking to organize routine channels of research and publishing for its own purposes and then make those services available to other departments within the university.[16]

- ACRS is developing a closer working relation with our Church of the Brethren neighbors by including Brethren in the ongoing series of Monday Morning Breakfast Stories. We are also looking for Brethren representation on the ACRS steering committee. In addition, we welcome Anabaptist-Catholics and others of Anabaptist spirit not identifiable with a religious label.

- We seek to support and promote "The Center for the Study of Abrahamic Traditions" (CSAT)—a concept currently under consideration by EMU to foster inter-religious relationships, specifically among religions within the Abrahamic traditions. What peace studies were to the re-imaging of the Mennonite Church in the sixties and seventies, inter-religious relationships, particularly those with Jews and Muslims, are in the beginning of this new millennium. ACRS, we believe, can bring a theological and historical perspective to the table. Realizing the full potential of such a center calls for a significant shift in our self-understanding and in our understanding of the church's mission. Paradigm shifts of this type are not created by individuals. They emerge out of the times—cultural, political, economic. Yet it is individuals and smaller groups of engaged people who serve as midwives to give birth to new understandings. We ask if ACRS can play the role of a good midwife.

Finally, as we envision the future, we ask where ACRS fits in the context of the larger university. Organizationally ACRS responds to the provost. This relationship has been positive and encouraging. Nevertheless, it would seem that many of the potential benefits are not being realized. In our earliest years several key members of ACRS were concerned about any direct accountability to the university lest the administration feel that it must be accountable for what we do, with the consequences that the freedom to express our thought or the positions taken on sensitive issues might be curbed. That has not happened.[17] But neither has ACRS been successful in establishing bonds that would allow us to be routinely engaged with the institutional guardians. Currently, therefore, the greater concern is that ACRS not be ignored, that we be given an institutional home on campus, and that, where training and experience equips them, members of ACRS be given advisory status on committees. In these tasks, ACRS has to date been all too ineffective.

From the vantage point of ACRS members, EMU is passing through a cultural and generational shift. What will the political shape and theological texture of the Anabaptist heritage come to be in this century? ACRS is attempting to raise critical perspectives essential to negotiate the shift into the new millennium. Using an agrarian metaphor out of our past, ACRS' current mission may be summarized thus: Through story telling, forums and colloquiums, research and publishing, cross-cultural exchanges and new ventures in inter-religious relationships, the seeds of a passing generation are being harvested. Our hopes are that these seeds will be treasured, not as museum artifacts, but as verdant elements of an inheritance that, when cross-fertilized with the creativity and commitment of the current generation and planted into the fertile soil of its culture, will spring forth into a new communal breed of twenty-first century Anabaptists—instruments of peace and well-being in the trajectory set by our ancestors.

Notes

1 From the opening statement (inside flap) of the brochure for The Anabaptist Center for Religion and Society, Feb. 2008.

2 Calvin W. Redekop, Appendix, "An Unfinished Story: The History of the Anabaptist Center for Religion and Society," in Robert and Nancy V. Lee, eds., *Making Sense of the Journey: The Geography of Our Faith* (Harrisonburg, Virginia: Anabaptist Center for Religion and Society, 2007), 320.

3 Redekop, 320.

4 The group, later known as the "founding members of ACRS," were holding weekly gatherings exploring two fronts: (1) seeking to determine the nature of ACRS; and (2) pushing the frontiers of what was conceptualized as the "core activity" to get ACRS off the ground—"Re-Imaging Our World." I had been given released-time from my teaching load and was chairing the group. What became evident to me after our meeting for about two months was that there were at least six or seven (depending on the number of persons attending) ways of re-imaging the world. These were overlapping visions, to be sure; yet we were not listening to each other—certainly not listening with the care and dedication necessary to meld our visions into a meta-framework of thought useful to pursue our perceived purpose. Elsewhere Cal Redekop affirms, "There were numerous chaotic meetings…" (*Making Sense …*, Vol. I, 318). Equally significant was the fact that although we had known and befriended each other (for many years in some cases), we were unfamiliar with each other's thought-constructs, philosophical presuppositions, and, yes, even our personal dispositions. I realized that unless the conversation and our presentations began to interconnect at a more primal and empathetic level of communication, our energies would rapidly sag and together we would fail in the venture of creating a novel organization whose larger purpose was yet to be discovered. Sharing our intellectual narratives was the group's redemptive therapy.

5 Nancy Heisey's report illustrates a common phenomenon: Universities harbor individuals involved in a wide range of activities of which not all are university sponsored and funded, but which at the same time have profound educational import. ACRS seeks to enhance the educational experience on campus by taking advantage of these special events and people.

6 Michael G. Cartwright and Peter Ochs, eds. (Grand Rapids, MI: Eerdmans, 2003). Following each chapter one or both of the editors offer their own commentary. The conference was held on March 16, 2007.

7 Gerald Shenk, October 5, 2006.

8 Thursday, November 30, 2006. Among the questions asked to provide focus were the following: Do we see people of other faiths as potential sources of wisdom for deeper insight into our own faith? Or are such persons first and foremost candidates for conversion to the gospel of Christ? Or, had we better just lovingly "live and let live?" (The less caring version of this is "Don't ask, don't tell.")

9 November 29, 2007. The procedures of this conference have been recorded but not published.

10 At EMU Professor of History Mary Sprunger hosted James Juhnke, Professor Emeritus of Bethel College, Newton, Kansas, March 3, 2008.

11 January 26, 2006.

12 Nancy Lee spent parts of twelve years teaching English at Northeastern University in Shenyang. Robert Lee is a specialist in East Asian religions and civilizations.

13 Myrrl Byler also arranged for the group of eighteen (of whom approximately twelve were ACRS members) to meet with MPC personnel at numerous teaching sites, as well as with their Chinese hosts.

14 Dr. Huaming Yang arrived on campus on December 31, 2007. Through the persistent work of Myrrl Byler, Yang's husband, Dr. Lin Li, was able to join her on campus by April 1, 2008. Although only Dr. Yang officially held the position, in practice both were given the status of Scholar in Residence.

15 The diplomatic work combined with other major assistance of Myrrl Byler and Robert Lee, coupled with the finances received from Mennonite Partners in China and ACRS, dare not go unmentioned.

16 Negotiations with Cascadia Publishing House LLC as the official publisher for ACRS-EMU are virtually finalized. But the internal structures to encourage and facilitate research and writing on a wider basis within the university are in their initial stages.

17 Whether this is because of the open-mindedness of the EMU administration and its respect for elders, or whether ACRS members are less radical than their self-image leads them to believe, are not issues essential to the current record.

NOTES ON CONTRIBUTORS

Kenton Kaylor Brubaker (PhD in Horticulture, Ohio State University) taught a wide spectrum of courses in biology and horticulture at Eastern Mennonite University for over thirty-five years. He also taught at Congo Polytechnic Institution and Free University of Congo under MCC, where he wrote a cell biology text in French. He married Emma Shetler in 1955, and they had four children: Karl, business manager at Hesston College; Kaye, professor of engineering at the University of Maryland; Jane, campus horticulturalist at the University of Oregon; and Annette, elementary teacher in Arlington, MA. Several years after Emma's death, he married Shirley E. Yoder, a pastor at Park View Mennonite Church in Harrisonburg, VA. During his career, Kenton developed a self-paced text in biochemistry, an international agriculture program, and a campus arboretum. He was active in ecological concerns, recycling, and alternative agriculture and participated in several national Science Foundation summer institutes in radiation biology, ecology, research in plant physiology, and genetic engineering. His principle avocations are watercolor painting, international stamp collecting, and tennis. His travels have taken him to many countries. He remains interested in the integration of science and religion and in a sustainable lifestyle. Currently he volunteers at Booksavers, an MCC program, where he cuts up and recycles books. He is an active, founding member of Shalom Mennonite Congregation.

George R. Brunk III (ThD, Union Theological Seminary in Virginia), named interim president of the Associated Mennonite Biblical Seminary in Elkhart, IN, for 2009–2010, is also Professor of New Testament at Eastern Mennonite Seminary, where he has taught since 1974 and has continued teaching part time since reaching retirement age. He was also the dean of the seminary from 1977 to1999. He served as field administrator and pastor in Italy under the Virginia Mennonite Board of Missions from 1964 to 1970. He has been involved in denominational service as a member of the Council of Faith, Life, and Strategy of the General Board of the (old) Mennonite Church and, more recently, of the Interchurch Relations Committee of the Mennonite Church USA. He was moderator of the Mennonite Church General Assembly from 1989 to 1991. He is an ordained Mennonite minister and overseer in the Virginia Mennonite Conference. He was married to Erma Hess (deceased), with whom he had two children, Douglas and Valerie (Hertzler). He is now married to Ruthann Miller, mother of Rachel (Jacobs), Eric, and Lynelle (Clark). George and Ruthann share a total of eleven grandchildren.

Omar Eby (MFA, University of Virginia) is Professor Emeritus of English at Eastern Mennonite University. Born on a farm near Hagerstown, MD, he received a B.A. in English from EMC(U) in 1957. He taught for six years in Africa—Somalia, Tanzania, and Zambia. He taught writing and literature for twenty-seven years at EMU before taking early retirement to pursue his own writing. His one break from the classroom was a three-year stint at MCC, Akron, PA. Eby has published books of fiction, biography, and personal experience, his most recent being *Fifty Years, Fifty Stories: the Mennonite Mission in Somalia, 1953–2003*, and *The Boy and the Old Man: Three Years in Somalia*. He also edited his brother-in-law Joseph Shenk's letters to him and published them as *Rafiki: Letters to Omar*. Eby married Anna Kathryn Shenk, and they have three children. They live near Harrisonburg, VA, and attend Weavers Mennonite Church.

Ray Elvin Horst (M.A. in Spanish, Temple University) has done additional studies in language pedagogy and Hispanic civilization. He developed tools for looking at economic and political issues as part of the language learning process in first and second year Spanish classes. He has led numerous student groups to Spain and Latin America. Three of those visits were semester long programs of Eastern Mennonite University, in which his wife Violet served as co-leader. In 1997 he initiated a two-week visit to Cuba as part of the semester in Central America. Since retiring from EMU in 2003, he has adapted his skills in the Spanish classroom to the teaching of English to immigrants in classes meeting two nights each week, and he regularly helps train new tutors under the Skyline Literacy Coalition. Ray and Vi are the parents of Heather and Stephanie Horst and are members of Community Mennonite Church in Harrisonburg, VA, where Ray is involved in the Sunday school and music activities. He also sings in the Shenandoah Valley Choral Society.

Vernon E. Jantzi (PhD in Sociology of Development, Cornell University), named interim dean for 2009–2010 at Eastern Mennonite University, served as professor of sociology at EMU for more than thirty years. As co-founder and former director of the Center for Justice and Peacebuilding, he brought together the fields of peacebuilding, development, and restorative justice. He has worked extensively at the interface of these fields in Africa, the Middle East, Latin America, Southeast Asia, and the South Pacific. In addition to his teaching, he has served as advisor to the Costa Rican government on land reform and the Peruvian ministry of education on Spanish-Quechua bilingual education. He has served as a member of the Board and Executive Committee of the Mennonite Central Committee for eleven years. Since his youth he has been an avid student of Spanish linguistics and Latin American literature—a significant asset in his relating to Latin American culture and immigration issues in the United States. In his retirement he has concentrated his efforts on creating spaces for interfaith dialogue and interaction. In 1963 he married Dorothy Leaman. They have two children, Terrence, married to Elizabeth Phelps, and Rosanne, plus granddaughter Valerie Lynn.

Jay B. Landis (D.A., Idaho State University) is Professor Emeritus of English at Eastern Mennonite University. Beginning at Eastern Mennonite High School in 1956, he transitioned after twelve years to Eastern Mennonite College/University's English department, completing fifty years of teaching in 2007. His decades of classroom experience, shading finally into three generations of students, have been the source of renewed inspiration. A native of Lancaster, PA, he received degrees in English from EMC, Case-Western Reserve University, and Idaho State University. He is married to Peggy Heatwole of Harrisonburg, VA, and they are the parents of two daughters, Ann Landis of Tallahassee, FL, and Jill Landis Snider of Broadway, VA, and the grandparents of Rebecca, Nathaniel, and Timothy Snider. Close residents of the university, he and Peggy are involved in the congregational life and mission of the Park View Mennonite Church.

He continues a bit of connection with EMU's Adult Degree Completion Program, volunteers in community agencies, sings in the Shenandoah Valley Choral Society, and enjoys growing roses.

John A. Lapp (PhD, University of Pennsylvania) wrote his PhD dissertation on *The Mennonite Church in India 1897–1962* (published in 1972). Recently he has written essays about the history of Mennonite World Conference and the Mennonite scene in the year 2000, both articles appearing in the *Mennonite Quarterly Review*. He taught history at EMC and served as dean, provost, and professor of history at Goshen College. Before becoming the executive secretary of MCC (1985–1996), he was the executive secretary of the MCC peace section and represented the Mennonite Church on the MCC executive committee. In retirement Lapp has been an occasional teacher, speaker, and writer. He is also the coordinator of the Global Mennonite History Project for Mennonite World Conference. Currently he is chair of the Lititz Mennonite Church and the Lancaster Interchurch Peace Witness. He has partnered with Alice Weber Lapp for fifty-four years, and together they are the parents of three and grandparents of six.

Robert Lee (PhD in the Study of Religion, Harvard University)—after serving in Europe and Korea under MCC, attending Goshen Biblical Seminary, and then serving in Japan under MBM—decided to go back to school in order to understand more fully the world, in particular China, Japan, and himself. Twenty-two years later, after studying, teaching, and doing research in the U.S., he returned to Japan to serve seventeen years under the Mennonite Mission Network (formerly MBM). In Japan he taught at Tokyo Biblical Seminary, directing its Asia Graduate School of Theology and its Tokyo Mission Research Institute programs, and also worked closely with both Japanese and North American Mennonites. During his seminary years, he met and married Nancy Burkholder, who went with him to Japan, where their three children were born: Steven, now a research scientist at MIT's Lincoln Laboratories; Suelyn, a church resource development coordinator in Madison, WI, and graphic designer of both volumes of the ACRS memoirs; and Robert (Bobby), a professor of medieval British literature at Indiana University South Bend. In addition, the Lees have four grandchildren. Now living in retirement at Virginia Mennonite Retirement Community in Harrisonburg, VA, the Lees remain active in ACRS, editing both volumes of this book, and hosting and counseling Chinese and Japanese students and scholars studying at EMU and AMBS.

James O. Lehman's (MLS, Kent State University) early interest in reading nudged him toward teaching and a being a librarian in Ohio and then moving into a professional library career for nearly four decades at Harrisonburg, VA. He served twenty-three years as the library director at Eastern Mennonite College/University in the early years of the revolutionary transformation of library automation and digitization of information availability. Thereafter he turned to archiving Virginia Mennonite materials. Love of local history led to a major book on his Kidron, Ohio, home community. Then followed an avocation of researching/writing eight congregational histories, one on Mennonite tent evangelism, and the 2007 Johns Hopkins University publication, *Mennonites, Amish, and the American Civil War,* which he coauthored with Steven M. Nolt. Now partially retired, he and Dorothy enjoy their family of five children, eight grandchildren, and one great grandchild. They have participated at Lindale Mennonite Church over nearly four decades, and he has served on regional and national historical committees.

Elmer S. Miller (PhD in Anthropology, University of Pittsburgh) and his wife, Anna Lois Longenecker, married since 1953, have two daughters and four grandchildren. From 1956 to 1963 they served in the Argentine Chaco under the Mennonite Board of Missions. Elmer taught anthropology at Temple University from 1966–1996, where he became full professor in 1980. In anthropology, his avocation since his studies at Hartford in 1956, his focus has been on the social transformation of belief systems in cross-cultural perspective. In addition to a textbook and more than twenty articles in professional journals, he wrote the book *Nurturing Doubt* about his personal experiences in questioning dogma in both theology and anthropology. His book, *Armonia y Disonancia en una Sociedad: Los Tobas Argentinos,* read widely in Latin America, is out of print, but The Human Relations Area Files at Yale University published his dissertation and the two-volume *A Critically Annotated Bibliography of the Gran Chaco Toba*. Since retiring in 1996, he and Lois have become active members of Germantown Mennonite Church. They also attend Covenant Mennonite Fellowship in Sarasota during the winter months.

Catherine R. Mumaw (PhD, Pennsylvania State University) is Professor Emerita of Human Development and Family Sciences at Oregon State University. She taught at Lancaster Mennonite School, Eastern Mennonite College, Goshen College, and Oregon State University and worked at Kathmandu University's School of Education in Nepal before retiring in Oregon. She was active in national and state professional organizations for fifty years, supported the International Federation for Home Economics for forty years, and was an Executive Committee member and/or external advisor to two World Congresses. She directed student programs in Jamaica and participated in scholar exchanges in Malawi and India. Her honors include the 1985 Indiana HEA Leader Award, 1994 Distinguished Faculty Award by the OSU Home Economics Alumni Association, 2002 Oregon Association of Family and Consumer Sciences Community Service Award, and EMU's 2006 Alumna of the Year. She served on the Board of Directors for Mennonite Community Association, Mennonite Mutual Aid Association, and Mennonite Economic Development Associates. Currently she is on the Steering Committee for ACRS. She has nurtured the hobbies of choral singing, amateur photography, and international travel. In 2005 she married Clair L. Basinger. They moved to Harrisonburg, VA, in 2007 and attend Harrisonburg Mennonite Church.

Laban Peachey (EdD, George Washington University), born in 1927 to Shem and Saloma (Bender) Peachey in Springs, PA, is the sixth of ten children. He and Helen Mumaw, whom he married in 1953, had four children; and the family now includes eleven grandchildren and one great-grandchild. Following his time in Civilian Public Service, Laban enrolled at Eastern Mennonite College in 1949. From 1953 to 1968 Laban taught psychology and was dean of students at EMC. He served as president of Hesston College in Hesston, KS, from 1968 to 1980. In the 1980s Laban and Helen made their home in Goshen, IN, where he was the vice-president of marketing at Mennonite Mutual Aid. Since 1990 Laban has held part time assignments at EMU and in various congregations as interim pastor. He was also involved in the beginning of the Casselman Historians in Grantsville, MD, and of The Valley Brethren-Mennonite Heritage Center in Harrisonburg, VA. Laban and Helen and their children were part of Mennonite congregations in the several communities where they lived. Upon returning to the Shenandoah Valley, they became members of the Lindale congregation, which Helen had attended as she was growing up. Helen was buried in the Lindale cemetery after her death in December of 2000.

Hubert R. Pellman (PhD, University of Pennsylvania) came to Eastern Mennonite School in 1936 as a student and in 1941 as a teacher. He retired in 1984 after forty years of teaching English and literature at the college. In those many years of teaching he had great satisfaction in relating to students and faculty. The Pellman Language and Literature Endowed Chair was established at his retirement when he was named Professor Emeritus of English. In 1964–65 while on sabbatical at Westmont College, CA, he was asked to consider writing a history of EMS/EMC. After his several years of research and writing, this history was published in 1967 for the fifty-year celebration of the school's founding. He was pastor of a small church near Grottoes, VA, for seventeen years. Hubert and his wife, Mildred, have wide-ranging friendships, local and international, and take pleasure in visits with family and friends in their retirement home in Harrisonburg, VA.

Lee Snyder (PhD, University of Oregon) has spent most of her career in Mennonite higher education. Growing up on a rye grass farm in Oregon and meeting her future husband, Delbert, at Western Mennonite School, Lee was determined to pursue further education. Choosing between science and literature was difficult, but inspired by a high school English teacher, she eventually chose literature. Looking back, she says, "Having no idea what I would do with my life, I discovered that English was the best choice I could have made." She served as president of Bluffton University (1996–2006), following a number of roles at Eastern Mennonite University (1974–1996), including being the vice president and academic dean (1984–1996). Lee, Del and their two daughters spent three years in Nigeria in a teaching assignment under Mennonite Missions Associates, an experience that shaped Snyder's international interests and Mennonite Church commitments. Currently she is serving as interim provost at Eastern Mennonite University (2008–09) and continues active in leadership development and board involvements.

A. Grace Wenger (M.A., University of Pennsylvania) is Professor Emeritus of Millersville University. Her teaching career of thirty-nine years ranged from a one-room elementary school through two Mennonite high schools—Eastern Mennonite School and Lancaster Mennonite School—to an associate professorship at Millersville State College (now Millersville University). She also served as the dean of women at EMC and as the faculty advisor of Scriblerus, the creative writing society there. Most of her writing has been in response to assignments from Mennonite organizations. One of these led to her book, *Frontiers of Faithfulness: The Story of the Groffdale Mennonite Church,* published in 1992. A member of this church, she has been active in Sunday school, summer Bible school, and sewing circle. Among her most significant accomplishments are helping underprivileged students succeed in college and working for fair housing for families facing discrimination. Because of the success of the program she developed for low-performing students, she received a Certificate of Excellence in Teaching from the Pennsylvania Department of Education and was awarded a Commonwealth Distinguished Chair for the academic year of 1976–1977. Now in an apartment at Landis Homes Retirement Community, she enjoys reading, volunteering, and developing new friendships. She attributes her cheerful attitude toward life to a happy childhood on a farm with supportive parents and four older sisters.

Carroll D. Yoder (PhD, University of Iowa) is Professor Emeritus of French at Eastern Mennonite University. The oldest of five brothers on an Iowa farm, he attended Iowa Mennonite School and later Eastern Mennonite College (now EMU), majoring in English and history. After language study in Brussels following graduation from EMU, he served two years with MCC's new Teachers Abroad Program in the Congo. That experience instilled a love of travel and determined his future career. Two sons and four grandchildren have kept him and his wife, Nancy, "on the move." Travel opportunities included involvement with a French high school in Paris, service as a country representative with MCC in Kinshasa, a Fulbright lectureship in Brazzaville, Congo, and sabbaticals in Paris and his home community in Iowa. He led eight cross-cultural programs to Quebec, France, and the Ivory Coast between 1972 and 2001. He is the author of *White Shadows: A Dialectical View of the French African Novel* (1991). His past and current activities and interests (education, service, writing, gardening, travel, and keeping up with his grandchildren) reflect Carroll's loyalty to his Mennonite heritage, his family and his community, be it local or international.

INDEX

beginnings of, 43
cultivated image of aid, not
    insurance, 43
life insurance included in
    portfolio, 43
Mennonite Partners in China (MPC),
    332, 350, 363
Mennonite Voluntary Service (MVS).
    See Voluntary Service, Mennonite
Mennonite women. *See* Women,
    Mennonite
Mennonite World Conference, 57
    in Basel, 122
Mennonites "in search of a home"
    Covenant Mennonite Fellowship, 332
    Germantown Mennonite Church,
        331-2
    Methodist congregation, 331
    Quaker Meeting, 340
    Unitarian gathering, 331
Mennonites in World War II, 8
Messiah College, 60, 102, 173, 331
Metzler, A. J., 46
Metzler, Edgar, 65, 66
Meyer, Albert J., 35, 82, 219
Milbank, John, 77
Mill Creek, 137, 140, 142
Miller, Ernest, 46
Miller, Ira E., 33, 60, 101-2, 150, 321
Miller, John W., 342
Miller, Lois Longenecker, 316-9, 333
Miller, Marlin, 354
Miller, Orie O., 29, 66, 128-9, 338-9, 341
Miller, Paul, 342
Miller, Ruthann, 86
Miller, Sam and Ella Mae, 324
Miller, Samuel, 274
Miller, Vern, 64
Millersville State College, 125-7
Milton, John, 109, 145
Mission activities, mission presence
    Argentine Chaco, 324, 328
    Congo, 123-5
    China, 58
    Ethiopia, 123
    India, 58
    Japan, 343-5, 350-7

Nigeria, 12
Palermo, Italy, 78-9
Tanganyika (Tanzania), 306
Viet Nam, 67
    as vocation, 79
Mobility of college faculty, 55
Mosemann, John, 299, 306
Multicultural worlds, 335-7
Murdock, Peter, 330
Mumaw, Esther Mosemann, 291
Mumaw, John R., 64, 78, 93, 98, 100-4,
    148, 151, 154, 296-7, 299
Mumaw, Grace, Lois, and Miriam, 292
Music
    as avocation, 293-6
    as gift that held family together,
        293-5
    as intergenerational bridge, 296
    Mennonite Songbooks and
        hymnals, 294-6
    as transcultural language, 296

N
Nagatomi, Masatoshi, 346, 349
Nation, Mark and Mary Thiessen, 354
National Institutes of Health, 34
Nepal, 191, 300, 309-10
Neufeld, Elmer, 23
Niebuhr, Richard, R., 346
Nishioka, (Billy) Yoshiyuki, 356-7
Non-Church Christianity, 348
Nonconformity
    black cars and plain coats, 169
    drawing Mennonite religious-
        ethnic boundaries, 269
    beyond dress, 63
    in non-essentials, 269
    as peace advocates, 63
    with patriotism of WWII, 63
    as value—a Mennonite
        "distinctive" alongside
        nonresistance, 73
Nonresistance
    "nonresistance and biblical
        teaching on peace"—focus of
        family teaching, 56
    as value—a Mennonite
        "distinctive," 73